THREATENING ANTHROPOLOGY

THREATENING

ANTHROPOLOGY

McCarthyism and

the FBI's Surveillance

of Activist Anthropologists

DAVID H. PRICE

DUKE UNIVERSITY PRESS

Durham and London 2004

FOR MY CHILDREN MILO AND NORA

May they share the insight, courage, and conviction

of conscience of Bernhard, Earle, Richard, Jack, Mary,

Melville, Gene, Morris, Kathleen, Philleo, and the

many brave others whose stories are recounted here

The widespread revulsion inspired even now, and perhaps forever, by the word *Communism* is a sane response to the cruelties and stupidities of the dictators of the USSR, who called themselves, hey presto, *Communists*, just as Hitler called himself, hey presto, a *Christian*.

To the children of the Great Depression, however, it still seems a mild shame to outlaw from polite thought, because of the crimes of tyrants, a word that in the beginning described for us nothing more than a possibly reasonable alternative to the Wall Street crapshoot.

Yes, and the word *Socialist* was the second *S* in *USSR*, so good-bye, *Socialism* along with *Communism*, good-bye to the soul of Eugene Debs of Terre Haute, Indiana, where the moonlight's shining bright along the Wabash.

—KURT VONNEGUT

CONTENTS

In this book I examine how the Cold War shaped the development of American anthropology. I use archival documents, correspondence, oral histories, published sources, and over thirty thousand pages of FBI and other government documents released under the Freedom of Information Act to document how the repressive postwar McCarthy era shaped and dulled what might have been a significant and vital anthropological critique of race, class, and the inadequacies of global capitalism.

While the primary subjects of this book are anthropologists, the basic description of the methods used to repress social activism reaches beyond the academically pigeonholed field of anthropology and beyond the time frame under consideration. The congressmen and senators who badgered witnesses at loyalty hearings and the college and university administrators who scrutinized their faculty for signs of thought crimes or activist inclinations did not care about anthropology per se but rather about begirding, discrediting, and disarming agitating social activists. Much the same story could be (or has been) told about American social workers, artists, playwrights, writers, historians, sociologists, longshoremen, essayists, cartoonists, physicists, actors, labor activists, educators, and psychologists. Anthropology's paradigmatic commitment to equality and relativism did make some of its practitioners easily visible targets, but the accounts of these attacks are relevant to all who are interested in the form and function of repression in stifling a needed movement for social justice.

It might seem that anthropology naturally attracts an inherently subversive element insofar as its notions of cultural relativism and enculturation critically undermine the principles and practices of nationalism or patriotism. But this is not the case. Many prominent anthropologists have supported conservative mainstream academic and governmental policies and programs, and some were comfortable being FBI informers. The repressive atmosphere of the post–World War II period redefined anthropologists' notions of public anthropology and provided positive reinforcements for anthropologists willing to think and act in "acceptable" ways (see Nader 1997a; Price 2002d).

A number of American anthropologists were Communist and Socialist activists.[1] That the discipline of American anthropology has deep connections to Communist and Socialist organizations should not be surprising to anyone who knows much about anthropology, Socialism, or Communism —but we are now in an era where people increasingly know little about anthropology and Marxism. False notions that Communists or Socialists were antidemocratic, inherently un-American or unpatriotic, cloud our understanding of the past. But as Lester Rodney—a journalist who campaigned for baseball's integration in the 1930s—recently noted, most Communist Party members were law-abiding patriots. Rodney questions the ability of present analysts to comprehend the motivations and beliefs of mid-century Communists without the smug historical baggage of the post–Cold War era by asking:

> are there any historians out there to say straight out that American Communists, despite their sins, were patriots who advocated something more humane than corporate capitalism for this land of ours and fought hard and effectively for social justice in the meanwhile?
>
> Yes, they were starry-eyed over the emergence of the world's first nation to proclaim itself socialist and place people above profits, and yes, they were lamentably slow to accept the reality that Stalinism had butchered the socialist dream. But when "liberal anticommunists" were doing diddly about the shame of raw racial discrimination, it was Communists who exposed the Scottsboro rape frameup, who put their bodies where their mouths were, going South to work for black rights, who with the black newspapers launched the campaign that ended the apartheid ban in our national pastime, who did the indispensable on-the-ground organizing in the creation of industrial unionism. (Rodney 2001:24)

Most American Communists and Socialists working as activists for social justice during the 1940s and 1950s *were* patriots advocating for something more humane than what capitalism had provided. In this book I examine the extent to which anthropologist activists *regardless* of their party affiliations became enemies of the state *because* they effectively challenged the economic and social order.

Writing about the Communist Party is still difficult. After publishing her fine book, *Many Are the Crimes*, Cold War historian Ellen Schrecker was pummeled from both the left and right for her analysis of political repression during the McCarthy period. She was criticized by those on the right (e.g., Weisberg 1999) who complained that she hadn't grasped that the Soviets' influence on the American Communist Party had discredited all that its members were striving to accomplish, while some on the left felt her stance on party links to the Soviet Union slighted party members and their efforts.

McCarthyism limited anthropologists' free academic inquiry by targeting, stigmatizing, and penalizing those working for racial, gender, ethnic, or economic equality. As red-baiting witch-hunts spread, a generation of social scientists learned to not overtly think under the rubrics of Marxist critique, while many in the discipline learned to ignore anthropology's natural, and ethically required, activist roles. In part, this book chronicles how McCarthyism helped mid-century American anthropology lose its way from a path charted by activist anthropologists who strove to establish a more threatening anthropology than survives today.

———

A few brief words on the book's organization are in order here. After opening with a brief overview of themes vital to an understanding of the Cold War and the political economy of mid-century American anthropology, in each of the chapters that follow I discuss some aspect of the public and private interactions between American anthropologists, McCarthyism, and J. Edgar Hoover's FBI, and I follow both chronological and thematic elements of this dark history. The first chapters use FBI documents and archival materials to examine how Melville Jacobs, Richard Morgan, and Morris Swadesh came to be attacked by localized loyalty boards and how the American Anthropological Association failed to offer meaningful assistance to these members whose rights to academic freedom were under attack.

In the following chapters I examine the congressional hearings subpoenaing Gene Weltfish, Bernhard Stern, Jack Harris, and Mary Shepardson, as well as the FBI background materials relating to these cases. While each of these episodes have key differences, those under attack shared common bonds of isolation because all were left to fend for themselves with no support from professional organizations or peers. The American Anthropological Association's abandonment of these scholars helped support a prevailing environment of isolation and fear that spread through academic and activist communities.

In chapter 9 I examine the methods used by the FBI throughout the Cold War to investigate anthropologists and others they deemed subversive. The FBI records of several anthropologists establish the methods and mindset of the FBI as it undertook extensive and expensive investigations of those they believed to be radical activists working for racial equality. The FBI investigations of anthropologists with apparent ties to Socialist or Communist organizations or parties are examined, with special consideration given to the numerous instances where such individuals were identified but never called before local or national loyalty or security boards.

The FBI's intrusive surveillance of liberal or moderate anthropologists such as Oscar Lewis, Margaret Mead, Philleo Nash, Ashley Montagu, Vilhjalmar Stefansson, Cora Du Bois and others establishes the extent to which America's secret police meddled in the academic and private lives of intellectuals who promoted racial equality and internationalist perspectives. I conclude the book with a brief consideration of but a few instances from the 1960s that indicate that these FBI suppressive tactics did not end in the 1950s.

My decision to conclude the book with a consideration of the early 1960s is largely one of logistical convenience and does not imply a significant break from what came next.[2] In fact, what we know about the FBI's intrusion in the lives of American activists for issues of racial and social justice indicates that the organization has continued to persecute, harass, frame-up, and attempt to murder[3] numerous loyal Americans devoted to resisting the inherent inequalities of American life. We can only expect an increase in these violations of law and civil liberties as the American presidency and Congress press further onward with their ill-defined war on terrorism—thus linking the activists of our age to those from this hidden past. To defend ourselves in the present we must build oases of knowledgeable hope in what Sigmund Diamond (1992:285) called the "desert of organized forgetting," and learn from these past well-funded and well-organized attacks on activists fighting for a better world.

Acknowledgments

During the first years of this research the late sociologist and historian Sigmund Diamond generously gave me valuable information, insight, and encouragement. A decade and a half of conversations and arguments with Marvin Harris helped me consider the infrastructural features of McCarthyism's witch-hunt. Marvin offered generous advice, insights, and recommendations throughout this project; I only wish he were around so we could argue about the final product. Laura Nader—who is in many ways the embodied moral conscience of post-Boasian American anthropology—helped me in ways too numerous to catalog, but most significantly her body of scholarly work provided a firm foundation for the ethic of this book. Her encouragement and advocacy helped bring this project into print. Nina Glick Schiller helped publish early seeds of this project and has continued to encourage me to focus my analysis; she also helped me delay infuriating an otherwise potentially sympathetic audience by segmenting my analysis of Cold War anthropology into two separate book projects (the second book examines anthropology's willing interactions with military and intelligence organizations). William Peace was a regular sounding board and a good friend throughout the writing of this book. He generously shared information and consistently warned me against being too blunt and strident, although I as often as not agreed he was right but ignored his sage advice. Eric Ross offered encouragement and good advice in helping me to remain focused on the key points of this project. Through years of mountaineering treks in the Olympic mountain range Thomas Anson patiently listened and argued through different arguments appearing in this book. Donna Smith's comments added important depth to the final manuscript. Several of my elected representatives helped me with Freedom of Information Act appeals; most helpful in these endeavors were Congresswoman Jolene Unsoeld, Congressman Brian Baird, and Senator Patty Murray. I would also like to thank the numerous elder anthropologists who allowed me to interview them about McCarthyism, the Communist Party, and the American Anthropological Association, many of whom agreed to do so under conditions of anonymity.

This project benefited from correspondence or dialogue with David Aberle, Matthew Amster, Geoff Bate, John Bennett, Russ Bernard, William Blum, Noam Chomsky, Gerry Colby, Charlotte Dennett, Andre Gunder Frank, Irving Goldman, Usama Goldsmith, James B. Griffin, Gustaaf Houtman, Janice Harper, Dell Hymes, Ruth Maslow Lewis, Antonio Lauria-Perricelli, Louise Lamphere, Robert Lawless, Robert Leopold, Richard Lingeman, Carolyn Fluhr-Lobban, Gary Lundell, Dan McGee, Scott McLemee, Ann L. Margetson, John Moore, Ashley Montagu, Mark Naison, the National Writers Union, Bob Patenaude, Tuz Mende and other staff at the Niebyl-Proctor Marxist Library, Mark Papworth, Tom Patterson, David Patton, various members of the Radanth-L group, Jerry Rauch, Steve Reyna, Jeff St. Clair, Nora Sayer, Mike Seltzer, Elman Service, Susi Skomal, George W. Stocking Jr., Carol Stabile, Sol Tax, Eric Wakin, Murray Wax, Gordon Willey, Louis Wolf, and Eric Wolf.

Many family, friends, and community members offered important advice, assistance, or support during the researching and writing of this book. These individuals include Boniface V. Lazzari, O.S.B.; Aaron Bonifield; Rex Casillias; Julie, Nancy, and the other women of the Common Ground CSA; Luke Devine, O.S.B.; Mike Extine; Aaron Goings; Lawry Gold; Dalia Hagan; Bob Harvie; David Hlavsa; Russell Hollander; Jacquie Johnson; Andrea Kueter; Dick Langill; Kilian Malvey, O.S.B.; Lura Montez Miller; Grace and Tom Nelson; Steve Niva; Linda Papworth; Jack Price; Fernell Price; Lisa Price; Michael Price; Midge Price; Lisa Queen; Jean Schuchardt; Bruce Schuchardt; Roger Snider; James Weaver; and Linda Weaver.

My research was to a significant degree unfunded[4] and thus financed largely by the kindness, love, and support of my dear wife Midge, who let me whittle away the manuscript a few hours at a time in stolen moments and who allowed me to clutter the house with piles of FBI files while frittering household funds on photocopies, phone bills, archival trips, and Freedom of Information Act requests and appeals. Saint Martin's College generously provided me with a semester sabbatical to finish the final book manuscript.

A NOTE ON REFERENCES

The format for citations of documents released by the FBI under the Freedom of Information Act follows that used in the FBI's central filing system. A citation such as "WFO100-354492-3:3" indicates FBI file number 100-354492-3, page 3. The letter abbreviation refers to the location of the file; e.g., "WFO" indicates "Washington Field Office," or FBI headquarters. (Other location abbreviations used are listed at the opening of the bibliography.) The first series of numbers—in the example, 100—indicates a "domestic security" file entry; "65" indicates "espionage"; "67" indicates "personnel matters," and so forth. For more on the FBI's central records classification codes, see Buitrago and Immerman 1981; Theoharis 1994. Some variations on this citation format are found in this book—for example, the letters "A" or "x" at times appear in citations, and page number citations are frequently missing. These and other variations only reflect my rendering of the exact FBI notations appearing on the cited files. I provide dates and page numbers where available, and do not attempt to interject this data where it is missing on the FBI files. Occasionally files from other federal agencies (such as the Department of Energy and the CIA) are cited using the archival formats of these agencies.

A list of archival and manuscript sources used also appears at the start of the bibliography, along with the abbreviation used for each source. Citations in the text are keyed to this list. In-text citations also include the location code information used by the individual archive or manuscript holder. For example, "MJ: 120, 52" indicates the "Melville Jacobs Papers, Special Collections, University of Washington"; "120" indicates box number, and "52" indicates folder 52. Correspondence and papers from other collections follow internally consistent formats used by specific archives or manuscript collections.

Periodical publications frequently cited are also indicated by abbreviations in the text keyed to this list in the bibliography. Those with no specific volume information appear as abbreviation and date. Those with additional facts of publication include such information in the cite; for example, "AAANB 1948 2(5): 72–73" indicates volume 2, number 5, pp. 72–73, of the 1948 *News Bulletin* of the AAA.

Personal correspondence is indicated in the text only, for example, "Doe to Price 12/1/99" indicates letter to the author from Doe on date given. Finally, interviews are also referenced directly in the text using a format such as "Peresypkin interview with Price 8/12/01."

CHAPTER 1

A Running Start at the Cold War:

Time, Place, and Outcomes

Since historical memory is one of the weapons against abuse and power, there is no question why those who have power create a "desert of organized forgetting." But why should those who have been the victims sometimes act as if they, too, had forgotten? — Sigmund Diamond

At first glance it might seem odd that anthropologists were among those citizens who were dragged through the shameful disarray of security and loyalty hearings of post–World War II America. American anthropology never had its "Hollywood Ten," although many more than ten of its practitioners were persecuted by congressional hearings and by J. Edgar Hoover's FBI. But the very premise of anthropology—with its commitment to cultural relativism and the inherent worth of all cultures—made it a natural target for these attacks. The nature of these attacks clarifies much about the real issues of McCarthyism and about the promise of what anthropology offered public policy makers regarding issues of racial, gender, and economic equality. Anthropology's radical view of racial equality made anthropologists obvious targets; and some anthropologists' ties to Communist, Socialist, and other progressive activist organizations made them easy targets.

The formative roots of McCarthyism are much more complicated than Richard Nixon rooting around the pumpkin patch; the entrance of the Soviet Union into the global arms race; or even the creation of a host of secret national security policies after the war. The appearance of McCarthyism was more of a mutant resurrection than it was a new birth sui generis. What came to be known as McCarthyism was part of a long, ignoble American tradition of repressing the rights of free association, inquiry, and advocacy of those who would threaten the status quo of America's stratified political economic system. Despite a general lack of proof of consistent ties to Communist organizations, the anthropologists who were paraded before various public, private, local, state, and national loyalty hearings shared the fundamental trait of progressive social activism.

The most common activities drawing the attention of anti-Communist crusaders included participation in public education programs, public advocacy, social activism, and protests, but the basic concerns of these actions were issues of racial equality. Throughout the twentieth century, American anthropologists argued against racial discrimination and against the biological basis of the notion of race. It is to the credit of the discipline that anthropologists during this period aggressively combated the racial prejudice permeating American society. In the end, these public actions mattered more than the presence or absence of demonstrable ties to Communism. Under these loyalty witch-hunts, Communists, Socialists, and liberal Democrats were equally recognized as a threat to the postwar status quo (and they *were* real threats to the systems of social and economic inequality they wished to demolish) and this threat provided the justification for persecution. McCarthyism's public spectacles transformed the development of anthropological theory, limiting both the questions anthropologists asked and the answers they found.

The seeds of the Cold War were firmly planted during the last days of World War II. America's entry into the war brought the application of anthropological methods and skills to the service of warfare at previously unseen levels. John Cooper (1947) estimated that over half of America's anthropologists contributed to the war effort. During the war, anthropologists found themselves doing everything from using their anthropological credentials as a cover for espionage (Madden 1999; Price 2000b; Price 2002b); conducting national character studies for organizations such as the Office of War Information (Doob 1947; Winkler 1978), the Office of Strategic Services, and the Ethnogeographic Board (Bennett 1947; Price 1998a; Leighton 1949:223–25; Mead 1941; Winks 1987); compiling important war-effort data;

undertaking dangerous cloak-and-dagger operations for the Office of Strategic Services (Chalou 1992; Coon 1980; Price 1998d); and assisting in the detention of Japanese Americans for the War Relocation Authority (Suzuki 1981; Drinnon 1987). The full range and scope of anthropological war work is too varied to recount here, but it is important to recognize that as the majority of the American public became immersed in America's war effort, anthropologists from all fields and theoretical orientations also joined in. These activities brought the FBI into their lives when background investigations were needed for sensitive war work.

In the mid-1940s few Americans could comprehend the brutal reign of domestic fear that soon followed. In 1945 anthropologist Ruth Landes wrote a piece for the *Nation* describing the morale and functioning of Washington's wartime bureaucracies. Commenting on Congressman Dies's loyalty committee, Landes lightly observed that "so little self-esteem is allowed indeed to many federal officers that they look to sources like the lists of the old Dies committee for assurance that they still matter. Only last year a Washington official showed me proudly a copy of testimony filed with the Dies committee about his alleged subversive opinions" (1945:365). By the end of the decade the consequences of such testimony before the Dies committee were severe, and such jesting and boasting became a thing of the past.

At the war's end most anthropologists returned to college and university campuses. But new fears and a new military industrial complex radically transformed these anthropologists and the universities to which they returned (Lowen 1997). These changes affected the world to be studied and the experiences of those who studied it, and the domestic political developments of this period cast shadows of distrust and jingoistic simplicity over all of American academia, thus limiting the nature of anthropological inquiry for decades to come.

The GI Bill of Rights brought the most significant postwar impact on American anthropology: it allayed an economic crisis, rewarded the war's victors, and set new standards of education for a generation of Americans. The GI bill created students—*lots* of students—thereby opening colleges and universities to a new generation. Under the GI bill any veteran of the armed services with an honorable discharge was eligible to receive enough financial assistance to cover the expenses of a college education. The record level of first-generation college attendance was a vital element in the coming retooling of America's workforce and class structure as the children of America's proletariat entered the halls of academia previously reserved for members of America's elite class (Murphy 1976:5).

As a result anthropology classes swelled, not just with a new breed of anthropology majors but with future engineers, chemists, teachers, historians, and other students needing to fulfill social science requirements. As the GI bill brought this mass of new bodies to campuses, however, it also negatively affected the opportunities for other individuals to work and study in America's universities: in all, 7.8 million World War II veterans used the GI bill's educational benefits and 2.2 million students flooded the country's two-year and four-year colleges and universities, thereby displacing a generation of women who had entered academia during the war (Bennett 1996:242). As a generation of male vets was welcomed into the classroom, a generation of women was all but excluded (Rossiter 1995:27).

The GI bill expanded the career opportunities for archaeologists and cultural, physical, and linguistic anthropologists (Patterson 1999:161–64). This new generation of anthropologists had grown up during the Great Depression, with many coming from families with ties to labor, Communist, and Socialist movements. They not only brought their political experiences and viewpoints with them but in many cases it was these experiences themselves that led them to the field of anthropology in the first place.

Walking on Eggshells: Postwar Reorganization of the American Anthropological Association

While American anthropology departments were poised to swell with this generation of bright new students, its oldest professional organization, the American Anthropological Association (AAA), was about to self-destruct by spinning into a half-dozen different scientific societies. In spring of 1945 a Temporary Organizing Committee was established, consisting of Homer Barnett (Chair), Julian Steward, John Provinse, Clyde Kluckhohn, and Frank Roberts (Frantz 1974:9). The dynamics of this reorganization weakened the association's ability to protect anthropologists facing McCarthyism's attacks. The reorganization was in part brought on because of subfield factionalism (as archaeologists and cultural, physical, and linguistic anthropologists had already created specialty associations) and the concerns held by the growing departments at the universities of Chicago, Michigan, and Berkeley, which were separated geographically from the increasing power base of the eastern corridor. Attempts to coordinate the reorganization of the association were complicated by numerous factors: the status of nonprofessional anthropologists, the impact of such a reorganization on a dozen regional and specialty associations, and the question of what was to be done with "professionals" not trained in anthropology.

In the end it was the obvious financial benefits for all that brought the AAA together for the reorganization. It was clear that the new wealth of funds available to researchers in the postwar and coming Cold War world could enrich anthropologists *if* they had an organized body both to represent them and to lobby for their inclusion in the coming funding feast. The prime concern of the reorganized AAA was to "mobilize the profession" to a position advantageous for funding (RAAA: "Committee of Nine Report," 3/9/46). Julian Steward helped bring various factions together for the reorganization by arguing that in a competitive funding environment "it is better to mobilize all anthropologists rather than just a section of them. The point of view that anthropology stands for is well known but it will be better in the final pay-off when the money is allotted if anthropology has made a case for itself" (RAAA: "Committee of Nine Report," 3/9/46). As the AAA's membership grew, diverse research interests created new pressures on the association. These pressures led to a postwar reorganization that ceded increased centralized power to the president and the executive board. The prerevised AAA constitution did not afford the executive board much authority to act on behalf of the general membership throughout the year, without the authorized approval of the rank and file at the annual meeting.

The Cold War brought a stunning variety of governmental agencies—and lots of money—to support anthropological research of interest to the new national security state. There was funding to study the languages and cultures of remote places that would potentially become the staging ground of the Cold War's many battles. Some of these agencies predated the war (e.g., the National Research Council, Office of Naval Intelligence) and were simply reinvigorated by this flood of cash and redirected with new purpose, but many others came into being in the postwar world (e.g., the National Science Foundation, Fulbright, and National Institutes for Mental Health) (Vincent 1990:292–96). There was also a postwar boom of private-foundation funding for anthropological research, although even these funds were not immune from the politics of Cold War interests (Saunders 1999; Ross 1999). After some conflicts over specific articulations of the AAA's reorganization, the promise of large amounts of funding—much of it conditional on the Cold War—was the glue that bound the association together.

The reorganized bylaws of the AAA charged the executive board to pursue funding opportunities for association members by specifying that "officers were obligated to maintain records of professional anthropologists, to serve as a clearinghouse for professional and scientific anthropological matters, to publish a bulletin for Fellows on activities of professional interest, to hold referenda on urgent matters, and to establish liaison with other scientific organizations and institutions" (Frantz 1974:12). The CIA covertly contributed to the maintenance of these rosters in the postwar and early Cold War period, and it was during this time that the FBI opened its file on the AAA (Frantz 1974:7; Price 2000a, 2003a).[1]

As the fragile coalitions comprising the reorganized AAA were hesitant to enter the frays of controversy, the newly reconstituted AAA was in a position weakened by its inability to defend the academic freedom of anthropologists suffering the attacks of McCarthyism. The surviving correspondence of the AAA finds members concerned that the association keep its distance from controversies involving AAA members. For example, in 1949, after the Committee on Scientific Freedom was formed, Harry Hoijer wrote to President Irving Hallowell with his concern that the committee would overstep the duties of the association by protesting the firing of accused Communists (RAAA: HH/IH 7/20/49). Similarly, as we will see, after Richard Morgan was fired from the Ohio State Museum under circumstances suggesting that his rights to academic freedom had been violated, Emil Haury wrote to President Shapiro that it was his "conviction . . . that our Association is a professional one and that we must proceed with the greatest caution in involving either the Board or the membership in matters lying outside of this area. Morgan's difficulty should be handled by the American Civil Liberties Union or by the American Association of University Professors although I am somewhat doubtful if Museum personnel falls within the scope of the latter organization" (RAAA: EH/HS 9/16/48). Such views were widespread. But in practice the ACLU assisted primarily non-Communist professors under attack, and at times it even privately cooperated with various loyalty boards and secretly turned over materials that had been given to them in confidence by Marxists, while the American Association for University Professors (AAUP) was weak and ineffectual in its defense of professors attacked as Communists (Salisbury 1984; Schrecker 1986:308–32). Some members of the AAA board and the association at large believed that if the accused individuals were Communists then they were probably getting their just desserts.

The association's executive board worked hard not to be distracted by McCarthy's intrusions into the terrain of academic freedom. It instead focused its energies on capturing the fruits of the Cold War economy for its membership. By ignoring these attacks, many of its members were rewarded through the increased availability of funding for this newly legitimized branch of the social sciences. Such were the benefits to be accrued by the academy in the Cold War economy.

The Postwar Economy

America entered World War II in a state of economic instability and uncertainty. But as the economies of Europe and Asia lay in ruins at the war's end, the United States, without substantial damage to its home front, emerged as the single most powerful economy in the world. But even with the spoils of a global victory, the immediate postwar domestic economic picture was dominated by a looming state of economic uncertainty. Although the mid-1950s to 1960s would find America in an unprecedented economic boom, the war had not so much solved America's fundamental economic problems as it had simply delayed the necessity of coming to grips with market capitalism's requisite peaks, valleys, and market collapses. Although Roosevelt had restructured Depression-era tax codes and nationalized large portions of the American economy, the war shifted the focus of such nationalization efforts to the all-consuming focus of warfare. The war economy brought new governmental programs that resisted adapting to the postwar era. The postwar 1940s were a period of crucial decision making for American policy makers committed to the economic programs of a now permanent war-based economy (Melman 1974). The armistice could have led to a rapid transformation from a nation preparing for offensive maneuvers across the globe to a scaled-back War Department focusing instead on defense, transforming the war-based economy to one producing goods for public need rather than publicly subsidized munitions and weapons of surveillance and mass destruction. But without open discussion the American economy continued on the established path of arms spending that had solidified the country and economy during the war, thereby augmenting a highly subsidized military industrial economy that did not provide a solution to the problems of the Depression so much as it delayed the need for finding a solution.

President Truman's, and later Eisenhower's, concern that the Depression could return provided some of the motivation for establishing the new make-work programs of the Cold War economy. By the time President Eisenhower warned of the dangers of the nation's military industrial complex, it was too late. The strategy of financing bombs over butter had been undertaken and many of those who questioned this strategy were easily construed as enemies of the state. American financier Bernard Baruch's speechwriter, Herbert Bayard, coined the term "Cold War" in 1947, and Walter Lippmann's *The Cold War* placed the phrase in wider circulation. In the Cold War's earliest days, policy makers outlined the roles and strategies of the conflict, and the conversion to a peacetime war-based economy was swiftly implemented without public debate or consent: those who questioned the need for this economic shift were often dragged before the loyalty and security hearings of McCarthyism.

The smoke and mirrors easing this shift to a military economy were finely crafted and the government's accounting system categorized expenditures in such a way that the extent of America's military spending was (and is) not easy to divine. The end result was that America's national security state devoured ever-increasing amounts of money yet public awareness of the costs associated with this economic shift steadily decreased until most citizens came to believe that the debts achieved by the time the Soviet Union collapsed were the result of domestic social programs and not the military industrial complex's special forms of corporate welfare (Vidal 1988).

The 1947 National Security Act set in motion a number of policies and dynamics designed to maintain a position of American economic and political dominance. With the work of articulate strategists such as George Kennan, America developed domestic and international strategies for dealing with those who would argue that the best hope for peace lay in peace rather than in perpetual war. Kennan argued this best in his secret 1948 State Department document known as "Policy Planning Study 23," where he argued that the United States should protect the interests of America's ruling elite through a policy designed to perpetuate the global imbalance of resources and power. He wrote: "We have about 50% of the world's wealth but only 6.3% of its population . . . In this situation, we cannot fail to be the object of envy and resentment. Our real task in the coming period is to devise a pattern of relationships which will permit us to maintain this position of disparity . . . To do so, we will have to dispense with all sentimentality and day-dreaming; and our attention will have to be concentrated everywhere on our immediate national objectives . . . We should cease to talk about vague and . . . unreal objectives such as human rights, the raising of living standards and democratizations" (1948:121–22).

Similarly, the adoption of National Security Council directive sixty eight, known widely as NSC-68, launched American foreign and domestic policy on an escalating arms race with the Soviet Union and built what would become the NATO alliance, while frightening the U.S. public by exaggerating the threat of the Soviet Union to the American way of life (Gaddis 1993; May 1993). Kennan and other Cold War policy strategists rationalized America's commitment to a military-based economy in which the public funding programs of the New Deal could be transformed into programs benefiting war industrialists, and an aggressive stance could be justified by the need to protect America's position as the wealthy victor of the world war.

The uncertainty of the postwar economy and the ascendancy of Soviet power in Europe brought a new national paranoia and concern for a creeping international red menace. As the Iron Curtain divided Europe and the Soviets maneuvered to stand toe to toe with Western technological advances, U.S. foreign policy engaged its former allies as opponents in arms races, space races, and humanitarian aid races as they fought each other using proxy nations as battlefields of contention for the hearts and minds of the world at home and abroad. From this perspective the Cold War can be seen as the twentieth century's unacknowledged third world war: raging for over fifty years, and claiming over six million lives in America's proxy and direct military engagements in the nations of the world from Afghanistan to Zaire (see Stockwell 1991:81).

On the American home front there was a lack of public understanding of the economic costs of living in a state of perpetual warfare, wherein peace was a vital stage of war. This constant state of military escalation required that the American public not consider military spending as optional, and those who spoke out about the absurdity of this situation were to be seen as deviant. Thus, in 1946 the FBI reported with contempt the predictions of Communist George Hickerson (father of anthropologist Harold Hickerson) that in the near future "a large American Army will be raised for only one purpose and that was to be the instrument in an aggressive American imperialism, bound on a course of world domination" (WFO100-354492-3:3).[2]

As America's military budget exponentially increased, so did its defense against those who pointed out the needs of domestic and international equality. Anthropologists had long studied such structural protectionist ideological regulatory systems, although they were much more comfortable describing the intricate patterns of social alienation and accusations of witchcraft among the Azande, Navajo, or Ndembu than they were establishing such relationships at home. But the mechanisms of identifying scapegoats for punishment in times of crises or change were remarkably similar in both exotic and local occurrences (see Harner 1973; Harris 1974; Hill 1995).

McCarthyism helped divide Americans into oversimplified categories of "loyal followers" and "enemies of state." All those who did not consent to support a gamut of policies ranging from an arms policy of mutually assured destruction to America's mid-century bigoted system of racial, gender, and economic stratification were fair game for the unchecked scrutiny of loyalty tribunals. But the magic of McCarthyism hid from view the essential fact that protest, dissent, and Socialist and Communist activism all had long, rich American traditions that could not easily be enveloped under the dismissive heading of foreign threat.

The Foundations of American Marxism

The roots of Communism and anti-Communism run deep in America. Historian Michael Heale argues that throughout the nineteenth century popular visions of America's violent revolutionary past, coupled with the American ideological commitments to equality and the influx of refugees and political outcasts, made the United States a natural home for a variety of revolutionaries. From the earliest nationalization, sedition, and alien acts of 1798 to the expulsion of immigrants during the Palmer raids and the mid-century Hatch Act (barring Communists from federal employment) there have been persistent baseless claims that radicalism was an imported phenomenon rather than derived indigenously from America's economic and social conditions. Even America's early labor actions in the 1850s were interpreted as linked to foreign ideas, as if standing up for a fair wage was somehow un-American. These efforts to organize the working poor "were thus immediately branded as both socialistic and foreign inspired, incompatible with the American philosophy of equal rights and equality of opportunity" (Heale 1990:16).

By the 1880s the abhorrent economic and social conditions of the Industrial Revolution fostered a widespread militant domestic labor movement. From its earliest moments the American labor movement was unsure of its commitment to activism directed at specific short-term piecemeal improvements, or of its devotion to establishing more radical changes in America's capitalist system. This division can be seen in the late nineteenth century's pronounced division between trade union Socialism and anti-Socialist trade unionists. Even among the trade-union Socialists there was great factionalism, as divergent forces birthed such diverse parties as the Socialist Labor Party, the Revolutionary Socialist Party, the Social Democratic Party, the Socialist Party of America, and even the Christian Socialists. When Columbia University professor Daniel DeLeon began to lead the Socialist Labor Party (SLP) in 1890 there were new possibilities for the development of a uniquely American form of socialism. The late nineteenth century found the United States open to the consideration of new radical alternatives: in 1892 Populist presidential candidate James B. Weaver received over a million votes (and 8.5 percent of the popular vote) running on a platform that would have nationalized the railroads and other holdings of the era's robber-baron capitalist elites. Eugene Debs formed the American Railway Union in 1893 and, the following year, President Cleveland called out troops to suppress the strike against the Pullman Car Company. In 1898, Debs formed the Social Democratic Party and, three years later, joined forces with Morris Hillquit to form the Socialist Party of America (SPA).

In 1905, after a quarter century of consistent factionalism among American Socialists, a new effort to form "one big union" dedicated to fight for Socialist goals emerged with the formation of the Industrial Workers of the World (IWW). The IWW was formed through cooperative efforts of William D. (Big Bill) Haywood (Western Federation of Miners), Eugene Debs (SPA), and Daniel DeLeon (SLP), although this alliance was short-lived. DeLeon was ousted in 1908 when the IWW shifted to a more anarcho-syndicalist approach to direct action. Four years later, Debs received 897,011 votes in his run for the presidency (5.9 percent of the popular vote) (Draper 1957:41).

The U.S. labor movement remained a diverse conglomeration of Socialist, Communist, and anarcho-syndicalist groups. The actions of these groups earned extensive workplace reforms including worker safety rights, labor standards, shortened work-day and work-week standards, and child labor laws. The widespread acceptance of Marxist views could be seen in the broad spectrum of American writers as diverse as Sherwood Anderson, Upton Sinclair, Sinclair Lewis, and Jack London, all of whom helped to propagate Socialist views among their readers.

After 1918, the Bolshevik revolution changed the way American Socialists and Communists envisioned the possibility of revolutionary change at home. Many Russian American Socialists left America for Russia and, as reports from John Reed, Anna Louise Strong, and others began to bring the revolution home to many Americans, the fear spread across America of the possibility of such revolutions developing elsewhere. By March 19, 1919, when the Third Communist International declared a new era of world communist revolution, there were already two Communist parties in America, the largest of which, the Communist Party of America (CPA), was estimated to have had 24,000 members, while the Communist Labor Party (CLP) had some 10,000. In 1921, the CPA and CLP merged under the guidance of the Comintern into one party, which in 1929 came to be known as CPUSA. After raids and crackdowns during the first "red scares" of 1919 and 1922 (in which J. Edgar Hoover's career was given a dramatic jump start), the party went underground to operate through the formation of secret cells, a tactic taken because party membership was illegal for foreign nationals, although it remained legal for American citizens. The Justice Department's Bureau of Investigation increasingly infiltrated and disrupted party activities. As the Depression made obvious the many problems of market capitalism, the Communist Party's membership blossomed.

In the early 1930s the Communist Party opposed Roosevelt's New Deal as mere reformist meddling in an economic system needing revolution. In 1935, Bulgarian George Dimitrov used his leadership at the Seventh Congress of Communist International to launch the Popular Front movement. The Popular Front was an adaptive, expansionist strategy helping Communists foster common cause with American liberal groups sharing their opposition to fascism. Suddenly the Communist Party became boosters of Roosevelt and his New Deal and there was a concomitant renaissance of Communist intellectualism across America. Labor unions (notably the Congress of

Industrial Organizations (CIO) which is estimated to have had significant Communist influence in its highly effective leadership), literary organizations, Hollywood, scientific federations, and professional associations all had prominent party members among their rank and file. Academics and intellectuals in metropolitan areas joined the party in large numbers.

In the 1930s, when the Communist Party organized rallies in support of the Scottsboro Boys,[3] Communism became increasingly associated with activism for racial equality (Heale 1990:105). During the 1940s and 1950s, the Communist Party became involved in a number of legal cases involving black Americans. In many instances it was the Communists' commitment to progressive activism that drew anthropologists into the party because of its stated commitment to racial equality.

The high point of the American Communist Party's membership reached about eighty thousand during the Depression. But the gains made through the Popular Front movement disintegrated with the signing of the Nazi-Soviet Pact in August 1939. As American intellectuals felt betrayed by the Nazi alliance they left the party in droves, and the FBI pursued American Communists at new levels. After Germany invaded the Soviet Union in 1941, the USSR returned to its support of Roosevelt and, on America's entry into the war, formed alliances with the United States and the Allied forces against the common enemy of Germany. Once America entered the war, the requisite security clearance investigations allowed the FBI to collect innumerable dossiers on American citizens with reported past ties either to the party or to hundreds of groups classified as Front groups by the attorney general's office. These wartime security clearance investigations formed the basis of much of the FBI's McCarthy-era investigations.

In 1944, Earl Browder reorganized the CPUSA as the Communist Political Association, but Stalin purged Browder in 1945 and the party returned to its old name. After the war, the party tried to reestablish ties with the left wing of the Democratic Party (Starobin 1972). Some have argued that the Communist Party members' support of Henry Wallace and his Progressive Party's campaign for the presidency helped fuel (through motives of political vengeance more than ideological grounding) the Democrats' anti-Communist policies. Harvey Klehr, John Haynes, and Fridrikh Firsov suggest that "the failure of the Wallace campaign (it garnered only 2.3 percent of the national vote), however, left anti-Communists in firm control of the Democratic party and American liberalism. CIO leaders such as Philip Murray and Walter Reuther, deeply angered by the Communist role in the Wallace effort, drove Communists and Communist-dominated unions out of the labor federation, destroying what had been one of the CPUSA's chief sources of strength" (1995:12). On campuses across the United States in the 1950s, professors who had supported the Wallace campaign found that such associations damaged their careers because they were interpreted as signs of links to Communism (Diamond 1992; Schrecker 1986).

The American Inquisitions: Torment by Committees

The red scares of the 1940s and 1950s have in some revealing ways been condensed in what remains of America's popular memory. First, almost two decades of disparate episodes of red-baiting have come to be incorrectly recalled as limited to the early 1950s. Second, most Americans conceptualize these attacks as being primarily on individuals with links to Communist organizations, rather than with groups advocating racial equality, arms reduction, or the progressive labor movement. Third, the wide range of public loyalty hearings is simply associated with what is imagined as the isolated ranting of Senator Joseph McCarthy of Wisconsin.

While the term "McCarthyism" usefully describes a variety of attacks on the American left, these practices predated and lasted well beyond Senator McCarthy's political reign. I adopt the term McCarthyism to describe events and red-baiting tactics used to harass and intimidate individuals even while recognizing that such antidemocratic, antilabor, and antiequality practices both predate and postdate McCarthy, but I use this term out of the recognition that it has come to generally describe these tactics.

The postwar McCarthy loyalty hearings had their roots in the 1939 Hatch Act that barred Communists from working for the federal government. On June 28, 1940, the Smith Act made it a crime for any individual to advocate the violent overthrow of the U.S. government, or to belong to any organization that advocated such an overthrow. In 1941, the Dies Committee of the U.S. Congress was charged with the task of identifying un-American activities linked with Communist organizations. Congressman Dies subsequently maneuvered to give his committee permanent status under the name of the House Committee on Un-American Activities (known colloquially as HUAC, an acronym that, as one of its hostile witnesses told me, should be pronounced as if one is preparing to "hawk one massive green loogie").

In June 1940, Attorney General Jackson created the Custodial Detention Program empowering the FBI to compile lists of American citizens and resident aliens believed to be affiliated with subversive organizations.[4] With this, the FBI's budget jumped from $8.7 million in 1940 to $14.7 million the following year (see Theoharis 1999:4–5, 2002:11–12) as the organization was given broad powers to conduct break-ins, tap wires, and use confidential informants to gather hearsay statements pertaining to the beliefs and actions of a wide range of Americans.[5] As we will see, anthropologists were frequently added to custodial detention lists.

In July 1943 (Theoharis 1999:21), Attorney General Francis Biddle instructed the FBI to discontinue its Custodial Detention Program. But after the Amerasia Foundation scandal broke in 1945, in which classified Office of Strategic Services (OSS) documents were published and leaked to the Soviet Union, there was a growing public distrust of any individual in the intelligence community who had links to Communism (see Klehr and Radosh 1996). In March 1946, Attorney General Tom C. Clark enacted the FBI's secret Security Index Program, which empowered the FBI to compile and maintain lists of Americans and aliens to be detained during a period of national crisis.

In March 1945, less than a month after Stalin's "Two Camps" speech declared that a peaceful coexistence with capitalism would be impossible, electorally defeated Winston Churchill spoke of the "Iron Curtain" and the "Sinews of Peace" in Fulton, Missouri, at Westminster College. Stimulated by such discourse, the war's end brought a new current of anti-Communism to America. Anti-Communism became such a part of the postwar world that Republicans adopted the slogan "Communism or Republicanism" for their 1946 elections. Across the United States, federal and state legislative assemblies held hearings in the late 1940s to investigate the private politics of citizens suspected of holding Communistic beliefs.

Hoover's FBI: History and Practices

The FBI was the law enforcement agency that most prominently investigated and persecuted Americans suspected to have ties to Marxist organizations during the 1940s and 1950s. In 1924 J. Edgar Hoover became the director of what was then the Bureau of Investigation, and he ran the agency as his personal fiefdom until his death in 1972. As one of the most powerful Americans of the twentieth century, Hoover ran the FBI for almost fifty years with little interference or oversight from presidents, Congress, or the judiciary.

The FBI infiltrated and monitored the Communist Party in America from its inception. As one anthropologist (a former member of the Communist Party) told me, "we used to say, there are 50,000 members of the CPUSA . . . and only 25,000 of them are FBI Agents" (although this anthropologist also added that the party knew this and used their labor by putting them to work). When the Communist Party of America was formed in May 1921, the FBI assigned Special Agent K-97 (Francis A. Morrow, under the party name "Comrade Day") to join the party as its eyes and ears. By rapidly advancing to the important post of district committee secretary Day fed the FBI invaluable information, including reports on party membership, structure, and secret codes used by members and leaders (Draper 1957:366–37). In 1922 Day was sent to the underground national convention. The FBI planned to raid the convention and arrest all in attendance, but the security measures taken by party officials prevented the bureau from locating the site of the convention until after it had adjourned.

From these earliest days of the party, the FBI infiltrated, monitored, instigated, and subverted the legal (until declared otherwise by the 1940 Smith Act) activities of the Communist Party. The FBI spent a fortune spying on formal and informal meetings, gaining access to party records, documents, and intelligence of all sorts. It hounded effectively, although it only crudely understood what it studied, making no distinctions about why American citizens or foreign nationals chose the way of Socialism or Communism: to the FBI they were all commie dupes.

J. Edgar Hoover was a law unto himself. At mid-century Hoover's FBI was well respected—and, more important, feared—across America. Hoover worked hard to foster an image of the FBI and his G-men as clever, honest, brave, and always victorious through dogged determination. He created a public image of himself as a straight-edged, uncompromising vigilante protecting truth, justice, and his American dream. The private Hoover, however, had little to do with the public projection of Hoover the bureau chief. The public Hoover was a no-nonsense, by-the-book, God-fearing patriot, while the private Hoover was a sophisticated blackmailer who abused his privileges as FBI director to control politicians, celebrities, and public figures. Whether this meant using his secret files on presidents Roosevelt, Kennedy, or Johnson's extramarital exploits, or his damaging information on members of Congress, Hoover privately created public policy by threatening the exposure of unflattering materials (Summers 1993; Theoharis 1991).[6] Hoover both cohabitated and vacationed with FBI Assistant Director Clyde Tolson for almost fifty years in what is sometimes interpreted as a homosexual relationship (Summers 1993, cf. Leopold et al. 1994; Theoharis 1995), a fact that would not be worthy of mention had Hoover not used his knowledge of others' sexual proclivities as a source of blackmail.

Hoover considered himself above the law. He considered the Bill of Rights to be a nuisance, and he trained his agents to conduct wiretaps or black-bag operations (breaking into homes or offices to look for "evidence") without the use of warrants (Marro 1982; Theoharis 1999:22; cf. Rosenfeld 1999). Although Congress enacted legislation in 1934 that prohibited the use of wiretaps by law enforcement agencies, the FBI ignored these injunctions. Eventually, the 1939 Supreme Court ruling of *Nardone v. the United States* held that this ban did indeed apply to the FBI and other federal law enforcement agencies. But the FBI ignored these bans and for decades thereafter conducted wiretaps without court authorization (Edwardson 1999).

Hoover's bigotry was apparent in his administration of the FBI. No Jews, blacks, Hispanics, or Catholics were allowed to be bureau agents until the 1940s (Sullivan 1979:49). Hoover openly said that "there will never be a Negro Special Agent as long as I am Director of the FBI" (quoted in Sullivan 1979:268). Aside from the five menial, personal servants that Hoover claimed he "made special agents to keep them from being drafted" in World War II, the few blacks in the bureau in the 1960s under Hoover's directorship were hired due to pressures brought by the Justice Department (Powers 1987:323–24; see also Summers 1993:56–60). Hoover's dislike of minorities was amplified in his distrust of civil rights organizations. He was "concerned with black civil rights organizations almost exclusively in terms of their potential as targets for Communist infiltration. His condescending attitude toward black intelligence and judgment made him inclined to see these organizations as easy prey for the skilled propagandists and agitators of the Communist party" (Powers 1987:324).

Hoover's former assistant director of Domestic Intelligence, William C. Sullivan, admitted that much of the FBI's supposed crime-sleuthing abilities were hyped beyond their actual capacity. For example, the reported abilities of the FBI's crime laboratory were pure hyperbole: "The laboratory, described in an FBI publicity booklet as 'the greatest law enforcement laboratory in the world,' is the highlight of the public tour of FBI headquarters in Washington, D.C. Over the years, millions of tourists have listened, awestruck, to glowing descriptions of the lab's capabilities and activities. Unfortunately, descriptions are nothing but a show-business spiel. The FBI Laboratory is in fact a real-life counterpart of the busy workroom of the Wizard of Oz—all illusion. Even the famous laboratory files were maintained for show. They look impressive, but they were really incomplete and outdated" (Sullivan 1979:95). The FBI's bureaucratic culture taught agents to at times falsify reports and evidence as a means of incriminating individuals they believed to be criminals. Former agent M. Wesley Swearingen reports how he was instructed to manufacture informants for reports. Once, prior to an annual inspection, his FBI supervisor called him into his office and told him to "develop some information for the forthcoming inspection" by FBI headquarters. Swearingen replied that this would be "no problem, knowing that I could fake my way through the task. Many agents took names from grave markers in the cemetery or names from the telephone book to refer to as potential informants in memos. I used names of janitors, bartenders, and newspaper delivery men to open informant files just before the inspection.

After the inspectors left town, I closed the files until next year. This was standard practice for most agents" (1995:54).

A combination of blind ambition and bureaucratic pressure to find or create evidence fitting the FBI's intransigent world view led the organization to routinely falsify reports and collect dossiers on individuals and groups that it (or often, J. Edgar Hoover) deemed to be subversive or somehow divergent from the American way of life. Needless to say, this knowledge should engender an attitude of caution when relying on any FBI documents—in this book or elsewhere.

Historian and sociologist Sigmund Diamond used the Freedom of Information Act to establish that Hoover's FBI infiltrated over fifty American college campuses in the 1950s (Diamond 1992). The FBI saw the prospect of free inquiry by intellectuals as a threat to national security and the American way of life (Fisher 1986), and the organization used a variety of methods and techniques to gather information on the opinions and actions of anthropologists and other professors it considered left-leaning. Among the FBI's methods of spying on the anthropologists documented in this book are wiretaps; rummaging through trash cans at subjects' homes or offices; monitoring the license plates of cars parked at meetings of interest; interviewing students, neighbors, colleagues, and supervisors of subjects; mail surveillance and mail opening operations; and tailing operations. These were the standard techniques used by the FBI in the 1940s and 1950s to spy on American citizens accused of subversive activities, and it may be decades until we learn the extent to which these unconstitutional practices are being used against Americans today.

After a group of unknown individuals called the Citizens Committee to Investigate the FBI broke into the Media, Pennsylvania, Resident Agency FBI office in 1971 and stole and distributed top-secret FBI documents, the world learned of the FBI's extensive domestic counterintelligence program known as COINTELPRO that had infiltrated and sabotaged left-wing political groups in America for years (Churchill and Wall 1990:xi). The stolen documents revealed that the FBI had used agent provocateurs, assassins, and an assortment of illegal and underhanded tricks to attack members of the American left. The FBI used COINTELPRO to target Communists, Socialists, racial integrationist groups, women's groups, the Black Panthers, the American Indian movement, and mainstream racial minority political candidates. Under COINTELPRO the FBI practiced warfare against democratic Americans struggling to change their own society. Tactics included death threats, poison-pen letters, smear campaigns, instigating violent attacks on activists, evidence-planting operations, suppressing the release of records that would clear accused activists, false arrests, and planting false stories in the press—all for the political gain of the FBI and the right-wing conservative political agenda they protected (Churchill and Wall 1990). The FBI used COINTELPRO to frame numerous black activists like Geronimo Pratt, who spent twenty-seven years in prison before being cleared by the courts in 1997 (Olsen 2000). As the scope of the FBI's illegal activities became known in the Church hearings, rules regulating the organization were adopted and the domestic surveillance of law-abiding American citizens was curtailed. The brief curtailment of these actions, however, was swept aside by a frightened Congress in the months following the September 2001 terrorist attacks.

Those few scholars who dared to criticize Hoover or the FBI found themselves to be targets of FBI investigations. In one instance, the FBI undertook an extensive (and expensive) campaign of surveillance and harassment directed against University of Colorado sociologist Howard Higman and his family after Higman had made a passing remark deriding Hoover to a student. The student (former Miss America, Marilyn Van Derbur) contacted the FBI, who decided it needed "to meet some of these academic punks in their own backyards" and began a prolonged campaign dedicated to hounding and harassing the offending professor (Summers 1993:174; Higman 1998:27–84). After playwright (and later, anthropology instructor) Donald Freed ridiculed, in his Broadway play *Inquest*, Hoover's role in the arrest and prosecution of the Rosenbergs, FBI agents saw to it that Freed lost his job—after which they attempted to provoke members of the Black Panthers to murder him (Swearingen 1995:116).

Academic Freedom and the Pall of Orthodoxy

As the FBI and the loyalty and security hearings investigated the politics of anthropologists and other professors, clear messages were sent concerning the inadvisability of research or extramural public work advocating for issues of social justice or equal rights (Holmes 1989). The principle of academic freedom holds that individuals must have the protected right to pursue academic enquiries independent of the political or economic controversies or consequences derived from their work. This most sacrosanct of academic principles—the very notion that knowledge must be pursued without fear of reprisal—is a product of the transformations of universities in the early twentieth century.

As Neil Hamilton's work clarifies, there are two components of academic freedom in America: constitutional academic freedom and professional academic freedom. Hamilton writes: "The two doctrines address similar goals about the importance of free inquiry and speech in the university, but each has different legal roots, and each presents different opportunities and constraints to address the goals. Constitutional academic freedom is rooted in the First and Fourteenth Amendments and prohibits government attempts to control or direct the university or those affiliated with it regarding either (1) the content of their speech or discourse; or (2) the determination of who may teach. Professional academic freedom is an employment law concept developed by the AAUP rooted in concerns over lay interference by boards of trustees and administrators in professors' research, teaching, intramural and extramural utterances" (1995:193). Historically, academic freedom has been promoted by academic professional associations and affirmed by the judiciary—but only weakly supported when the controversies of a given age draw in teachers, lecturers, instructors, or professors (McCormick 1989; Melby and Smith 1953; Meranto et al. 1985). Supreme Court Justice Brennan, in the majority decision in *Keyishian v. Board of Regents* (1967), affirmed the central importance of academic freedom when he wrote, "Our nation is deeply committed to safeguarding academic freedom, which is of transcendent value to all of us and not merely to the teachers concerned. That freedom is therefore a special concern of the First Amendment, which does not tolerate laws that cast a pall of orthodoxy over the classroom" (Keyishian v. Board of Regents 385 U.S. 589). The loyalty hearings of the 1940s and 1950s and the FBI's investigations brought just such a pall, although it fell beyond the classroom into the private lives and politics of activist anthropologists.

The AAUP was the body primarily responsible for the codification of principles of academic freedom in America, and the reassertion and reformulation of these principles appears tied to American military actions. In 1915, with the onset of World War I, the AAUP produced a weakly written policy that championed the principles of academic freedom but tied the judgment of appropriate views to a discipline-based peer review concept. In 1940, as Europe raged in war, the AAUP produced a simple, clear, and powerful statement concerning the rights of academic freedom, writing: "Freedom in research is fundamental to the advancement of truth. Academic freedom in its teaching aspect is fundamental for the protection of the rights of the teacher in teaching and of the student to freedom in learning." The weak link of the AAUP's 1940 —and present—statement is its insistence that along with the rights of academic freedom come inherent "responsibilities." Thus the AAUP offered academic freedom to "responsible" faculty who agreed to "at all times be accurate," "exercise appropriate restraint," and "show respect for others." In 1970 these "responsibilities" came to include the need of faculty "to foster and defend the academic freedom of students and colleagues" (AAUP 2001:133–34).

While the stipulations that professors have the responsibility to strive for accuracy is paramount to any academic endeavor, and while each of the identified "responsibilities" appears reasonable under principles of collegiality, the notion that freedom is contingent on social definitions of "responsibilities" illuminates the AAUP's view that academic freedom is an allotted privilege, not a fundamental right, available only to those who act and think in a "responsible" manner. The requirement of "responsibilities" clarified that academics are only leased the alienable right of academic freedom under the condition that they agree to problematically undefined standards of "responsibilities."

As shown by the cases of Gene Weltfish, Bernhard Stern, Melville Jacobs, and others discussed in this volume, interpretations of these "responsibilities" were subjugated by a given era's sense of crisis. Thus outspoken pacifists in times of war, activists fighting for economic equality, scientists measuring American racism, and Cold War American Communists were judged as irresponsible and ineligible for the same protections of academic freedom afforded to their colleagues whose views are aligned with the status quo (Rogin 1967; Horne 1986).

On March 25, 1949, the regents of the University of California required all employees to sign an anti-Communist loyalty oath. This decision was in part a reaction to the then recent anti-Communist hearings at the University of Washington (see chapter 2), but the California oath generated national repercussions. Initially, most faculty strongly opposed the regents' demand for loyalty declarations, with a majority of faculty calling for the oath to be rescinded. During the 1949–1950 academic year, professors refusing to sign the oath were paid but were not issued letters of appointment—thus explicitly undermining the notion of tenure. The following year the regents declared that all who did not sign the oath would be fired. On March 22, 1950, the faculty voted 1,154 to 136 (with 33 abstentions) to abolish the loyalty oath. At the same time it endorsed by a similar margin (1,025 in favor, 268 opposed, 30 abstentions) its own faculty-generated anti-Communist statement in a move designed to assure the regents that academic freedom rather than Communism was the reason for opposing the loyalty oath (Schrecker 1986:119).[7]

Thirty professors were fired from the University of California system as a result of the loyalty oath. Because they were not demonstrable Communists but were considered to be "men and women of principle fired for their stand on principle," numerous civil libertarians denounced the oath, although many of these fair-weather civil libertarians were not in principle opposed to firing actual Communists (see Schrecker 1986:117).

Outside of the academy revelations of several Soviet spy rings brought the notion of a "Communist threat" to the American public's imagination. While a number of Soviet espionage arrests had occurred in Canada in the postwar period, such arrests did not occur in the United States until March

1949 when Soviet citizen Valentine Gubitchev and Justice Department employee Judith Coplon were arrested on espionage charges. America's fears multiplied as the power of the atomic bomb spread beyond the proprietary domain of the United States. The following year brought the nuclear espionage arrests of Klaus Fuchs in London, as well as David Greenglass, Ethel and Julius Rosenberg, Abraham Brothman, and Miriam Moskowitz in the United States. In 1952 Guy Burgess and Donald Maclean defected from the British Foreign Ministry to the USSR. Soon after CIA Director Walter Bedell Smith announced that Soviet agents had penetrated every American intelligence organization, including the CIA, President Eisenhower secretly authorized the U-2 spy plane to fly over the Soviet Union. Once the Rosenbergs were executed in 1953, America entered a new era of fear and distrust.

It was the Democrats who unleashed the power of loyalty witch-hunts on mid-century America—although it would be the Republicans who by terror and innuendo developed these trials into a true art form of the absurdist inquisition. With the Truman Doctrine, America embarked on a commitment of fighting Communism both at home and abroad. President Truman planted and fertilized the seeds of McCarthy's rise to prominence and reckless power by requiring all federal employees to sign loyalty oaths proclaiming whether or not they had ever belonged to any of the organizations deemed subversive by the Attorney General. Truman initially intended that these loyalty oaths would be used to monitor security aspects of federal employment, but the recklessness with which loyalty hearings were conducted led to the destruction of hundreds of careers (Bernstein 1989).

In February 1949 congressmen Karl Mundt and Richard Nixon introduced the Mundt-Nixon Bill requiring the registration of all American Communists. That summer, just three days after the Soviets detonated their first atomic bomb, Pope Pius XII excommunicated all Communists. The 1950 Internal Security Act (aka the McCarran Act) was a Cold War legislative watershed strengthening the federal government's ability (largely through the FBI) to persecute individuals in the name of national security. The act created a Subversive Activities Control Board endowed with the discretionary power to divine which educational or political organizations were un-American. The McCarran Act created mechanisms for the arrest and "custodial detention" without trials of "radicals" during times of national crisis, empowered the State Department to limit passports and rights of travel for suspected radicals, and allowed for the arrest and deportation of foreign radicals.

Joseph McCarthy was elected to the U.S. Senate in 1946. It was not until February 1950 that he made his first public accusations against a vast Communist conspiracy, wildly claiming that 205 Communists had infiltrated the

State Department. It did not matter that his later testimony before the Senate Committee on Foreign Relations failed to identify a single "card-carrying" member of the Communist Party. His power and appeal were tied to his ability to generate fear and intrigue, not to the establishment of any factual connections to Communism (Oshinsky 1983).

McCarthy used his position as the chairman of the Government Committee on Operations of the Senate and his membership on the Permanent Subcommittee on Investigations to parade hundreds of witnesses accused of having links to the Communist Party or to front organizations. By 1953 McCarthy's ever-widening scope of recklessness came to include persons and agencies of real power and, as he strayed from the more vulnerable targets of the liberal and radical left, his power and appeal quickly dissipated. He veered so far off course in 1954 that he began accusing members of the army and the CIA of being part of the Communist conspiracy, and he even claimed that President Eisenhower was soft on Communism. Senator McCarthy's fall from power was even quicker than his rise, with a 67 to 22 senatorial censure vote in 1954.

In McCarthy's heyday the theatrics of anti-Communism were always more important than the findings. The media recorded his posturing innuendos without focusing on the damage caused by such hasty behavior. When on February 9, 1950, McCarthy waved his sheets of paper before the Wheeling, West Virginia, Republican Women's Club, the press uncritically reported the event as if it were news, and in the years that followed they sold newspapers as accomplices to his theatrics of shame and fear. When his list of names dropped from 205 to 57 the following day, it mattered little as long as the drama of accusations and charges sold papers and advertisements for toothpaste. The melodramatic success of the McCarthy and McCarran hearings paved the way for the passage of the 1954 Communist Control Act, which further restricted the rights of individuals in Communist organizations both real and imagined.

Hiram Bingham in his five-year role as chairman of the Federal Loyalty Review Board developed important repressive policies and procedures that were further refined by senators McCarthy, McCarran, and others.[8] Bingham used the attorney general's list of subversive organizations to hound American progressives from all walks of life, and his FBI file indicates he coordinated his efforts with the FBI to harass American progressives employed in the federal government (WFO62-82273-672). Although HUAC was not disbanded until 1975 (Criley 1990:77), the Smith Act (of 1940) was overturned by a Supreme Court ruling in 1957, which made it once again legal to belong to the Communist Party. By then, however, news of Khrushchev's 1956 revelations about Stalin along with the ravages of McCarthyism had reduced the membership of the CPUSA to fewer than 25,000. Whatever threat the party had ever represented to the American status quo was gone.

The Nature of McCarthyism

The forms and functions of the 1940s and 1950s loyalty and security hearings need to be considered here. Although forms varied somewhat depending on time and place, these hearings were commonly staged with witnesses parading before boards of elected or nonelected officials asking questions designed to insinuate that the subject was disloyal to the United States. The legal standing of these local, state, or national hearings was often questionable and the legal protections afforded witnesses varied greatly. Frequently the questions asked were not intended to be answered so much as they were meant to imply high levels of unspecified guilt.

The ritualized nature of these hearings did not escape the notice of anthropologists and sociologists. In 1956 sociologist Harold Garfinkel described "status degradation ceremonies" in which structured ceremonies are used to shame and denounce persons in otherwise good social standing in order to reduce their social stature. The subjects of the degradation process are systematically represented as frauds that have misrepresented themselves, and they are thus systematically reduced in stature to take on a downgraded social status marked with stigma. These ceremonies transform the individual identities diminishing the basic trust afforded to other members of a society. Garfinkel observed that all societies have degradation ceremonies of some type, noting that "only in societies that are completely demoralized, will an observer be unable to find such ceremonies, since only in total anomie are the conditions of degradation ceremonies lacking" (1956:420).

Victor Navasky observed that there are obvious applications of Garfinkel's theory of degradation ceremonies for the loyalty and security hearings of the 1940s and 1950s. He states: "Their job was not to legislate or even to discover subversives (that had already been done by the intelligence agencies and their informants) so much as it was to stigmatize" (1980:319). Thus, under Garfinkel's rubrics HUAC's badgering of witnesses served to "effect the ritual destruction of the person denounced" and helped to foster social solidarity among those who were not the subject/victims of these ceremonies (1956:421).

Steven Spitzer recognized that a social notion of deviance "emerges from and reflects the ongoing development of economic forces (of the infrastructure)" and that superstructure functions to manage and regulate members of society, particularly "problem populations" (1980:179). One of the strengths of Spitzer's theory is that by focusing on general principles rather than specific acts, we can account for cross-cultural instances of deviance. Spitzer theorized that actions and beliefs supporting a society's mode of production are construed as nondeviant, while those that threaten the development and free functioning of its economic sector become deviants. Thus, in an economy that is dominated by productive forces requiring intense focus in a demanding, high-stress environment, drugs (e.g., coffee, cigarettes) that help employees focus on the labor requirements of a demanding workplace will be selected for, as well as those (e.g., alcohol) that allow for a controlled distancing of unwinding. However, those (e.g., LSD, marijuana) that foster responses of hyperindividualism or apathy will be deemed deviant. Likewise, in a society based on intense ethnic, gender, economic, and racial segregation, individuals who advocate the abolition of such systems of stratification will also be seen as deviant.

To the credit of the field, anthropologists were among Senator McCarthy's suspects from the very beginning of his witch-hunt. Just hours after his Wheeling, West Virginia, speech McCarthy confided to journalists that chief among the names on his list of 205 known communists "was a professor of anthropology, a woman" (Reeves 1982:235). Although McCarthy did not further identify this anthropologist, the controversy surrounding the publication of Ruth Benedict and Gene Weltfish's (1943) *Races of Mankind* made both women likely contenders. When Weltfish was later subpoenaed to appear before McCarthy he made no secret of the contempt he held for her, Benedict, and their work demonstrating that northern blacks had higher IQs than southern whites (see chapter 6).

Most hearings allowed witnesses to be accompanied by members of legal counsel, who usually had little function other than to advise their clients, under the protection of the Fifth (and occasionally First) Amendment, to avoid answering questions. These committees at times used professional witnesses, or FBI informants, who made careers out of producing lists of citizens allegedly involved in Communist Party activities. As Victor Navasky (1980) observed, prominent among these informer types were reluctant informers, unfriendly informers, enthusiastic informers, informed and philosophical informers, uninformed informers, truth-telling informers, combative informers, denigrating informers, noisy informers, comic informers, husband-and-wife informers, informers-by-dispensation, and even resister informers. Philosopher Barrows Dunham understood that HUAC gained its strength through fear and that the committee "lived on names. The more names they had, the more hearings they could have, the more people they could drag to the pillory before the public to spread the terror. They lived on names until they ran out of names, and then they died of inanition" (quoted in Schultz and Schultz 1989:131). Although the informers gave the committees their strength and power, it was the Cold War's national security state that incubated the conditions for terror.

This witch-hunt was based on the premise that Marxism, Communism, and Socialism represented fundamental threats to the American way of life. But the "American way of life" in the 1940s and 1950s was predicated on a fundamental stratification of race, gender, class, and wealth. While American Marxists and non-Marxists challenged this structural system of prescribed inequality, the conservative forces of government, industry, and bureaucratic power demonized those who fought for a society of equal rights, equal worth, and equal opportunity. Although the various red hunters of Congress, the Senate, and assorted school boards made much of the Communist Party's commitment to revolution by any means, many members of the party were nothing more than committed localized activists who joined a group promoting progressive change.

The most important functional outcomes of these hearings were that they helped terrify and divide the American left. The bonds that had been formed during the Popular Front period were severed as many liberal Democrats redefined themselves as anti-Communist, or even anti-anti-Communist, while others became silent in the climate of fear. Some on the left objected to McCarthy's tactics more than they did to his assault on the rights of free thought and free association. For some Americans, like playwright Lillian Hellman, this brought divisions among those on the left that were not easily repaired. It made naked the fickle nature of freedom of belief in America, while it exaggerated the idea of the harm brought by those with Communist affiliations. As Hellman wrote years later: "I am still angry that the anti-Communist writers' and intellectuals' reason for disagreeing with McCarthy was too often his crude methods . . . Such people would have the right to say that I, and many like me, took too long to see what was going on in the Soviet Union. But whatever our mistakes, I do not believe we did our country any harm. And I think they did" (1976:154–55).

Beyond the National Lawyers Guild, most civil rights and civil liberties organizations such as the ACLU did little to assist Communists under attack by HUAC or other boards. The ACLU was generally squeamish when it came to defending Communists in the 1940s and 1950s, and it regularly tried to determine if clients accused of party membership were falsely accused before taking their cases. Perhaps the most disturbing revelation about the ACLU is that its board member and lead general council (1929–1955), Morris Ernst, carried on a secret correspondence with J. Edgar Hoover in which Ernst "sent Hoover and Nichols scores of confidential letters written to him by friends and associates" (Salisbury 1984:579). Ernst purged party members from the ACLU and prevented it from defending Communists. These were harsh decisions, as Ernst and the ACLU "drove the veteran Communist Elizabeth Gurley Flynn off its board, declared war on fellow travelers and approved a resolution that put party members beyond the pale. They were deprived of A.C.L.U. support or sympathy because, in effect, they were part of a foreign conspiracy. The line was drawn exactly" (Salisbury 1984:577). It is tragic that this was the organization that the executive board of the American Anthropological Association thought would defend the rights of anthropologists accused of Communist connections. But an organization that would not tolerate Communists in its own ranks could hardly champion the rights of academic freedom of anthropologists attacked by the agents of McCarthyism.

Party Bogeymen

There are heated and prolonged debates among contemporary scholars of the Cold War concerning the nature of the relationship between individual American Communists and the Soviet Union's control over the central party's apparatus. The early post–Cold War period produced a flurry of books by right-wing scholars using previously unavailable materials from the KGB, CIA, FBI, and other agencies to argue that McCarthy and other fanatics of the 1950s were correct in their view that American Communists were working for a secret global network of Communists. There are variations in these works but the basic approach can best be seen in Klehr, Haynes, and Firsov's *The Secret World of American Communism* (1995), where files from the KGB's archives are used to argue that the actions of CPUSA were carefully orchestrated from Moscow. These documents suggest to Klehr et al. that all party members acted at the beck and call of Soviet masters. While Klehr's archival work sheds important light on contacts between American and Soviet Communism, the files can also be interpreted in ways less conspiratorial (e.g., Navasky 2001). The documents examined by Klehr et al. suggest a far less successful and centrally powerful Soviet-based party than is claimed by most red-baiting McCarthyist cold warriors of the 1940s and 1950s. Instead of an effective foreign-organized political machine, we find a weak, frequently ignored, and poorly funded apparatus that accomplished little of note at the beck and call of Moscow. Most of the activist successes of the party were based on efforts of American progressives not Muscovite controllers.

Because a few American Communists were involved in espionage, the likes of Klehr, Haynes, Firsov, and others impugn the motivations and actions of all of the party's rank and file. Such accusations make for convenient historical justifications for the widespread attacks on individual lives and progressive civil rights work, but they have little to do with the historical realities of these times. The CIA, National Security Agency (NSA), FBI, and other branches of America's intelligence community still control the self-serving, selective release of an astounding amount of espionage documents, so the release of selected documents—such as the Venona documents—clarifies little about most party members. As Victor Navasky argues: "Venona half-documents that some CP leaders knew about and may have been middlemen for the receipt of secrets, and perhaps they even recruited some spies. *But missing from Venona is the experience of 99.9 percent of the million comrades who passed through the* CPUSA *during the 1930s and early 40s—stay-at-homes who contented themselves with reading (and sometimes shouting at) the Daily Worker, demonstrators who sang along with Pete Seeger and social activists who organized trade unions and rent strikes in the North and fought lynching and poll tax in the South*" (2001:40; emphasis added). A wealth of autobiographical writings and oral history documents by party members describe a wide range of personal motivations for party membership, and there were diverse individual responses to policies and principles originating from the party's central committee (see Schultz and Schultz 1989; Miller 1987; Navasky 1980; Hook 1987; Gornick 1977). Most individuals joined the party to patriotically work toward the goals of equality and equal opportunity for all. While American Communists did at times operate under party discipline, most operated outside the sphere of direct Soviet influence.

The loyalty hearings and FBI surveillance issues discussed in this book are joined by common instances in which the loyalties of various anthropologists were questioned after they engaged in activism for issues of social justice. An anthropological lens is used here to focus on the plight of individual anthropologists belonging to substantially different political parties. At times these groups' differences are ignored (although these parties adhered to different strategies, goals, and beliefs, and often viewed each other as bitter enemies) in an effort to cast light on the FBI's view of them as a shared threat to the domestic economic order. I am not arguing that the differences between the Communist, Socialist, Socialist Labor, Socialist Workers, Progressive, (or even in some cases) Democrat and Republican Parties were insignificant (they weren't), but in many ways when it came to attracting the attentions of the FBI, party membership mattered less than one's commitment to activism. Although the political affiliations of these anthropologists were varied, the extent to which they behaved as activists by speaking out and acting against social injustice largely determined how they were treated by the FBI and a variety of loyalty boards.

For some non-Marxist anthropologists (see, for example, Philleo Nash in chapter 13) this meant that the FBI observed their opposition to racism and economic inequality and undertook extensive investigations into their private lives. For others who had known ties to Marxist organizations (for example, Socialist Labor Party member Leslie White) but no apparent links to activism, the FBI maintained little interest in their activities and did not undertake effective investigations of them. Whether it was Melville Jacobs's vocal opposition to the Hobbs Concentration Act of 1941, Bernhard Stern's highly confrontational work opposing various eugenics groups, Morris Swadesh's support for Native American rights, Gene Weltfish's and Richard Morgan's work for racial equity, or Franz Boas's opposition to the misapplication of IQ tests, it was activism more than red politics that brought the spotlight of inquiry on anthropologists.

Progressive social activism was the issue that drew the attentions of witch-hunting politicians like Albert Canwell, McCarthy, McCarran and others. To see the strength of this point, consider the plight of then-Methodist seminary student Frank Wilkinson, who amassed the largest-known FBI surveillance file for his work on Los Angeles's Citizen Housing Council which struggled to end the racial segregation of housing in the 1940s. Wilkinson's advocacy led Hoover's FBI to compile over 132,000 pages of a "surveillance and disruption" file on him—at an estimated cost of over $3 million. It was not party membership that led to Wilkinson's appearance before HUAC as well as the FBI's hounding—it was his activist efforts to curtail racial and economic injustice (Criley 1990; Schultz and Schultz 1989:263–78). As Wilkinson himself notes: "At twenty-eight years of age I became the manager of the first integrated housing project west of the Mississippi. When you read the FBI documents *that* was the month J. Edgar Hoover and the FBI began following me. From then on, my work in the housing authority was disrupted. Hoover was out to get me fired from the word 'go.' All of that is in my FBI files." (quoted in Schultz and Schultz 1989:270).

Mark Geller, who himself came under fire during the Truman loyalty hearings, stresses that these purges were designed to discredit and remove individuals who were activists and advocates for equality, not to hunt actual Communists:

> I never was a Communist Party member but I was charged with disloyalty. You have to understand everything against the background of what was taking place. Otherwise there is absolutely no meaning—except in the context of that period. All these informants and all these charges that don't mean things, et cetera, were really unimportant. *What was really important, at least from my point of view, was the fact that the whole thing was a vehicle for driving everybody out of the government, or everybody out of private industry, or everybody who had some idea in mind of trying to inhibit the development of the Cold War.*

We were so unimportant really. We were zeros, I mean who the hell were we? We were not in top agency positions. We were ordinary union members. But we had a point of view, on the question of race and the question of unions. You have to remember that Washington was a Southern town; it was Jim Crow including the government. All of the government agencies had separate dining rooms or separate dining areas for blacks and whites. *In a sense we were radicals in that we were breaking Southern traditions. And there were some who also came with a point of view of politically coming out of the war and not wanting to see a recurrence of an international debacle.* . . . *Everybody who's for equality has to be a Red: that was the attitude.* So you get a list of the active members of the union and ipso facto they are Communists. We were the eternal enemy. If you understand that, you understand everything. Everybody in opposition had to be driven out. (quoted in Bernstein 1989:180; emphasis added)

Those who fought for equality were labeled Communists and their efforts were demonized, thus strengthening the status quo of imbalanced race, economic, and gender relations. This strategy worked well, and it left a regressive legacy that marks the American landscape even to this day.

Silence, Self-Censorship, and the Politics of Fear

By many measures McCarthyism was a smashing success. It succeeded in broadcasting clear messages that it was dangerous to study and work to change domestic systems of inequality—a lesson most anthropologists learned all too well. As Dell Hymes recalls, during the 1950s, "it was risky to discuss [Marxist thought] with people you did not trust. (As a graduate student, I kept Marxist books off my shelves and out of sight)" (1999:vi). The specter of McCarthyism hung over American anthropologists as they formulated theories of culture and studied various peoples around the world. This specter limited the questions they asked and answered. Many of these limitations were obvious although unstated, others were not so obvious. American anthropologists learned to ignore the ways that predominating neo-Malthusian models of development and the so-called Green Revolution were linked to American Cold War policies of dominance and dependency (see Ross 1998:79–104).

When practiced properly, anthropology is a threatening science. Its dictums of equality and its distant view of stratification threaten claims of legitimacy and dominance; but in the mid-century its critique of the abuses of race in contemporary society was a direct threat to America's status quo. Throughout the twentieth century anthropologists like Ruth Benedict,

Franz Boas, Marvin Harris, Margaret Mead, and Ashley Montagu brought anthropological views of race—or more properly the nonbiological existence of race—to a broad popular audience, but during the 1940s and 1950s this was a message that threatened the power relations of American inequality.[9]

Some aspects of anthropology's theoretical perspective potentially threatened Cold War America's national security state. Marx's influence on twentieth-century social science was far reaching. Anthropology's roots in Lewis Henry Morgan's evolutionary approach, and the materialist and crypto-Marxist theories of anthropologists like V. Gordon Childe, Julian Steward, and Leslie White brought Marx-influenced perspectives to the core of the field—although the absence of an emphasis on class conflict, comodification, and praxis marked these theoretical developments. It was not until the 1960s that anthropologists began to openly acknowledge the discipline's epistemological debt to Karl Marx and Friedrich Engels. Even today there continues to be a hesitancy to acknowledge the impact of Socialism or Communism on the development of American anthropology. Although Marxist and materialist theories did enjoy a critical rebirth during the 1960s and 1970s, the manifestation of this was directly affected by the lessons of McCarthyism (Harris 1968a, 1979; cf. Ross 2002).

Anthropological theory was hampered at least as much as anthropological praxis during the McCarthy period. Although anthropology is perhaps the branch of the social sciences best suited to examine Marx's grand observation of the cross-cultural causal linkage between social structure, consciousness, and production, in the 1940s and 1950s anthropologists could not openly explore Marx's assertion that "the mode of production of material life determines the general character of the social, political and spiritual processes of life. It is not the consciousness of men that determines their being, but, on the contrary, their social being determines their consciousness" (1859:20–21).

It is unclear to what extent the writings of anthropologists during the 1940s, 1950s, and early 1960s intentionally muddled their own theoretical analysis as a result of the threat that scholars like Morris Opler might issue. As Eleanor Leacock observed, "the influence of Marxist theory upon neoevolutionary formulations was complicated by the fact that until the 1960s it was virtually impossible for an academic to discuss Marxism as such" (1985:249). It is unknown to what degree Julian Steward's inconsistent notion of a cultural core—an unsatisfying amalgamation of cultural features that at times functions as Marx's Base and at others as Marx's Superstructure—was derived from Marx.[10] Some of Steward's correspondence indicates a direct but hidden influence of Marx. In reply to Marvin Harris's speculation in *The Rise of Anthropological Theory* that Steward's cultural ecological theory had been primarily influenced by A. L. Kroeber, Carl Sauer, and Robert Lowie at Berkeley (see Harris 1968a:662), Steward wrote to Harris that

> speculation about how I [came to develop my conception of "cultural ecology"] is only partly correct. First, I was interested in causes before I really got into anthropology, and was quite disturbed that Kroeber repudiated this interest. Second, the key factor of the national intellectual climate was the Depression, which started after I finished my studies at Berkeley in 1928. I had taught at Michigan two years, 1928–1930, and Utah 3 years, by the time the Depression became so acute that everyone was asking Why? . . . and thinking generally took a sharp Marxist turn. It was during the thirties that Columbia became a communist cell far more than people knew, and curiously, many adopted the political and economic orientations yet remained thorough-going relativists in their anthropological work[.] I too read Marx and others but it was dangerous to proclaim a Marxian position. (Julian Steward to Marvin Harris 3/8/69)

In *Anthropology and Politics* Joan Vincent examines the subtle changes in language as Marxist-influenced Columbia-trained anthropologists published their dissertations (1990:238–42). Vincent established consistent shifts in Preston Holder's 1951 dissertation when it was published as *The Hoe and the Horse on the Plains*—shifts that purged the language and analysis of Marx. Vincent notes that "the political language of the dissertation—references to evolution, class, the program of colonialism, and power—was transformed into discussions of development, status, pattern, and 'those in high places'" (1990:239). Vincent observes that even references to Marxist archaeologist V. Gordon Childe were excised from Holder's book (Leacock 1990:239; cf. Peace 1995). Eleanor Leacock later notes that when she "discussed the impact of the fur trade on native Canadian society and the significance of the transformation from production for use to production for exchange, I cited, not Marx as I should have, but a chance statement of the far-from-Marxist Herskovits" (1985:255).

But this vetting of Marx and self-censorship of views was not limited to students—professors equally felt the pressures (see Lazarsfeld and Thielens 1958:192–217). There is some evidence that anthropologists self-censored their publicly declared opinions regarding the propriety of Communists teaching at universities. For example, Robert Redfield's statements on this topic at the University of Chicago's sixtieth anniversary vary from his unpublished writings on the topic. While his publicly stated view bravely championed his sincere civil libertarian views regarding the danger of McCarthyism on American campuses, he nonetheless also stated that "no investigation of the university has turned up any Communist teachers because there are none, and indeed a great free university is not a place where a reasonable man would expect to find them because the life of such a university is freedom of thought and expression which is just what Communism cannot practice or tolerate" (1951:161). A draft paper titled "Communists Should Teach in American Universities," preserved with Redfield's professional papers, expressed a more progressive view of this situation:

> It occurs to me that by reason of the fact that we have no Communist on our faculty my university may be incomplete. A university is a place where all intellectually significant points of view are presented and criticized. Communism, as a theory and doctrine about society, is intellectually significant. It exerts a powerful influence and it does so in part because it has important ideas. I do not see that astrology or other views of the Klu Klux Klan require serious consideration in a university, because these ideas are feeble, incoherent and [easily] shown of little worth. But the ideas expressed by Marx, and ideas later expressed by Lenin, are coherent, and are defensible by men who have scientific principles and scholarly capacity. I do not say that these ideas withstand criticism—I say only that they are respectable enough to deserve criticism. (n.d.:1)

Thus Redfield *publicly* proclaimed that Communists could not tolerate freedom of expression, while his *private* thoughts on the need for Communist professors remained muted (see Hook 1949). While evidence of the distribution of such self-censorship is by its very nature difficult to document, it is not surprising to find in an anthropology department so frequently visited by roving FBI agents (see chapters 9 and 10).

Some of anthropology's collisions with McCarthyism were public and well known, while other incidents were extremely private and were either publicly unknown or recognized only with private whispers. Very few of these episodes have been the subject of scholarly inquiry, and there are a number of reasons for this. There is a general reluctance to acknowledge the discipline's historical ties to Communist and Socialist organizations. There are basic misunderstandings of the nature, goals, and scope of McCarthyism. The methodological complications inherent in studying any secret process makes fact gathering difficult. Because many anthropologists and organizations acted out of fear there is a general reluctance to examine these troubling events. Finally, there is hesitancy because some of the actors in these events are still living, and there is discomfort in examining instances where prominent anthropologists cooperated with the forces of McCarthyism. And so the topic of anthropology's intersection with McCarthyism remains a topic of significance but rarely of detailed consideration.

Contemporary anthropology is still marked by McCarthyism in many ways. There are retired professors who taught or studied anthropology during the 1940s and 1950s who witnessed McCarthyism's lessons of self-censorship first and second hand. In anthropology departments across the country, from Columbia to UCLA, there are practicing anthropologists who were themselves red diaper babies—children of Communists—during the McCarthy period. Many of these descendants of the McCarthy period have personal histories unshared with their colleagues and students although the impacts of their pasts continue. The lessons of the dangers of activism remain well learned. Ellen Schrecker observed that by the late 1950s there was a significant decline in hearings and dismissals, "not because . . . [of] resistance but because they were no longer necessary. All was quiet on the academic front" (1986:341).

McCarthyism took a large chunk out of American anthropology—a chunk so deep it continues to affect and limit the scope and approach of anthropology today. The ravages of McCarthyism profoundly changed mid-century American academic discourse and, more important, altered some possibilities of radical anthropological activism and advocacy. As we will see, the AAA's approach to defending the rights of scholars under attack moved from a position of syncopated incompetence to a stance of distracted indifference. Scholars who were under attack were left to fend for themselves, and some came to be marginalized as academic pariahs.

McCarthyism tamed the classroom—for a while. In the 1950s a chill fell over the classroom; as one professor observed, "you no longer get the Marxist view brought up in class. In 1946 to 1949 they made this place hum. I don't know whether they believe differently today or if they are unwilling— they may have changed positions. Vigor and extremeness of position are gone" (quoted in Lazarsfeld and Thielens 1958:216). Perhaps most significant, contemporary anthropology continues to be marked by the absence of a wealth of voices of those who were led to exit the field due to the pressures of McCarthyism. We cannot know what contributions individuals like Jack Harris, Richard Morgan, Morris Swadesh, Melville Jacobs, Gene Weltfish, or Jerome Rauch (and the countless others who are not known to us) would have made to the field if they had been allowed the full freedom of inquiry needed for science to function properly.

CHAPTER 2

Melville Jacobs, Albert Canwell, and

University of Washington Regents:

A Message Sent

The threads of the Marxist tradition in political

anthropology are still difficult to discern, let alone

unravel. — Joan Vincent

The belief in the inherent equality of all people is a touchstone of Boasian anthropology, and Franz Boas's early-twentieth-century scientific critique of the social abuses of "race" launched American anthropology on a course of political activism. Boas and his students understood that the seemingly straightforward biological category of race was inevitably wrapped in a highly stratified social context. Thus, supposedly objective measures of innate abilities, such as IQ, were inevitably linked to cultural realities. Boas and his students saw it as their duty to bring this perspective to the streets, newspapers, radio broadcasts, and governmental agencies.

While Boas and the later Boasians of the mid-twentieth century held very progressive antiracist views, they fell short of contemporary understandings of race. Ashley Montagu was the Boasian responsible for most clearly formulating the contemporary anthropological view of race.[1] Montagu's 1942 *Man's Most Dangerous Myth: The Fallacy of Race* established and popularized the anthropological framework of race as social construct. Most anthropologists view race as consisting of culturally identified physical features—that is, it is culture that recognizes certain physical traits (e.g., skin color, facial features, hair type) as belonging to certain culturally imagined distinct racial groups. This view holds that biological variation is real but that the grouping of physical traits into "racial groups" reflects cultural, not biological, realities, and as such this view threatened the normative racist justifications for inequality in postwar America. As Boas wrote in a 1941 essay for the Communist-controlled literary magazine the *New Masses*: "How can we expect the Negro race to take its proper place in our culture as long as economic and social discrimination persist? We must demand equality, not equality on paper, but equal rights in life, equal opportunity for education, equal economic opportunities, and the breakdown of social barriers that oppress even those who in character and achievement are often infinitely superior to those who will not acknowledge for them the claim that is so often heralded as the basis of our society, the claim that all men are born with equal rights" (1941:6).

Melville Jacobs was a gifted anthropologist and linguist whose private politics became the focus of a postwar red-baiting Washington State congressional committee. Jacobs (Ph.D. 1931) was trained by Franz Boas at Columbia University in the 1920s, where his cohort of fellow graduate students included Anita Brenner, Henry Carey, Reo Fortune, Frederica de Laguna, and Gene Weltfish (Ebihara 1985:106–7). Jacobs's ethnographic work with Pacific Northwest Sahaptin and Clackamas Indian peoples produced some of the most important regional Indian linguistic texts of the Boasian and post-Boasian era. Ultimately it was Jacobs's professional work and private activism on race and equality that led to two public loyalty trials and decades of FBI persecution and surveillance.

Like many Boasians prior to the postwar period, Jacobs thought of race in terms of a biological category—but one with no bearing on an individual's mental potential. Melville Jacobs and Bernhard Stern's 1947 *General Anthropology* textbook's examination of "the plasticity of human behavior," and their critique of racism and of the inherent cultural biases of IQ tests are issues consistent with contemporary anthropological critiques of race. But their analysis of the "eleven races of mankind" has been replaced by an appreciation that the social categories of race are not so easily delineated. Despite such inevitable analytical shortcomings, Jacobs and Stern's analysis of race and racism was succinct and hard-hitting, leading them to unfavorably compare America's racist practices with those of the Nazis: "In Germany, the creed of

Aryan superiority among the Nazis led to the extermination of millions of Jews and helped to incite World War II. In the United States, racism serves primarily to sanction and to perpetuate discrimination against Negroes and other dark-skinned peoples. In colonial areas it has impeded the efforts of submerged peoples in their struggle towards equal opportunities, justice and independence" (1952:75). Whatever the specific faults a contemporary anthropologist might find in the half-century-old writings of anthropologists like Jacobs and Stern, the kernel of the present critique of race as a social construct was there, and it was a *radical* critique that threatened the social order of the day.

The FBI Notes Jacobs as Subversive

Jacobs came to the FBI's attention in July 1940 after "a confidential informant submitted information listing Professor Melville Jacobs among about twenty-one professors and instructors of the University of Washington whom [the informant] described as being radical reds or who have been mixed up with Communism or radical activities" (WFO100-26050 5/19/41). The FBI's central files listed Jacobs as belonging to such "subversive" organizations as the National Federation for Constitutional Liberties and the American League for Peace and Democracy.

The FBI conducted an investigation into the activities of Communists at the University of Washington in May 1941 (WFO100-4082-1). At the suggestion of Assistant U.S. Attorney Gerald Shucklin a conference was convened with Shucklin, a Seattle FBI agent, and two members of the University of Washington's board of regents. One regent told the FBI that "the Board of Regents, especially during the present disturbed international situation, is anxious to remove from the faculty any members who can be proven to be Communists." The Regent added, "that great difficulty was encountered in producing sufficient evidence of Communist affiliation to warrant discharge of an instructor, due to the tradition of tenure which practically guarantees an instructor a permanent position at the University after he has taught for at least three years" (WFO100-4082-1). Regent members asked the FBI and U.S. attorney's office to provide information that would help them determine the identity of secret Communists at the university. There is no record, however, of the regents expressing any concern over issues of academic freedom or the dangers of investigating the private politics of instructors.

When the FBI told the regents that their policy precluded the sharing of bureau records, the regents "indicated that they might attempt to secure authorization of the United States Attorney General for the disclosure of such information" (WFO100-4082-1; cf. Diamond 1982). Shucklin said he would forward their request to the attorney general, but added he "could give them no encouragement, or hope for favorable results." The memo concluded with a report that local right-wing radio broadcaster Lester Hunt had identified Jacobs as a Communist during a broadcast (WF00100-4082-1).

Jacobs was identified as a Communist when the FBI interviewed a self-described pacifist professor at the university two months later (WF0100-4082-2 8/4/41). Another report from 1941 indicates the FBI was aware that Jacobs spoke on "Race and the National Situation" at a Communist Party meeting in West Seattle (WF0100-4082-4).

After America entered World War II, Jacobs offered to the U.S. military his skills as a linguist and scholar. Correspondence from this period indicates that he contacted a number of old acquaintances in various branches of military and intelligence service, but despite the need for linguists no offers were forthcoming. It is unknown if the FBI's knowledge of his membership in the Communist Party damaged his chances of working on sensitive projects during the war, but this seems likely. It is surprising that Jacobs's FBI file does not contain information on his public protests and opposition of the internment of Japanese Americans by the War Relocation Authority (see Goldfrank 1977:197; AA 1942, 44(1):286). It seems unlikely these actions escaped the scrutiny of the FBI, and it is probable that such records existed but were either destroyed, not indexed, not locatable, or withheld for reasons not disclosed by the FBI.

In coordination with the Civil Service Commission, the National Defense Detail, the Seattle Police Department, and the Office of Military Intelligence, the FBI interviewed a former Communist member of the university's faculty on April 27, 1942. The faculty member recounted how he was solicited for Communist Party membership in 1935 through his activities in the teachers' union (WF0100-4082-7). On joining the party he was "given a Party membership book and a Party name," and was expected to pay approximately 10 percent of his income as party dues. He provided the FBI with a list of sixteen Communist professors, instructors, and teaching fellows. Due to the protections of the Privacy Act the identities of all but four individuals are not disclosed herewith—these four are Melville Jacobs, Joseph Butterworth, Dorothy Butterworth, and party dues secretary, James Norie.

A month later the Seattle FBI office sent a nine-page "Internal Security-C[ommunist]" report on Jacobs to bureau headquarters. A portion of this report appears to have been provided by a university employee with access to personnel records. Most of the report consists of information gathered from interviews with several informants. The first "confidential informant" had studied anthropology at Columbia University under Boas with Jacobs, taught at the University of Washington since approximately 1930, conducted fieldwork in the Pacific Northwest with Jacobs, and had since retired in the Seattle area. The informant reported details of Jacobs's personal and professional life, and indicated that while conducting fieldwork with Jacobs, "Jacobs mentioned the work of the Washington Commonwealth Federation and seemed to be more conscious of social and economic problems. At that time and subsequent thereto, JACOBS frequently discussed the conditions of the working man and how they should be better. In 1938 and up to the present time, JACOBS became more active in the discussion of political questions, and informant has had very little dealing with him" (WFO100-4082-9).

The FBI's suspicions of Jacobs intensified with news of his interest in the Washington Commonwealth Federation (WCF), a liberal interest group established by Democrats in 1935—although within three years Communist Party members controlled its leadership. Most of the federation's activities involved supporting Democrat candidates, but in 1936 it helped elect four Communists to the Washington State legislature, and another five Communists to the state legislature in 1938. The WCF worked under the Communist Party's Popular Front strategies of the 1930s, and its suspected ties to the Communist Party brought inquiries into its involvement with the Washington Pension Union (Acenca 1975).

One informer told the FBI that there were inevitable ties between anthropology and Marxist thought, and added that, "in 1848, at the time ENGELS and MARX wrote the Communist Manifesto, it was the generally accepted anthropological theory that man passes through certain stages from a savage beast into an educated human being. Anthropologists generally have repudiated this theory today. However, the Communist Party accepts this theory and at all times in scholastic arguments with informant, JACOBS has endeavored to justify this theory" (WFO100-4082-9:3). Thus Jacobs's professional work was suspect as influenced by Communist thought.

Nine other informants were interviewed for this report. They described Jacobs as a "left-winger," a "fellow traveler" involved with various Communist Party fronts, and as developing "undercover" political views. Some informants reported seeing Jacobs at Communist Party meetings in the 1930s, others remarked on his activism opposing racism. One reported that "on several occasions within the last four or five years bills have been introduced in the Washington State Legislature preventing the inter-marriage of races. JACOBS has always been one to lead a group to Olympia to lobby against such legislation" (WFO100-4082-9:4). Another memo identified Jacobs as a long-active member in the Communist Party (WFO100-27050-2 5/26/42).

Hoover instructed the Seattle SAC (Special Agent in Charge) to add Jacobs to the bureau's Confidential Custodial Detention Card File on November 3, 1942 (WFO100–4082-14; WFO100-27050-9). A memo from Lawrence M. C.

Smith, chief of the Special War Policies Unit of the War Division, to Hoover confirmed Jacobs's "tentative dangerousness classification" (WFOI00-4082-15 12/3/42), a status he held until Attorney General Francis Biddle abolished the custodial detention program eight months later (WFOI00-27050).

For the remainder of the war the FBI recorded little interest in Jacobs, but in October 1945 his name appeared on a security report indicating that he was a member of the "Rogers branch," an elite core of influential Communist Party members who held positions of power or high stature in Washington State (WFOI00-4082-22). As I show in my discussions of Richard Morgan, Paul Radin, and Mary Shepardson, these "professional branches" of the Communist Party were special party sections for prominent community members. In theory, professional branches protected the identities of party members with a visible public presence, but the branches were as infiltrated by FBI agents and informants as any other section meeting of the party.[2] A portion of a 1943 report on the Rogers branch found,

> with reference to the professional unit mentioned above concerning ████
> ██████ the informant stated that this was a "very super-duper" group
> of communists. Informant declared that every precaution was taken to
> protect the identity of members of this unit and informant declared that
> the members to his knowledge were highly educated persons who were
> generally employed in the professional fields. Informant stated that per-
> sons who were prominent in public life, such as members of the state
> legislature, were not admitted to this unit lest their activities be traced
> and other members be identified. The professional unit makes its con-
> tributions to the party, according to this informant, by way of financial
> gifts and also by way of writings.
>
> In connection with the latter matter, the informant stated that the
> professional members who provide this material never permit their
> names to be attached to it but rather the name of some other individual is
> attached as author. The informant voiced the opinion, although he had
> no positive information to substantiate it, that the following were mem-
> bers of the professional unit of the communist party: Professor MEL-
> VIN [sic] JACOBS, Professor ████████, and Professor ██████████
> of the University of Washington. (WFOI00-4082-19)

Another memo indicated that a meeting of the professional branch was held at Jacobs's home (WFOI00-4082-32 4/21/45).

As the FBI geared up for the century's second red scare, it refused to disentangle party Communism from the progressive causes that many Communists, Socialists, and nonaligned progressives joined. The FBI cared little whether individuals involved in progressive activism were Communists or not, or whether American Communists operated independently of international Communists. In practice, the FBI monitored and suppressed equally the actions of all activists fighting for economic, racial, or social equality, whether they were Communists or not.

The FBI had already infiltrated Seattle's Communist Party branch, and it had free access to records inside of Seattle's party headquarters located in the Empress Building on Second Avenue. A memo dated May 5, 1945, recorded Jacobs's payment of ten dollars a month into the party's "Day's Pay campaign" as a member of the "Rogers Club" (WFO100-4082-33). A "highly confidential source" with access to the party registration cards at party headquarters, took photographs of membership cards including Jacobs's card for the Rogers Club, and thus documented his party status (WFO100-4082-42).

The FBI routinely staked out "subversive" meetings, writing down the license numbers of cars parked near homes where meetings were held. Many of these meetings were nothing more than labor campaigns or public talks on the dangers of racism—but the FBI believed that the free exchange of ideas on these topics threatened the fabric of American life. In 1943 Jacobs's car license plate was recorded in the neighborhood of a meeting of the teachers' branch of the Communist Party (WFO100-4082-24) and at various other "subversive" meetings (WFO100-4082-26). Jacobs's file also contains partial transcripts of wiretapped telephone calls in which Jacobs called a second party whose phone was tapped by the FBI.

During the 1940s and 1950s the FBI routinely scanned newspapers for information on subversive activities; even the most innocuous references to "subversive" individuals were clipped and added to their files. One FBI clipping from the *Seattle Daily Times* (8/18/43) announced a talk by Jacobs to the Young Men's Business Club on the topic of "Races and the War" (WFO100-4082-21). Another clipping from the *Seattle Star* (9/15/44) announced a talk to the Retail Credit Association of Seattle, on "Race Problems and World Peace." There are photostat reproductions of church handbills advertising Jacobs's talk at a meeting of the Christian Friends for Racial Equality (WFO 100-4082-53). The FBI also noted Jacobs's regular comments on the local KJR radio program "Science Headlines" (WFO100-4082-56 12/4/47), most of which dealt with the anthropological critique of the concept of race or the misuses of the concept of "intelligence" (WFO100-4082-58).

In November 1946 J. Edgar Hoover requested that the Seattle bureau reexamine Jacobs's party status to determine whether or not his Security Index Card should be canceled (WFO100-4082-45). On June 13 the Seattle office compiled a list of information collected during the previous four years indicating that Jacobs was still involved in Communist Party activities. The Seattle SAC then indicated his desire to "retain the subject on the Security

Index list" (WF0100-4082-49). This information established that Jacobs was involved in numerous radical causes affiliated with the Communist Party, but it would be a public official who used Jacobs's affiliations to try and destroy his reputation and work.

Fear, Racism, Paranoia, Senator Albert Canwell, and the University of Washington

In 1947 Senator Albert Canwell, Republican chairman of the Washington State Interim Committee on Un-American Activities, held hearings to un-cover what he believed to be a ring of Communist professors at the University of Washington (Frederick 1997; Scates 2000). From the beginning of these attacks the University of Washington's president, Raymond Allen, took the position that all faculty must be forthcoming about any "questionable" past political activities. Allen's narrow view of academic freedom held that all faculty must "not only cooperate with Canwell, but refrain from criticizing him as well" (Schrecker 1986:95).

Eleven professors were called before Canwell's committee, including were Maud Beal (English), Joseph Butterworth (English), Joseph Cohen (Sociology), Harold Eby (English), Garland Ethel (English), Ralph Gundlach (Psychology), Melville Jacobs (Anthropology), Angelo Pellegrini (English), Herbert Phillips (Philosophy), Melvin Rader (Philosophy), and Sophus Winther (English). Of these eleven only one identified other party members and only a few discussed their private politics (Countryman 1951; Sanders 1979).

Jacobs refused to identify or discuss others accused of maintaining Communist connections. When he was asked by committee investigator William Houston to identify who had "solicited" his membership in the Communist Party, Jacobs replied that he "wouldn't phrase it as a—as a solicitation. I would put it somewhat in this light, Mr. Houston, if I may, that in the period of the Depression and in the course of visiting around in the country, riding about in my car and seeing poor devils starving or walking along the Bowery of New York, I became aware [of an] aspect of life I had never had any occasion to be interested in. Furthermore a professional anthropologist has to work with people who have taken the most indescribable beating, our American Indians or other natives in various parts of the world" (State of Washington 1948:245). Houston regarded this answer as unresponsive— and he apparently missed Jacobs's suggestion that anthropologists studying minority populations might naturally be drawn to radical critiques of American inequality. After being repeatedly pressed to name who, other than his wife (previously identified as a party member), was present at party meetings, Jacobs finally said, "I simply cannot be an informer on people who, in my judgment, have always been completely loyal to our country, and who do not believe in force and violence, who have never done anything illegal, and who are my friends" (MJ: 120, 52). Against the advice of council, Jacobs refused to answer any further questions. His decision to discuss his own political inclinations and activities while refusing to discuss those of others paved the way for his future problems with the University of Washington's Faculty Committee on Tenure and Academic Freedom.

It was at this second hearing at the University of Washington that Canwell pressured President Allen to investigate these party connections and to determine what should be done with the six professors with documented past affiliations with the Communist Party. Allen did little to resist Canwell's attacks on academic freedom, and AAUP official William T. Laprade likened Allen's behavior to that of "a sheriff who, seeing a mob bent on action, takes the leadership of a lynching party" (Schrecker 1986:321). On campus Allen was pressured to resist Canwell's drive for a campus show trial, but Allen could not resist such a prospect (Sanders 1979; Jenkins 2000). In fall 1948 Edward H. Lauer,[3] dean of the College of Liberal Arts and Sciences, filed complaints against six of the eleven faculty members who had appeared before Canwell's committee.[4] These faculty members were ordered to appear at hearings of the Faculty Committee on Tenure and Academic Freedom, which would investigate whether they had lied to the administration about past party membership. The committee was charged with fact finding and with making recommendations for possible disciplinary action to President Allen and the board of regents. Jacobs found himself in a precarious position because of his initial failure to confirm to President Allen his past party membership (Sanders 1979:67–68).

It is not clear what communication the FBI had with Senator Canwell or President Allen. In 1948 one former University of Washington student told the FBI about a supposed network of Communist professors who recruited him into the party. This informant, "advised that when he was a freshman on the campus in ▮▮▮▮▮▮▮▮ he was picked up by a group of professors including JOSEPH BUTTERWORTH. ▮▮▮▮▮▮▮▮ and MEL JACOBS, who he identified as COMMUNISTS. . . . He stated that these individuals and others who were primarily professors and graduate students, formed an off campus discussion group. He advised that ▮▮▮▮▮▮▮▮ was in their confidence to the point where MEL JACOBS and JOE BUTTERWORTH told him they had lists of key men who were their responsibility to be assassinated should the occasion arise. He [believed] that these men were employed in such fields as telephonic communication" (WFO100-4082-64). This is a highly suspect claim. It is clear from Jacobs's writings and his later interviews with FBI agents that he was cautious concerning with whom he discussed his political activities, and he was careful not to politically indoctrinate students. It is ridiculous to think that people such as Butterworth and Jacobs had been involved in such a plan, but the FBI considered this report credible and they intensified their investigation of Jacobs.

Anthropologists from around the country wrote letters to President Allen in support of Jacobs. Letters were written by anthropologists E. A. Hoebel, Harry Hoijer, W. D. Wallis, Ralph Linton, Margaret Mead, Erna Gunther, Melville Herskovits, John Cooper, and Bernhard Stern, as well as anthropology students Robert Lane, Wayne Suttles, and Richard Daugherty (MJ: 121, 9). Bernhard Stern tried to coax President Allen into seeing the dangers of rendering to the state the authority to regulate intellectuals. Stern argued that,

> as a Sociologist, I made several studies on the effect of the pressures of such groups [i.e., the Canwell committee] upon the teaching process. I have found that they are invariably detrimental. There is consensus among educators as you know, that scientific inquiry and honest teaching require an atmosphere of freedom, a sense of security on the part of the teacher that he can be forthright in the expression of his intellectual convictions and other finds which he has arrived at through scholarly inquiry and contemplation. Such committees create fear and tension and so undermine academic morale.
>
> I have found that when University administrators support their faculties when they are attacked by such groups the cause of scholarship is advanced, but when they yield the results are baneful to intellectual inquiry for some years following.
>
> The decision which you make in the situation confronting the University of Washington will, I feel, be crucial, not only for education in Washington, it will have its repercussions throughout the United States. It is for this reason that I am taking the liberty of writing you to tell you that those of us who have read your volume on medical education are looking to you to support your faculty against those who would subvert the traditions of academic freedom and political liberty in this country. (MJ: 120, 51)

Even Ralph Linton wrote President Allen, saying that "the attack on Mr. Jacobs is part of the general campaign of terrorism now being carried on against all intellectuals by reactionary fascist groups" (MJ: 121). Melville Herskovits wrote Allen stating that the policy threatened the reputation and autonomy of the University of Washington, and adding that he had "learned with regret of the attacks of the Canwell Committee on various members of your faculty under the guise of attempting to ferret out un-American activities. This seems to be a part of a movement which feeds on a refusal to recognize the academic principle that problems must be looked at from all sides, and misinterprets this as taking sides. I am writing this letter to express the hope that the University will stand firm against these attacks." (MJ: 120, 51). President Allen, however, was unmoved by these letters.

On July 15, 1948, Jacobs wrote to President Allen, summarizing a meeting with Senator Canwell two days earlier. Jacobs reported that he, Professor Eby, and their mutual lawyer, Edward Henry, had discussed procedural matters pertaining to the upcoming hearing. Jacobs wrote that it was clear that Canwell intended to use the hearings for opportunistic speechmaking and to humiliate all who appeared before the committee. Jacobs wrote that Canwell committee chief investigator William Houston

> indicated that unless they went the length of a public denunciation of the party, Communism and Russian Communism, they would of course be judged—by his group—still "Communists at heart" if not actually party members.
>
> [Houston] described how the committee was bringing west some authorities who would portray communism and all its works, and how everyone subpoenaed would be required to be present in order to be "educated" about such matters. He indicated no little delight in the spectacle of the enforced presence of professors who would have to sit and learn at the feet of the authorities he was importing, and that no partial absences would be tolerated. . . . Mr. Canwell informed us that every person who had ever joined the party was either a prospective saboteur or a dupe. Mr. Houston at several points indulged himself in the employment of various expletives not customarily employed by gentlemen.
>
> Mr. Houston concluded that the only useful thought he had for the remainder of the afternoon was that Dr. Eby and I each proceed to sit privately with an investigator, without benefit of the presence of an attorney, and tell all.
>
> Mr. Canwell's final assertion was that his committee "did not play many tricks." (MJ: 120, 51)

Jacobs understood the danger that both he and the University of Washington faced from the tenure committee's proceedings, and he took some calculated comfort in his perception that the university faced a possible blacklisting if it ruled against him and the other professors. His wife, Bess, wrote to a friend a week before the hearings, saying that "both Harold [Eby] and Mel cannot see how this committee can fail to give them complete exoneration from all charges, after weighing the evidence. And of course, if Allen goes ahead and requests firings in spite of such exoneration he will guarantee a national black-

listing of the university by the American Association of Univ. Professors"
(MJ: 121, 6 10/16/48).

The University of Washington hearings lasted from October 27 to December 15, 1948.[5] In the end, the committee concluded that while Jacobs had been less than forthright concerning past Communist affiliations, his political activities had not interfered with his teaching responsibilities. However, the board of regents fired three of the other faculty members under investigation (Butterworth, Gundlach, and Phillips) because President Allen believed all three had lied about or continued to maintain their party memberships. The regents adopted President Allen's recommendation to retain Jacobs as a faculty member if he would comply with two conditions: that he sign an affidavit stating he hadn't been a member of the Communist Party since 1946, and that he be placed on probation for two years. Jacobs complied and remained on the faculty of the University of Washington for the rest of his life (MJ: 121, 6).

Jacobs's victory came at a great price, including a $1,325 legal bill—an amount approximately 40 percent of his annual salary (WFO100-4082-9:2). There were also personal and psychological repercussions. A careful reading of Jacobs's papers makes it clear that his view of academic freedom, his colleagues, and the American political system was forever altered. As with other victims of witch-hunts, his willingness and capacity to trust others were greatly diminished. One document shedding light on these feelings was originally drafted as "An Answer to Charges," and was later presented to the committee in a highly edited version, titled "Statement to Faculty Committee of Tenure and Academic Freedom." In this narrative Jacobs summarizes his journey from party membership to leaving the party to his surreal encounter with the inquisition. He clarifies his own outrage and examines the hypocrisy of his colleagues, and at one point he wryly compares the treatment of former Marxists with the treatment of scholars who have undergone paradigmatic shifts:

> My gradual change of orientation of the early 1940's regarding the world and national picture, symbolized by eventual disaffiliation from an organization that had long given a degree of support to the New Deal, is surely not [an] unusual occurrence among persons who attempt to keep growing and who remain independent in their thinking. Nor would any understanding person presume that an earlier orientation, or personal affection for some of its protagonists, had so permanently conditioned a scholar that he was henceforth incapable of sincere or creative thinking in terms of new evidence. The history of scholarship, science, and politics provided innumerable instances of persons whose veering in some

new direction of thought has warranted no hue and cry that had once been so wrong that they could never be trusted or right again.

My own scientific field offers as witness to striking changes in point of view the distinguished careers of Professors Kroeber, Sapir, Benedict and a number of others. In politics we find, for example, that a former sincere and scholarly Communist, John Strachey, is now a member of the British Cabinet and most certainly is now no Communist. Many [such] patriots of Britain appear to suffer no misgivings because of . . . [their] continued presence in an important position in the State, and as far as I know . . . [they have] made this transition without a public [crossed-out text appears here, which states: "display of aggression towards his former confreres"] undignified and sadistic outburst directed against his former confreres. Nor do religious denominations invariably turn away with expressions of hatred or disdain [for] those who had earlier rejected their theological premises.

Every scientific or scholarly specialist could offer additional examples of civilized and accepting rather than provincial and rejecting responses. He could cite noted and respected figures in his field who had interested themselves in a partial or fuller support of creeds, scholarly, scientific or political, which they later abjured with dignity. The maintenance of self respect during a process of change of that kind is a common, accepted, and often admired feature of academic, cultural and political life.

My own career in anthropology has, I think, been to some extent an example of such a change. From 1922 to about 1940 I was confessedly an adherent of the Franz Boas group in anthropology: Boas had been my main teacher. During seventeen or eighteen years I thought in terms of many of the premises of this school of scientific thought, although I was also critical of a number of items. Over a period of years, during the early 1940's I moved so far away, like scientists such as Kroeber, Sapir, Benedict, Mead, Hallowell and some others had done, that I can no longer be identified as a Boasian. My Textbook illustrates this fundamental change.

An analogous process, no less far reaching, occurred in my thinking and action in non-anthropological issues, although these matters were, as everyone who knows me appreciates, peripheral to my central interests which have since 1924 been in scientific work.

Scientists of my field do not urge that since I was an active supporter of the most important portions of Boas' thinking, the fact of that earlier adherence still hangs over me like a threatening black cloud and my several recent writings must therefore be dismissed as irrelevant to a dispassionate discussion of my present worth.

But there appear to be politicians and some others who pray that my path is now so darkened by certain occurrences of the period of my growth that I cannot be trusted to have advanced from such sinister shadows, nor can any confidence ever again be accorded me.

Scientists who are no longer Boasians are, I believe sufficiently respectful of the considered opinions of others that they give vent to no denunciations of Father John Cooper, Professor Herskovits, Reichard Speck, and Lowie, who remain little if at all changed from the Boas position. The reaction is one of respectful attention not magical exorcism. Our science is not disgraced by pleas for inclusion of either former or still unrepentant Boasians in a list of those who are to be forever damned. Nor do the publications of our science exhibit Complaints which argue for expulsion from the American Anthropological Association of persons who adhere to positions of a decreasingly popular doctrine, or who thought in some of its terms for a time in the past.

Scientists do not indulge in a priori or deductive judgments of the point of view of their colleagues. Anthropologists do not assume naively that a present or past supporter of Boas subscribed to every line and paragraph of even most of what Boas wrote during some fifty five years of intensive research and in some six hundred books, monographs and papers.

But the Complaint appears to deduce that I have subscribed to the validity or worth of everything published, here or abroad, in terms of thousands of books, monographs, articles, editorials, official statements, manifestos, constitutions, speeches, or other forms, whether written long before I was born or since, whether sane or extreme, whether correct or incorrect, whether I read them or not, whether I knew of them or not, providing that some then outstanding Communist was the author. Need there be further discussion of the preposterousness of such a deduction?

The characterizations of Communists in general, offered in the Complaint, are exemplary illustrations of reasoning from the general to the particular, reasoning which takes for granted the truth of a number of not necessarily proven assumptions and generalizations regarding the Communist movement. These formulae, which are the slogans and battle cries of many politicians too, warrant scholarly study in order to ascertain their degree of probability, if they seem to have such probability.

The generalizations regarding the Communist movement, as noted in the Complaint, also imply an absence of variability of mind, opinion and behavior in the membership. But everything known today about the psychological responses of human beings indicates that they vary from person to person.

In other words, the Complaint exhibits false generalization, ingenuous stereotypes and an inept adherence to syllogistic inferences.

[paragraph below is crossed out, but legible, in the original]

My own record proves that the application of certain formulae to me as in the Complaint, involves a display of some kind of deductive idiocy, or some combination of libel, slander, and falsehood.

In effect the Complaint says, (1) all Communists took orders blindly from Moscow. (2) Jacobs was a Communist too long. Therefore (3) Jacobs took orders blindly from Moscow too long. That is, he did so for so long a period that further utilization of him now by the university cannot be warranted, even though everyone knows he never took such orders even indirectly, were there such orders. And that if there were such he could not possibly have known their source. That had he known of or suspected the fact of such a source he would not have stayed in the organization another minute. That syllogism symbolizes the essential argument as well as the absurdity and dishonest[y] of the Complaint.

[text following is crossed out, but legible, in the original]

The only dignified response that is possible in the presence of such balderdash and untruths is that of shock, sorrow and anger. I know that were its phrasings ever published their reception among the cultured and liberal people of the State, not least among the many thousands of students and citizens who know me, would be such as to cause damage to the university, which I have tried so long to serve faithfully and which all these people know I have served and am now serving with credit.

It is hard to accept the indisputable fact that in permitting itself to express such absurdities and intemperateness in writing, the university administration has endangered everything a university stands for and has guaranteed a lessened degree of respect for its officials for years to come.

The astonishing public announcement by the administration that it was issuing a Complaint against me for handling by the Tenure Committee, resulted at once in a remarkable display of expressions of unbelief and horror by large numbers of professors as well as by outstanding persons in the community, and what was especially remarkable was the fact that many or most of them [were] hitherto unknown to me. Nothing can be more certain than that the administration would long have withdrawn the Complaint had it realized the extent of repudiation of its policy. One wonders why it has remained so isolated from its own staff as well as the people of the State and has adopted a policy of asking for ex post facto convictions for crimes that it itself must know were never committed.

Can it be that it is overawed by the power of a certain newspaper that some years ago assigned a roving political reporter to do what was needed in order to set up the equivalent of a Tenney Committee for this State? Can it be that my dignified classroom comments, upon query of students who wished to know the worth of the frequent anthropological articles in that paper, were such as to discredit it as a source of information?

Or can it be that my pioneering work in the temperate reporting of the scientific evidence relevant to racial topics and interracial relations was effective over the years, and consequently some of the citizens who remain uninformed about matters of race are supporting those who are resorting to the presently employed means of removing me from the community's public services?

I believe that the Committee should pursue some sort of inquiry in order to determine whether or not such possibilities are germane to this case. I sincerely hope that they are not, but there are many who are persuaded that they are, and therefore it might be well to satisfy those who fear that there is more to the Complaint than meets the eye. The university should be protected lest it be attacked on the grounds of having retreated in the face of pressurings of that kind. (MJ: 121, 8)

Unfortunately, the end of the hearings by the University of Washington's Faculty Committee on Tenure and Academic Freedom only marked the beginning of a new reign of intimidation of academics committed to fighting racism and economic injustice. In the months and years that followed, anthropologists found themselves in increasing danger of being scrutinized by similar local and national loyalty boards. As these attacks continued, professional associations such as the AAA faced important choices regarding both their responsibilities to members whose academic freedoms were under attack and their need to distance themselves from these scholars and the associated scandals in order to protect their members' access to the rolling gravy train of coming Cold War research dollars.

The success of the University of Washington's purging of Marxist and once-Communist scholars sent a message to right-wing politicians and university board members across the country. If such show trials could successfully intimidate progressive and radical scholars in Seattle—then one of the most pro-labor, progressive regions in the nation—then these purges could be implemented with success elsewhere.

CHAPTER 3

Syncopated Incompetence: The American

Anthropological Association's Reluctance

to Protect Academic Freedom

The academy did not fight McCarthyism. It contributed
to it. — Ellen Schrecker

From a contemporary stance it seems odd that the
American Anthropological Association did not
more actively offer Melville Jacobs assistance during his troubles at the University of Washington.
The most common explanations for the AAA's inaction stress the "inappropriateness" of the association becoming involved in political matters. But
another important dynamic of this silence was the
widespread belief that the postwar reorganization
of the AAA created an easily fractured set of coalitions that could be damaged if the organization
adopted positions of controversial public advocacy.

The AAA's archives document its reluctance to
become involved in accusations that its members
were Communists or Socialists. The surviving record shows that officials such as the organization's
president Irving Hallowell were interested in offering limited assistance only if the accused individu-

als were *wrongly* accused of being Communists, but real Communists were to be left on their own.[1] Issues of academic freedom were understood in terms of how non-Marxists were affected by these loyalty oaths and hearings—there was little concern about the impacts of such actions on real, live Marxists. As the tensions of McCarthyism increased, so did a widespread silence that some interpreted as a consensus that accused individuals were simply getting what they had coming to them, while others deciphered the message that all who spoke out against this resounding fascistic chord would become its next victims.

The Morgan Story: "Get the Bastard"

In the months following Melville Jacobs's appearance before the University of Washington's Faculty Committee on Tenure and Academic Freedom, Richard Morgan, an archaeologist educated at the University of Chicago, was fired from the Ohio State Museum under accusations that he was either a Communist or a Communist dupe. Morgan's situation was a complicated one, and the AAA's disorganized inquiry and coordinated inaction further complicated his situation.

Morgan grew up in Middletown, Ohio, and later studied geology and archaeology at Ohio State University. He undertook doctoral studies in anthropology at the University of Chicago, but after becoming a curator at the Ohio State Museum in Columbus he didn't complete the doctoral degree. Morgan's archaeological work was well respected and his archaeological chronology of the Ohio Valley was groundbreaking. During the decade he worked at the museum, he produced a number of significant archaeological monographs, including *Fort Ancient* (1946) and *Fort Hill* (with E. S. Thomas, 1948).

Richard Morgan married Anna Rubio late in life; their marriage was his first and her second. Rubio was a well-known activist who openly held radical views, and many considered her home to be the Communist Party headquarters for Franklin County (Sayre 1995:401). The FBI first became aware of Richard Morgan in 1943 when they noted his contacts with Rubio, then treasurer for the Indianapolis section of the Communist Party, and they recorded that Morgan was paying Rubio $25 each month in party dues (WFO100-6109-1). As FBI agents began to make inquiries to Morgan's associates, they learned he was a quiet, private man who rarely interacted with his colleagues. He was reported to be bright—if not a bit odd—although no one believed him to be a Communist and no one reported hearing him express Communist views. After this initial, limited investigation of Morgan, the FBI undertook a thirty-day mail cover surveillance operation on him. In 1944, the FBI learned that Morgan was a registered member of the Franklin County Communist Party Professional Club (WFO100-238370-37).

One member of Chicago's anthropology department told the FBI that Morgan was "a clean-cut, conscientious, quiet, and reserved individual, who worked hard for his education. He said that at the time [Morgan] attended the University, there were no Communist activities on the campus, and that [Morgan] was not active in student affairs. He said that [Morgan] has never expressed any radical ideas or shown any interest in world politics. He said that [Morgan's] primary interest is anthropology and archaeology, and that he believes that [Morgan] is 100% loyal" (WFO100-13775-2). The FBI's suspicions concerning Morgan were raised after an informant with access to the private records of Chicago's midwest regional office of the Joint Anti-Fascist Refugee Committee in Chicago (JAFRC) provided the FBI with documentation linking Morgan and Anna Rubio to JAFRC—a supposed Communist Party front (WFO100-13775-2).

One Indianapolis FBI informant reported in July 1945 that Anna Rubio planned to sell her Indianapolis rooming house "so that she and her husband could start a 'progressive bookstore' in the downtown area" (WFO100-238370-37). This bookstore was later established in Columbus and would play an important role in the troubles that would befall Richard Morgan.

In mid-1947 an FBI informant—apparently a trusted member of the Cincinnati Communist Party branch—gave the FBI a comprehensive roster of all branch members. This roster indicated that Morgan's party membership name was Marvin Dillingham (WFO100-238370-3X 8/19/47). FBI records indicated that "Marvin Dillingham" contributed $100 to the Columbus party section in January 1947 and $150 in February 1948 (WFO100-238370-8).

After years of covert FBI surveillance, the Morgans' public troubles began when Anna's son, Alfred Rubio, rented his house to Frank Hashmall, an industrial organizer who belonged to the Communist Party. In early March 1948 a right-wing scandal sheet known as the *Bulletin of the General Orton Chapter of the Reserve Officers Association* published an article identifying Richard and Anna Morgan as dangerous, radical agitators. The bulletin identified Anna Morgan's bookstore as a hotbed for local radical activity, stating: "For your sober amusement and to debunk the adage that it can't happen here, our Security Committee invites you to visit the Goodale Bookstore at 38 E. Goodale St. Go into the back room if you can. Also, the house where some of the radicals, fellow travelers etc., on the campus live, is at 220 W. Seuth Ave" (JBP: transcribed note taken by J. Bennett, ca. 1948).

Within days of the bulletin's publication, the *Columbus Dispatch* published an interview with Anna and Richard Morgan concerning the bulletin's allegations. Erwin Zepp, director of the Ohio State Museum, then wrote to Morgan demanding that he clarify his involvement in this scandal (JBP: EZ/RM 3/25/48). Soon there was a small riot at the bookstore and at the home owned by Anna, as summarized by Nora Sayre:

> The Columbus newspapers were among the most zealous in the nation in chastising subversives. In 1948 Frank Hashmall, a district organizer for the Communist Party sent to revitalize the mall branch in Columbus[,] visited the Timken Roller Bearing plant with a few colleagues. They tried to distribute leaflets criticizing the Truman administration: a couple of steelworkers assaulted them and the leaflets were flung into the gutter. The police were called in and Hashmall's address was published in *The Columbus Dispatch*; *The Columbus Citizen* printed a picture of the home he had rented, also his unlisted phone number. Two weeks later, when Hashmall was away, the house was stoned and the windows smashed, the doors were battered down, Venetian blinds were ripped from their frames, and the furniture was broken to bits by some thirty men while a mob of about a thousand cheered from the street outside. (1995:400)

The police were present during this riot and they eventually dispersed the mob—although not until the crowd tossed books and other possessions all over the lawn. No arrests were made. Sayre notes that groups of these men photographed at the scene of destruction were wearing American Legion caps.

On March 25 Richard Morgan learned by way of the local media that Zepp had fired him. Later that day Zepp sent Morgan a simple letter requesting his resignation in order to make matters easier for all involved. Zepp wrote:

Dear Mr. Curator:

The last Bulletin of the General Orton Chapter of the Reserve Officers Association with headquarters in the Army and Navy Club at Fort Hayes, calls attention to certain activities at the Goodale Book Store and a house at 220 West Tenth Avenue. The Bulletin mentions "radicals and Fellow Travelers" in this connection.

It is known that the group or groups in question, have been and are under federal scrutiny, and that certain newspapers in possession of the facts are withholding publication as a matter of public policy.

You must realize the effect of the foregoing facts upon your status in a *state position*, and your responsibility to relieve the Society, preferably in your own way, from the damning publicity which is sure to follow the army officers spark.

It is desirable for all concerned that you take the Initiative and act without delay. (RAAA: EZ/RM 3/25/48)

The next day the *Columbus Dispatch* carried a statement by both *Dispatch* editor and museum chairman Arthur Johnson stating that Morgan had been fired. Morgan maintained that he was still a museum employee because Zepp had not actually fired him. During the next month Morgan and John Bennett, an assistant professor of Anthropology in Ohio State's Department of Sociology, published a small mimeographed handbill outlining the case and calling for letters of support directed at the board of trustees. As letters of protest from the AAA's membership poured in to the museum, the board decided to keep Morgan in his curator position on a special "limited current service basis" while the board investigated the facts of the case (AAANB 1948 2[4]:51).

It was widely known that Morgan held progressive views concerning the equality of races, and in the 1940s in conservative, racist Columbus these views contributed to a perception that he was a marginal or dangerous figure. Morgan had campaigned to desegregate housing developments in Columbus, and there were reports that he "had been tutoring black children 'after hours' at the museum" (Sayre 1995:403). As John Bennett recalls, Morgan was tied to these activities largely through his wife, and that he was "certainly a member of the political circle, but Anna was the leader." According to Bennett, "Dick was in some respects a victim of his wife's activities, as well as a victim of a Columbus right-wing cabal. It was Anna's activities that led the 'cabal' (the Columbus Dispatch newspaper and the statehouse reactionaries, not to mention the fearful Museum Board) to fire Dick. He was the only person they could act against, since Anna was not employed anywhere" (Bennett to Price 4/28/97). Bennett believed that Morgan's troubles hit some deep, Ohio cultural roots, and that the "Morgan case was really a throwback to World War I—early 1920's—red baiting—some of the same Ohio creeps involved in the 1919–1923 episodes were involved in the 40's in the Morgan case. That is, this was native American redbaiting and witch hunting, pure and simple. Pre-HUAC. Ohio was a hotbed of right-wing sentiment, with Honest John Bricker—perhaps the most reactionary Republican of the Interwar years, former Governor and later Senator, at its head. The story around the University at the time was that when Bricker was told that Morgan and his wife had opened a Communist cell in Columbus, he slammed his fist on the desk and said 'get the bastard'" (Bennett to Price 6/9/97).

On April 13, 1948, Bennett sent a six-page statement to the board of the Ohio State Archaeological and Historical Society reporting that he had been working for several years with members of the Ohio State faculty to develop a cooperative archaeological research program, and in this capacity he had come to know Richard Morgan and he could "vouch for his excellent professional standing" (JBP: Bennett Report 4/13/48). Bennett detailed Morgan's contributions, publications, professional association memberships, and his work as an associated editor of *American Antiquity*. Bennett also wrote to the board that he had learned the AAA, the Society for American Archaeology, and the American Association for the Advancement of Science "had expressed interest in the case." Bennett received numerous letters from top-ranked anthropologists from around the United States inquiring into the Morgan case,[2] and he warned the board to anticipate problems replacing Morgan as word spread concerning the circumstances of his firing. He argued that "the position of Curator cannot be filled for an indefinite period—perhaps never—by a qualified professional, if Mr. Morgan's dismissal is upheld. A somewhat analogous case occurred at the University of Illinois . . . where only last Fall, after 15 years, was a professional anthropologist induced to accept a position. It should be understood that anthropologists and archaeologists, like lawyers, doctors and other professional people, have their codes of ethics and their means of protecting their members. And aside from any direct professional action, individual anthropologists would not wish to accept a job where they would be exposed to summary dismissal for vague charges without a hearing or consolation" (JBP: JB/Board 4/13/48). Bennett was concerned that Morgan had been fired without a fair administrative process, and that there was a lack of direct evidence tying Morgan to any wrongdoing. After all, Morgan had not been "accused (nor his wife) of any *direct* affiliations or connections with Communist elements, even in newspaper stories which carried a note of hostility toward the whole affair. This lack of direct accusation, presumably reflecting an absence of any definite evidence, makes the circumstances of his dismissal all the more serious from a professional point of view" (JBP: JB/Board 4/13/48:3).

Bennett closed his report with a threat, writing: "If reinstatement is not made, I am afraid that the professional societies, possibly including the American Association for the Advancement of Science, will enter into the case very energetically. In addition, the position of Curator will be boycotted and the archaeological reputation of the Society will sink very low. I am led to these conclusions by the increasingly serious note in official and unofficial letters of reactions I continue to receive from professional people, within and outside of the field of anthropology" (JBP: JB/Board 4/13/48:3).

Fighting Back: Morgan's Mail Campaign

Richard Morgan did not wait for the AAA to take action; he instead mimeographed a summary of the events leading to his dismissal and mailed out copies to the AAA's membership and to several civil rights groups. His April 1948 memo is as follows:

Fellow Anthropologist

I regret that because of the shortage of time I cannot write you a personal letter. A serious situation has developed at the Ohio State Museum. On March 25, I received the enclosed letter from the director, Mr. E C Zepp. That afternoon I read in the papers, heard on the air and was informed by reporters on the telephone that Mr. Zepp had "fired" me from my position as Curator of Archaeology.

We are faced with the question of academic freedom. I do not consider Mr. Zepp's letter a dismissal. I feel it most unjust that a museum director should accept the vague insinuations of a Reserve Officer's report without consulting me on the question or giving me an opportunity for explanation.

To be brief, and beginning with what may seem irrelevant but which has become a part of the entire picture, I should state that some five months ago my wife opened a little book store at 38 East Goodale St. Although she carried a full line of current fiction the emphasis was on Negro and labor literature. (Mr. Zepp was never in that bookstore). Last year my wife purchased a house as an investment. This year when her son, a returned navy veteran, wished to move to Columbus she sold the house to him. He changed his plans and did not move in, but rented the place to a man who proved to be an officer of the Communist party.

The General Orton Chapter of the Reserve Officers Association is a private club not connected with the government in any way. Its president, Henry B. Van Fleet, is a local termite exterminator. Prof. William Warner of the Dept of Education at Ohio State University is Department Security Officer of that organization for the State. Their "Security Officer" in addition to condemning the Goodale Book Store and a house at 220 West Tenth Ave. (a student rooming house) also stated that the Fellowship of Reconciliation, American Friends Service Committee, National Council against Conscription and the American Veterans Committee, should be carefully watched.

Through this group's prompting the press, hysteria reached such a pitch that after four attempts a mob attacked the Communist's home, wrecked all the furniture and smashed every window. When alarmed citizens protested police failure to protect the man and his family, other organizations were declared suspect and ordered up for investigation. The University, instead of defending its own against reaction, ordered an investigation of the YMCA, Socialist Club, Student Federalists, Wallace Committee and the Progressive Citizens' Committee.

I realize that we are facing a much more serious problem than my reinstatement in my position (if Mr. Zepp's letter can be considered a dismissal). It is now a point of academic freedom in the USA, the right of a man to work in his field without having to defend himself against the slanderous sniping of a semi-military clique. It becomes a question of freedom of thought, freedom to live one's private life, the right of the professional man to feel a reasonable security in his position and to enjoy the peace of mind to do better work in his field. If we fail to act now we are doomed to go down the road that German scientists followed.

The Board of Trustees of the Ohio State Archaeological and Historical Society is meeting on the 16th of April and will consider my case at that time. I would appreciate it very much if you would write a letter on my behalf protesting the undemocratic action taken in my case. If you are familiar with my academic background and archaeological contributions it would help greatly if some statement evaluating my work could be made. Letters may be sent to [E. Zepp and John Bennett]. (RAAA: 3, Shapiro Presidential Correspondence)

News of Morgan's firing quickly spread through the anthropological community. After receiving one of Morgan's mimeographed mailings, Sol Tax wrote to John Bennett expressing his concerns over Morgan's recent firing. Tax described Zepp's actions as "Un-American": "I have known Dick for 18 years and I have never heard any suggestion that he is not a thoroughly loyal citizen of the United States, and I find it impossible to believe that any charges could possibly be sustained against him. This appears to me a case, therefore, in which he is being made to suffer for activities in which he had no part or for which he had no responsibility. This certainly is against the spirit of our American democracy and is, instead, in the very spirit of the totalitarian police state that we are so anxious to protect ourselves against" (ST: ST/JB 47, 10 4/10/48).

At the annual meeting of the Museum's board of trustees on April 16, 1948, a revised policy on tenure and employment was contrived in a closed-door session so that Morgan could be fired in accordance with an ex-post-facto tailor-made policy. This new policy included a clause allowing the firing of Communists or individuals who kept company with Communists, for the reason that the museum was "supported by the State . . . to preserve the heritage and traditions of Ohio and through its program of research, exhibits, lectures and publications, to encourage understanding and good citizenship among our people. Communism is hostile to these purposes, and it is the policy of this Society not to have in its employ a member of the Communist Party, or one who by close and continued and sympathetic association with such members, indicates his approval of their plans and purposes" (RAAA: 3, policy document sent to Richard Morgan 7/28/48). Publicly, the museum board wished to appear more circumspect, and they announced that they would retain Morgan until his case had been properly investigated and a special committee to investigate the case was appointed.

Morgan's mail campaign began to have some impact in the months that followed. Cora Du Bois wrote AAA Executive Secretary David Stout in April urging a position of support for Morgan and suggesting that the AAA try to blacklist the Ohio State Archaeological and Historical Society (RAAA: 3, 2 [Shapiro] Pres. Corr., 1948, N-Z). W. W. Howells wrote President Shapiro endorsing the AAA's resolution in support of Morgan: "Later on, with more dope, I think we might send a communication to *Armed Forces*, a paper primarily for reservists and veterans and their organization and a very good one. It is high time these local patriots left the public safety in the hands of the FBI" (RAAA: 3, HS/Board 4/12/48).

There was some friction between President Shapiro and Executive Secretary David Stout after Stout independently drew up a resolution concerning Morgan and sent it out to the executive board without consulting Shapiro (RAAA: 3, HS/Board 5/12/48; HS/WH 5/12/48). Shapiro wrote Stout that he opposed a vote of censure for the museum (RAAA: 3, HS/DS 4/12/48). Shapiro wrote Howells that he was upset with Stout for two reasons: first, "the resolution struck me as being too similar to the action taken by Doctor Zepp which we were condemning" and, second, because Stout took action without consulting Shapiro.[3]

David Stout wrote a reply to President Shapiro and the executive board concerning the resolution he had recently distributed, in which he stated: "Subsequent to mailing the resolution, I had a letter [and a] telephone conversation with our President. He pointed out, very correctly, that the resolution as originally worded by me left little room for further action concerning Mr. Morgan, should the association desire to take it. He suggested certain changes of wording, which I wholly agreed were desirable and the statement was then sent to the Board of Trustees of the Ohio State Museum and Historical Society in the following form, in time to reach them by April 16, the President concurring" (RAAA: 3, DS/HS 4/20/48). Increasing numbers of AAA members were outraged over Morgan's treatment and wrote to Shapiro asking him to take action in the matter. President Shapiro responded to these letters by stating that the situation was troubling but the association could do little. In June 1948 Ralph Beals suggested that a permanent committee be set in place to deal with these sorts of issues (RAAA: 3, RB/HS 6/8/48).

The Museum Board: Flip-Flopping on a Done Deal

John Bennett wrote President Shapiro on June 30, 1948, requesting that the AAA appoint a committee to investigate Morgan's predicament. Although Bennett was a junior member of the faculty, he volunteered his own services for this committee. Further, he recommended that James Griffin, Fay-Cooper Cole, Robert Redfield, or Fred Eggan be added to the committee roster (JBP: JB/HS 6/30/48). On July 6 President Shapiro appointed a fact-finding committee in order to assure that Morgan was afforded a fair and due process (JBP: JB/HS 7/9/48). The committee consisted of John Bennett (Ohio State University), Fay-Cooper Cole (University of Chicago), and James Griffin (University of Michigan) (AAANB 1948 2[5]:72–73).

While the reasons for selecting these individuals are not recorded, it seems likely that Bennett was chosen because his employment at the university gave him an inside view of the situation. Cole was the best known and the elder of the group, he was well respected and had plenty of experience in academic politics. James Griffin had known Morgan since their days together as graduate students in Chicago; the two worked together on projects over the years; and Griffin was one of the most respected archaeologists in the region.

On July 20 Bennett requested that the museum board allow him to attend the board meeting to be held three days later. On July 22 the board notified Morgan by telegram that he was to appear before the board on the following day, but Bennett was not allowed to attend the meeting.[4] A portion of the unsigned draft of an AAA report on the board's meeting of July 23 survives in the AAA's papers. It reports that

> Morgan felt, wisely or not, that he [must] decline to attend the meeting unless an impartial observer were present. Since this request was not granted, he retired. The Board then decided to dismiss Morgan, stating without qualification that he had "refused to discuss the merits of the matter" and that he was in [violation] of the stated employment policy of the Society. This policy had only been adopted at the April 16 meeting and had not been sent to the [delegation(?)] at that time. This states that it is contrary to its policy to have in its employ "a member of the Communist Party or one who by close or continued or sympathetic association with such members indicates his approval of their plans and purposes." The Board went on to say that "if Mr. Morgan wishes to make further response or reply he shall have full opportunity to do so." (RAAA: 3, Shapiro "Special Meeting")

The executive committee's draft report noted that Morgan wrote to Johnson on July 29 asking for an opportunity to respond to the board, but as of August 22 he had not been given an opportunity to do so. After once again awkwardly proclaiming the AAA to be a scientific society, not a political organization, the draft report summarized that "from the review of the evidence available to the Executive Committee of the AAA, it was felt that the handling of Mr. Morgan's ["dismissal" crossed out] case was a ["probable" crossed out] violation of his ["civil liberties" crossed out] rights as a citizen and that the facts available to it should be turned over to some properly organized association to defend these basic rights ["of an American citizen" crossed out]. This ["action" crossed out] conclusion seemed all the more appropriate since Mr. Morgan's professional competence was not in question" (RAAA: 3, Shapiro "Special Meeting").

After Bennett failed to gain access to the museum board's minutes, he recommended that the AAA committee convene in Columbus for an audience before the trustees. Griffin wrote AAA President Harry Shapiro, Fay-Cooper Cole, and John Bennett that he saw no reason why he, Cole, and Bennett should bother meeting in Columbus much less with the museum's board of trustees. Griffin seemed squeamish at the prospect of confronting the board, writing, "If the Board of Trustees would not see fit to allow Bennett to participate in their meeting while Morgan was present, it is extremely unlikely that they will see fit to turn over to our committee the actions of the Board or the data submitted to them on Morgan's case. Since our committee is supposed to be a fact-finding committee, and since the Board has refused to recognize that the committee has any rights in the matter, I do not see how our presence in Columbus will cause the Board to change its mind" (Peace to Price 7/15/00).[5] Griffin's cautious approach further sealed Morgan's fate.

Although the chair of the AAA's investigatory committee, Fay-Cooper Cole, was the least active of the committee members, on July 26, 1948, after learning the outcome of the recent board meeting, he wrote a panic-stricken letter to President Shapiro urging him to take action by making public his own position that "Morgan's statement to the Board was entirely correct and it should be emphasized" (RAAA: 3, FC/HS 7/26/48). It is unfortunate that Cole, as chair of the committee and the most senior and well-established scholar, did not make the effort to travel to Columbus and become involved in the workings and confrontations of the investigation. Instead, most of the risk and exposure was left to Bennett who pursued the case as diligently and as far as he felt advisable.

Three days after the board's meeting, Bennett interviewed Dean Hatcher. Hatcher believed that Morgan made a strategic mistake in not attending the meeting. He believed the board might actually have found in Morgan's favor had he appeared before them. Hatcher viewed Morgan's decision as an act of "suicide." Bennett paraphrased Hatcher's remarks as follows: "After all, this

Board was not so hostile. I know of 2 men in there who were open minded. Peters and myself were in Morgan's favor—as far as getting him a hearing went at the time. Why a man should not take advantage of an opportunity to talk things over with his own Board is something I cannot understand. Why, here we wanted to talk things over with him in a friendly way, to give him a chance to have his side heard, and he turns around and walks out" (JBP Hatcher Statement to Bennett 7/26/48). At the end of July 1948, Bennett officially withdrew his participation in the AAA's investigation of Morgan's firing, citing conditions under which "liberals cannot afford at the present time to defend [radical] groups" (JBP: JB/HS 7/31/48). In a second letter written the same day, Bennett wrote to Shapiro and the committee that he had "stuck [his] neck out as far as I am able to without having it cut off, and I must pull out" (JBP: JB/HS 7/31/48).

Zepp told Bennett that the board's plan was to allow Morgan to keep his job while he searched for another appointment, but that Morgan's stance throughout the situation had left them with no option but to fire him (reported to JBP: Bennett to Cole, Shapiro and Griffin 8/2/48). Bennett wrote to the committee that he had been troubled by Anna Morgan's political activity, stating: "I hate to say this, gentlemen, but we must face the fact that we are dealing with Communists" (JBP: Bennett to Cole, Shapiro and Griffin 8/2/48), thus clarifying the bias held by many in the association that civil rights and due process should be afforded only to non-Communists.

"A F——ing Mess if Ever I Saw One"

Some members of the AAA's executive board believed that Morgan weakened his case with the museum by, as Charles Voegelin put it, "insisting the AAA representative be present at his hearing" (RAAA: 3, CV/HS 8/18/48). Homer Barnett wrote to AAA President Shapiro, stating that "it appears to me . . . that the American Anthropological Association through its Executive Board, is on the point of setting an ill-advised and hazardous precedent in the case of Mr. Richard Morgan of the Ohio State Museum. The seriousness of this situation did not occur to me until . . . I received a circular letter from Mr. Morgan in which he reviews his position at length. It was only in the light of this statement that the report on the Board's action . . . takes on significance" (AAANB Sept. 1948 2[4]:51).

Barnett argued that Morgan's problems had nothing to do with his profession but rather were only of a personal nature, and therefore the association should not undertake an investigation. Barnett referred to ongoing discussions during the AAA's reorganization that a centralized executive board could easily overstep its authority and unilaterally adopt policies not shared by the greater membership body. The executive board quietly adopted Barnett's stance, declaring the matter a private one between employer and employee. Of course, the association could have stressed that Morgan was fired for personal rather than professional reasons, but it instead interpreted the events in ways that justified a position of concerned inaction. Sadly, this limited view of what did or did not constitute a political policy of the association was a key feature of its position on issues of academic freedom during the McCarthy period.

Griffin wrote to Morgan that given the political climate he had little hope for a legal or administrative reversal of these decisions. Regarding the AAA's position on this matter, he doubted "very much that the AAA will take any active steps in your defense. The appointed committee was simply a fact-finding body to present what evidence it could get to the Executive Committee of the AAA. It is my opinion that the AAA will feel that the evidence submitted would not justify taking further action. Indeed, I don't know what action it would take. It is not a union, nor even the AAUP. It can deplore, but it cannot denounce" (WJP: JG/RM 8/5/48). But severe damage had been done to the Morgans. When reporters—even those sympathetic to their plight, such as Scripps-Howard's R. A. Blackburn—called them for comments, Richard and Anna Morgan were prone to lash out with a rage stoked by the injustices they had suffered, thus alienating those who might have become allies.

On August 8, Bennett wrote to Griffin and Shapiro that there was no direct evidence that Morgan was indeed a Communist, although it was clear that Morgan had been "a fairly faithful attendee to meetings of liberal and radical groups in attendance at meetings of CP members in the Morgan home" (JBP: JB/JG&HS 8/8/48).

The AAA had made a strategic error in asking John Bennett—a junior, untenured assistant professor—to become involved in the investigation. Bennett had been forthright in writing President Shapiro that his freedom to investigate the Morgan case was severely limited and that he himself faced some risk for engaging in this activity. Bennett expressed these concerns to Griffin and Shapiro, noting that

> Ohio is run by a powerful and small group who control the University and practically everything else. They can put pressure on almost anyone they choose to, although they are not omnipotent. I could never have lost a job over this, but I could have suffered some embarrassing and unfortunate publicity.
>
> Although technically, as Shapiro says, my role was an "impartial observer" it must be understood that in light of the conditions now existing

in this country, there is no such thing as an "impartial observer" in anything having to do with communism. The impartial observer, politically speaking, becomes de facto a communist sympathizer, whether he is or not.

Johnson or no one else has actually threatened my official status. I have a friend in Dean Hatcher, recently appointed vice president of the university. I have no fear about an undercover or overcover attack on me succeeding. I simply was unable to continue to run the risk of involving anthropology and the university in a smear campaign. One will begin here just before the elections, and we have to be careful to [not] add anything that can be used as fuel. (JBP: JB/JG&HS 8/8/48)

Just a day prior to this letter Morgan had written to Griffin stating that Bennett had "withdrawn from all participation in this case," claiming that Bennett's "academic freedom has also been violated" (WJP: RM/JG 8/7/48).

When Sol Tax read in one of Morgan's mailings that the AAA investigatory committee was no longer pursuing its investigation, he wrote John Bennett asking if this were the case (ST: ST/JB 47, 10 8/16/48). Bennett replied cautiously, suggesting that Tax ask Cole for details on the status of the investigation, adding that a report to the AAA's executive board was being drafted. Suggesting that things were not as plain and clear as presented in Morgan's latest epistle, Bennett added, "Morgan's letter is only the last item in the whole tragedy, and makes our job only so much more difficult. One wishes for a neat and categorical judgment upon the affair, but such is impossible. In short, Morgan is both guilty and not guilty; the [AAA] the same. From beginning to end the case has been a series of misunderstandings and stupidities. With some danger and nastiness lurking in the background" (ST: JB/ST 47, 10 8/23/48). Bennett's response was strained by a guarded tone with a sense of frustration in not being able to frankly come forth with the details of the emerging mess.

On August 23, Morgan mailed a report to President Shapiro detailing his treatment by the museum board. Four members of the AAA's executive board met in New York to consider the accumulated correspondence and the finding submitted by Bennett, Cole, and Griffin relating to the Morgan matter. The board decided that "this was a civil matter, lying outside strictly professional interest of the Association, that they were therefore in such a matter not empowered by the constitution to take action that would commit the membership without an opportunity for it to express its collective wishes" (AAANB 1948 2(5):72–73). As far as the association was concerned, Morgan was on his own.

In a letter to Fay-Cooper Cole, Morgan commented on his own work as an activist for equal rights, noting that his public activism for civil rights must have marginalized him and his position: "In my civic life for the past several years I have worked actively for equal rights for all minority groups. I have fought especially for the rights of the Negro, particularly against restrictive covenants. I am a member of the Association for the Study of Negro Life and History, the N.A.A.C.P., and other groups seeking to improve the condition of the Negro people. I have had a Negro girl student from the University working as a technician in the Archaeological Laboratory for several years. I have also consistently combated anti-Semitism. I can assure you that my activities along these lines, which have been strongly reinforced by my training as an anthropologist, have not been popular with those in authority" (RAAA: 3, RM/FC 8/14/48). Morgan was not going quietly. After he launched another mimeographed letter campaign to the AAA membership, John Bennett wrote Griffin that they were in "a f——ing mess if I ever saw one" (JBP: JB/JG 8/26/48).

Griffin believed the committee should abandon its investigation and invest its energies in helping Morgan find other employment. The desire to abandon the investigation prevailed, and the fact-finding committee quietly withdrew. Emil Haury encouraged President Shapiro to distance the association from Morgan and ask the ACLU or the AAUP to take the lead in the matter (RAAA: 3, EH/HS 9/16/48). A month before the annual AAA meetings Bennett wrote to Griffin that he felt some guilt—although he had withdrawn his participation at the suggestion of Morgan himself—because he "answered questions from the Committee and Shapiro which revealed some of the facts the Morgans apparently were not inclined to reveal" (JBP: JB/JG 11/16/48). Morgan was portrayed as despondent and defeated, willing to fight the matter in court as his last and only hope. Bennett passed on reports from third parties that Morgan "feels that he is finished professionally, and cannot ever get another job in archaeology. Therefore his only alternative is to fight the case publicly. If he does the latter, he really may be 'finished' professionally. But actually the important thing would seem to be his attitude, which prevents him from making and preserving contacts in the field" (JBP: JB/JG 11/16/48).

Bennett again tried to organize a meeting between Morgan and some of the principal figures, with hopes that Morgan could provide "some clarification of the comedy of errors and misunderstandings that resulted in his dismissal" (JBP: JB/JG 11/16/18). Clearly still upset by Griffin's efforts to avoid undertaking any meaningful investigation in Columbus, Bennett added a lengthy parenthetical scolding to Griffin: "(If you guys had only come to town to conduct a hearing, and had talked to these people, things might have been entirely different. Our collective official status, plus your outside prestige, would have cracked open so many things and would probably have led to an immediate conference between ourselves, the Society, and Morgan. The more I think about it, and discuss it, the more this is evident. The Committee bungled the thing)" (JBP: JB/JG 11/16/48). Griffin replied that he had no intention of contacting Morgan, noting that Morgan had not sought out his advice during the entire episode and he had no intention of giving unsolicited advice at this late date. Griffin grudgingly acknowledged that it would have indeed been better if the committee had met in Columbus, although he persisted in maintaining that by the time the committee had been formed it was simply too late to effect much change.

Bennett recommended that Griffin write to Morgan as a friend to emphasize that his career was by no means ruined and to tell him that "court action will only make things worse" (JBP: JB/JG 11/16/18). Bennett asked Griffin to assure Morgan that the recent comments by Homer Barnett in the AAA's *News Bulletin* did not reflect the views of the AAA, and that many in the association still supported him. Barnett had argued in the *News Bulletin* that the AAA had gone beyond its duties in investigating Morgan's firing because "the issue was over personal liberties and did not involve the question of professional abilities" (AAANB 2[4]:52).

James Griffin wrote the final report of the AAA's investigatory committee, compiling a chronology of the events leading up to Morgan's dismissal and the board's mishandling of the July hearing. Griffin noted that

> it has been stated that President Johnson and later the Board wished to remove Morgan to avoid unfavorable publicity which would reflect upon the security of the Ohio State Museum. It has been said that the Scripps-Howard paper, the competitor to Johnson's paper in Columbus, had been gathering evidence on the Morgan affair and were ready to expose Morgan's connection with the Communist group. It is evident, however, that a considerable amount of publicity which has resulted came about through Johnson's dismissal of Morgan which was done through the press in the most public manner possible. Both Johnson and the Board of Trustees have acted in such a way as to give Morgan most excellent reasons for violently objecting to their actions. It is evident that no better case could be found of the refusal of an employer to give his employee a fair hearing. On the other hand, it has become extremely unhealthy or unwise in this country for individuals to become associated with the Communist party. While legally it is recognized as any other political party, from the standpoint of public opinion, it is regarded as an illegal act which approaches treason. This attitude is appar-

ently particularly strong in Columbus. (JBP: Griffin, Final AAA Report, p. 15)

Griffin's report ended with a statement that the committee had not been empowered with making recommendations for the AAA's executive board, but nonetheless pointed out that "Morgan's civil and human rights were certainly violated by the President and the Board of Trustees of the Ohio State Museum" (JBP: Griffin, Final AAA Report, p. 16).

John Bennett's supplement to this report added a few details and new interpretations of the events recounted. Bennett closed his supplement noting that "Morgan has some clear moral and probably legal issues on his side; yet his course of action is unrealistic and dangerous to him. The Society has a right to request resignations of employees with connections deemed undesirable for public institutions; yet the methods used to secure a dismissal were of the clumsiest and most inhumane sort" (JBP: Bennett's "Supplement to Report of Special Committee on the Dismissal of Richard G. Morgan," p. 3). Bennett's summation came close to arguing that Morgan had brought on his own problems by adopting aberrant views on racial and economic stratification, and while the museum had muddled the way they sacked him, they had every right to do so.

Bennett's memories of the process are not positive ones, and decades later there is some bitterness toward the association and the committee (see Price 1997a). He recalls:

> There was no coordinated "investigation" by Bennett, Cole and Griffin. Each of us, so far as I know, worked independently. I believe that the AAA people appointed the three names as a committee, but they never met or issued a single report. I was on the "committee" because I was on the spot. I did submit a couple of documents, one a fairly long summary of events which was read at the AAA meeting, which I could not attend because I was in Japan at the time. So far as I know this document was not kept by the AAA. . . . The gist of the piece was to the effect that it was impossible to work with the Morgans and their associates because they were simply not candid and would not cooperate with an "AAA investigation." I was personally disturbed by this since I had worked with Dick Morgan on archaeological matters and considered him a friend.
>
> My memory contains a residue of resentment over the way [the] AAA handled the whole thing. The president at the time was a physical anthropologist [Harry Shapiro] from the American Museum. . . . One can sympathize since the AAA had never had to cope with anything like this, but they really did not support the "investigation," either financially or with any other form of backup; did not send a qualified representative to

Columbus; left the whole thing up to me, basically. And so in a vulnerable position (first job after doctorate). And so on. They simply fumbled the ball—but then neither Griffin nor Cole showed up, either. The atmosphere at the time—the fear that McCarthy [later?] managed to instill all over—led most people to consider the affair as a very hot potato. Remember for example, that the Ohio State Museum, while independent, was actually located right on the university campus, and one or two major OSU administrators were on the Museum and Historical Society Board. I think everybody in the University environment was scared silly the thing would infect the campus. (Bennett to Price 4/28/97)

From Hesitancy to Syncopated Incompetence

President Shapiro concluded that the association's executive officers did not, "regardless of their personal sympathies, have the authority to commit their organization in matters involving civil liberties" because the organization was seen as a professional one that did not involve itself in politics (RAAA: 3, HS/Walsh 11/10/48).[6] More accurately, the AAA selectively chose when to assert itself politically, while it publicly claimed it was not involved in political matters. The AAA's political action in support of the status quo of America's shift to a full-time military-industrial economy was appropriate, while political action undermining or questioning this order was not worthy of support.

Prior to leaving for fieldwork in Japan in late 1948, John Bennett submitted a detailed proposal suggesting ways that the AAA might deal with future civil rights cases involving the AAA members. Bennett directly critiqued Homer Barnett's stance regarding Morgan noting that contradictorily this position wanted the AAA Board to have "the right to make a protest, [yet] he denies it the right to intervene [on] an individual's behalf" (JBP: Bennett Memo, 12/48). Bennett understood that other anthropologists were likely to find themselves in similar difficulties in the near future, and he recommended that the AAA prepare for such cases, recognizing that it would be "extremely difficult to establish a fixed policy in cases of this kind. Each case is a unique situation, for one thing, and the extent of the Board's intervention would appear to be governed by the particular situation. The prohibition against investigation of the individual is also a difficult question, since some investigation may be necessary in order to determine whether the Board should do anything at all" (JBP: Bennett Memo, 12/48). Bennett's memo should have been a warning for the association to adopt a defensive posture for the troubles that were silently to befall its fellows in the following decade, but this warning fell on institutionally deaf ears. Bennett wrote that "the Morgan case provides another cogent example of the dangers of formalism. Mr. Morgan could call on no professional organization other than the AAA to assist him. His case was beyond the jurisdiction of the AAUP and similar groups. Yet he was a reputable professional who had been crudely and unfairly treated. In cases where other, perhaps more efficiently-equipped bodies could be called in, the AAA might confine its efforts to a simple protest. But in cases like Morgan's, the AAA should perhaps enter more intensively" (JBP: Bennett Memo 12/48). Bennett recommended that the AAA "draft for incorporation in its constitution or bylaws a strong statement concerning its interest in the professional and civil right of its members," and he proposed that future investigations insist that senior local representatives be chosen as investigators, or if junior anthropologists were chosen, that their role as observer be carefully delineated (JBP: Bennett Memo 12/48).

As Morgan was left to fend for himself, a variety of nonanthropological organizations watched with concern from the sidelines. Clyde Miller, director of the Bureau on Academic Freedom (BAF), wrote President Shapiro that his organization considered Morgan's "dismissal so gross a violation of both academic freedom and tenure that [the BAF] brought him to New York City for a conference and meeting" (RAAA: 3 CM/HS 12/21/48), at which Morgan told a sympathetic crowd of 2,300 how he had come to be fired after his decade of "fighting racial and religious discrimination" under circumstances in which he had been portrayed as guilty by association (WFO100-238370-37; cf. *New York Post Home News* 10/11/48). Miller reported that Morgan's case was sympathetically received and that scholars such as Robert Hutchins (chancellor of the University of Chicago) had called for the conference to review these new threats to academic freedom.

Miller advised the AAA to take two specific courses of action concerning the Morgan case. He believed that, first, the association needed to "set up a Committee on Academic Freedom," and second, they needed to take "specific action in the case of Dr. Richard Morgan" (RAAA: 3 CM/HS 12/21/48). The AAA did go through the motions of carrying out this suggestion—although, as we will see, regarding the first action the validity of the committee's work is seriously to be questioned given committee member George P. Murdock's covert role as an FBI informant. The second action, meanwhile, was ignored.

One of the most troubling aspects of Richard Morgan's story is the degree to which academic and professional associations such as the AAA or the AAUP refused actively to come to his aid. We find a very different association depicted in its archival records than the one represented in its official publications during the 1940s and 1950s and today: in the archives, instead of finding an organization protecting its members we find it running for cover. But even today the AAA's official publications continue to rely on brief accounts in the association's newsletter rather than on the available archival resources to construct a protectionist mythic representation of the association as protector of academic freedom (see, for example, Trencher 2002). Certainly the AAA's reactions were complicated by a general climate of fear mixed with the tenuous alliances that had recently been forged during the association's postwar restructuring: indeed, with the passing of years, John Bennett came to view the association's mishandling of the Morgan affair as having more to do with incompetence than either cowardice or maliciousness. Bennett came to believe that the AAA "simply didn't have a clue as to what to do or how to do it, so they faked it" (Bennett to Price 7/7/97). But inexperience cannot explain the association's later silence when an increasing number of anthropologists were attacked publicly and privately for engaging in "un-American activities."

The tragic fact is that the association actually did more to investigate the circumstances of Morgan's firing than it did in *any* of the many later instances of anthropologists being accused of Communism, Socialism, or a variety of vague charges of un-Americanism that were to come in the 1940s and 1950s. In the chapters that follow we will see that the association did not learn from the Morgan case how to deal with similar attacks on other anthropologists. Instead it learned to avoid even going through the motions of such investigatory inquiries or advocacy stances, and instead it buried its head in the sand, ignoring anthropologists being fired, blacklisted, and taught the valuable lessons of self-censorship.

CHAPTER 4

Hoover's Informer

Informants are a useful and valuable part of any internal
security or national defense program and liberals and
intellectuals need to face reality and recognize this. . . .
It is in the interest of all intellectuals and liberals that they
cooperate fully with the FBI if they are to continue to
enjoy the freedoms which make their academic interest
possible. — W. C. Sullivan

While the American Anthropological Association's leadership increasingly distanced itself from
Richard Morgan and his problems, there was a
growing movement by many of the association's
rank and file to take action in support of Morgan. In Toronto in December 1948 at the association's annual meeting there were discussions about
Morgan's troubles. After what is described in the
AAA's *News Bulletin* as a "lengthy discussion" of
the Morgan case at the annual AAA business meeting (by three hundred nonvoting members and
ninety-three voting fellows), the council passed a
motion resolving "that the American Anthropological Association go on record as favoring investigation by the Executive Board in cases where
the civil rights, academic freedom and professional

status of anthropologists as such have been invaded, and take action where it is apparent that injustice has resulted that affects their rights as citizens and scientists, and be it further resolved that the Executive Board appoint a Committee on Scientific Freedom which shall submit for consideration by the Council at its next meeting recommendations as to what action (publication of the facts, etc.) shall be taken in such cases" (AAANB 1949 3[1]:1). It was further resolved that, "the Executive Board continue to regard the situation of Mr. Richard G. Morgan as an order of business under the resolution concerning professional freedom passed on December 28, 1948" (AAANB 1949 3(1):1; see also AA 1949 [51]:370).

These resolutions were reactions by the AAA's progressive wing designed to counter the conservative stance taken by the executive board the previous summer. In the weeks prior to this meeting Morgan wrote to many prominent anthropologists who had expressed sympathy for him and his case, asking for their help in persuading the AAA to take a stand with him and his cause (e.g., ST 47, 10 RM/ST). President Shapiro planned for a "general policy discussion on civil liberties cases among the membership" (JBP: JB/JG 11/16/48), and there was a general awareness among the association's membership that between the Jacobs and Morgan cases the encroachments on academic freedom raised questions that needed answers.

Naming Names: George P. Murdock's 1949 Letter to J. Edgar Hoover

A document released to me by the FBI under FOIA reveals that on the day following the 1948 annual AAA meeting, anthropologist George Peter Murdock sent a letter to J. Edgar Hoover detailing his suspicions that members of a Communist conspiracy had taken control of the AAA's business meeting. Murdock's letter sheds light on the seldom-mentioned realpolitick conditions that impacted the conduct of normal science during this period.

Murdock wrote to Hoover of his concerns that Communists had used subterfuge, had taken advantage of the meeting's agenda rules, and had secretly orchestrated seemingly individual actions to push through their agenda of support for Morgan. Murdock's letter reads as follows:[1]

January 1, 1949

Mr. J. Edgar Hoover
Federal Bureau of Investigation
Washington, D.C.

Dear Mr. Hoover,
    At the annual convention of the American Anthropological Association in Toronto this week the Communist members of the Association

took the first important step aimed at the conversion of our scientific organization into a propaganda tool subserving [*sic*] their interests. They secured the passage of a motion whereby the Association will set up a special committee on civil liberties to investigate infringements thereof and to take action in behalf of members of the Association who are victimized thereby.

The methods by which this action was achieved were typical of those by which certain labor unions and liberal organizations have been penetrated. At the annual business meeting of the Fellows (voting members) of the Association they called for an intermission at about 10:30 P.M. after all the regular business of the Association had been concluded. Large numbers of the Fellows, because of fatigue and the late hour, took advantage of this lull to leave the meeting, but all the party members and fellow travelers were present when we reconvened. The rest of the meeting was beautifully stage-managed by a small nucleus of party members, who guided a much larger number of genuine liberals who were quite innocent of how they were being maneuvered and used. The discussion and action revolved around the case of Richard Morgan [text here is redacted, but probably says, "who was recently fired from his position as Curator"] of Anthropology at the Ohio State Museum, and how to deal with this and similar cases in the future.

The objectives are clearly apparent. The affairs of the Association are administered by an elective Executive Board, which includes no party member or fellow travelers. It was hoped that the President and Executive Board, in appointing the special committee on civil liberties, would choose at least one of those who took the initiative in the meeting, i.e., a party man, and that he would be in a position to swing the whole committee in its future actions. It is fairly likely that at least one Communist member of the Association will be involved in a civil liberties case during the coming year. In such a case, the committee could be expected to swing the whole weight of the Association behind the Communist victim. Since anthropology is in many respects the most central of the social sciences, and has hitherto been one of the most objective and least politically tainted, the propaganda value of swinging its official organization behind an accused Communist would be enormous.

It is highly unlikely that these objectives will be accomplished. The Executive Board and the newly elected President, A. I. Hallowell of the University of Pennsylvania, seem to be fairly well aware of what is at issue, and there is little likelihood that any party member or fellow traveler will be appointed on the new committee. There is every probability that the Association will act with great circumspection in any civil liberties case that may arise, and that it will not allow itself to be used as a tool. The potential dangers to anthropological science are, I believe, fairly adequately realized.

There is always a possibility, however, that things may go astray. The members of the Association are predominantly liberal in their political orientation and place a high value on civil liberties, and I include myself very definitely with this majority. The number who are politically astute, however, is not large, and there is always a chance that the rest can be stampeded into injudicious action if an important and highly publicized civil liberties issue should arise in the near future. It is to prepare your organization for this possibility that I am writing.

The individual members of the American Anthropological Association number about 1500. Their names and addresses are published in the last issues of our official journal—American Anthropologist, n.s., Vol. 50, No. 4, Part 1, pp. 731–747 (October-December, 1948). Of these 1500 members, those with active Communist affiliations probably do not number many more than 15, or one per cent of the total membership. Fellow travelers would add from one to two per cent more. Approximately 97 per cent of our membership, I am sure, would not knowingly do anything to advance Communist interests, and probably 95 per cent would actively oppose any movement which they knew to be Communist sponsored. Many of them, however, are capable of being duped.

For a number of years I have made a special effort to identify the members of the Association who are or have been actual members of the Communist party. Careful examination of the list referred to above reveals twelve individuals whom I can place in this category with full assurance that I am correct. Guesswork and inference would add several more names, but I prefer to mention only those about whom I have what seems to me positive evidence. All of these except Morgan I know personally very well, being on a firm first-name basis with all. Most of them are actually very capable people, and I would defend their right to hold any academic position for which they are qualified. I feel strongly, however, that none of them should hold a government position where they might participate in policy decisions or where they might be a danger to security. Nearly all of them are personal friends, and I should certainly not mention them to you if I thought your organization would use the information to jeopardize them in their present or future civilian positions. Contacts with FBI men and observation of FBI activities over a number of years have convinced me that you are not engaged in a "witch hunt" and are solely concerned with vital national security. I am giving you these names primarily to protect American anthropologists as a group, because if our national organization should get into a political jam in the future, investigation will certainly reveal that these twelve people, or some group of them, have engineered the matter. The names, with a few comments, follow:

[the first name and accompanying text, approximately 3 lines, is missing, but it would appear to be Irving Goldman given the alphabetical arrangement of the list and the mention of the name Goldman that appears in the paragraph on Lesser][2]

Jules Henry, Washington University, St. Louis Mo. He played a modest role in the affair at Toronto, but is probably not very important.

Melville Jacobs, University of Washington, Seattle, Wash. Has publicly admitted (after an original denial) that he has been a party member. There is good evidence that he is an extremely important figure, a genuine big shot in the organization. He appears to be the only one of the twelve who has the unusual authority to express minor criticisms of Russia or of Communist activities when these are adjudged to be tactically or strategically useful. Characteristically, he remained completely in the background during the Toronto meeting, though [he was] observed in conference with the active leaders just prior to the important discussion.

Alexander Lesser, Association of American Indian Affairs, 48 East 86th St., New York, N.Y. Lesser was another of the group released by the State Department.[3] Unlike Goldman, however, he has for many years been an active organizational leader. He was in the forefront of the discussion at Toronto. He is a very intelligent man and an important figure though certainly junior to Jacobs in the organizational hierarchy.

Oscar Lewis, University of Illinois, Urbana, Ill. All I am certain of about Lewis is that he has been a party member in the past. It may well be that he has retired from all participation, and no longer holds his former views. At least, I know of no recent activity. He is certainly not an under-cover leader, for he is essentially timid.

Richard Morgan, 154 East Kelso Road, Columbus, Ohio. Morgan was the focus of our discussion. From everything I can ascertain, he has been a party worker or a Communist at heart, and was not such at the time when he was fired from his job at the Ohio State Museum. His wife, however, is and has long been a Communist. Morgan probably has less professional competence than anyone else in this list. He seems to have been primarily a pig-headed and uncooperative Welshman, who has never had any real friends. Craving love, he has found it only from his wife and has thus become putty in her hands. Though probably not a Communist in the past, he will certainly be one in the future. For a person of his obstinacy, the loss of his job under the conditions would probably be enough to convert him. This tendency will be strongly confirmed by the attention and apparent affection which all the party members and fellow travelers showered on him at Toronto. He has found unexpectedly a group of new and warm friends, and can be expected to respond to them as to his wife."[4]

██

██

Morris Siegel, 45 Siegel St. Brooklyn, N.Y. He is probably not an important figure.[5]

████████████████████████████████████[6]

████████████████████████████████████

████████████████████████████████████[7]

In addition to the above twelve, there are probably a handful of other active party members in our Association and there are still others who are confirmed fellow travelers and can always be counted upon for assistance. Several took leading roles in the Toronto action. Altogether, there are about two dozen upon whom the leaders of the Association have their eyes fixed, and whose machinations they are at least prepared to circumvent. This year's action is important not in itself, but because it is certainly the groundwork for a more serious step to be taken a year hence. A number of us have agreed to give the matter a good bit of thought during the coming months in the hope of being able to anticipate what the next attempted step will be and of being able to devise measures to thwart it.

For purposes of identification, I may say that I am Professor of Anthropology at Yale University. I was the chairman of our Department of Anthropology from 1938 to 1943, when I entered the service (I am a commander in the U.S. Naval Reserve). I was vice president of the American Anthropological Association in 1946 but hold no office in the organization at present.

I have been in some personal conflict as to whether to write this letter or not, and I very strongly hope that nothing I have said will be used in any way to damage the purely academic and scientific careers of the persons I have named. I am concerned only that their political careers will not injure anthropological science or the national interest.

Very truly yours,

George P. Murdock (WFO100-4082-69)

I wish to make three points regarding this remarkable letter. The first concerns the disturbing implications of one of anthropology's leading scholars secretly informing on other top scholars to the chief of America's secret police. This act is especially disturbing because Murdock was wrong about the party membership status of some of these named individuals, and thereby was making his decision to turn informer solely on the basis of suspicion and innuendo, or worse. Second, we do not know how common such secretive tirades by informers were, or are. We simply do not know to what extent these relationships helped to shape the specific nature of the social (and physical) sciences in the postwar period. Third, Murdock may have been correct to observe that some Communist Party members of the AAA did indeed use co-ordinated tactics at AAA business meetings to pass controversial motions— this was certainly a common practice used by party activists elsewhere, and one later used by radical members of the association at business meetings during the Vietnam War.[8]

It is important that Murdock's letter be viewed from within the historical context in which it occurred before judging its propriety, although even with a careful consideration of this historical milieu Murdock's action appears careless. While 1949 was marked by an increase in public paranoia concerning the dangers of Communism, we are left to wonder what other factors may have contributed to the composition and posting of this letter. Murdock appears disingenuous to end the correspondence with a stated hope that the letter would not damage the careers of the anthropologists on whom he informed, and it is odd to read that he considered himself to be "personal friends" with nearly all those on his list. Even in 1949 it would be difficult to imagine that anything other than harm for these colleagues could be achieved by penning such a letter to J. Edgar Hoover.

Murdock's letter raises questions concerning the commonality of such correspondence between disgruntled scholars and the FBI. Lazarsfeld and Thielens's classic study of academic freedom and reticence during the McCarthy period recorded instances of professors informing the FBI of students whose classroom comments suggested they might be Communists. When one professor at a military-base extension campus encountered a student whose comments suggested "the Communist *Pravda* line," the professor first, "hinted and hinted and warned him in this one class session to be careful. His rejoinder was, 'In the university anything goes, any idea—just so it's within the bounds of propriety and decency.' At the end of the session [the student] announced that he knew the incident would be reported since there were unknown intelligence men in the class. I felt that I ought to report this incident, but I felt like a rat. A friend who is also teaching in the military told me to cover myself. I phoned the next day to the civilian security man, and explained the situation to him. I later learned that the F.B.I. had already heard most of the conversation. I didn't have to repeat the story to them. They had already received reports of the incident" (1958:210). The outspoken student in this incident understood the principles of academic freedom better than his professor—who seemed relieved to have cleared himself by ratting-out a student whose academic freedom he was ethically bound to protect. Given the lack of thorough FOIA research into questions of Cold War academia as well as the nature of secretive communications between informers and the FBI, it is not possible to know how common such informing episodes were. We do know from the work of other FOIA scholars studying academia (Diamond 1992; Schrecker 1986, etc.) that such actions were far more common than the normative historical renderings of the discipline's history would suggest. The records of the FBI, CIA, and other federal agencies are being destroyed at an alarming rate (see Price 1997a), and we are rapidly losing an unknown amount of historical data. Accusations like Murdock's may have reduced funding opportunities for individuals, just as rumors from unidentified sources at times lessened some anthropologists' chances of professional advancement (see Peace and Price 2001; Price 1998a).

Finally, regardless of the motives and actions of Murdock it is possible that he was correct in his assessment that some Communist or Socialist members of the association had orchestrated the annual business meeting's discussion of Richard Morgan's firing. Radical fellows of the association may well have worked together in "fraction sessions" to set the agenda adopted by the assembled body. It is well known that liberals and conservatives have also "conspired" for decades by building coalitions and orchestrating motions outside of the walls of the association business meeting—it seems that only when individuals with leftist politics carry out such practices that Murdock became concerned. As those familiar with the archival correspondence of AAA fellows from this (or any) period know, it was quite common for fellows to try to gain the support of their colleagues on specific positions and to orchestrate the introduction of motions prior to the business meeting, a practice known as caucusing.[9]

Throughout his career, Murdock expressed contradictory views concerning academic freedom and the relationship of the AAA to political positions. Almost two years after he became an FBI informer, he became a vocal opponent of the University of California's loyalty oath. In responding to then AAA President Ralph Beals's challenge that he was reversing his position on academic freedom (from the Morgan case), Murdock responded that he disagreed, as "we were then faced with a bogus issue, not a genuine one. . . . I feel that a scientific association should not take a stand on political issues unless they seriously threaten the social foundations of science and teaching as I am convinced the present one does" (RAAA: 5, GM/Velas 12/18/50). Later, as turmoil grew over AAA declarations condemning the Vietnam War, Murdock criticized the merging of politics and anthropology, although he had no such qualms when it came to using the Human Relations Area File to supply the U.S. army and CIA with anthropological data (Price 1998a; Ford 1970; Mel Ember to Price 7/18/95).

Murdock corresponded with other conservative anthropologists who were also concerned that Marxism was tainting American anthropology. Esther Goldfrank shared her concerns with Murdock that anthropologist Edward Haskell was using his position in the Society for Applied Anthropology to alter policies "to coincide with the Stalin line." She also believed that Conrad Arensberg betrayed a deep commitment to Marxism, and, no doubt drawing on her husband Karl Wittfogel's analysis of oriental despotic societies, she passed on concerns that Jacobs, Stern, and others were subtly shaping their analysis in Marxist ways:

> It is dreadful to think that such persons are still being placed in positions where they can manipulate politically unaware social scientists. Jacobs and Stern have done it neatly in their popular Outline of Anthropology and apparently the Linguists are now also doing their bit. Even if Jacobson's [sic] paper was not too well organized, he is certainly correct when he points out that linguistics, like biology and social science, are now being pressed into Stalin's developmental scheme.[10] This means an emphasis on Slavery as an early form everywhere and the elimination of the concept of Oriental society which is characterized by the bureaucracy as the ruling class—and this concept as you know does not stem from Marx, but was developed by Adam Smith and John Stuart Mill as well as others in their times. (EG: EG/GM 9/14/49)

Goldfrank believed that liberals such as Ruth Benedict, Cora Du Bois, Donald Collier, Laura Thompson, and John Gillen had fallen for Stalinist trickery because of their support for integrationist policies.

The full impact of Murdock's 1949 letter on the lives and academic careers of the twelve individuals named therein is not fully understood, but the FBI files of some of those named indicates that the FBI increased their surveillance and monitoring as a result of the letter. As I describe later, Murdock's letter prompted the FBI to begin an extensive mail-monitoring program and intensify its efforts to monitor and track Oscar Lewis's movements, scholarship, and politics, and it also coincided with increased FBI monitoring of Melville Jacobs. Perhaps the most shocking aspect of Murdock's situation is that later this reckless FBI informer was appointed to "protect" the academic rights of the AAA's membership.

A Farce at Best: The AAA's Committee on Scientific Freedom

Among the first items of business undertaken in January 1949 by A. Irving Hallowell, the new president of the AAA, was the formation of the Committee on Scientific Freedom. There was a concerted effort to seek out individuals who could be agreed on as being considered "fairly level-headed, middle of the road people" (RAAA: 4, Hill/AH 1/8/49), but those selected were far from middle of the road given the appointment of George Murdock, an FBI informant, in the catbird seat. In selecting Murdock, President Hallowell passed over such individuals as Harry Shapiro, George Foster, John Gillin, John Embree, Robert Redfield, Frederica de Leguna, Douglas Haring, V. Ray, Loren Eisley, and Fred Eggan (RAAA: 4, President Hallowell 1949).

Four months after writing to Hoover, Murdock was appointed chair of the AAA's Committee on Scientific Freedom along with committee members E. G. Burrows and A. I. Hallowell. The committee was charged with establishing principles of scientific freedom and the criteria to be used in investigating alleged violations of academic freedom. This committee was the very one whose formation Murdock had secretly bemoaned to Hoover could threaten the credibility of the AAA. The committee formulated a series of conservative policies limiting consideration of cases to those of AAA fellows and delegating most of its responsibilities to the AAUP and the ACLU. It is unknown if Hoover was consulted regarding the policies of the committee because the bureau has not been forthcoming with all of its files on the AAA and Murdock.[11] Murdock declared the committee's charge "a dirty job, and those of us who are members can expect only grief," but the nonposthumous grief received by Murdock and the committee was minimal, and their approach to the problems of academic freedom advanced their conservative agendas within the association and the academy (RAAA: 4, GM/AH 6/13/49).

After examining statements made by Richard Morgan, the general secretary of the AAUP, Ralph Himstead, reported to the executive board of the AAA "that Morgan had not had the advantage of *due process* in the legal sense" (emphasis in original). Himstead "believed that there were underlying principles basic to American life that had been violated." An internal AAA memo reports that "Himstead said that the case had been pretty badly muddled but that this was no doubt due to the inexperience of the association in such matters. They found it inexpedient to appoint a local man on any committee of investigation. He thought it was quite evident that there was misunderstanding between Morgan and the Board as to the nature of the so-called hearing at which he refused to testify. Partly on account of this ambiguity he can appreciate both the refusal of Morgan on the one hand and the critical attitude of the Board on the other because Morgan refused to testify" (RAAA: 4, AAA

Executive Board memo 1/6/49). Himstead stressed that the AAA should use caution in this case because they could easily make things worse than they already were.

Ralph Beals wrote President Hallowell from Ecuador to support the establishment of another local fact-finding committee, stating: "It seems to me that in the Morgan case, we must continue to act as the committee on scientific freedom and that we must have a good fact finding committee; we cannot wait until a general committee on scientific freedom is created" (RAAA: 4 RB/AH 2/3/49).

But President Hallowell, a fair-weather civil libertarian, was frightened by the prospect that the charges against Morgan might have merit. He sent a memo to the executive board explaining his strategy of "deliberately . . . stalling insofar as making any further commitments on the part of the Association," adding that he had recently

> heard that Morgan is acting as secretary or treasurer of a Communist Party group. Whether this is true or not I cannot say at the moment but I am trying to find out. Any information you may have would be greatly appreciated, if this intimation is correct, the case takes on a new angle since heretofore Morgan was reputedly free of direct C.P. associations. In view of the recent expressions of the C.P. in France, Italy and the United States, with respect to cooperation with Russia in the event of an armed conflict it seems to me that any gesture on the part of the AAA with respect to anyone having direct relations with the C.P. becomes an extremely delicate matter, to say the least, if not a real danger to the status of our Association. Do you not think, therefore, that it is necessary to discover whether or not Morgan has direct C.P. connections before any other move is made? (RAAA: 4, AH/Board 3/10/49)

Once the association decided to worry more about the party status of individuals than the ongoing assault on the academic and personal freedoms of all, the freedom to pursue political or academic positions of one's own choosing was abandoned.

A Resounding Whimper: The AAA Strikes an Action Pose

Morgan's firing was discussed in an article on the campus red purges published in the Communist-affiliated *Masses and Mainstream*. The article, written by Samuel Sillen, characterized Morgan as one who was "long a leader of the fight in his community for decent race relations," but who was fired "after twelve years of service because of anti-fascist activity" (1949:7). In discussing Melville Jacobs and the other victims of the University of Washington's red hunt, Sillen focuses on how the governing boards of universities controlled university presidents and the activities of faculty. Sillen examines a study by Hubert Beck on the racial (no blacks), gender (only 3.4 percent women), and class composition of university boards and concludes that "almost half . . . of the 400 largest business organizations of the country had among their officers or directors persons who were . . . also members of the governing boards of [the] 30 leading universities" (1949:14; Sillen citing Beck 1947).

In the article, the polling data of university boards indicated political views that were significantly more conservative than those of the general public. Sillen cited a 1936 poll of university trustees indicating that 26 percent favored Franklin D. Roosevelt while 63 percent favored Alfred Landon, whereas actual voting figures indicated a reversal of this elitist mindset with Roosevelt capturing 61 percent of the popular vote and Landon capturing 37 percent. Sillen questioned the commitment of such conservative board members to defending the premise of free inquiry on American university campuses.

In a memo to the AAA's executive board, President Hallowell reported that Erimine Voeglin had written to Ohio State political scientist Harold Zink "to make local inquiries with particular reference to Morgan's direct affiliation with the C.P." Zink reported that his contacts said Morgan was not an officer in the Communist Party and that he was probably not directly affiliated with the party. But Zink's report on Morgan did not remove him from the realm of Communist Party influence. Hallowell informed the executive board that Zink believed that "there is a widespread feeling here that although not a member of the C.P. Morgan has been active in behalf of the party or at least has been exploited by the C.P. to a distinct degree. This has been increasingly apparent since his 'experience'—at least that is the opinion of one well informed person. There is probably a difference of opinion as to whether he is aware of such activity or more or less a dupe." Hallowell interpreted this information to mean that the executive board "must assume Morgan to be free of direct C.P. connections" (RAAA: 4, Hallowell to Executive Board 3/24/49).

A few weeks later President Hallowell informed the executive board that he "discovered that one of the organizations which Morgan has requested to supply a [legal] brief [is] Civil Rights Congress—[which] appears in the Communist category on the list of organizations furnished [by] the Loyalty Review Board by the Attorney General" (RAAA: 4, AH/Board 4/8/49). Concerned that Morgan might actually have Communist ties, Hallowell decided to postpone until June any AAA action concerning the Morgan case (RAAA: 4, AH/Board 4/29/49). Thus Morgan was not given legal aid by the AAA, yet was criticized and abandoned by them for taking what legal assistance he could muster.

On July 14, 1949, President Hallowell submitted a report on the Committee on Scientific Freedom to the AAA executive board. In an accompanying memo, Hallowell advised the board that, in accordance with the second motion passed at the 1948 AAA annual meeting, the report would be considered by the fellows of the upcoming annual meeting. Hallowell asked the board to consider approving the report as written, and to consider if the report's recommended procedures should be put into effect at once.

The "tentative recommendations" of the Committee on Scientific Freedom consisted of six separate points along with two "supplementary resolutions regarding Communism" (RAAA: 4, AH/Board 7/26/49). First, the committee proclaimed its support for the "principle of freedom of opinion and speech for professional anthropologists" as both scientists and citizens, as protected by the legal guarantees of civil liberties. Second, it advised that the association adopt a policy of taking "positive action investigating possible violations of scientific freedom and in initiating remedial measures to the extent warranted by its financial resources," but only in cases involving AAA fellows. This recommendation was designed to limit the extent that the AAA could become enmeshed in such battles, effectively limiting the resources and clients available for its limited protections. Third, it would be the responsibility of individual fellows to bring complaints to the Committee on Scientific Freedom.

The fourth point, the most politically revealing of the committee's recommendations, relegated any proactive power the association might have brought to the fight for academic freedom and basic civil rights to either the AAUP or the ACLU. The committee recommended that if it could be determined that either the ACLU or AAUP was involved in an investigation, the AAA could then contribute funds—not to exceed one hundred dollars—to support an investigation. After putting the onus of investigation on these other bodies, the committee recommended that "only if the resulting [ACLU or AAUP] report is adjudged unsatisfactory, will the Association act independently. If neither of the above-mentioned organizations is active in the case, the Executive Board will appoint two Fellows to conduct an investigation. The investigators shall not be associated with the institution concerned in the case. In general, two days on the scene will be considered a normal period for a preliminary investigation, but further investigation can be undertaken if it seems necessary" (RAAA: 4, AH/Board 7/26/49). By relegating the investigatory responsibility to other organizations—organizations such as the ACLU that at times secretly worked with Hoover's FBI, or the AAUP that passively provided guidelines on the proper decorum for campus inquests rather than defending attacked professors—the AAA's commitment to academic freedom was doomed from the start (see Salisbury 1984; Schrecker 1986; McCormick 1989:199–203).

Fifth, an investigatory committee would be created for specific cases and would submit its findings to the executive board. Sixth, in instances where anthropologists lost their jobs, three categories of "treatment" by the AAA would be established. The first category involved instances where individuals with tenure or similar contracts of long-term employment were involved. In these instances "the burden of proof will be assumed to rest upon the employer to show that the dismissal was due to a violation of law, or to moral turpitude, exceeding the accepted bounds of civil liberties" (RAAA: 4, AH/Board 7/26/49). The second category involved instances where employment contracts were limited. The burden of proof would then rest on the individual employee to establish that his or her civil rights had been violated. The third category covered instances where anthropologists had evidence that they would have been reappointed to a position of employment had not issues of academic freedom led to problems. In these cases the burden of proof would "rest upon the employer to show why the anthropologist should not be reappointed." The sixth point in the final version of this report (as reported in AAANB 1950 4[1]:2) differs from the initial text described above by collapsing these three categories into one, thereby empowering the executive board to adjudicate under what grounds an employee was terminated. This point is followed by a new paragraph declaring essentially that "over and above the[se] specific situations . . . the Executive Board is empowered to consider and take appropriate action on any case presented to it" (AAANB 1950 4(1):2). In cases where the board established that an anthropologist's scientific freedom had been violated, it would send statements to the employer, to national and local news services, and to civil liberties organizations as well as report findings to the AAA's *News Bulletin*.

The two "supplementary resolutions regarding Communism" were attached to these six recommendations. The first resolved "that membership in the Communist Party, or acceptance of its views, shall not be regarded as sufficient grounds for the termination of an anthropologist's employment, unless so provided by the laws of the United States or of the state concerned." The second resolved "that preoccupation with any outside interest to an extent prejudicial to the adequate performance of professional duties shall be regarded as sufficient grounds for the termination of an anthropologist's employment at the conclusion of a term appointment" (RAAA: 4, AH/Board 7/26/49). These two resolutions did not progress beyond the committee, and thus the association was not given the opportunity to vote on the issue as a collective body.

In March 1949 Richard Morgan's attorney filed a petition for writ of mandamus in the Ohio State Supreme Court, requesting that he be reinstated in his position of curator of archaeology at the Ohio State Museum. Morgan requested that the AAA submit a brief supporting his position that he had been fired for reasons unrelated to his work performance (RAAA: 4, RM/Board 8/15/49). In August the board decided not to submit a brief, publicly stating that the executive board "decided that we did not have the legal talent or means required for the preparation" (AAANB 1949 3[3]:2–3). The board offered to submit letters of support, and Morgan responded on August 24, 1949, that letters of support would be valuable to his case (AAANB 1949 3[3]:2–3; cf. AA 1950 [52]:136).

President Hallowell wrote Frank Shearer, Morgan's lawyer, documenting Morgan's professional status and background. Hallowell established that Morgan was a fellow in the AAA, and that he had made scientific contributions to the understanding of the prehistory of indigenous Americans. Hallowell also noted Morgan's work as an editor of *American Antiquity*, his membership in Sigma Xi, and his graduate training at the University of Chicago. Hallowell closed the letter with statements asserting that Morgan's curator work demonstrated a strong record of serving the public and representing the museum in a favorable light (RAAA: 130, AH/FS 8/18/49).

Morgan wrote President Hallowell that his case would be presented before the Ohio Supreme Court in early October. He added that the jurisdictional linchpin in establishing his case of wrongful dismissal lay in establishing that the Ohio State Museum was a "public or state institution" (RAAA: 4, RM/AH 9/20/49). Although the museum's location is on "state owned land, [and] is supported by direct appropriations from the State Legislature[,] and its staff members belong to the Public Employees Retirement System," the state attorney general maintained that the Ohio State Archaeological and Historical Society was not a state or public institution. In an effort to establish that the society did consider itself to be a public institution, Morgan requested a copy of a letter that Arthur Johnson (president of the society) had mailed to then AAA President Harry Shapiro on July 8, 1948, in which Johnson had claimed that the Ohio State Archaeological and Historical Society was a state institution. Morgan believed that "if this letter could be submitted by my lawyer as evidence in the case it would be of great value. Therefore, I wish to make a formal request of the American Anthropological Association for a photostatic copy of the letter in question" (RAAA: 4, RM/AH 9/20/49).

FBI records indicate that Morgan's lawyer later violated his duty to protect his former client's rights to confidentiality by agreeing to talk to the Columbus Resident Agency concerning his involvement in Richard Morgan's legal defense. It seems likely that this lawyer's previous membership in the Communist Party made him vulnerable to pressures to cooperate with this body. An FBI agent reported that Morgan's onetime lawyer

> voluntarily appeared at the Columbus Resident Agency and advised that he first became interested in communism in 1939 at Dayton, Ohio, but reverted back to Democracy during his military service, 1942 to 1945. He stated that in May, 1948 he obtained his law degree and passed the Ohio Bar in June, 1948. He added that he had practiced in Columbus since that time. He continued that he could not, however, get rid of his communist tag easily and that after starting his practice found himself involved in litigation that concerned CP members in Columbus. ▬▬▬▬▬ stated that he was "retained" to represent Richard Morgan in his fight to regain his position at OSU. Morgan was the "misguided husband of Anna Morgan, an avowed, sincere communist." He further stated that Anna in his mind was a real "Commie" but would never do violence. He claimed that he advised Morgan to fight for reinstatement on a procedural ground, win, as he certainly could, on the merits and then once reinstated, immediately resign. When Morgan failed to take his legal advice, ▬▬▬▬▬ dropped out of the case. (WFO100-238370-37)

The *Columbus Dispatch* records that Morgan and his lawyer failed to appear before the Ohio Supreme Court for a mandamus hearing in October 1949 (10/5/49). The AAA's executive board adopted and endorsed a report from the AAA's Committee on Scientific Freedom, censuring the administration of the Ohio State Museum and the Ohio State Archaeological and Historical Society (Beals 1950a). The ACLU supported and "commended this statement" (AAANB 1950 4[4]:4), although it was too little, too late for all the good it did Morgan.

On July 14, 1950, President Ralph Beals of the AAA wrote to the ACLU asking for assistance with the Morgan case. George Stoll, associate staff council for the ACLU in New York replied to Beals that the Morgan case seemed to "offer the general rule that the law does not provide remedy for every injustice," adding that the Supreme Court's decision on this matter clarified that there were no further legal actions to be taken (RAAA: 5, GS/RB 9/22/50).

On Not Seeing the Best Minds of a Generation

Amateur archaeologist Raymond Baby later filled Morgan's position at the museum, a position he held for the next thirty years. While some have suggested that Baby facilitated Morgan's firing in hopes that he would advance his career (see Sayre 1995:403), I see no reason to conclude that Baby was in any way involved.

Alhough Morgan became an obscure figure in American archaeology, the FBI continued to monitor and harass him for decades, filing regular reports noting his employed or unemployed state, examining evidence of supposed party activities, and recording his attendance at meetings of the Progressive Party (WFO100-23870-10 12/28/49). The FBI regularly conducted "telephone pretext calls" from the 1940s through the 1960s to confirm his whereabouts and his employment status (WFO100-238370-41). The FBI updated his security index card noting changes of address or occupation and his contacts with the political left (e.g., WFO100-238370-7). For example, when Richard and Anna Morgan took a carload of activists to a Civil Rights League rally in Washington, D.C., in mid-January 1949, the FBI monitored and noted the identities of their companions (WFO100-238370-8).

The FBI recorded that from 1951 to 1956 Richard Morgan operated a chicken farm at a rural homestead in Worthington, Ohio. The FBI spied on the Morgans as Richard tried his hand at farming and Anna continued to earn her living as a nurse. The FBI worried that "a trash cover could not be established on the Morgans as they resided on a farm" (WFO100-3-63-1872:6). Their home was used as a meeting place for a variety of political causes involving the party as well as nonparty causes, and their home was at times a stopping-off point for various progressives passing through the Midwest. A Cincinnati FBI agent noted that a 1951 meeting of the Franklin County Communist Party held at Anna and Richard Morgan's house "featured Pete Seegar [*sic*], who sang progressive songs," and that Pete Seeger and his wife spent the night at the Morgans' farmhouse (WFO100-238370-37 4/27/51).

The Morgans' names occasionally appeared in the local press linked with progressive causes and campaigns. The FBI speculated that they were responsible for the circulation of various political handbills in the early 1950s. In winter 1952, the FBI recorded Anna and Richard Morgan's financial contributions to the National Committee to Secure Justice in the Rosenberg Case (WFO100-387835-314:15). At one point the FBI concluded that Anna and Richard Morgan had written and printed some "250 [free speech] circulars and had sent many of these to the faculty members at OSU. According to the same source, Anna Morgan stated that she and her husband went to Springfield, Ohio, to mail the circulars so that the FBI would not detect that the mail actually originated at Columbus" (WFO100-238370-37 11/25/53). In 1953 the FBI speculated that the Morgans might use their rural farm "as a hideout for underground functionaries" (WFO100-238370-37 11/13/53). Further FBI reports indicate that during 1953 Richard Morgan was section organizer and executive committee member of the Franklin County Communist Party (CI100-3-11-10089:2 4/20/53). On January 18, 1954, a report filed by the Cincinnati SAC indicated that the FBI had begun a physical surveillance operation (known as FISUR in FBI bureauspeak) on the Morgans' home (WFO100-237370-22).

In 1954 Anna Morgan appeared before the Ohio Un-American Activities Commission and, eventually, she was fined $500 for contempt charges (Sayre 1995:402), but Richard Morgan was not called to appear before the commission. While Anna Morgan was coping with her contempt charge, the FBI noted that Richard took on Anna's responsibilities of registering local Communist Party members. He was reportedly cautious due to his wife's legal difficulties and he became increasingly "nervous," although "he continued to be frequently contacted by Party members for advice and to receive their monetary contributions" (CII00-3-11-1109:4 10/19/54).

In August 1955 an FBI informant reported to Cincinnati FBI agents that Richard and Anna Morgan's home in Worthington, Ohio, contained a secret "hidden, padlocked, windowless room." This FBI informant (perhaps an FBI agent) broke into the Morgans' house, entered their windowless room, and reported that "this room, in addition to containing an abundance of printed material relating to Communism, also contained two portable typewriters and two Speed-O-Print duplicating machines" (WFO100-231370-30). The informant also recorded the serial number of the typewriters and duplicating machines.

Reports by the FBI included the fact that Richard Morgan underwent a series of serious medical procedures in 1956, which left him under the ongoing care of his physician (WFO100-231370-30). The FBI also noted that Morgan published some correspondence in the Communist Party front publication the *Reporter* (WFO100-231370-30), and they regularly monitored the Morgan finances, and conducted periodic mail-cover operations (e.g., see WFO140-0-27959 6/25/56, CII00-3-63-1872:6). Richard Morgan's Security Index Card indicates that in early 1959 he and Anna had moved to Chicago, where Richard worked as a part-time clerk at the Universal Insurance Agency (WFO100-238370-38). The FBI continued to track Richard Morgan's activism on issues of racial and social justice into the 1960s. In one report the FBI noted that

> [Richard] Morgan stated that the Party wanted and was struggling to get low income housing, [and] open occupancy and integrate housing for lower and middle income whites and Negroes. He related that this created quite a problem inasmuch as it was difficult to keep the whites from moving out of the neighborhood when the Negroes moved in.
>
> In regard to the schooling problems. Morgan related that the Party was for integrated schooling. He stated that he knows personally that Negro enrollment in local schools has increased and white enrollment

has not. This was not due to the whites moving out of the neighbor-hood, but the fact that the whites were not attending these schools with large Negro enrollments. (CGI00-13775:3 2/12/60)

The FBI learned in fall 1962 that Morgan was working for the American Friends Service Committee in Chicago (CGI00-13775:2 2/28/63). In February 1964 the Chicago field office notified FBI headquarters that Morgan worked as a clerk at Chicago's Ebony Museum (WF0100-238360 2/24/64). Pretext phone calls by the FBI indicated that in October 1964 Morgan quit his job at the Ebony Museum in Chicago and moved to the Boston area (CGI00-32951:2 11/30/64).

When Anna and Richard Morgan left the United States in 1968 to live and travel in Mexico the FBI tracked their movements and associations. The bureau reported that the Morgans "expressed an interest perhaps in living in Mexico in the future. Richard Morgan stated he was a retired archaeolo-gist and expressed an interest in doing study and research in remote areas in Mexico. The subjects indicated that their activity in the Communist Party in Chicago in recent years had been reduced practically to 'a standstill'" (WFO 100-23870-70 11/26/68). The FBI determined that the Morgans still owned their Greenwood Avenue home in Chicago, that they were renting it out and living off of the rental income and their Social Security benefits, and that they planned to stay in Mexico throughout the 1968–1969 winter. But while living in Oaxaca, Mexico, Richard Morgan suffered a ruptured aorta and died in November 1968 (FN 1969 10[6]:4). The FBI dutifully filed a report noting the death of the object of their years of surveillance and concern.

It is impossible to determine what the life and career of Richard Mor-gan might have been like had he not run afoul of conservative mid-century Ohio politics. It is likewise unknown to what extent his Ohio travails warned other anthropologists, academics, and would-be citizen activists of the dan-gers of becoming involved in progressive politics and the incipient civil rights movement. While these elements of Morgan's story are unknowable with any degree of certainty, they are nonetheless questions of central importance to an understanding of the impact of McCarthyism on the development of American anthropology. Regardless of the speculative nature of such state-ments, had Morgan not been associated with activist politics in Columbus, he would have had a long and distinguished archaeological career. With his training in Marxist social science, in a climate free from the oppressive and antiscientific milieu of his time and place he might have developed the sort of rich and complex materialist approach to archaeological understanding that would not emerge in America for decades.

Many deeply troubling questions remain concerning George Murdock's correspondence with J. Edgar Hoover. Murdock's letter provides direct and incontrovertible evidence of the social sciences' ties to the interests and policies of America's Cold War national security state—in effect limiting the promise of science's ability to transcend the limits of social context. The inability of the social sciences to critically examine Marxist or materialist lines of inquiry without the threat of being reported to Hoover's FBI limited the nature and scope of the social scientific mode of inquiry in ways that have had long-term effects. Social activism brought heavy penalties, while informing clearly had its rewards. Although Morgan was left to fend for himself on his chicken farm, Murdock the informer capitalized on the Cold War's funding opportunities as he and his Human Relations Area File profited from government-funded research of use to America's Cold War national security state.

As I discuss in the next chapter on Morris Swadesh's troubles at the City College of New York, there were negative consequences for anthropologists who dared to critique the AAA and academic institutions that did not defend the academic freedom of Morgan and of Melville Jacobs. While Jacobs's public persecution ended with the University of Washington's tenure committee hearings, a series of lower-profile, private trials began after the public spectacles concluded.

CHAPTER 5

Lessons Learned: Jacobs's Fallout

and Swadesh's Troubles

To comprehend the pernicious effects of the Cold War on

anthropological understandings today, requires a renewed

realization of what Aldous Huxley meant by *Brave New*

World. Colonization of the mind by self-censorship is

the most efficient effect of repression or censorious

relationships. — Laura Nader

The FBI's interest in Melville Jacobs did not end with the conclusion of the hearings by the Canwell Committee or the tenure committee. Indeed, fallout from these hearings affected him for the rest of his life. Jacobs retained his professorship on probationary status, but he had grave misgivings that remained with him for decades about his colleagues and the university administration.

In spring 1949 Jacobs and Bernhard Stern sought a publisher for an edited collection of anthropology essays to accompany their successful anthropology textbook (Jacobs and Stern 1947). During the Canwell hearings, William Houston had claimed that Stern was a Communist, but this statement was presented without proof as part of a bizarre tirade that included claims that then Columbia University President Dwight D. Eisenhower was part of a Communist plot to subvert higher education in America, so no real attention had been paid to this accusation (BSC: MJ/BS 10/1/48). Stern wrote that Ralph Linton had undertaken efforts to make sure that their book would not be published. Stern also reported that he sent a copy of a prospective edited volume to Barnes and Noble as well as to Ralph Linton

> to get his OK on it because as you remember, he had praised our *Outline of Anthropology* as the best available text in anthropology. The letter from Linton was the most shocking document that I have seen in my long experience with skullduggery and character assassination. (I was shown the document by Smith in confidence but since it concerns you indirectly I think you should know its contents). I don't remember its exact wording . . .
>
> It began by saying that he had changed his mind about Outline, because his attention had been called to the fact that our Chapter on Primitive Economics was straight out of Stalin. Then he discussed the readings and stated that while it seemed innocuous, he did not believe that anything that I would do could be free from the intention to indoctrinate and that therefore he would not recommend that they publish anything by me. Moreover they would see that this judgment would be reflected in the sales of the Outline. All in the name of freedom!
>
> At no time in the letters of Linton was your name mentioned nor was any reference made to what happened at the University of Washington.
>
> Two weeks ago I gave a paper at the meeting of the American Ethnological Association, at which I learned what Linton meant about the chapter on Primitive Economics. In my paper I had criticized Murdock (see my contribution to the book, out yesterday, published by Macmillan entitled, *Philosophy for the Future: TQFM* edited by Roy Wood Sellers et al).[1] In his discussion from the floor, Murdock said that the issue I raised would involve too long a comment, but he wanted to call attention to the fact that the political bias of the speaker and his collaborator could be found in the Outline. And then he revealed the great conspiracy. In our discussion of primitive economic life among the simple food gathering peoples we speak of work bands or *committees*. Never in all his cross cultural research has he ever encountered "committees." Ergo, with our organizational predilections we superimposed the concept of committees on our material. As for him, he said "I prefer freedom." This really happened, absurd as it may seem, and it is on this basis that Linton acted as he did. (MJ: 7, 7 5/25/49)

Stern and Jacobs failed to find a publisher for their volume, and as we will see, Stern had his own troubles with McCarthyism.

Post-Canwell FBI Fallout

Although FBI records are often nothing more than collections of rumors and innuendos, such reports often provide the basis for comprehensive surveillance campaigns. For example, after one informant made the dubious claim that Jacobs had shown him "a small black book containing the names of numerous people in and around Seattle, who JACOBS stated were to be assassinated at the outset of the Communist Revolution" (WFO100-4082-90), the FBI intensified its surveillance of Jacobs for years.[2] Unfortunately, the FBI's practice of protecting its informants (even fifty years later) prevents us from examining the credibility of this slanderer, but the notion that a low-level functionary such as Jacobs—known to have publicly diverged with party doctrine on several occasions—would be given such a hit list is nothing short of ridiculous.

But Jacobs's FBI file also documents the private fallout that came after his public trial by the Canwell Committee and the tenure committee. Documents released by the FBI in 1999 led me to modify my previous view that Jacobs refused to provide information concerning his previous comrades in the Communist Party (see Price 1998a). These documents establish that ongoing pressure from the FBI eventually did lead Jacobs to tell the FBI about other members of the Communist Party.

We cannot know how Jacobs might have reacted to the FBI's intimidation had organizations such as the AAA, ACLU, or AAUP offered him some assistance. The FBI's records of Jacobs divulging information that he had refused to discuss with the Canwell and tenure committees show a man betrayed by his colleagues and terrorized by FBI agents. These agents would suddenly appear without warning at his home and workplace, bringing with them the threat that at a moment's notice they could resurrect a show trial and end his career. Jacobs's coerced cooperation with the FBI was unfortunate but understandable given the lack of support he received from colleagues.

The month after Murdock identified Jacobs as a Communist in his letter to Hoover, the FBI created a report entitled, "Communist Activities in U of W," identifying Jacobs as a likely Communist (WFO100-4082-78 2/15/49). One source reported that another unnamed professor at the University of Washington was going to resign unless MELVILLE JACOBS was given a clean bill at the University of Washington" (WFO100-4082-80). A brief mention was made in Jacobs's FBI file of Murdock's letter to Hoover concerning the

1949 AAA meeting in Toronto, noting that "it is fairly likely that at least one Communist member of the Association will be involved in a civil liberties case during the coming year. In such a case, the committee could be expected to swing the whole weight of the Association behind the Communist victim. *Since anthropology is in many respects the most central of the social sciences and has hitherto been one of the most objective and least politically tainted, the propaganda value of swinging its official organization behind an accused Communist would be enormous*" (WFO100-4082-83; emphasis added). The FBI's belief that anthropology was somehow "one of the most objective and least politically tainted" branches of the social sciences makes the AAA's abysmal efforts to assist Morgan, Jacobs, and others all the more pitiful.

On December 6, 1949, an FBI agent interviewed Jacobs concerning a colleague at the university. Because any report of noncooperation made to President Allen would have brought renewed unwanted attention to his provisionary status, Jacobs's discussions with the FBI must be seen as occurring under conditions of coercion. According to this report,

> JACOBS advised that he joined the Communist Party in approximately 1935 and was a semi-active member until approximately 1946. He was recruited into the party by an individual named ▆▆▆▆▆▆ who was at that time a student at the University. He stated that it was ▆▆▆▆▆▆ who first organized the "Rogers Club" on the University Campus. JACOBS advised that so far as he knew, the "Rogers Branch" of the Communist Party was named for a person by the name of ROGERS who was a liberal and a former governor of the State of Washington [John R. Rogers, elected in 1896]. JACOBS advised that he was of the Jewish faith and in about 1935, anti-Semitism became a force to be [concerned] with throughout the world. This was brought to his attention mainly by the Nazi government in Germany which had taken drastic measures against those of the Jewish faith. He advised that he and other members of his faith became fearful of Fascism and anti-Semitism; and Communism offered an avenue through which they might combat these forces.
>
> He had always considered himself a liberal, and the Communist Party offered him the ideologies nearest to his own political beliefs. At the time he joined the party, there was a liberal movement on the campus which induced many members of the faculty to join the party. He advised that without exception those who were active members of the party and were on the faculty of the University of Washington, had recently been publicly exposed. Contrary to the popular concept of branch meetings, there was no uniformity of thought among members of the branch. There

were those few fanaticals such as ▨▨▨▨▨▨▨▨ and JOE BUTTER-
WORTH who "swallowed party line" without question; but there were
also those who did not agree with party line in its entirety.

JACOBS advised that he, along with many others, disagreed often
with party edicts as they were handed down, and the branch meetings
were often bitter sessions of "tug of war." So far as he knew, reports of
dissension within the branch did not leak out. He advised that it was
doubtful that such "divisionist Tactics" would be tolerated today in the
Communist Party. Party officials had always been somewhat skeptical of
the Rogers Branch, and had felt that if pressure were brought to bear on
these professional members of the party, they would forsake the party to
"save their own skins." JACOBS pointed out that the party was for the
most part correct in these suspicions because the majority of the members of this branch had in fact forsaken the party to protect their own
skin. He stated that he had formed the opinion that the Rogers Branch at
the University of Washington was unique in CP activities in the United
States. There was somewhat of a "[word illegible] club" attitude on the
part of party members in that they assumed a somewhat philosophical
view toward the party and with the exception of a few student supporters, they did not put forth a great deal of effort toward proceeding [with]
party interests. On the other hand, he discerned an entirely different attitude on the part of Communists on the East Coast. He advised that he
had met Communist friends in New York, Brooklyn, Chicago, etc., and
for the most part, they had a much more fanatical view toward Communism, ie., almost without exception, they rang doorbells, gave speeches
and passed out literature for the party. He advised that he had never done
this and had never had any intention of doing such things for the party.

He suspected that he and many of his friends would never have joined
the CP had they been located on the East Coast. He perceived more of a
liberal attitude on the part of local Communists without the religiously
fanatical attitude encountered in the East. (WFO100-4082-92:1–2)

Jacobs insisted that he had always kept his academic and political life separate. He noted that his professional demands left him with little time to read
Marx or Communist Party literature, and that he seldom attended meetings
although he had paid party dues on a regular basis. He told the FBI about the
political participation of a number of university Communists, and he provided details on individuals' adherence to party doctrine and attendance at
meetings. Jacobs reported that one former party member "was often critical of tactics and doctrines of [the] CP and did not hesitate to criticize. He
stated that ▨▨▨▨▨▨ was a deep thinker and an independent one; and he

was convinced that he had totally severed connections with the party. He stated that charges that ███████████ was a member of the CP were absolutely ludicrous" (WFO100-4082-92:3). Jacobs indicated that one fellow professor "was also unjustly branded as a Communist while JACOBS knew of his own personal knowledge that ███████████ was never a dues paying member of the party. He advised that he was familiar with the testimony given against ███████████ at the Canwell hearings and that the testimony was an honest mistake" (WFO100-4082-92:3). The FBI report noted this mistake without commenting on the damage the accusation had wrought.

In 1950 Jacobs told the FBI that one of his acquaintances from his Communist days was still "a sincere idealist and is completely 'sold' on the Communist philosophy. In his opinion it would be a long time before ███████████ would ever break away from the CP" (WFO100-4082-94:2). Jacobs told the FBI that if an "all-out war" broke out, "it would take on the aspect of a religious war. It would be a fight to the bitter end, with atrocities on both sides, and the Communists in the country would go to any extent to assist in the overthrow of the Government. *He believed that the wisest thing to do could be to lock up enemy Communists in the country not only to protect this country from sabotage, but to protect the Communists from violence from non-Communists"* (WFO100-4082-94:2; emphasis added). He described his own plans to flee with his wife to Idaho in the event of such a war. Jacobs told the FBI that while he was willing to discuss these matters in private, he would never testify to these events in public.

The FBI noted that "throughout the entire interview JACOBS was most cordial and even anxious to discuss the above matters. He advised that the writer was welcome to call on him at any time and he would give whatever assistance he could" (WFO100-4082-94:5). But in another report dated July 25, 1950, one FBI agent noted how his sudden, unannounced appearance at Jacob's office seemed to unnerve or frighten Jacobs. As one agent observed:

> It should be noted that the writer has seen Jacobs coincidentally numerous times on the campus and he always appeared affable and cooperative. On the occasions of this meeting, however, he gave the impression of being quite nervous and upset.
>
> When the writer walked into his office, he was toying with a pencil and upon seeing [the FBI agent] he dropped the pencil and was at a loss for words for some few moments. His nervousness was sufficient to be noticeable to the writer.
>
> After some conversation, JACOBS stated suddenly, as if the recollection just struck him, that ███████████ [obviously an individual of interest to the FBI] had just been out to visit him.

He appeared somewhat embarrassed to make this admission but stated that ███████ was apparently out calling on his old friends.

███████ called at JACOBS' home and visited approximately three hours with JACOBS and ███████ some other professor who "was coincidentally" at JACOBS' home at the time ███████ called. (WFOIOO-4082-94)

Jacobs told the FBI that all accused Communist Party members appearing before the Canwell and tenure committees had their defense organized without the assistance of the Communist Party. Jacobs remained critical of Senator Canwell, and he did not hesitate to critique him and his committee. As the FBI states, Jacobs's

comments concerning the Canwell Committee were particularly vitriolic. JACOBS advised that the Canwell investigators who called on professors on the campus, were incompetent, unintelligent, domineering and threatening. They incurred the instant disgust of most people they met on the campus. He advised that instead of imbibing their interviewees with a desire to give information, rather they had the effect of convincing them they should say nothing. JACOBS advised that the entire course of the hearings were handled in an awkward bungling fashion by incompetents. He believed that the purpose behind the investigation was good, and did not resent that at all, but the personalities with whom he and other professors were forced to deal, made it difficult for them to follow the "route" they deemed the most desirable. He described investigator ███████ as a big blundering, strapping, threatening "boob" and ███████ as incompetent, patently incapable of handling the job set out for him. (WFOIOO-4082-94)

It is easy to read an air of sycophantic terror into the statement that "the purpose behind the investigation was good."

The FBI maintained contact with Jacobs throughout the 1950s. An internal bureau memo (WFOIOO-4082 5/27/52) indicates he was contacted on numerous occasions to provide background information relating to acquaintances that were seeking clearance for governmental work. A neighbor of Jacobs came to the Seattle FBI office on July II, 1952, to provide information on what he considered to be suspect activities at the Jacobs's household. This neighbor wanted to contribute to the fight against communism by reporting his belief that Jacobs was a Communist, and he added that he had previously reported this information to the Canwell Committee. The neighbor reported that he had "noticed on several occasions, out of State automobiles parked in the vicinity of JACOBS' home, and that young men have visited JACOBS' home for extended periods in the recent past. He also learned [from] ▆▆▆▆▆▆▆▆ that their radios have been fading, and there has been some distortion in the reception recently. He explained that much of this information is hearsay, but he is passing it on for appraisal" (WFO100-4082/ 6/18/52). The FBI agent reported these suspicions concerning Jacobs as if it were an actual possibility that he might be transmitting information to red controllers from a clandestine radio station at his house.

Throughout the 1950s and into the early 1960s Jacobs became more subdued in his academic writings on race, and his public appearances advocating racial equality occurred much less frequently. He concentrated on his linguistic research and did not enter the public controversies of his age, instead preferring to remain silent in the background. During the campus uprisings of the 1960s Jacobs took care to counsel students to be careful when engaging in public protests, quietly referring to his own past troubles (De Danaan to Price 3/15/01). His approach to public advocacy and activism appears forever dampened by his encounters with Canwell, his colleagues, his own university, and the FBI.

The Third Time's a Charm: Morris Swadesh's Troubles at City College

The Jacobs and Morgan cases had far-reaching consequences for anthropologists across the country. The news of these episodes broadcast a clear message that it was open season on any anthropologist or academic involved in activist progressive politics—whether Communist or not. These scholars were so thoroughly lanted[3] that other academics avoided them, their views, and their problems. The lesson to be learned was unmistakable: those who refused to restrain from radical or Marxist analyses or to refrain from racial or economic activism could easily be the next witness to be called before the growing host of loyalty and security committees. Anthropologists around the country knew that activist members of their profession had been accused of being Communists, and that one anthropologist had already lost his job for political activism without due process or a proper investigation by the AAA.

Anthropologist Morris Swadesh's problems at the City College of New York (CCNY) were linked to Morgan's troubles at the Ohio State Museum. Swadesh's contract was not renewed after he used class time to discuss issues of racism on the CCNY campus and the details of Morgan's firing, as well as the threats to academic freedom precipitated by these events. But Swadesh's case was fundamentally different from either Jacobs's or Morgan's because his was a direct challenge to classroom academic freedom.

Morris Swadesh studied linguistics under Leonard Bloomfield and Edward Sapir, earning his B.A. (1930) and M.A. (1931) degrees at the University of Chicago. He then followed Sapir to Yale, where he completed his Ph.D. in 1933 with a dissertation on the Nootka language. In the late 1930s he was invited by President Cardenas of Mexico to help implement an innovative Indian education program using indigenous Indian languages for classroom instruction. During World War II he served in the language section of the Army, and in the Office of Strategic Services where he taught both Russian and Mandarin Chinese (McQuown 1968:756). According to his surviving family, that service included hazardous frontline duty in the China-Burmese theater. His service period culminated in the preparation of training methods and materials for armed services personnel to achieve fluency in foreign languages including Russian and Chinese. His manuals were used extensively and their insights on learning language became the basis for methods such as the Berlitz language series. After the war he was hired by CCNY's Department of Sociology and Anthropology, where he was a popular and successful lecturer.

Swadesh first came to the attention of the FBI in 1946 when a fellow veteran anonymously accused him of having (in a wartime conversation aboard a ship) "openly proclaim[ed] that he was a Communist. . . . [He] stated that if it were necessary to obtain the aims of the Communists he would participate in an attempt to overthrow the Government of this country by force and violence" (WFO100-344641-1 4/5/46). The informer stated that Swadesh regarded force as a last, rather than a first, resort. Morris Swadesh's family found the notion of him using force and violence risible and the allegation doubtful. He was, they said, a conscientious objector who returned to the United States and volunteered for military service only because of the great perfidy of the surprise attack at Pearl Harbor.

Swadesh had sent a gift subscription of the *Worker* to this informer friend, who told the FBI that he rejected the gift because he did not agree with the party's aims (WFO100-344641-1 4/5/46). The FBI acquired a letter from Swadesh to this informer in which Swadesh explained he wanted to send the *Worker* because it was "a useful wedding present, something you can't get along without." Swadesh explained that much of the Western press was propaganda and couldn't be trusted. He added, "I could go on, because I know there are many issues that have been raised in the headlines the past few months. Later on, when the explanation or denial comes out, it appears on Page 19 if at all so that the reader may never know that his newspaper has admitted reporting a false statement or a misrepresented fact. That is why I'm getting you the Worker (it is a weekly edition of the Daily Worker, with a survey of the week's news). . . . The Worker and the little man in general have nothing to gain by twisting the truth. It is only special interests that can gain by kidding the public. Perhaps you will feel that the Worker represents a special interest too. Of course, it does. It represents the opinion of the Communist Party of the U.S." (NYI00-80694:2 12/18/46).

This letter caused the FBI to reexamine records from Swadesh's three and a half years of wartime army service, as well as his academic records, employment status, and known addresses since the 1930s. The New York City SAC recommended that Swadesh be added to the Security Index as a native-born Communist, and a report indicated that in 1947 Swadesh had been the Washington Heights CP press director, that he had marched in the New York City May Day parade the previous year in his military uniform, and that he was one of the anthropologists identified by Murdock as a Communist agitator at the 1948 AAA meeting (NYI00-80694 5/10/49). The FBI recorded Swadesh's letter to New Jersey Governor Driscoll protesting the trial of six blacks accused of killing William Homer in January 1948 (NYI00-344641-18 11/2/53). The FBI noted that he had marched in the 1948 New York City May Day parade and that he had braved the violent 1949 Peekskill rally in support of Paul Robeson.

At CCNY Swadesh was a lively, popular instructor who mixed in with his classroom lectures discussions of current events and contemporary social problems. As his friend and colleague Stanley Newman later eulogized, Swadesh's willingness to engage in political discussions at CCNY "embarrassed the administrative powers" because he "vigorously champion[ed] student demonstrators. Being a man of powerful convictions, he was inclined to be as uncompromising in battle for a social or political idea as he was in advancing a linguistic theory. As a result of this episode and of other less publicized ones, he became labeled unambiguously as a 'leftist' during the nosiest period of the McCarthy Era, and university administrators were unwilling to take the risk of hiring him" (Newman 1967:949).

It was just nine days after Swadesh was added to the FBI's Security Index that a letter of complaint was issued to Swadesh by five administrative figures at CCNY (including former Bureau of Indian Affairs chief John Collier) that provided the basis for the nonrenewal of his contract at CCNY (see *Daily Compass* 6/8/49). There are no records indicating that the FBI illegally notified any administrators at CCNY that Swadesh was added to the Security Index, but the timing of these events suggests this to be a likely possibility, and records of such action could be among the redacted or unreleased records pertaining to Swadesh or could have been unrecorded in any file.

As an untenured professor, Swadesh taught under a year-to-year contract at CCNY. A month after learning that his contract would not be renewed, Swadesh wrote to AAA President Hallowell requesting that the association investigate the events leading up to the nonrenewal of his teaching contract. Swadesh's letter outlined the pertinent facts of his case, and remarked on his surprise when,

on May 27, 1949, [the] last class day of the school year, I was suddenly notified that I was denied reappointment as Associate Professor in the Department of Sociology and Anthropology of City College—despite the unanimous recommendation of the departmental Appointments Committee. Besides being in disregard of the procedure provided by the By-Laws of the Board of Higher Education of New York, this action violates customary norms of personnel practice, particularly as to the late date of notification, making it practically impossible to locate a new position for the coming year.

The pretext was that some members of my department claimed to have spontaneously changed their minds about me in the last few weeks. Incredible supporting reasons were claimed to explain this alleged phenomenon. Among them was the slander that I allegedly do not believe in verification of scientific fact, and other equally ridiculous slanders. A close examination of the facts will prove this last-minute reversal of reappointment to be a flagrant violation of academic freedom, probably motivated in part by my refusal to collaborate in certain improper maneuvers of the departmental chairman in violation of the professional rights of certain other members of the department, in part by my disapproval of the discriminatory practices of the administration. I submit under separate cover several documents which will facilitate study of my case. . . .

Of most interest to anthropologists is the false accusation brought against me of "improper use of a regular scheduled class time for the organization of a protest to the Governor of Ohio concerning the dismissal of an employee of that state." The "employee" refered to here is evidently Mr. Richard G. Morgan, member of the Anthropological Association, whose case was referred to the Scientific Freedom Committee by the Toronto Meeting. My action in class was not "the organization of a protest" but the discussion of pressures to which anthropologists are subject today and the inevitable effects on anthropological teaching. As an outgrowth of the classroom discussion, students were moved to prepare and circulate a petition to the governor of Ohio, urging an investigation of the Morgan case and his restoration to this position "if the investigation so warrants." This was an extracurricular activity carried on outside of class time and sponsored by the student Sociology Society.

At the time of the Toronto meeting I had already been recommended for reappointment by my department; since such recommendation is normally tantamount to actual reappointment, I had no reason to anticipate the present circumstances. I was pleased at our action in providing for a Scientific Freedom Committee because I knew that the moral influence of such a group would greatly aid in securing Richard Morgan's professional rights and would generally strengthen the position of all anthropologists. If the Executive Board had acted promptly to set up the Committee, it might well have avoided the problem of my present situation. The fact is that the Board's delay has created doubts in many minds as to [whether] it intends to set up any serious committee. I am sure that my anthropological colleagues at City College might well have refused to make themselves parties to a violation of academic freedom in my case, if they thought it might result in the official censure of their professional organization. Considering this I hope that you will now hasten to get up the Committee and in so doing give it the orientation and personnel that will enable it to function effectively.[4] (RAAA: 4, MS/AH 6/29/49)

A few days later Hallowell informed Swadesh that the "resolution passed at the last Annual meeting places the investigation of such cases squarely in the lap of the Executive Board" and that the Committee on Scientific Freedom had only been charged with "recommending procedure to the Council at its next annual meeting" (RAAA: 4, AH/Board 7/1/49). Thus the AAA's position was that it was unable to take any action until the next annual meeting, thereby effectively abandoning Swadesh to fend for himself. Hallowell passed on a copy of Swadesh's letter to the board, noting that "since both Aginsky and Swadesh have prepared quite voluminous documents in support of their respective positions, I have asked them to send you these documents. I hope you will take time to examine them at once and make specific recommendations as to the next step that seems appropriate in this particular case. I hope you will agree with me that this procedure seems to be required because of the fact that the council cannot act on the report of the Committee on Scientific Freedom until the next Annual Meeting so that at the moment we have no established procedures" (RAAA: 4, AH/Board 7/1/149).

A number of important developments transpired during the month between Swadesh's nonrenewal of contract and his letter to President Hallowell. On June 13, 1949, Bert Aginsky, sociology and anthropology chair at CCNY, wrote to the New York Board of Higher Education of his regrets over the handling of the Swadesh case, which he characterized as "contrary to the basic principles espoused by academic institutions" (AES: 6, 6/13/49). Yet Aginsky then advanced charges that Swadesh had misrepresented the basic facts of the case claiming that Swadesh had originally admitted to present-ing a biased version of the Morgan episode in class. Aginsky believed that Swadesh's charges of anti-Semitic racism were irrelevant in this case, and were only broached to obfuscate the facts of the case to distract attention from Swadesh's own wrongdoing.

Jay Powell (1995:663) suggests that Swadesh was not given the same assis-tance by the AAA as Richard Morgan had received. Swadesh had experienced anti-Semitism at Yale and believed that an element of Aginsky's action against him was discriminatory. The charge was difficult to credit because Aginsky was, as Morris Opler sarcastically put it, "what the man in the street calls a Jew" (RAAA: 4, MO/AH 6/18/19). Swadesh's family believes that Aginsky at-tempted to coerce Swadesh into informing on another professor to get rid of him, and that the harsh feeling between the two originated in Swadesh's re-fusal to buckle under. Without denying that anti-Semitism may have played some role in Swadesh's firing, I would stress that Swadesh's case was given at least as much serious consideration as those such as Jacobs, Stern, or Weltfish who found themselves under fire—the problem was that the consideration wasn't much at all.

There also may well have been personal issues between Swadesh and Agin-sky,[5] and anti-Semitism may or may not have been a factor in the firing. The climate of the country in the postwar years was increasingly xenophobic and politically intolerant. The biases evident in the list of suspected Communists that Murdock gave J. Edgar Hoover makes it plain that distinguishing anti-Semitism from a broader xenophobia or from political intolerance can be difficult.

A number of anthropologists wrote to Hallowell and the AAA executive board to weigh in on the Swadesh case. Morris Opler wrote President Hal-lowell urging him not to get involved in the Swadesh matter, recommending instead that the New York Board of Higher Education adjudicate the case as a contractual dispute (RAAA: 4, MO/AH 6/18/49). This suggestion was far from an apolitical one, as it was obvious that the conservative board of education would find against Swadesh. Opler claimed that Swadesh had "slanted" the version of the Morgan case that he'd presented in his class. A month later Opler again wrote to Hallowell arguing that even tenured professors can get fired if they do not fulfill the duties of their contract through such neglect of contractual responsibilities (RAAA: 4, MO/AH 7/22/49). Gabriel Lasker wrote the AAA executive board arguing that there was probable cause for Swadesh's dismissal. On July 6, 1949, George Murdock wrote President Hallowell that he'd just "learned from Burt Aginsky that Morris Swadesh has officially ap-plied to have his case investigated" (RAAA: 4, GM/AH 7/1/49). Meanwhile Swadesh broadened his requests for assistance beyond the AAA by also seeking support from the American Ethnological Society—whose president was Burt Aginsky.

In July 1949 a pamphlet titled "The Lorch and Swadesh Dismissals: Discrimination and Thought Control at City College" was mailed to academics across the United States.[6] The pamphlet described the circumstances under which Morris Swadesh and Lee Lorch (of the mathematics department) had not been given continuing contracts at City College. Both Lorch and Swadesh had been vocal critics of racial-bias policies in the greater New York area and on the CCNY campus. The pamphlet argued that Swadesh's problems resulted from his battles against anti-Semitism, his protests over the college's decision not to hire a black job applicant, and his use of class time to discuss "the dismissal of a fellow scientist who opposed racist theories." The pamphlet stated that Lorch was "well-known for his opposition to discrimination," and described how one college employee had been found to discriminate against blacks and had been rewarded with promotions and a pay raise, and how Professor William E. Knickerbocker, a well-known racist, had been subjected to a vote of removal by the New York City Council yet retained his position as professor and department chair. The pamphlet called for a letter-writing campaign in support of Swadesh and Lorch, directed at the New York Board of Higher Education (EG: 2, pamphlet).

On August 10, 1949, Swadesh wrote President Hallowell that the New York Board of Higher Education had rejected his appeal. Swadesh was clearly angry at the AAA for their inaction in this matter. He complained that "the situation at City College is not isolated. The anthropological profession has in a little over a year suffered at least three serious violations of academic freedom (no one knows how many cases have taken place but screened from public notice): Melville Jacobs threatened with dismissal and actually subjected to the humiliation of a 'probation,' Richard G. Morgan dismissed after many years of service. Morris Swadesh dropped after being assured of reappointment" (RAAA: 4, MS/AH 8/10/49). Swadesh's anger seeped through in discussing the association's inaction in his case as well as Jacobs's and Morgan's cases. He wrote that he felt that "three fellows of the American Anthropological Association were evidently pressured into making themselves accomplices of the action in order to make it look legal. Still other fellows and other members have indicated to me that they are afraid to come out in my support because their own administrations would look unfavorably upon any signs of concern for academic freedom" (RAAA: 4 MS/AH 8/10/49).

Swadesh asked the AAA executive board for emergency fellowships for himself and for Richard Morgan, but the AAA did not seriously consider his request. It is difficult to gauge just how pervasive was the fear of openly supporting Morris Swadesh, but the correspondence of various anthropologists from this period indicates that the AAA's inaction contributed to the veil of fear that cloaked anthropology and other disciplines. The AAA announced in their October 1949 *News Bulletin* that the executive board had found "no grounds for further action in this case," and thus the AAA relinquished to the New York Board of Higher Education the responsibility for any further action (AAANB 10/49:3; cf. Hallowell 1950:136–37).

President Hallowell wrote to Ralph Himstead inquiring if Swadesh had asked the AAUP to take up his case (RAAA: Pres. Correspondence AH/RH 10/6/49). In a move typifying its consistent inaction during the McCarthy period, the AAUP took no action in this matter. President Hallowell appeared relieved to have rid himself of Swadesh's case, writing Alfred Kroeber that "since the Board has acted officially on the Swadesh case, my own view is that it might not be reopened except on the basis of some new facts" (RAAA: 4, AH/AK 11/1/49).

At the annual meeting of the American Ethnological Society (AES) on November 18, 1949, Bernhard Stern moved that the society coordinate its own investigation into the circumstances surrounding Swadesh's termination. The motion passed and the AES's Committee on Academic Freedom was formed. Two days later Burt Aginsky stepped "aside as presiding officer of the [AES] Executive Board while the Swadesh matter [was] under consideration, leaving the Chair in Dr. [Julian] Steward's hands" (AES: BA/JS 11/20/49; AES: BA/AES Board 11/20/49).

In the end, the AAA and the AES did little to help Swadesh. Publicly, members of these associations expressed regrets, stating that they were helpless to intervene in such matters of contractual negotiations, while privately some of them maintained that Swadesh was a troublemaker who had gotten what he had coming to him. However, while anthropological and linguistic associations did little to aid Swadesh, colleagues like Charles Voegelin and Zellig Harris did what they could to offer sympathy and assistance (Hymes to Price 1/16/98).

Swadesh's firing made the headlines of the *Daily Worker*, where in one story he was quoted as saying that "possibly there is some basis for explaining [the department's] part in the non-reappointment as due to my stand against bigotry and racism in the College, which they seem to be more interested in covering up than correcting" (DW 8/8/49, p. 14).[7] Meanwhile, without comment the FBI updated his Security Index Card to note his unemployment (9/5/50). In 1951 Columbia University's Department of Anthropology granted him a research affiliation and he found work as an editor at Columbia University Press (WFO100-344641-89 12/21/61). In addition, he continued his lexicostatistical research in New York and later Colorado under the limited sponsorship of the American Philosophical Society. His Security Index

Card was updated on January 7, 1953, to specify a "TAB for DETCOM" and a "TAB for COMSAB" (which designated that he should be detained as a Communist in the event of a national emergency, and that he was considered to be a potential Communist saboteur) (NYI00-344641-18 11/2/53).

Morris Swadesh and his wife and children moved to Denver in September 1953 (WFOI00-344641-19 11/19/53). The FBI learned that Swadesh had enrolled in two anthropology courses and a mathematics course at the University of Denver in fall 1953. The FBI monitored Swadesh's increasingly active involvement in Denver Communist Party meetings, and they noted he also held meetings to protest the Rosenberg's execution and to support arrested Smith Act violators from the Denver area (WFOI00-344641-29).

A February 17, 1956, message from the Denver SAC notified J. Edgar Hoover that Swadesh had moved to Mexico City and requested that the FBI continue its investigation of him in Mexico (WFOI00-344641-31 2/17/56). In the following months the FBI monitored Swadesh's activities in Mexico and confirmed that he was teaching at the Escuela Nacional de Antropología e Historia. In June 1956 the FBI learned that Swadesh was in Chiapas (WFOI00-344641-35 6/25/56) and later tracked his brief return to Denver in December 1956 (WFOI00-344641-44 1/2/57). Informer members of the Mexican Communist Party reported to the FBI that Swadesh was unknown to them, but the FBI made inquiries about Swadesh to potential employers at Mexico City museums and colleges thereby spreading apprehension and fear and limiting his hiring possibilities.[8] In all, throughout the 1950s the FBI generated dozens of reports tracking Swadesh's status and travels (WFOI00-334641-64 2/6/59).

Just as Swadesh's decision to move to Mexico derived from his problems at CCNY, his decision to remain there was linked to fears of future reprisals for his political views and associations if he returned to the United States. In 1961 an FBI informer reported that Swadesh "remains in Mexico associated with the national University. They advised that he reportedly was offered a post or scholarship at Johns Hopkins University, which he refused because he was afraid of going to the United States" (WFOI00-344641-91 11/14/61). Despite such reported fears, he did return to the United States in 1962 to teach summer school at the University of Washington (WFOI00-344641-97).

When Swadesh applied for a new passport in 1963 he acknowledged that he had been a member of the Communist Party in the past but would not provide any detailed summary of his past political actions because it "would be contrary to his principles to subscribe to the required affidavit on the ground that an individual's political beliefs or affiliations should have no bearing upon his eligibility to receive passport facilities" (WFOI00-344641-105 12/26/63). It is not known how Swadesh resolved his passport problems, but in 1965 he spent half a year traveling in Europe and Africa (WFO100 344641-105 2/12/65) and he taught as a visiting professor at Syracuse University after his return.

The FBI's interest in Morris Swadesh ended when he died of a heart attack in Mexico City on July 20, 1967. Although his political activism and Marxist affiliations had brought him numerous obstacles in the United States, his career still left a tremendous impact on anthropology and linguistics (see McQuown 1968; Newman 1967; Rendon 1967). He was a prolific scholar who made important contributions to the analysis of Native American languages, publishing over twenty books and monographs and over one hundred scholarly articles (Lonergan 1991:679; Swadesh 1971). Swadesh's contributions to language training, glottochronology, and lexicostatistics were substantial and seminal, and they are the works of extraordinarily high intelligence. He was beloved in Mexico both by the Indians with whom he worked and by his colleagues and students. His work with the Indians raised literacy and converted their indigenous languages to written form, helping their cultures to survive as Mexico modernized. Twenty-five years after his death, colleagues held a symposium in his honor. In driving Swadesh out of the United States, the profession of linguistics and the credibility of the United States in Latin America were both diminished, and we can only wonder what Swadesh might have accomplished had he been given fair treatment by his native land.

Issues of Professional Assistance, Advocacy, and Abandonment

While Jacobs and Swadesh were left on their own to fight for their academic freedom, there were other instances of prominent leaders using their authority to successfully assist scholars under attack. One such case even involved the AAA. In 1950 when Ralph Beals became president of the AAA, he brought a new courageous aggressiveness with which he and the AAA defended scholars under attack by the red scare.[9] The success of efforts by Beals raises questions about the possibility of different outcomes for Morgan, Jacobs, or Swadesh had the AAA's presidency or board positions been filled by less fearful and cautious academics. Beals's presidency came during a period of increased red-baiting, with widespread attacks on academics across the country, but Beals's tenure demonstrated the difference that a courageous individual can make in addressing crises of academic freedom.

Soon after Beals stepped into the AAA presidency he began to assist anthropologist Leonard Broom in his efforts to obtain a passport to conduct fieldwork under a Fulbright grant (see RAAA:4 "L. Broom Passport Case"). The State Department had refused to issue Broom a passport because his name appeared on a list of subversive scholars. However, because of Beals's aggressive efforts, a passport was forthcoming and Broom was allowed to conduct his research (Beals 1951:436).

In striking contrast to former President Hallowell's approach to the attacks on Morgan's or Swadesh's academic freedom, Beals dealt with issues proactively and aggressively by addressing the academic merits of the case without concern over the specific accusation against Broom's political affiliations. Beals understood the suppressive nature of the threat to all members of the discipline, and he approached Broom's fight as a fight for all by writing strongly worded letters of support to Secretary of State Acheson while eliciting the aid of Washington anthropologists such as Philleo Nash to work whatever inside angles were available to them. Beals made a difference, and his impact stands in marked contrast with the (in)actions of other leaders during this period, actions that had real impacts on scholars like Melville Jacobs and uncounted others who watched from a distance.

The lack of support from colleagues and organizations weighed heavily on scholars like Jacobs. Had Jacobs received support from his colleagues he might have reacted differently to the pressures of FBI harassment. It is difficult to blame Jacobs for succumbing to such pressures; after all, his peers and professional organization had abandoned him. Despite his cooperative approach with the FBI, they do not appear to have ever returned this trust, instead continuing to compile such unlikely reports as his involvement in clandestine radio broadcasts or his role as part of a ludicrous assassination faction. It did not matter that Jacobs was willing to play ball with the FBI, he was never considered trustworthy.

One of the problems in tracking and measuring assaults on academic freedom is that in few instances can one find a smoking gun firmly establishing acts of reprisal on individuals for specific actions. There are many reasons for this—not the least of which is that academic administrators are frequently malevolent but seldom stupid, and they do not tend to leave paper trails documenting the suspected motivations for their actions given the possible bureaucratic and litigious consequences. There were few instances during the 1940s and 1950s in which tenured professors were explicitly fired for political actions; more often than not, accusations of repression involve the gray areas of contractual relationships. When professors held only ongoing contracts and were not engaged in active tenure review processes, it was much easier to terminate their contracts without holding messy investigations. Likewise (as will be seen in Kathleen Gough's experiences at Brandeis University), it is even more difficult to concretely establish that political considerations were responsible in cases where promotions or raises were denied for reasons other than those stated by institutions and administrators.

The FBI had been aware of Swadesh's Communist sympathies since 1946, and they spied on him as he established himself as a professor at CCNY.[10] His advocacy for racial minorities and for the causes of academic freedom marked him as a threat to be dealt with. If the FBI wanted to push Swadesh to the margins it succeeded domestically, although he was still an important and influential linguistic theoretician outside of his country's borders. But the FBI's years of monitoring and harassment succeeded in planting the seeds of fear in Swadesh that prevented him from seriously pursuing a prestigious position at Johns Hopkins or elsewhere.

Swadesh clearly felt that his problems stemmed from his stance on the issues leading to the firing of Richard Morgan. Because he occupied such a tenuous position at the college it was easy for the administration to remove him, and because he held no contract he was in fact never actually "fired." As most untenured professors know, becoming involved in controversial political matters can be fundamentally maladaptive. In effect, Swadesh's numerous letters to the AAA were attempts to persuade the association to engage in behavior similar to that which got him in trouble in the first place. His protests regarding the lack of justice and due process in the Morgan case in turn initiated a similar chain of events leading to his own dismissal. He had seen an egregious example of social injustice become a crude template for his own experience.

CHAPTER 6

Public Show Trials: Gene Weltfish

and a Conspiracy of Silence

Shortly after my arrival in Zandeland we were passing
through a government settlement and noticed that a hut
had been burnt to the ground on the previous night. Its
owner was overcome with grief as it had contained the
beer he was preparing for a mortuary feast. He told us that
he had gone the previous night to examine his beer. He
had lit a handful of straw and raised it above his head so
that light would be cast on the posts, and in so doing he
had ignited the thatch. He, and my companions also, were
convinced that the disaster was caused by witchcraft.

—E. E. Evans-Pritchard

During the early 1950s several fellows of the American Anthropological Association were subpoenaed to appear before congressional committees
investigating national security issues, loyalty, and
the activities of a long list of subversive organizations accused of Communist connections. As these
committees grew in number and power in the early
1950s, the AAA adopted and implemented policies

that increasingly positioned the organization at a safe distance from anthropologists accused of links to Communism. This stance was facilitated by the association's catechism that it was a professional association and that it did not become involved in political matters.

When Jacobs, Morgan, and Swadesh came under fire in the late 1940s the association at least went through the motions of investigating events and supporting the principles of academic freedom, but with these later cases the AAA put forth even less effort to investigate facts or support the accused anthropologists. In searching for references to these later persecutions in the AAA executive board's private correspondence, and in the published items in the association's *News Bulletin*, there is little record of hearings and firings. This conspiracy of silence does not mean that these persecutions went unnoticed by the association's membership—indeed, the membership knew about these attacks on academic freedom and generally watched from a distance without venturing to get involved. Under the leadership of individuals like George Peter Murdock, the AAA institutionalized policies clarifying that scholars caught up in loyalty or security dragnets were on their own and they could expect no meaningful support or investigation from the AAA.

Although the individual experiences and outcomes of anthropologists appearing before loyalty committees differed they did share several commonalities, including a common thread of racial activism, a refusal to answer any questions that could lead to questions about political associates, and difficulty securing or retaining employment after testifying. Further, each of their experiences before these committees changed the way that they viewed their colleagues, the academy, and their society.

Gene Weltfish: The Stifling of a Critical Voice

In 1902 Regina (Gene) Weltfish was born on New York's Lower East Side into an extended family of Russian-German/Americans. She benefited from a liberal arts education at Barnard College in the 1920s, and in the mid-1920s she started a graduate program in anthropology under Franz Boas and Ruth Benedict at Columbia University. After her ethnographic fieldwork among the Pawnee, Weltfish wrote her dissertation on aesthetic designs in Native American basketry. She completed the dissertation in 1929, but at that time Columbia required that all doctoral students publish their dissertations, and the prohibitive costs of doing so prevented her from formally completing her degree until 1950, when the university eliminated the publishing requirement. Because she was not able to seek employment as a Ph.D., Weltfish taught as a lecturer at Columbia from 1935 until 1953. However, in 1953 her contract was suddenly terminated after she received a subpoena to appear before Senator McCarthy's Governmental Operations Committee (cf. U.S. Congress 1953b:118; Bloom 1990:31).

The FBI first became interested in Weltfish in the late 1930s, and they maintained an active interest in her throughout World War II. In December 1944 the FBI interviewed Ralph Linton, then chair of Columbia University's Department of Anthropology. According to the interview, Linton told the FBI that Weltfish was

> an energetic and industrious scholar who had accumulated a good reputation as an instructor at Columbia University. [Linton] advised further that at the time the subject first became associated with Columbia University Anthropology Department, the Dean [sic] was Franz Boaz [sic], a noted Anthropologist who became well known as a Communist. At this time the Anthropology Department was well infiltrated with Communists who actually dominated Boas and the Department.
>
> In the opinion of Linton, Boas was merely a "tool" and because he had attained his late 70's, had become somewhat senile [and] thus was easily led by his Communist associates. One of the members of the department at that time was Alexander Lesser, an alleged Communist. Gene Weltfish married Lesser. However, Linton later heard that these two had become divorced. He was not certain of this fact. Linton was unaware of Lesser's present whereabouts. The latter was dismissed from his employment at Columbia University subsequent to Dean [sic] Linton's appointment as head of the department. This dismissal was the result of misconduct on the part of Lesser who had [identified] himself as a Ph.D. in Anthropology when actually he had not attained such a degree. In addition, Lesser had been unable to properly account for University funds given to him for research purposes.
>
> Dr. Linton was not certain that Gene Weltfish was ever a member of the Communist Party. However, he believed it likely that she may have been a member during Boas' regime in the Anthropology Department. He was of the opinion that it would definitely have been to her advantage to have become a member of the Communist Party at that time. Since the subject received favorable attention during that period, Linton drew the inference that Gene Weltfish had been a member of the Communist Party or at least a fellow traveler. (NY100-64734:3 12/7/44)

There was a level of mutual hostility during this period between Linton and many of Boas's students. In 1936, when Boas prepared to retire as anthropology chair, university president Nicholas Murray Butler appointed an ad hoc committee to select a replacement, making sure that no anthropologist from the department was a member of the committee. Columbia's administration had long since tired of dealing with Boas's progressive stances on political and social issues such as racial equality and America's involvement in World War I. Butler had strained relations with those department members that he viewed as politically radical, and Boas's retirement was an opportunity to bring a more conservative perspective to the department.

Ruth Benedict was appointed acting head of the department for the 1936–1937 academic year by Dean Howard McBain. But McBain died shortly thereafter, leaving Benedict without an administrative patron during the search for a permanent chair. None of Boas's students were seriously considered for the position, and Linton came to Columbia the following year as a visiting professor with an understanding that he would be considered as chair after a trial year. In Linton, Butler found the conservative operative he was seeking.

Linton's appearance at Columbia was problematic for several reasons. He had briefly been a graduate student at Columbia before World War I, although his approach to anthropology was decidedly non-Boasian. When he returned to Columbia after the war in full uniform he was reportedly rebuffed by Boas, who disdained such jingoistic displays in the classroom (cf. Linton and Wagley 1971:13–14; Lewis 2001:458). Linton then left Columbia to teach at Harvard, but legends of the Boas-Linton encounter in 1919 were still circulating when Linton assumed the post of the great man with whom he'd clashed.

Many of Boas's students felt slighted that one of Boas's protégées was not selected for the position. It was no secret that Linton did not get along with Ruth Benedict, Margaret Mead, or Gene Weltfish, and it is not surprising that he felt comfortable passing his speculations on to the FBI. When the FBI asked Linton about Ruth Benedict, he described her as "being on the fringe"—clarifying that in using this phrase he meant to characterize her as being almost fanatical but not intentionally a fellow traveler of Communist or other radical organizations (NY100-64734:4 12/7/44; cf. Buhle 1994).

During this period, the FBI monitored Gene Weltfish's correspondence under a mail-watch program, recording the return addresses of all of her correspondence (NY100–64734:10 12/7/44). The FBI noted that she lived alone with her fourteen-year-old daughter, Anne Lesser, and they recorded her apartment address and the general hours that she was not at home. The reasons for including these details in the report are not explicitly stated, although the bureau's practice of conducting illegal, no-warrant searches of the homes of suspected subversives seems the likely motivation. Records of such break-ins are not included in her file, but testimonials of former FBI agents clarify that records of such illegal actions would not be kept in retrievable files (Swearingen 1995).

The FBI catalogued numerous references to Gene Weltfish in the Communist Party's newspaper, the *Daily Worker*. These references ranged from notations that she'd signed civil rights petitions to articles discussing her involvement in the Congress of American Women (DW 5/26/46) or discussions of interviews with her on radio station WNBC (DW 5/28/46). The FBI also noted that Weltfish conducted seminars at the Marxist-oriented Jefferson School for Social Science.

FBI Racism and The Races of Mankind

The 1940s were a time of increasing discomfort for Weltfish at Columbia. In 1940 university president Butler "called a special meeting of the faculty to tighten academic freedom of speech. He told them that when an individual's position on an issue clashed with that of the university, that individual should leave the university. He called his position 'before and after academic freedom'" (Caffrey 1989:302). While the faculty successfully challenged Butler's policy—leading Butler to retract the harsher elements of his statement—the campus's increasingly intolerant climate was clear to progressive faculty. Many of Weltfish's colleagues tempered their speech and actions under these restrictive conditions, but she continued to speak out and publish academic research dealing with controversial subjects such as racial intolerance in America.

In 1943 Ruth Benedict and Weltfish coauthored a thirty-one-page booklet, *The Races of Mankind*, which examines the physical and social realities of race. The Public Affairs Council funded *The Races of Mankind* as one of eighty-five pamphlets in a popular series, and was designed to popularize anthropological views and critiques of American racial views. *Races of Mankind* differentiated between racial, national, ethnic, and religious differences and presented qualitative and quantitative data demonstrating that differences between American racial groups were due to cultural rather than biological differences.

Weltfish and Benedict's work on the pamphlet was part of their contribution to the U.S. war effort. But as Benedict biographer Margaret Caffrey notes this contribution was not welcome by all: "*Races of Mankind* had originally been written to be distributed in USO [United Service Organization] centers and copies had been ordered by the Army for use by leaders of orientation courses. It became a *cause celebre* when the chair of the House Military Affairs Committee, Congressman Andrew J. May, prohibited its distribution in the Army. May was from Kentucky, and Kentucky was one of three Southern states specifically cited in the pamphlet from the Army World War I intelligence tests to show that Northern blacks had scored higher than Southern whites" (1989:298). May's racist sensitivities and his powerful political position led the army to rescind its commitment to distribute *Races of Mankind* to soldiers, but the publicity resulting from the army affair helped the pamphlet to sell at record levels, with almost a million copies sold in the next decade. In addition to its impressive sales, *Races of Mankind* was widely translated, adopted for use by labor unions, and made into a comic book and an animated film (Caffrey 1989:299).

When Chester Barnard, president of the USO, ordered the pamphlets to be removed from USO reading rooms around the globe, he was taken to task by mystery writer Rex Stout, then chairman of the Writers War Board (Rice 1944), along with other writers. In the *Saturday Review of Literature*, Elmer Rice wrote that the USO's censorship presented "a striking example of the woeful lack of courage displayed by Americans in positions of power, when they are brought face-to-face with our most urgent and social problem" (1944:13).

The *Daily Worker's* commentary on the War Department's censorship of *Races of Mankind* bluntly observed that scientific research was being suppressed by powerful military and political forces that supported the same sort of "superstition" and "quackery" being promulgated by the Nazis. The March 8, 1944, editorial "Upholding Superstition" reads as follows:

> Patriotic Americans are rightly indignant at the War Department for its rank conduct in regard to "Races of Mankind." The department now acknowledges that it has actually prohibited the use of this pamphlet in Army training courses.
>
> It is difficult to reconcile such an act with the cause for which we are fighting. Immediately there is impressed on one's mind certain similarities between this book-banning in the interests of racists and the race theories which have been the heaviest artillery of our deadly enemies. We cannot combat Hitlerism with full force and effect, and at the same time ape Hitlerism even in part.
>
> By barring "Races of Mankind" from its courses, the War Department has withdrawn factual information from our soldiers which would give them heightened morale in their grapple with the foe. It is science which is being suppressed. It is superstition and its offspring, falsity and quackery, which are being upheld.
>
> Race superiority theories have ever been the favorite tool of the agents of ignorance and iniquity. Those theories have been the logical foundation stone of the hideous Nazi state, that Moloch in the slaughter of mankind's souls and bodies. In the South, the version of the race su-

periority idea known as "white supremacy" has kept in power the most degraded personalities, perpetuating poor schools, poverty and the poll tax.

The scientific facts brought forward in "Races of Mankind" put to rout such intellectual dry-rot. The pamphlet tells truths America should know. Notwithstanding the horrible handicaps under which he has labored, the Negro has marked up remarkable records of achievement. This is the case in such diverse fields as science, literature, the theater, political life and now in our armed forces. Pearl Harbor had its Dorie Miller just as Boston's battle had its Crispus Attucks.

What is vital at this moment is that the great mass of the white people now recognize this and that the Negro people are more and more insisting on using their rights. In that recognition and insistence there is being built up a unity which is born of a common interest and common necessity. This is strikingly shown by the CIO, which has distributed this pamphlet and has furnished in its own organizations an example for the nation.

This matter of War Department suppression of democratic material has to be fought out. Americans everywhere will have to insist that the War Department's attitude and practice in this respect be changed. They will have to make certain that this attitude is likewise fully defeated through the widest distribution of the banned pamphlet.

Every individual and organization has now the duty to join with the CIO and bring "Races of Mankind" to the attention of all members and friends in the armed forces and elsewhere. This pamphlet must be carried to the whole American people. (DW 3/8/44:6; cf. WF0190-1065467-417A)

While the *Daily Worker's* views on the War Department's suppression of Benedict and Weltfish's work seems reasonable to contemporary readers, they were read as radical and provocative for their time. The FBI reported the editorial with concern and noted with unease that *The Races of Mankind* had been circulated at the New York Communist Party headquarters (WF0190-1065467-417).

New York FBI agents reported that on January 4, 1945, Weltfish protested in a public lecture the American Red Cross's policy of segregating blood plasma donated by blacks (WF0100-2872252-4). The War Department established this policy during the war to placate racist politicians who held superstitious views regarding racial groups mixing blood. Someone attending the lecture told the FBI that Weltfish's arguments "made a deep impression . . . and indicated it had impaired her faith in the Red Cross program"—a dangerous occurrence during a time of world war (WF0100-2872252-4).

Such unsolicited FBI informer letters were common during this period. Among the tens of thousands of pages of FBI files on anthropologists that I have read, there are dozens of such unsolicited citizen-informer letters. Most are addressed directly to J. Edgar Hoover, many are handwritten, and most have handwritten notations by FBI personnel or attached reports indicating that FBI background investigations were undertaken on these individuals as a result of these letters. While the specific content of these citizen-informer letters varied, there was a general pattern wherein authors relayed comments or actions they observed and then added that they were writing because it was their civic duty to report such facts to the FBI. Reported statements or actions often involved unpopular notions of racial equality, and those holding such views were generally described as "communists." These letters also frequently contain testimonials of patriotism and duty, and some note doubts regarding the propriety of turning informer on a fellow citizen. The formulaic structure links these various letters as part of a greater cultural phenomenon of duty-bound informing and reveals the public fear that red-baiting figures like McCarthy and Hoover successfully harnessed and promulgated.

Other Americans felt duty-bound to inform on what they saw as the Communist views of Weltfish. In May 1947 a soldier wrote to J. Edgar Hoover with a detailed report on a talk at Hunter's Girls College by Weltfish on anthropological research supporting the inherent equality of all races—views the soldier believed betrayed Communist biases. With a declaration of his own commitment to Americanism, he signed off with "hoping you put an 'H' Bomb under all them Reds, I am . . . [signature redacted]." A few years later (February 1949) another concerned citizen-informer wrote Hoover that while on vacation in New Hampshire she had overheard discussions by fellow vacationers that indicated Communist sympathies. After identifying these individuals to Hoover, she added that she wanted to call attention to Professor Gene Weltfish, stating, "She is [a] definite connection with the Communist Party here. The direct influences that she exerts over her students make her doubly dangerous" (WFO100-1287225-11).

FBI agents filed a detailed summary of a talk Weltfish presented to the East-West Association in Pittsburgh on February 16, 1947. According to the report, Weltfish told the group that

> about six or seven years ago, American Scientists woke up and saw that Hitler was using our material for destruction. These scientists have been called inhabitants of "ivory towers" but they woke up too late. Going back to 1938, she said we placed an embargo on goods to Spain. Dr. Weltfish felt there was something wrong when these people who were fighting for lives were unable to purchase necessary goods. Then came Hitler,

misusing people and things and, in the end, somebody else grabs the treasure and everybody is left confused.

She said that in the field of anthropology, a large committee was appointed who studied this subject to decide what was best to teach in the schools. After putting this idea of brotherly love into practice, they learned that the parents objected, so they realized they would first have to teach the parents and adults. She said that Scientists sort out facts in an orderly fashion and pigeonhole these new facts. (Judging people is a pigeon-holing game that human beings are [fond] of doing). This judging is a bad habit for it [is] so often wrong.

Anthropology is the science of mankind. First we say, this one has Italian blood, then we say, that one has Greek blood and another has Chinese blood. The truth is that there are only four types of blood[:] A, B, AB and O. You can't classify according to family, country, race or color. (WFO100-287225-5)

The report further stated that Weltfish discussed the failures of scientists to ascertain any meaningful differences in brains, bones, and other features, and she described nutritional and environmental features that contribute to IQ measurements. She spoke of the "pecking order" that permeated stratified American society and discussed the lack of evidence that "race mixing" had any deleterious effects on populations—arguing that racist beliefs were embedded not in biology but in class conflict. In discussing the suppression of free inquiry of race she mentioned how U.S. Representative Andrew J. May had banned the distribution of the *Race of Mankind* within the armed services. Weltfish believed that the pamphlet "would not have attracted much attention but for the prejudice of some of the high-ranking men of the Army and the Congressmen they sought to interest. [Andrew J.] May was on one of the Committees in connection with the defense of the United States and as a result her book was banned for distribution because some of the material was thought improper . . . Confusion was put into the minds of people by design because the wrath of Congressmen and military leaders had to be listened to" (WFO100-287225-5). The FBI recorded the exchange between Weltfish and the audience on the topic of race.

Later, the FBI somehow obtained a fourteen-page single-spaced transcript of the address Weltfish presented on March 26, 1949, at the Waldorf Astoria's Cultural and Scientific Conference for World Peace (NY100-64734:20–33; see also Gillmor 1949; Weltfish 1949). The Waldorf conference was a watershed for the postwar intellectual left, although the conference was disrupted and subverted by the CIA (Saunders 1999:45–56). Weltfish's remarkable address demonstrates the complexity of her analytical abilities and shows her to have anticipated many of the critiques of colonialism to be developed decades later by such scholars as Kathleen Gough (1968) or Talad Asad (1973).

At the Waldorf conference Weltfish described how international economic markets thrived under conditions of racism, and she identified the neocolonialist economic conditions prevailing in the postwar world by describing the role that public and private American interests played in these emerging conditions (NY100-64734:20–25). She focused on the expropriation of raw materials in Africa, and the imprisonment of indigenous journalists who challenged these exploitive economic relations, and she issued a call for indigenous rights and a greater equity of economic and social justice: "In all this," she states, "is the underlying viewpoint that production is an end in itself and that raw materials are the means to its achievement, but the most essential part of the equation is left out—the people who work the raw materials—their wants, their rights, their needs and their power. If the racist-tainted mind in the U.S. and in the colonial countries believes that the colonial peoples do not see this error, he is mistaken. There is in some colonial peoples a certain refinement of mind that is foreign to our Western civilization" (NY100-64734:30). Needless to say, such talk of Third World liberation and economic independence deepened the FBI's suspicions of Gene Weltfish.

The FBI compiled extensive lists of dozens of subversive organizations to which Weltfish belonged, including the Women's International Democratic Federation, Congress of American Women, Jefferson School of Social Science, Civil Rights Congress, International Women's Organization, American Committee for Protection of Foreign Born, National Council of American-Soviet Friendship, Veterans of the Abraham Lincoln Brigade, Committee for a Democratic Far Eastern Policy, American Council for a Democratic Greece, Council on African Affairs, American Slav Congress, and United May Day Committee (WF0100-287225-53). When a photograph of Gene Weltfish appeared in a LIFE magazine article, the FBI added it to their centralized files (WF0100-287225–22).

Weltfish and the Party Question

For many scholars of the Cold War, determining whether or not a specific individual was a member of the Communist Party is of critical importance in interpreting specific interactions with congressional committees such as HUAC or the Internal Security Committee. I do not share the view that knowledge of an individual's party status necessarily improves our understanding of the investigations and inquisitions examined here. I am instead interested in questions of an individual's party membership status insofar as such information adds some depth to our understanding of the individual's actions and the role of the party in laying the foundation of the American civil rights movement. My lack of interest in establishing the status of Gene Weltfish's party membership is not meant to minimize the contributions party members made to activist causes. Further, it is not meant to distance Weltfish from any stigma associated with party membership, nor is it to argue against the position that questions of party membership can shed important light on an individual's motivations. Instead, I note that the central reason that Weltfish and the other anthropologists discussed in this text were identified for investigation by the FBI, and by congressional and senate committees, is because they were committed activists for racial, economic, gender, and global equality. In understanding the FBI's obsession with Weltfish, the status of her possible Communist Party membership was of secondary importance to her activism.

Some scholars suggest that individuals wrongly identified as Communists by Hoover or McCarthy took on the status of double victims—that is, as victimized by the inquisition they encountered and by mistaken identity. But focusing on party members falsely and accurately accused infers that some individuals could legitimately be asked about their private and public political beliefs and actions (e.g. Krook 1993), and this position subtly supports the view that the agents of McCarthyism had the right to monitor or attack members of subversive organizations such as the Communist Party. I do not share this view.

I do not know if Gene Weltfish was a member of the Communist Party, nor do I consider it directly relevant to issues of academic freedom. The FBI believed she was, as do some anthropologists who were members of the Communist Party during the 1960s and 1970s. However, Weltfish's daughter, Anne Margetson, unequivocally states that her mother was never a party member. Margetson maintains that her mother refused to cooperate with McCarran's and McCarthy's committees simply out of principle (Margetson interview with Price 6/1/98). If Margetson is correct this does not change my interpretation of these events but it does arguably add a level of tragic irony to Weltfish's persecution, because fair-weather civil libertarians like George Murdock and the power-base members of the AAA (who only wanted to assist non-Communists attacked by loyalty and security committees) would have come to her aid if they were true to their stated principles of "academic freedom."

Weltfish was one of the dozen anthropologists identified as Communists in Murdock's January 1, 1949, letter to Hoover. Murdock's letter caused the New York field office to reexamine what it knew about Weltfish. The FBI reported that "on February 21, 1949 Confidential Informant ▬▬▬▬ of known reliability, advised of Communist Party activity at Columbia University. According to the informant two organizations, 'Marxist Society' and the 'Progressive Student Organization,' are the instruments for spreading Communist Party doctrine within the university. Gene Weltfish, a professor, conducts the majority of the Marxist Society activities, according to this informant" (WFO100-287225-23). Another informant contacted the FBI and "advised that Professor Weltfish was not merely sympathetic to the Party but was under Party discipline" (WFO100-287225-23).

Louis Budenz was one of the most important professional witnesses used by Hoover and by congressional and senatorial committees to generate names of supposed members of the Communist Party. After leaving the party he "came under the protection of the Catholic Church, from which he received the financial and spiritual support he had once gotten from the party" (Schrecker 1994:43). Although Budenz incorrectly identified a large number of non-Communists as Communists, he was a celebrity witness whose testimony was sought out across the country in the late 1940s and 1950s (see Schrecker 1994:173–87). With time Budenz's embellishments and lies became so numerous and outrageous that even the FBI eventually stopped using him as a witness.

Budenz told the FBI in 1950 that Weltfish was a "concealed Communist"— that is, a party member who kept her membership secret (WFO100-287225-24). This report includes a statement, apparently by Budenz, that described Weltfish's ties to the party: "From the late 1930's or early 1940's on, I constantly advised officially that Dr. Weltfish was a very active and effective member of the Communist Party. Her name came up during a New York State Party meeting and was also mentioned in the Politburo. These references arose from her many activities among the teaching groups and also her participation in many Communist fronts. According to ███████ she was one of the most reliable Communists in the educational ranks of the country" (WFO100-287225-24). The FBI also used public resources to compile information for Weltfish's FBI file. Her file includes an article from the *Columbia Spectator* (11/30/50) with the front-page headline "Gene Weltfish Asks Fight on Anti-Red Act" (WFO100-287225-25), and other articles record her involvement in housing, racial, and gender equity movements.

On January 19, 1951, an unidentified woman, likely a Columbia graduate student, approached Weltfish in order to secretly gather information for the FBI on Weltfish's involvement in the Women's International Democratic Federation (WIDF) meeting to be held in East Berlin the following month. Weltfish told the informer of her commitment to working and fighting for peace, explaining how she saw her involvement with the WIDF as working toward this goal. Weltfish told the informant that "peace is a dynamic situation which must be fought for, the members of the WIDF are all set to take part in a fight for peace. As conclusive evidence of this I can state that I have one million women in Italy and one and one-half million in France, who have guns and caches of ammunition. If things get much worse late this spring my two and one-half million women in France and Italy know perfectly well how and when to shoot" (WFO100-287225-27). The New York SAC asked the Washington field office to check the Passport Division to see if Weltfish had been issued a passport for the upcoming February WIDF meeting (WFO100-287225-27). Six days later FBI headquarters reported that no passport had been issued for this meeting, and Weltfish's name was placed on a "Flash Notice" alert within the Passport Division (WFO100-287225-28).

A highly redacted report from the New York SAC to Hoover dated February 5, 1951, expressed concern over Weltfish's reported knowledge of arms and ammo caches in Western Europe. Although much of this report is withheld, it appears that an FBI informant (apparently the same woman who contacted Weltfish on January 19) contacted Weltfish to gather more information on the WIDF. The report contains a summary of the informant's interview with Weltfish. The informant paid special attention to an interruption by an unidentified man carrying photographs. The informant reported that,

> at the inception of the interview a man came into the room and gave several photographs to Dr. Weltfish. She described this man as being about ▀▀▀▀▀▀ and ▀▀▀▀▀▀ in appearance. According to ▀▀▀▀▀▀ this individual had the photographs in a brief case in between pieces of loose-leaf paper. ▀▀▀▀▀▀ stated she could see the outlines of the negatives and on one she noted a mountain in the background. ▀▀▀▀▀ recalled that Dr. Weltfish started to state to this individual "Is this all you have on Soutrh [sic] Car . . ." at which time she stopped and added on "South Caledonia. ▀▀▀▀▀▀ got the impression that [Weltfish] actually started to say South Carolina but purposely changed the designation because she was in the room.
>
> ▀▀▀▀▀▀ later checked the "Atlas" and learned that there is no country named South Caledonia.
>
> After showing Dr. Weltfish the first group of pictures this individual took out another small envelope in between a sheet of loose leaf paper and gave it to the subject. She stated to him "You will get more for those. These are still better." The subject indicated that she wanted more of the pictures that this individual had made.
>
> After the man, described above, left the room, the interview with Dr. Weltfish commenced. Mrs. Weltfish explained to the subject the exact purpose of the interview and indicated to Dr. Weltfish sympathy with

the Russians. Dr. Weltfish then stated, "The present is the fruits of the struggles of the past." She explained to ▆▆▆▆▆ that in ▆▆▆▆▆ she should accentuate that ▆▆▆▆▆ does not effect [*sic*] people but that people effect ▆▆▆▆▆. She stated that ▆▆▆▆▆ was the most advanced country of the world, Russia. She added that she, Dr. Weltfish, devotes her entire life to the cause of women and she then told ▆▆▆▆▆ that she should join "our organization," the WIDF with 81,000,000 [!] members. (WF0100-287225-30 2/5/51)

Weltfish reportedly again commented on the extent to which women in Western Europe were armed and ready for action. Weltfish was portrayed as waiting for an international women's uprising, stating that "women now exercise effective control and today while many men in many lands are asleep[,] wide awake women all over the world are prepared to act and shed blood for what they want" (WF0100-287225-30:3 2/5/51). As I discuss below, in 1952 the FBI passed on this information to the U.S. Senate Judiciary Subcommittee, where the mention of "South Caledonia" took on a paranoid importance with both the FBI and the subcommittee as they looked for evidence that Weltfish was involved in some vaguely articulated massive Communist conspiracy.

Weltfish, Germs, and the Media

On June 12, 1952, a member of the McCarran Senate Judiciary Subcommittee to Investigate the Administration of the Internal Security Act requested that FBI agent L. L. Laughlin make available any information that the FBI held regarding Gene Weltfish. The committee was "particularly interested in any foreign travel engaged in by Weltfish and her employment" (WF0100-287225-40). In response, a "blind memorandum" was prepared for McCarran's committee on June 24, 1952.[1]

Gene Weltfish appeared before the McCarran Committee in fall 1952 (U.S. Congress 1952b). After being sworn in by Senator Ferguson, she identified herself and proceeded to assert Fifth Amendment protections for refusing to answer all questions concerning past or present membership in the Communist Party. Senator Ferguson then produced a copy of the June 10, 1952, *Daily Worker* and read aloud the headline: "Woman Scientist Offers to Prove Germ War Charge," asking Weltfish if she had written this article. She replied that she hadn't. Committee attorney Robert Morris asked if she had written other articles on the subject of germ warfare and the Korean War. She again replied that she had not, and then Morris asked her if she had issued a press release on this topic. Weltfish replied that she had, and on further questioning stated that she did not have a copy of the press release with her but she did list the names of various newspapers and reporters who had been given a copy.

The apparent basis of Ferguson's repeated questions of whether or not Weltfish had authored the article in the *Daily Worker* is that about 80 percent of the article was a written response by Weltfish to an article attacking her that had appeared in the *World Telegram and Sun*. In her statement she carefully discussed the horrors of biological warfare agents and mentioned reports of the *possibility* that such agents could have been deployed in Korea, but she did not make accusations of American uses of these weapons.

Senator Ferguson discussed newspaper reports of Weltfish's talk at the Pythian Temple, pointedly asking her if she had said that "germ warfare has been used against the Koreans and the Chinese" by the United States. Weltfish denied making such statements, saying she had been misquoted in the press. When Ferguson further pressed her concerning what she had said at this public talk, she replied, "in the Pythian Temple, all I can say is that I was speaking about the plight of children during war, about the problem of the death of parents and the difficulty of children in such circumstances. I cannot say what I said in that public meeting in any exact words. My point was that the danger to children was something that we must all pay attention to, no matter what weapons are used" (U.S. Congress 1952b:233). The committee again pressed Weltfish concerning whether she had claimed the United States had used biological agents in Korea, and again she denied making such statements and denied having access to information proving such a claim. Morris then questioned her concerning an affidavit by former missionary to China, Dr. James Endicott. Weltfish confirmed that she delivered Dr. Endicott's statement to the press.

> Mr. Morris: Did that affidavit say that the Americans had used a large leaflet bomb for the dissemination of insects and a small porcelain-type bomb for the spreading of germs?
>
> Miss Weltfish: As I do not have that before me, what the affidavit said, I do not know. It seems to me it was not so much material what was in the affidavit. What was material to me was, as I pointed out in my first release, that Dr. James Endicott was a man of conscience, a Christian missionary, and what he felt he had seen was of some importance to pay attention to. The important thing was the fact of the integrity of the man that interested me. (U.S. Congress 1952b:233–34)

Weltfish said she did not personally know Dr. Endicott, but she had received this information from him by mail. The committee next focused on how Weltfish came to know Albert Kahn—the journalist who had introduced Weltfish to Endicott—asking her if Kahn or Endicott were Communists.

Morris read an excerpt from a *New York World-Telegram* article entitled "Germ Warfare Charge Laid to Columbia Prof," which read: "The hall was jammed and many women and children were present. A number of the spectators said they were shocked at some of the anthropologist's statements . . . After the meeting they sent wires to Dr. Kirk and Frederic Cuykendahl, acting president of Columbia, telling them that Dr. Weltfish has said she had seen documentary evidence that the United States is waging bacteriological warfare in Korea. They said she accused the United States of 'committing the crime of dropping bubonic plague bombs on innocent children in Korea'" (U.S. Congress 1952b:236). Weltfish denied making the statements reported in this article.

Scott Endicott, the son of the Canadian missionary who gave Weltfish the reports on bioweapons, coauthored a book in 1999 examining available evidence supporting his father's claims that biological weapons were deployed by American forces in the Korean War (Endicott and Hagerman 1999). In *The United States and Biological Warfare*, Endicott and Edward Hagerman piece together a well-documented historical narrative establishing that biological weapons testing occurred in Asia during the Korean War. They examine a number of problematic documents suggesting that U.S. military forces may have used these weapons in Korea—although these claims are controversial. As Christopher et al. reported in the *Journal of the American Medical Association*, these allegations of biological warfare use during the Korean War "were supported by a series of investigations conducted by the International Scientific Commission, a group of scientists, and other organizations not part of the commission. Although these investigations were described as impartial, they were carefully controlled by the North Korean and Chinese governments. The United States admitted to having biological warfare capabilities, but denied using biological weapons" (1997:414). Much of the United States biowarfare history is still classified, and according to Daniel McGee, a scholar of U.S. biochemical warfare systems, "given the current situation, in which the U.S. is very actively expanding its research on 'defensive' biological warfare and countermeasure programs (to supposedly protect us against 'terrorists' and 'rogue nations'), I seriously doubt that they will be forthcoming regarding many of the events relating to this chapter in the history of the United States biological warfare program" (McGee to Price 10/11/97). Under these conditions we can only suspend questions on the veracity of Endicott's claims until the appropriate historical documents are made available, and note the possibility that Endicott might have been correct in his claim.

Senator Ferguson questioned Weltfish about comments on germ warfare that she might have made to any of her classes or to her colleagues at Columbia. Weltfish insisted that she had not made any such comments to her classes and that the only colleague she had spoken with was W. Duncan Strong, chair of her department, in order to clarify what she had and had not said.[2] Morris read from a *New York Post* story (6/13/52:48) describing Dr. Endicott's affidavit in which he stated that:

> In the part of China where I investigated . . . the Americans had used a large leaflet propaganda bomb for the dissemination of insects, and a small porcelain-type bomb used for spreading germs.
>
> Another bomb "still had not been properly investigated" wrote Dr. Endicott, "and I discovered in the head, covered by a steel plate, two large handfuls of dirty cotton soaked in a glycerin-like substance. The Chinese doctors who were with me were horrified when they saw me handling this stuff, and immediately sterilized my hand."
>
> Dr. Weltfish found this impressive, she said, because, while not a biologist, she was a social scientist specializing in human relations, and having asked "What manner of man was Dr. Endicott?" had learned that he had been a missionary in China for 22 years before returning to his native Canada. "What would he have to gain from currying favor with China?" she asked herself. (U.S. Congress 1952b:238)

Morris eventually shifted his questions from germ warfare to Weltfish's knowledge of Nina Popova (U.S. Congress 1952b:239). Citing the protections of the Fifth Amendment, Weltfish refused to answer these questions. Morris asked if she knew that Popova was a Soviet representative at the United Nations. Weltfish stated that Morris was mistaken, and then she returned to her refusal to answer questions under the Fifth Amendment protections. Morris stated that Popova was "the Soviet delegate to the Women's International Democratic Federation" (U.S. Congress 1952b:240), and he remarked that this was an organization wherein Gene Weltfish held the office of American vice president. Morris then asked a series of bizarre questions about whether or not Weltfish had received microfilm from anyone concerning South Caledonia. Weltfish insisted she had not, but because neither Morris nor any other committee member presented any explanation of these strange accusations, they surely left an impression of espionage-laden intrigue while not providing any evidence of any wrongdoing (U.S. Congress 1952b:241).

Morris's seemingly disjointed line of questioning was the result of an FBI informant's confused account of observing a conversation Weltfish had with an unknown individual. Clearly the FBI briefed Morris on this matter, coaching him to ask Weltfish these questions—most likely with the hope of trying to later trap her with a charge of perjury. Providing a member of congress or their staff with such classified and confidential information was illegal, although the FBI frequently leaked such information to congressional bodies during the course of these investigations (Theoharis 2002:199–210).

April Fools' Day 1953 with Senator Joseph McCarthy

A month after President Eisenhower took office in 1953 the State Department issued six directives calling for the removal from governmental libraries of hundreds of books written by controversial American authors (Robins 1992:272; Mitgang 1988). Senator McCarthy and the Senate Committee on Governmental Operations held hearings ostensibly to identify subversive books to be purged under these directives. Authors believed to be Communists, or influenced by Communist ideologies, were the primary targets of this search. McCarthy and his committee faced little opposition to these actions from either Democrats or Republicans in the House and Senate. This bipartisan complacency provides some measure of the degree to which the whole of America's House and Senate were passive partners in these witch-hunting expeditions.

On April 1, 1953, Gene Weltfish appeared before McCarthy's Government Operations, Permanent Subcommittee on Investigations. Accompanied by her attorney, Gloria Agrin, Weltfish was interrogated by senators Joseph McCarthy (chair), Karl Mundt, John McClellan, Stuart Symington, and staff member Roy Cohn. Only a few days earlier Earl Browder had provided some engagingly hostile testimony to the committee, and on the previous Friday, Bernhard Stern had appeared as a hostile witness. A few weeks earlier police had been called after one witness, William Marx Mandell, "accused the subcommittee of attempting a Nazi-like 'book-burning'" (Reeves 1982:485).

Senator McCarthy and staff members Bobby Kennedy and Roy Cohn used these hearings to examine accusations that U.S. funds had been used to purchase Communist-influenced books for use in American libraries located around the world (Reeves 1982:482–91). McCarthy and Cohn accused a variety of American scholars of writing Communist-influenced books that had been purchased by the federal government for use in foreign State Department Information Program information centers. Committee staff members Cohn and G. David Schine traveled through Europe visiting United States Information Services libraries compiling lists of books to be purged from libraries (Reeves 1982:490).

McCarthy's committee pursued novelists, artists, and poets who violated his personal standards of racial and economic decency. As a result of these intransigent, amateurish investigations, the books of many well-known American authors such as Langston Hughes, Lillian Hellman, Dashiel Hammett,

Edgar Snow, and Howard Fast were removed from U.S.Information Agency libraries around the globe (Robins 1992:272–73). This same year, McCarthy subpoenaed Rockwell Kent before the committee because overseas libraries contained copies of his books *Wilderness* and *N by E* (Capra 1996).

It was in this climate of intimidation that Gene Weltfish appeared before McCarthy's committee. Having recently lost her teaching position at Columbia, one can only imagine the anger that must have seethed within her as she calmly fielded a stream of questions. An intensely accusatory atmosphere designed to shame and humiliate Weltfish was sustained by the fact that most of the questions were asked with the expectation that they would not be answered, but the hearing transcripts clearly show her exposing the political nature of the attack against her.

The committee identified Weltfish as one of eighty-five Communist authors of interest to their investigation. Members of the American Legion assisted in the legwork of tracking down supposedly Communist books.[3] Because 228 copies of Benedict and Weltfish's *The Races of Mankind* (1943) and the children's book *In Henry's Backyard* (1947) were held in State Department information centers, McCarthy focused on these writings on the inherent equality of all races.

After being sworn in, Weltfish spent several minutes invoking the Fifth Amendment in reply to a string of questions about her past and present political and personal affiliations. After asking and reasking these questions for some time, Roy Cohn appeared to grow tired and moved on:

> Mr. Cohn: Now, under the Fifth Amendment, the privilege against self-incrimination, you decline to answer whether or not you were a Communist at the time you wrote that book. Is that right?
>
> Miss Weltfish: That is right.
>
> Mr. Cohn: Are you currently an instructor at Columbia University?
>
> Miss Weltfish: I am a lecturer at Columbia University.
>
> Mr. Cohn: A Lecturer at Columbia University. When were you served with a subpoena to appear before this committee?
>
> Miss Weltfish: Monday at 5 P.M.
>
> Mr. Cohn: Has anything happened between that hour and now concerning your status at Columbia?
>
> Miss Weltfish: I am still at Columbia. My tenure will terminate at the end of this semester.
>
> Mr. Cohn: When were you notified as to that?
>
> Miss Weltfish: About 2 weeks ago.
>
> Mr. Cohn: You were notified that your tenure at Columbia will terminate. Is that correct?

> Miss Weltfish: That is correct.
>
> Mr. Cohn: From whom was that notification received?
>
> Miss Weltfish: The Chairman of my department.
>
> Mr. Cohn: I see. Can we have his name?
>
> Miss Weltfish: Prof. Duncan Strong.
>
> Mr. Cohn: For how long a period of time have you been lecturing at Columbia?
>
> Miss Weltfish: Since 1936.
>
> Mr. Cohn: Were you a member of the Communist Party in 1936? (U.S. Congress 1953b:117–18)

Weltfish refused to answer all questions relating to her personal political affiliations, and for several minutes Cohn showboatingly questioned her about her alleged comments regarding the U.S. military's use of biological weapons in Korea. Although Cohn did not raise the issue, Weltfish's firing from Columbia was linked to the publicity she and the university received after her appearance before the Internal Security Committee. Then, after another long diatribe and questioning by Cohn there was an interesting moment where after a period of inactivity Senator McCarthy seemed suddenly to come alive and demand that some Communist-inspired passages be read from Benedict and Weltfish's *The Races of Mankind*. The transcripts indicate Roy Cohn tried to dissuade McCarthy from this—telling him that there had been no time to select a passage—but McCarthy seemed hell-bent on this course of action. Ignoring the advice of his handler Cohn, McCarthy grabbed the book and swaggered forth in a reckless attack:

> Sen. McCarthy: Just opening at random, I find something on page 18 of the book entitled, "The Races of Mankind" which should interest my southern colleagues to some extent. It shows the intelligence tests of the
>
> Southern Whites: Arkansas: 41.55 [and]
>
> Northern Negroes: Ohio: 49.50
>
> Miss Weltfish: May I state that this came from Army records?
>
> Sen. McCarthy: Pardon?
>
> Miss Weltfish: That this material came from Army records. (U.S. Congress 1953b:119)

Even in the Senate's sterile transcripts one can sense an air of panic and loss of control as the committee realized that McCarthy's carelessness had revealed the biased nature of these hearings—if not the fundamental strain of racism that fueled these attacks. At this point Roy Cohn returned from the sidelines and did his best to retrieve the lost point, although Weltfish had seized the moment—if in the end only to be appreciated by posterity. Struggling to rescue McCarthy from himself, Cohn ridiculously clarified for the record that "all of the material in the book did not come from Army records, did it?" Weltfish replied that it had not. Cohn then made sure that this was the last that the committee would hear about any of the specific ideas found in Weltfish's writings. Instead the remainder of the hearing was spent with panel members making speeches directed at Weltfish, who generally replied by evoking the Fifth Amendment. The committee was not only interested in smearing the reputations of witnesses, it enthusiastically smeared the reputations of those who could not defend themselves. At one point Senator Mundt tried to besmirch the reputation of deceased anthropologist Ruth Benedict by suggesting that she was somehow an agent of communist doctrine.

The committee seemed to believe that those who fought for racial equality should be suspected of being Communists. Their attacks indicate that they would have subpoenaed Benedict had she been living, and that they would have accused her of being a Communist for the simple reason that she held progressive views regarding the inherent racial equality of humankind.[4] The transcripts show that the committee pressed Weltfish for information on Benedict's beliefs and politics:

> The Chairman: Do you know whether she [Benedict] was a Communist?
>
> Miss Weltfish: As I say, I know nothing about her political beliefs. We didn't discuss them together.
>
> The Chairman: I am going to have you answer that question, unless you think it will incriminate her. I am not talking about her political beliefs. I am talking about whether or not she was a Communist. Do you know whether or not she was a Communist?
>
> Miss Weltfish: As I say, I know nothing about her political beliefs.
>
> The Chairman: Well, you see, this particular chairman does not consider the Communist Party as a political party. I agree with the Supreme Court decision, which has found that it is an international conspiracy, not a political party. Therefore, I am going to ask you whether you know whether she was a Communist, regardless of what you knew about her political beliefs. It is very simple. Either you knew she was a Communist—
>
> Miss Weltfish: As I say, I know nothing about either her political beliefs or any activities that she may have been engaged in. I have no way of determining such a thing. She was my senior colleague at Columbia. This is all I know about her.

> The Chairman: You will be ordered to answer the question. Do you
> know whether or not she was a Communist?
>
> Miss Weltfish: I have no way of knowing what her political outlook,
> beliefs, activities were.
>
> The Chairman: I am going to order you to answer the question. It is a
> very simple question. Do you know whether she was a Communist?
> This woman who helped you write the book?
>
> Miss Weltfish: I helped her write the book.
>
> The Chairman: All right. Do you know whether she was a Communist?
>
> Miss Weltfish: Of course not; no.
>
> The Chairman: You do not know whether she was Communist?
>
> Miss Weltfish: I have no way of knowing such a thing.
>
> The Chairman: Do you know?
>
> Miss Weltfish: I do not know. (U.S. Congress 1953b:120–21)

And so on.

The committee believed it possessed the skills to divine the political standing of any individual, and they found it preposterous that Weltfish would not have likewise weighed the words of Benedict—the recipient of one of the largest American military intelligence grants given to any social scientist in the postwar period—to search for pink adjectives and red verbs or nouns.

Toward the end of her testimony Weltfish was drawn into a rhetorical exchange with Senator John L. McClellan (Democrat from Arkansas) regarding truth, justice, and America. McClellan insisted that Weltfish tell the committee if she had changed any of her views of Americanism or Communism over the years. Weltfish replied that she had "never changed [views] with regard to [her] identity as an American" (U.S. Congress 1953b:127). McClellan snidely countered that he would accept her statement if she told the truth, but her testimony would surely incriminate her. Weltfish replied:

> The truth has many interpretations, as everyone who works with
> words and concepts knows; and as I say, the implication here that it is
> possible to develop truth in a context of this sort, where opinions are
> being frozen instead of allowed the fluidity that they should have—I
> think I have covered the question.
>
> Sen. McCarthy: Doctor, I have in my hand an issue of the *New York Times*
> for April 1, 1953, and I do not quote from it because it happens to be
> my favorite paper at all. [Reading:]
>
>> "Dr. Weltfish has served as president of the Congress of American Women. She could not be reached for comment yesterday.
>> Dr. Weltfish, in speeches in Vienna and New York, in June 1952,

offered to prove the Communist charges that the United States Forces used germ warfare in Korea."

I am curious. Is that a correct quotation?

Miss Weltfish: I have never been in Vienna.

Sen. McCarthy: So then you never spoke in Vienna?

Miss Weltfish: I have never been in Vienna, nor have I spoken there.

Sen. McCarthy: You say you never have been there and you could not very well have spoken there. Well, how about New York? Did you make a speech in New York in which you offered "to prove the Communist charges" —

Miss Weltfish: I refuse to answer the rest of that material on grounds of possible self-incrimination. (U.S. Congress 1953b:127–28)

On establishing that Gene Weltfish would not answer this question, Senator McCarthy dismissed her as a witness.

The committee learned little by subpoenaing Gene Weltfish. She resisted without a fight their attempts to oppress her, although this caused her significant personal and professional problems. Throughout her testimony she remained composed, even when pressed by the committee. But her appearance before the committee and before the Security Committee the previous year led to the loss of her job at Columbia and created obstacles for her future employment prospects (*Time* 4/13/53).

Fired without a Rally of Support from Colleagues

Weltfish's Columbia contract ostensibly was not renewed because of the newly enacted policy changes governing the university's prolonged use of lecturers (although this same policy was also used to advance other lecturers to tenure-track positions), but in actuality Weltfish was fired because Columbia's trustees considered her to be a political liability. Due to the FBI's refusal to fully comply with Freedom of Information Act requests pertaining to Weltfish and Columbia, it is not possible to determine that the FBI was directly involved in her firing. Regardless of the presence or absence of any FBI interference on campus, Gene Weltfish was on her own. Unlike Richard Morgan's firing, the AAA did not even go through the motions of making inquiries into the circumstances leading to Gene Weltfish's termination from Columbia, and unlike Bernhard Stern, Weltfish did not emerge from her appearance before McCarthy with her position as a lecturer at Columbia intact.

When I discussed Weltfish's life with numerous anthropologists who were students at Columbia during the 1950s, some stressed that she was not actually fired by Columbia University because she was on a year-to-year contract. But the term "fired" is appropriate because her lengthy employment was terminated by Columbia's administration—an act that fits the standard definition of the term. Weltfish's termination was publicly presented by the university in the context of the policy change regarding lecturers: "Dr. Gene Weltfish, lecturer in anthropology, is one of those who under the amended statutes, is ineligible for reappointment for the next academic year. The amendment provides that exceptions may be 'by permission of the president.' In considering last December the case of Dr. Weltfish, Dr. Grayson Kirk, then Vice President of the university decided no exception could be made" (Lissner 1953:19). Further, university provost W. Emerson Gentzler rationalized that the changes leading to Weltfish's firing were similar to policies adopted at Harvard, Yale, and New York University (Lissner 1953:19).

Thirty lecturers at Columbia lost their jobs as a result of the new policy, while another twelve lecturers were allowed to continue teaching on a year-to-year basis. While it cannot be documented that the university created the new policy as a means of getting rid of Weltfish, it is clear that they could easily have kept her as a lecturer if they had wished to do so. Indeed, chair of her department, W. Duncan Strong, defended her as a "popular instructor" and argued that there was a need for another tenure-track line in the department, which Weltfish certainly would have been qualified to fill (Lissner 1953:19).

Although historians of anthropology have not analyzed the events surrounding Weltfish's firing, her termination has become part of the informal canon of the discipline replete with a fair share of misinformation and hyperbole. In the sparse published mentions of Weltfish's firing there are inconsistencies in the date of her firing, and a number of writers recycle the error that she was fired in 1952 rather than in 1953 (e.g., Bloom 1990:31; di Leonardo 1998:224; Pathé 1989:377). Some of the stories about her colleagues gallantly protesting her firing may have an element of truth, although a few of these tales have elements of supernatural heroism in which favorite ancestors rise from the dead to do battle with Columbia administrators (see Pathé 1989:377). In another errant account, passed on to me in the 1980s by a graduate student at the University of Chicago, Alexander Goldenweiser (who died in 1940), reportedly attempted to organize a strike by Columbia's anthropology students. It is easy to understand how such stories enter into circulation; indeed, it is difficult to understand how a well-respected scholar such as Gene Weltfish could be fired without one of her colleagues bursting into the dean's inner sanctum and shouting for the recognition of academic freedom. That no heroes came forward speaks volumes of the degraded political climate where such atrocities occurred unchallenged.

As a graduate student in the department at the time, Marvin Harris remembered students circulating a petition for Weltfish's tenure—although it was ignored by Columbia's administration—and students were cautioned against signing the document (Harris interview with Price 3/14/97; see also Murphy 1991:75). Others recall being told to keep quiet and to not get involved, which certainly was the approach of organizations such as the AAA.

After leaving Columbia Weltfish continued her research. In 1953 she published a speculative treatise on the origins of art in past societies, *The Origins of Art*. Given Weltfish's interest and involvement in human rights and women's rights issues, the relatively apolitical topic of the work seems out of character. Weltfish had a longstanding interest in artistic motifs, and the theoretical framework developed in the book is clearly one of interest to her, but the choice of this project at this time is clearly linked to the pressures of McCarthyism and the severe consequences for scholars studying inequality and injustice.[5]

In 1954 Weltfish accepted an invitation from former student John Champe to study Pawnee materials at the University of Nebraska. Weltfish received some support from the Nebraska Foundation and the Bollingen Foundation between 1954 and 1958, as she compiled historic, prehistoric, and ethnographic data for her 1965 book *The Lost Universe* (Pathé 1989:377). The FBI aggressively tracked her movements during this time: they monitored her Pawnee scholarship, noted her income from various publishing and writing projects, and monitored her change of address and her unemployment status (WFO100-287225-61; WFO100-287225-72 7/13/59). In January 1960, FBI agents staked out her residence to establish her contacts, movements, and the topics of her research, determining that she was generating some income through the sale of articles and other publishing ventures (WFO100-287225-77).

In 1961 Weltfish returned to the classroom to teach anthropology at Fairleigh Dickinson University in Madison, New Jersey. She was an active presence on campus and advanced through the ranks quickly to become a full professor in 1968, although she took mandatory retirement in 1972. The FBI tracked her career moves until March 31, 1972, when they entered their last report. After retirement Weltfish continued to maintain her affiliation with Fairleigh Dickinson University as a professor emeritus, and she taught at a variety of regional colleges and universities until her death in 1980 (Pathé 1989:378).

A Final Note from the Margins

In 1980, Carol Ann McBride interviewed Gene Weltfish as part of an ambitious master's thesis project of examining anthropological notions of objectivity and subjectivity (McBride 1980). McBride reports that Weltfish was resistant to being interviewed, and the brief interview took place over the telephone for an hour and fifteen minutes. McBride wanted to talk about objectivity and subjectivity, but Weltfish believed anthropology's obsession with the topic largely to be a distracting fad,[6] and she shifted the conversation to a discussion of China, which she described as "a quarter of the world's people . . . in a government that's in agreement" (180). Weltfish described China as the great hope of humankind, proclaiming "China is a resource that shows what is possible. Compare it with another part of the world. The point is—God! What we're doing with children in the United States! It makes my gut turn around. So wake up! Say what I have to say: there is China with her children" (181). McBride asked Weltfish how she tried to aim her writings at specific audiences, and Weltfish curtly replied that she didn't "owe anybody anything" (182). McBride argued that the question was not one of owing anyone anything but rather "it is a question of putting to use our visions; a question of *implementation*" (182, emphasis in original). This statement then led to an exchange revealing some of the impact of all that Weltfish had endured from the 1940s onward. McBride writes that Weltfish replied angrily:

> "Therefore *I* should have to break my neck? Don't you think I've been chased enough?
> "What do you mean chased?"
> "I mean that in this society I've been kicked in every corner. You don't know my history?"
> At this I quiet. Yes, I do know her history. I'm aware of what happened to her during the McCarthy scare. I know she was booted right out of Columbia, and I'm aware there's more. "Yes, I'm aware of your history."
> Chiding me she says, "*You* haven't been kicking for 77 years. My part is to tell people." (182–183)

Gene Weltfish died two months after her interview with McBride. While long honored by her students and close colleagues (Diamond 1980a; Parks and Pathé 1985), anthropology has yet to acknowledge either the importance of her contributions to the advancement of racial, gender, and economic equality and the lack of involvement by professional associations like the AAA in defending her. As Bob Murphy later reflected, Gene Weltfish "was not only the last of the Boas students at Columbia, but one of the last of the old-time radicals, which is why she was dropped" (1991:75).

Questions of Weltfish's possible Communist Party membership cloud contemporary understanding of the nature of the threat she represented to 1950s American society and to the conservative visions of the role of academics. Those who focus on supposed political affiliations over political actions reduce and dismiss science-based activism to emotive, simplistic caricatures. While America's dominant political parties supported Jim Crow racism, the Communist Party's position on racial equality was in total alignment with the scientific findings of biological and anthropological research. What were scientists like Gene Weltfish to do when they found their positions ridiculed by the mainstream capitalist press but supported by the Communist press? When the *Daily Worker* published a cogent defense of Weltfish and Benedict's critique of American racism, mainstream newspapers such as the *New York Times* or the *Wall Street Journal* remained silent with indifference, refusing to confront the prevailing racist positions of many in the Senate.

Gene Weltfish paid dearly for her activism, but her efforts were not in vain. Her efforts and those of her colleagues helped to establish a base that would be built on by the civil rights movement and further evolve and develop in the decades following.

CHAPTER 7

Bernhard Stern: "A Sense of Atrophy

among Those Who Fear"

The danger of Communism in America lies not in the fact

that it is a political philosophy but in the awesome fact

that it is a materialistic religion, inflaming in its adherents a

destructive fanaticism. Communism is secularism on the

march. —J. Edgar Hoover

Bernhard Stern, the third of seven children, was born in Chicago 1894 to Jewish-German immigrants Hattie and Herman Stern (Bloom 1990:19). Stern's father owned a small department store staffed and run by the family. Samuel Bloom notes that patriotism and a love for democracy were important values in the Stern household, where "similar to other immigrant families, the Sterns were strongly linked to their ethnic origins but also enthusiastically patriotic about their newly acquired nationality" (Bloom 1990:19). Stern earned a rabbinical degree from the Hebrew Union College of Cincinnati, and a master's degree from the University of Cincinnati. After his marriage to Charlotte Todes, Stern worked as a rabbi for a few years then decided to pursue a career in medicine, for which he moved to Europe because of policies prohibiting Jews from attending American medical schools. A serious illness prevented him from completing his studies, and he returned from Europe in 1924. Soon thereafter he began graduate studies at Columbia University under Franz Boas and William F. Ogburn.

After teaching for a year at City College, Stern received a departmental recommendation for a tenure-track position. However, his application was rejected by the college president because of his sponsorship of a controversial campus talk by Yale economist Robert Dunn on the economic and social advances then being made in the Soviet Union (Bloom 1990:21).

After completing a Ph.D. degree in sociology in 1927, Stern was hired as an assistant professor at the University of Washington where he soon became enmeshed in controversy. After only two years in Seattle, Stern wound up on probation. According to Bloom:

> Local religious groups, angered by Stern's classroom advocacy of a scientific approach to the problems of life, had been pressuring the University to dismiss him. In addition, the business community was disturbed by Stern's criticism of capitalist institutions and his sympathetic discussions of the achievements of the Soviet Union.
>
> A group of Seattle ministers had the greatest influence on Stern's dismissal. They were critical of a speech he gave before the Auto Mechanics Local in which he claimed that environment was a greater force than heredity. What convinced them that Stern, already on probation, was beyond redemption was an analogy he drew between Easter sunrise services and the pagan rites of Indian idol worship. (1990:22)

The University of Washington fired Stern in 1930. Despite campus protests by students and a formal request by the sociology department made to the ACLU for an investigation, the decision to terminate Stern was final. Stern's FBI file notes that university president M. Pyle Spencer later maintained that Stern was fired for financial reasons. Downplaying the role that public protest had played in Stern's firing, Spencer told the FBI that "Stern's resignation did not come as a result of protests from various leading citizens about particular theories advanced by Stern" (WF0100-58316).

Stern returned to New York City and began his five-year stint as an associate editor of the *Encyclopedia of the Social Sciences* while also writing an ethnographic account of the Lummi Indians of Puget Sound (Stern 1934). He became a lecturer at Columbia University's Department of Sociology, a position he held until his death in 1956, although he temporarily taught at a number of other institutions (including Yale and the New School) during the intervening years.

The FBI began collecting information on Stern in the 1930s, but they did not centrally analyze the information until mid-1941 when an individual at the Chrysler Corporation wrote the FBI inquiring if one Bernhard J. Stern was the same individual named as a Communist by Congressman Martin Dies in a speech on American Communists. The FBI identified Stern as a contributing editor to several "communistic" publications (WFO100-306864-X 7/25/41). In response, Hoover produced an extensive list of subversive organizations to which Stern belonged, including Stern's participation at the 1938 national Communist Party conventions, as well as his contributions to such moderate groups as the Pan-American Democracy Conference and a variety of human rights groups. In all, the FBI's list of itemized organizations filled more than seven pages.

The FBI noted that a *New York Times* article on May 11, 1933, identified Stern as participating in a protest march from the Columbia campus to the home of Columbia President Butler. A small riot had ensued as "unsympathetic" students clashed with the protesters. The FBI also recorded references in the *Daily Worker* to Stern's activities in the New York College Teachers' Union (DW 12/31/38). Other FBI records indicate that Walter Steele testified before HUAC on August 16, 1938, that Stern supported Stalin's killings of government workers (WFO100-306864-1). The FBI also filed a *Washington Post* article dated December 2, 1939, reporting that Rabbi Bernard Stern, a Columbia university instructor, and M. I. Finkelstein, "a notorious Stalinist in the History Department at the College of the City of New York," worked for the Committee for Intellectual Freedom and Democracy. This FBI file included a 1940 FBI Comintern report listing Stern's association with the independent Marxist journal *Science and Society* (NY100-58316-1),[1] and a copy of the 1943–1944 catalog of the New School for Social Research listing him as an instructor.

FBI agents summarized Stern's academic writings in book reports for the FBI's Publication Services Division,[2] one of which was about Stern's book on Lewis Henry Morgan (1928). The author of this report had a reasonably coherent understanding of Marxism, and comprehended that Morgan's writings had influenced Engels's analysis of class. Morgan's views of property relations in America's capitalist political economy were accurately summarized.

Bennett Stevens: The Church as a Stupefying Corporation

The FBI noted that "Alexander Trachtenberg, President of International Publishers, Inc., testified before the Dies Committee on September 13, 1939, that he knew Stern. He said that Stern had used the pen name of Bennett Stevens and International Publishers, Inc. had published some pamphlets by him" (U.S. Congress 1939–1940:4928–29). In January 1940 the FBI acquired and analyzed a thirty-one page pamphlet, "The Church and the Workers," by Stern writing as Bennett Stevens (WF0100-306864-1).[3] It is interesting to consider the reactions of FBI agents as they read such sacrilegious passages as: "The doctrines and rituals of the churches are powerful means of developing attitudes of subservience among the workers, since the worker is taught to reconcile himself to his poverty . . . and be dutiful to his employers . . . and be submissive in the presence of his 'betters.' A supernatural power is pictured that will punish workers if they disobey the rules of order and self respect which their rulers have established to keep them docile and expedient. Capitalism and its morals and practices are taught to be God-given creations; it becomes irreligious and wicked to challenge them" (WF0100-306864-1).

In this tone the pamphlet analyzed the Christian church's opposition to labor movements throughout history. Although the tone is strident, Stern provided a forceful historical argument linking Protestant and Catholic teachings with the economic interests of the bourgeoisie. The pamphlet condensed and popularized a radical critique of religion's role in suppressing labor movements and the rights of the masses. As Stevens/Stern wrote:

> The churches have always used their influence and resources to maintain reactionary rulers in power. The Peasants' Revolts at the close of the Middle Ages against the feudal princes were crushed by great slaughter with the active aid of both the Catholic and Protestant leaders. During the revolutions of the eighteenth and nineteenth centuries in Europe when the rising bourgeoisie was arrayed against the landed aristocracy and monarchy, the churches again joined the reactionary forces. The French Revolution of 1789 and the revolutions of 1848 throughout Europe were all surging with anti-church spirit because the churches, as buttresses of the established order, passionately resisted the rise of the middle class. But when the bourgeoisie became the ruling class, it in turn allied itself with the churches against the rising working class. (1932:3)

In addition to this social conflict analysis, Stern offered a structural functional view of the workers' exposure to the messages and rituals of the church. According to Stern, "religious ritual with its mystic emotionalism is given as solace and consolation to offset the monotony of the hard working day" (4).

Lyrics from common prayers and hymns were presented by Stern to illustrate the link between capitalism and the Christian church. To show what he described as the church's declaration "that economic and political change would be futile because it is not the fault of capitalism that the workers are exploited, but due to erring man who 'does not live according to the laws of Christ'" (5), Stern quotes the following hymn:

> I think Heaven's punishments are due
> To Atheism and Sedition too
> I think for these 'tis God's own sending
> And not because our laws need mending. (5)

Stern further argues that such forms of complacency maintaining thought control enabled the church to prevent the masses from focusing on the injustices surrounding them in their daily lives. He provides quantitative data on the size and wealth of American Catholic and Protestant churches as well as Jewish synagogues and briefly discusses J. P. Morgan and J. D. Rockefeller's monetary investment in Protestant causes.[4]

In analyzing Christianity's response to the Great Depression, Stern cites statements by clergy that it was a sin for "starving, penniless workers" to not participate in the doomed "Buy Now" campaigns, thereby making not only a duty but a sacrament out of consumption in a capitalist society (8). He criticized the joint pronouncement by American Catholic cardinals, archbishops, and bishops proclaiming that the Depression's widespread unemployment was due to "lack of good will" and "neglect of Christ" (8). Stern observed that Protestants blamed the Depression on faith rather than on the inherent failures of the capitalist economic system. Indeed, one Protestant clergyman is quoted as declaring that "unemployment will cease when people are converted to a belief in the Incarnate Christ" (8–9). Even the involvement of churches in charity work for the unemployed was interpreted as part of the larger capitalist plot. Stern declared that the church helps with charity "because they realize that charity is a safety-valve against discontent and that it checks revolutionary struggle" (9).[5]

Additional discussions in the pamphlet include the church's role in opposing labor strikes throughout the United States in the early twentieth century. Stern criticizes Sherwood Eddy and others in the Christian Socialist movement by calling them "counter-revolutionary" (14–15). In analyzing the Catholic view of private property and capitalism, he quotes Thomas Aquinas, Pope Leo XIII, and Pope Pius XI to illustrate the church's view that workers must accept their lot in life and toil for their masters without rising up (16–19). Stern also notes the uses of church doctrine in the service of imperialist expansions, and states that the conquest of the Philippines, missionary work in China, and the subjugation of American Indians are part of a recurring pattern wherein missionaries assist in capitalists' campaigns of global economic and cultural domination (22–24). Stern also lashes out against Orthodox and

Reform Judaism for their role in subverting revolution and propagating the status quo.

To illustrate how the American Christians used the Bible to subjugate black Americans, Stern quotes from what he characterizes as a "southern Negro work song":

> While nigger, he busy, wit' Bible and pray
> White folks dey's stealing de whole Eart' 'way.
> White folks use whip, white folks use trigger
> But 'twere Bible an' Jesus made slave of the nigger. (20)

Stern recounted white Protestant policies denouncing abolitionism and the financing of black churches by white landowners as a means of "Keeping the Negro in his place" (21). He further notes that in the American South, Protestantism was a central component of the rise and spread of the Ku Klux Klan, and white Protestant churches played vital roles in organizing mob violence against Communist Party activists working for racial and economic equality in the South (21).

The role of religion in the United States is contrasted by Stern with that in the Soviet Union, and he concludes that religious leaders have betrayed the class interests of the workers. He states that in times of war, religion is, "used as a lubricating oil to speed up the workers, to increase production and to make them pliant to increased exploitation" (6).

Stern closes his pamphlet with his own altar call—inviting others to join in his efforts to combat religion: "It is necessary to link the fight against the church and religion with the fight against capitalism and imperialism. As long as capitalism exists, religion and the churches will be used for the ends of the capitalist class" (30). He concedes that churches fulfill an important role in contemporary societies as centers for citizens to socialize and engage in recreation and conversation with a wide range of community members. Stern also recommends that trade unions organize social events to fill this need, and he insists that "a militant worker's anti-religious movement must be organized under the leadership of workers who have already freed themselves from church influences, which will have for its purpose the emancipation of the masses from religious domination" (31).

The quotes included in the FBI's report emphasize church bashing and his characterization of the Soviet Union's position on religion. Needless to say, the FBI's comments on Stern's religious views clearly indicate an institutional bias opposed to his constitutionally guaranteed freedom of religious belief.

The FBI compiled volumes of information on Stern throughout the 1940s. One confidential source told HUAC that Stern was paid four hundred rubles by the Soviet government on February 10, 1940 (U.S. Congress 1939–1940: 4928–29). The FBI intercepted unidentified correspondence referring to Franz Boas and Stern in which someone from the Workers Library Publishers wrote Stern that "in regard to the Boas manuscript, will you please get in touch with ▬▬▬▬ on this and arrange to see him? I spoke with him on the matter and he thought it would be advisable to get more detailed information from you as well as a glance at the manuscript itself" (NY100-58316:17). Stern's article on Boas appeared in *Science and Society* in fall 1943 and the FBI noted that in it Stern labels Boas "a 'Progressive' in that he was 'anti-Fascist' and lent the prestige of his name, time and strength to such 'Progressive Causes' as organizing intellectuals in defense of 'Loyalist Spain', supporting the national Federation for Constitutional Liberties, heading the American Committee for Democracy and Intellectual Freedom, signing the petitions to release Earle Browder, etc" (1943:18). Stern summarizes Boas's significant scientific contributions to the study of race, closing the ten-page overview of Boas's contributions with a quote from a piece in the *New Masses* where Boas argues that "we must demand equality, not equality on paper, but equal rights in life, equal opportunities for education, equal economic opportunities, and a breakdown of social barriers that oppress even those who will not acknowledge for them the claim that is so often heralded as the basis of our society—the claim that all men are born with equal rights" (299).

Although half of the article politely discusses and critiques Boas's contributions to cultural anthropology, Stern reprimands Boas for his dismissive approach to cultural evolutionism and his inability to discern anything resembling the deterministic pattern of cultural development as discovered by Marx and Engels. Stern further faults Boas for his refusal to adopt a Marxist view of history and for his conclusions that "it is no more justifiable to say that social structure is determined by economic forms than to claim the reverse" (305). Stern expresses disappointment that after four decades of research Boas could not discern any "general laws relating to the growth of culture" (308), and he laments Boas's support for "democratic individualism, not on a theory of social classes" (317). Indeed, Stern states that "in his social views Boas shows as little Marxist influence as in his anthropological writings" (316).

The Public Investigation of Stern

An August 8, 1950, memo from the New York SAC to FBI Director Hoover describes a letter in which Louis F. Budenz identified Stern as a "concealed" Communist who was "very active in many capacities, writing the party's influence among professors and in raising money, and also in the infiltration of the scientists, which had an underground character. I know this because of conferences with him, by ███████████, who was assigned to work among the Communists for some time, and by official references made by ███████████ " (WFOI00-306864-15).

The FBI's interest in Stern was piqued after Budenz identified him as a Communist. In the 1950s, the FBI expanded their collection of Stern's "Association with Communist Front Organizations and Communist Front Activities" to include almost fifty organizations. The FBI's list also categorized his "Association with Communist Publications" such as *Science and Society*, which in point of fact was not a Communist-aligned publication (WFOI00-306864-16).

In the 1950s the FBI interviewed Stern's current and former students. In one report, a student informer, "who attended classes at Columbia University, advised that Dr. Bernhard Stern at the beginning of a course . . . made a statement to the effect that he, Stern[,] was a leftist. The informant advised that Stern is considered to be radical and students sometimes walk out of his classes during the first few lectures. ███████████ also stated that Stern has been known to recommend the Jefferson School of Social Science for the study of Marxism. The informant also advised that he had heard that Dr. Stern and his daughter . . . were to go to Camp Unity during the summer" (WFOI00-306864-17:19 5/21/51). Another informer-student reported that

> although the course was nominally one in ███████████, he, the informant, would consider it to be actually one in Communist indoctrination. The informant stated that he recalled students in the class were given readings in Lenin, and that frequent references were made to Russia and the five systems in effect there under Communist leadership.
>
> According to [the informant], Stern made mention of trips he had made to Russia and compared [the] cultural, economic, and physical advancements made there and in the United States. These comparisons were usually in favor of Russia.
>
> Confidential Informant ███████████ stated that Stern never mentioned revolution or any method of bringing about a change in ideologies in this country, but according to ███████████, [Stern] used innuendo and ridicule as his weapons, making a particular point of ridiculing religion and Christianity. He reported that Stern cited the high war profits as an evil of the capitalistic system, and pointed out how the racial and religious minorities were more fairly treated in Russia. (WFOI00-306864-17:19 5/21/51)

As the FBI intensified its investigation of Stern in the early 1950s, they tried to amass evidence indicating that he had abused his position as a college professor by indoctrinating students in Communist ideologies. Despite the failure to produce evidence of such classroom behavior, the claim that Stern had abused his position as a professor was a central theme in his later appearances before congressional hearings.

"I Am Going to Take Care of Your Rights"

In 1952 Stern was subpoenaed to appear before the U.S. Senate subcommittee to investigate the administration of the Internal Security Act hearings on "Subversive Influence in the Educational Process." During Stern's appearance he was questioned about his past membership in the Communist Party, but by citing the Fifth Amendment he refused to tell the committee anything regarding his past party membership and whether he'd ever used a pseudonym or the name Bennett Stevens. Stern did state, however, that he did not then belong to the Communist Party.

The committee tried to use Stern's connection to *Science and Society* to find him guilty by his associations with other Marxists and Communists. The Committee clumsily interrogated Stern about the journal, confusing Marxist analysis with Communism.

> Mr. Morris: To your knowledge, is Science and Society a Communist publication?
> Mr. Stern: It is not.
> Mr. Morris: It is not a Communist publication?
> Mr. Stern: That is right.
> Mr. Morris: To your knowledge do you know any persons associated with Science and Society who have been Communists?
> Mr. Stern: To my Knowledge I don't know.
> Mr. Morris: You do not know?
> Mr. Stern: To my knowledge, no.
> Mr. Morris: Do you know anybody presently associated with Science and Society who has been in the past a member of the Communist Party?
> Mr. Stern: Not to my knowledge.
> Senator Ferguson: Do you believe that it is a violation of the Code of Ethics of the College Teachers, the professional teaching, to answer the question that a person is not a Communist, as you have answered it?
> Mr. Stern: I have not answered anything of that sort.
> Senator Ferguson: Yes; you said that you were not now a Communist.
> Mr. Stern: But I didn't answer anything about the ethics.

Senator Ferguson: No. But I am asking you whether or not it is a violation, in your opinion, of the Code of Ethics, of the Teachers profession to admit that you are not a Communist? I say, do you find in the Code of Ethics of the Teaching Profession, the College Teachers, anything that would make it a violation of that Code of Ethics for a teacher to admit that he is not a Communist?

Mr. Stern: In answer to that question, I would say that these questions have had a very baneful influence on American Academic life. *They have destroyed the essence of academic freedom. They have created a sense of atrophy among those who fear that whatever creative ideas they may have might be labeled Communist*, and therefore the entire profession is aroused by the drive toward loyalty oaths by the holding of these hearings.

Senator Ferguson: This is not a question of loyalty oaths. This is a question of whether or not it is a violation, in your opinion, of the Teachers' ethics to admit that he is not a member of the Communist Party, or to say that you are not. You have answered it that way, that you are not now a member.

Mr. Stern: Well, it is clear then by the fact that I have answered it, that I do not regard it as a violation of my ethics; but on the other hand, I do want to say that the asking of that question by this committee of a member of the faculty of a private institution is clearly a very distressing development in American academic life. Here we have the Government invading private institutions, and trying to determine what their faculty should think.

Senator Ferguson: Where do you teach?

Mr. Stern: Columbia.

Senator Ferguson: Is that a private institution?

Mr. Stern: I have always known it as such.

Senator Ferguson: It gets no public funds?

Mr. Stern: I have no control of the funds of the university. I would assume it does, but nonetheless, all of the private institutions have been particularly worried about accepting Governmental funds on the grounds that the Federal and State governments would interfere with their academic freedom. (U.S. Congress 1952b:182–83, emphasis added)

After repeatedly being questioned regarding the propriety of Communists being allowed to teach in colleges and universities, the committee turned its attention to life in the Soviet Union. Senator Ferguson then asked about the nature of Communist repression in the Soviet Union. Stern conceded that there were differences in the types of freedom of speech between the United States and those allowed in Soviet Russia.

After asking a series of questions about religious and academic freedom in the Soviet Union and the Soviet bloc, Senator Ferguson asked "whether or not the teacher or scientist has academic freedom in Russia." Stern used his reply to comment on some of his own academic freedom restrictions, stating that "my answer is that as far as I know, [given] the evidence, there is full as much academic freedom in the Soviet Union as there is [in the United States] at the present time, in the light of the loyalty oaths, in the light of the investigations of the various committees. In the light of the things that I have seen in the last few years in my teaching experience, the blanketing of the thought of the younger men because of the sentiment which has been aroused by the recent investigations" (U.S. Congress 1952b:185). If Senator Ferguson comprehended Stern's point, he did not acknowledge it. He instead launched into a passive-aggressive series of questions designed to get Stern to admit that America provided greater freedoms than the Soviet system. Ferguson asked Stern if he believed that professors "have a greater academic freedom at the present time in teaching in Russia than they have in America." Stern replied that the question was too simple for such a complex situation—he would need a great deal of time to straighten out all the issues involved in this matter.

The committee then discussed a list of about fifty subversive groups with which Stern was reportedly associated, a list that appears to be the same as that given in Stern's file. The committee asked Stern to take a look at the organizations identified on their list, at which point Stern asked the committee if he would be allowed to invoke the Fifth Amendment in this matter, and he was instructed that he should consult his attorney. After Stern replied that he had no attorney, Senator Ferguson informed him, "I am going to take care of your rights under the Fifth Amendment" (U.S. Congress 1952b:186). After Stern was given time to examine the list, he asserted his Fifth Amendment rights to avoid answering further questions. He then told the committee that the list was a complicated one, adding that some of the information was correct, some of it wrong, and much of it had serious mistakes. The committee gave him ten days to look at the list and write a response, and further testimony was taken from Stern in an executive session.

The Torquemada and the Great Heads of Plutonis

On March 27, 1953, Stern appeared before Senator McCarthy's Committee on Government Operations, where he was questioned as part of the committee's investigation of subversive books held in American libraries abroad. A month earlier, American novelist, essayist, and critic Granville Hicks testified to HUAC that Stern recruited him to join the Communist Party in 1935 (Bloom 1990:25). In the transcripts of this hearing, Stern comes across as unafraid, and at times he even seems to have taken charge of the discussion—at which point staffers Buckley or Cohn reassert control by asking questions that force him to assert his Fifth Amendment privileges.

Anthropologists and sociologists who knew Stern at Columbia report that he was a gentle person with a great patience for students with problems understanding topics of study or discussion, but that he expected students to be prepared for classes and he would not suffer a fool—as Sig Diamond put it, "he was quite outspoken though soft-spoken" (Diamond to Price 2/28/99). This quality can be seen in Stern's dialogue with committee members, when at one point they attempted to get him to identify even a single element of Soviet society with which he found fault. Stern appeared to enjoy asking them to be as specific as they could with their questions, thereby creating the atmosphere of a guessing game. This maneuver allowed Stern to keep some control over an otherwise helpless Kafkaesque situation. The passage of dialogue quoted below occurred after pages of just such a protracted guessing game. At this point Stern had refused to answer a string of Senator McCarthy's questions, and a frustrated McCarthy accused him of being a Communist on the basis of his Fifth Amendment assertions. To this charge, Stern replied:

> Mr. Stern: My answer is, Senator, that since no inference can be drawn from a refusal to answer under the Fifth Amendment, that your question is irrelevant. Or my answer would be the whole question, the whole question is irrelevant.
> Senator McCarthy: Well, I think it is a relevant question and you will be ordered to answer it unless you think your answer might tend to incriminate you.
> Senator Symington: It is relevant to me because I have a son at Columbia.
> Mr. Stern: He is not in one of my classes. I am sorry. You better send him around.
> Senator Symington: I would like to ask you some more questions. . . . Let's narrow it down a little further, then. Let's say, Are there any policies of the Politburo, expressed policies that you don't agree with?
> Mr. Stern: On what?
> Senator Symington: I'm not answering the questions.
> Mr. Stern: These questions are meaningful to me.

> Senator Symington: Let's say on anything. Are there any policies of the
> Soviet Politburo and the Kremlin on anything that you don't agree
> with?
>
> Mr. Stern: There are many things I don't agree with.
>
> Senator Symington: What are they?
>
> Mr. Stern: It is hard to list them in a situation like this and define—
>
> Senator Symington: How about just one or two illustrations of what
> you don't agree with that the Kremlin is doing today?
>
> Senator McCarthy: Senator, the witness puts me in mind of a divorce
> case I tried once as the judge, and the wife was on the stand telling
> what an awful husband she had. I asked her if she had any faults and
> she said, "Yes, I have my faults." And I said, "Name one." She said,
> "Judge, I can't think of any off hand."
>
> Mr. Stern: That is a very clever anecdote. But I am not a divorcee, I
> am not in a divorce court. I am concerned rather with more careful
> thinking you see. (U.S. Congress 1953b:105–6)

After several rounds in which the committee dramatically asked and re-asked
Stern if he had ever disagreed with Communist Party doctrine, Stern finally
appeared to see some purpose in answering the questions in his own way.
Stern addressed Senator McCarthy and said:

> Mr. Stern: I will answer your question. Do you [Senator McCarthy]
> want to ask another question before I answer Senator Symington's
> question, because he has been after me for such a long time that I
> think I will tell him.
>
> Senator Symington: I don't think the expression is quite fair. I have been
> trying to find out what you think because you are teaching in the
> university.
>
> Mr. Stern: Several years ago, during the Lysenko controversy, I wrote an
> article in which I evaluated the Lysenko controversy in a very critical
> fashion. I appraised it in a scholarly way not in the arbitrational way
> whatsoever. I evaluated both sides and formulated a position which
> asked Lysenko certain questions which he had failed to answer in re-
> lation to genetics. I was cognizant of the value of Lysenko's work in
> plant breeding and increasing the food supply of the Soviet people,
> but I didn't like—I pointed out that he was using the materials of the
> geneticists wrongly, quoting from materials in 1932, and assuming
> that they were 1952. This is my scholarly approach you see.
>
> Now I did, in a scholarly way, appraise Lysenko in an article called
> "Genetics Teaching and Lysenko," which had international recogni-
> tion, quoted by Huxley, quoted by all the various people; unfortu-

nately in some ways that I didn't approve of. It was critical of the Lysenko approach to genetics as of that time.

You see, this is what I am speaking of. When you asked this question as you did, I didn't want to be drawn into a long analysis of my position.

Senator Symington: On genetics?

Mr. Stern: On anything you see. I will be glad to give you a lecture on genetics because I have written considerably on it.

Senator McCarthy: I think we will get along without the lecture.

Mr. Stern: Thank you. I prefer not to give it too. (U.S. Congress 1953b: 106–7)

It appears that none of the senators or members of their staffs had ever heard of Lysenko, and that they were ignorant of the importance that allegiance to Trofim Lysenko's doctrine had played. Lysenko's Lamarkian evolutionary theory of the inheritance of acquired characteristics so dominated Soviet genetics that criticism of Lysenko was seen as a direct act of anti-Soviet dissent. For the sake of posterity, it is unfortunate that McCarthy did not allow Stern to lecture them on his critique of Lysenko.

Later in the testimony McCarthy read the following quote from Stern's edited reader, *The Family: Past, Present and Future*: "The family of the wage earner and salaried employee, deprived of land and a friendly neighborhood to give security and status, as is the case usually in industrial urban surroundings, finds this lack met in Russia by a highly developed system of social insurance and public service" (U.S. Congress 1953b:110). Senator McCarthy then asked Stern how he knew the facts in this passage. At first Stern defended the passage, but then paused and asked Senator McCarthy if he could look at the book he was quoting from. McCarthy replied:

Senator McCarthy: You certainly may. The passage is marked which was read.

Mr. Stern: Your quotation was not from me.

Senator McCarthy: Who is it from?

Mr. Stern: It is from Mildred Fairchild.

Senator McCarthy: May I see it? It is not in quotes; it is written in your book and not in quotes. Where does it indicate it is from Mildred Fairchild?

Mr. Stern: It is right on top.

Senator McCarthy: Let me see it. In other words you are quoting someone else?

Mr. Stern: I am quoting an article published in a reputable journal. (U.S. Congress 1953b:110)

Senator McCarthy was apparently unfamiliar with the format of scholarly edited volumes, indeed, McCarthy and his staff rarely read the books or articles of those they questioned—if they had in this instance they would have noticed that the authors' names appeared at the first page of the chapter. Instead, the committee staff's primary research aid for these investigations consisted of skimming through books and indexes looking for key words like "communism," "Marx," "USSR," and "fluoride"; then these pages were selected for use in hearings (see Reeves 1982).

At one point Roy Cohn asked Stern to read a passage from his edited book *The Family: Past, Present, and Future*. Senator McCarthy interrupted, and instructed Cohn to tell him if Stern wrote the passage. Cohn replied that it was "difficult to tell." Stern then entered the discussion, saying,

> Mr. Stern: No; it is not. On the top of the page it says who the author is.
>
> Mr. Cohn: Could you come up here? Maybe you can help us out. Would you say what I am going to read is from you or a citation of what somebody else said?
>
> Mr. Stern: That [is a piece] I wrote; that is [the] introduction telling what the contents will be.
>
> Mr. Cohn: You said that ["]the Socialists Marx and Engels saw beyond the misuse of women's labor by capitalists and contended their participation in large-scale production was the potential basis of their emancipation and thus of a higher form of family life; and that the efforts of women to achieve this emancipation through organized movements will be discussed in the editor's article which ends the section["]. And that subsequent article is by you as well, is that right?
>
> Mr. Stern: I have to see it.
>
> Mr. Cohn: You say the editor's article which ends this section. You are the editor?
>
> Mr. Stern: That is right. . . .
>
> Mr. Cohn: Are [these] your words?
>
> Mr. Stern: Those are my words, and this is what it means in the article, if you follow on through. In the early days of capitalism there was a tremendous criticism of capitalism, you see, on the basis of the older family, the feudal family, which I hope you are not supporting, Mr. Cohn?
>
> Mr. Cohn: Sometime you can question me.
>
> Mr. Stern: And I said that at that time, in this particular book, there were different schools, and I quote one school that saw nothing but evil in capitalism, you see. Then you go to a short quotation from Marx and Engels in which I show that they saw not merely the de-

structive factor of capitalism, but also the fact that when women were employed it would give them the opportunity to develop to become emancipated, under capitalism. (U.S. Congress 1953b:112)

The transcript does not indicate whether or not Cohn or the committee understood Stern's point. Cohn then asked a number of questions about the Pope, Catholicism, and organized religion—apparently the FBI had informed the committee that Stern had published his critique of religion under the pseudonym of Bennett Stevens. Stern had little to say on this matter.

Columbia's Stern Reaction

Stern's appearance before these committees created problems at Columbia University. But while Columbia had fired Gene Weltfish with little fuss or opposition, an extraordinary opposition was mounted to block Columbia's firing of Stern. President Kirk formed an ad hoc "committee on conference," a six-member advisory group that conducted its own investigation, met with Stern, and advised Kirk on whether or not Stern had committed an offense punishable by termination (see Bloom 1990:26–29). The committee's findings proved to be favorable, and the report states that Stern was "not a member or otherwise under the subjection of any group to which he has surrendered his intellectual freedom," that he had not violated his commitment to "the community of scholars to which he is a part," and that his refusal to answer the congressional committee's questions did not negatively reflect on his academic or personal integrity (Bloom 1990:27). After the committee on conference's findings in support of Stern, President Kirk wrote to some of the trustees that it was his own feeling that "since Stern is a relatively unimportant individual in the University community, and since we can retire him in about two years, that it might be wise to accept these findings without further inquiry" (Bloom 1990:27).

Although many members of the Board of Trustees would have preferred to fire Stern as they had fired Weltfish, Stern was allowed to keep his job. Stern's position at the university was under a slightly different bureaucratic structure than that of Weltfish: while both Stern and Weltfish held lecturer positions, Weltfish was hired as a "statutory lecturer" (technically a part-time position, although its thirteen-hour teaching load was that of a full-time faculty) in the university's School of General Studies, while Stern's position was administered through the university's sociology department. This administrative difference added an obstacle hampering the efforts of those administrators wishing to fire Stern, as they would first need to cut through the protests of his sociology colleagues who had hired him, whereas Weltfish was a relatively easy target because her position was administered outside of the anthropology department.

Some scholars argue that the decision not to fire Stern demonstrated Columbia's commitment to intellectual freedom and academic integrity (Bloom 1990). But the overall similarities in the ways that both Stern and Weltfish testified before these committees—with such divergent outcomes—suggests that such proclamations of Columbia's virtue in this matter are shortsighted.

It is not clear why Weltfish was fired while Stern kept his position when many of their circumstances were so similar. Certainly the differences between Wetfish's at-large statutory lectureship and Stern's departmental lectureship influenced the form and course of Weltfish's firing, but it does not account for all of the differences in these two cases. Some anthropologists have commented that gender accounts for these divergent outcomes, and this seems likely to have played an important role in the decision to terminate Weltfish. Others believe that it was simply the last straw for Weltfish, and that years of being publicly associated with radical political causes had taken its toll.

It seems likely that Weltfish's comments on the possible use of biological warfare agents by the United States were simply too disturbing to be ignored by Columbia's trustees. The press coverage linking Columbia with Weltfish's claims of biological warfare was clearly the sort of publicity that the university wanted to avoid.

One of the most important differences in the Weltfish and Stern cases was that faculty from across the campus joined forces to speak as one voice telling the administration to not purge Stern. Columbia's administration listened when Thomas Drew (chemical engineering), Walter Gerhorn (law), James Gutmann (philosophy), Mark Van Doren (English), Isador Rabi (physics), and Carl Shoup (economics) came together in the Columbia committee on conference and supported sociologist Robert K. Merton's finding that it was vital that Stern's academic freedom be protected.

No such broad effort was made to support Weltfish as Columbia prepared to fire her. It may well be that her fate served as the wake-up call that mobilized faculty to support Stern when he came under attack. It may also be that differences in their personalities created different reactions from across the campus, or perhaps that the networks of campus power were gendered in ways inaccessible to her. Whatever the chain of events that led Stern's colleagues to support him, their actions demonstrated the power held by a group willing to stand up and oppose the inclinations of their governing board. Had others taken such a defensive stance while Jacobs, Morgan, Swadesh, and Weltfish came under fire, their attackers would not likely have made the advances that they did.

In the end, Stern remained a lecturer in Columbia's sociology department. In 1955, just two years after his appearance before Senator McCarthy's committee, his card was withdrawn from the New York FBI field office's Security Index, and his status as a security threat was canceled. The last page of Stern's FBI file contains a copy of his November 1956 obituary in the *New York Times*.

CHAPTER 8

Persecuting Equality: The Travails of

Jack Harris and Mary Shepardson

Together, the Security Index and the Communist Index
totaled approximately 50,000 names in Chicago . . . I
estimated at one point in time in the mid-1950s that if
there had been a national emergency it would have been
necessary to set up tents in Soldier Field on Lake Shore
Drive to house all those to be arrested. —M. Wesley
Swearingen

As the cases of Bernhard Stern and Gene Weltfish demonstrate, appearances before loyalty and
security hearings altered for decades the lives of
witnesses. Some witnesses found themselves unemployed, divorced, or suddenly disenfranchised
and friendless. Others later found themselves unable to regain trust in their colleagues, friends, and
associates, while still others committed suicide.
To the general population the hearings broadcast
messages of fear and compliance, and to anthropologists and other scholars who wished never to
appear before the committees were sent messages
of self-censorship and political deactivism.

In this chapter I examine Jack Harris's and Mary

Shepardson's encounters with McCarthyism as well as the divergent impacts of their appearances before these hearings. While the specific experiences of Harris and Shepardson differ in many ways, both were subpoenaed because of their efforts to fight for the equality of minority peoples (in one case at home and the other abroad), and their experiences before the committees directly led them to pursue significantly different career paths. Although Jack Harris was led to pursue work outside of anthropology, Mary Shepardson's experiences led her to curtail her work as an activist and to pursue a career in anthropology.

Jack Sargent Harris: A Lesson Learned—Leaving the Radar Screen

When the Great Depression hit in 1929, Jack Harris lost his job as an assistant production manager for a Chicago publishing firm. After three years of a life at sea as a merchant sailor, he earned a scholarship to Northwestern University, where he first encountered anthropology in an introductory course taught by Melville Herskovits. At Northwestern, Ralph Bunche befriended Harris while they both studied anthropology and African colonialism under Herskovits (Edelman 1997:8; Henry 1999), and Bunche and Herskovits influenced Harris's decision to study the effects of colonialism on the developing world. After graduating, Harris entered graduate school at Columbia University's Department of Anthropology. In his correspondence with Herskovits, Harris recounts the liberal and radical atmosphere at Columbia in 1936, where he participated in activities such as labor activism on the New York waterfront, walking supportive picket lines, and fundraising for labor causes (Madden 1999:5).

Harris received a Ph.D. in anthropology from Columbia in 1940 and then taught at Ohio State until the war broke out (Edelman 1997:8–11; Harris 1941, 1942). Early in the war Ralph Bunche asked Harris and William Bascom to work for him at the Coordinator of Information (COI), the organizational predecessor to the Office of Strategic Services (OSS). There Harris and Bascom received an assignment to

> go to the Gold Coast together under the cover of a phony anthropological expedition to West Africa. The cover was well prepared. There was a letter from the president of Northwestern University and another from the president of Ohio State University saying that we had been selected to undertake this mission. . . . I had a conflict, because during my days at Columbia I was told by associates of Boas that he violently opposed using our scientific reputation as a cover for intelligence activities in war. He based this on an incident in which a student of his had been involved in World War One.

However, our feelings were so strong, I felt that whatever capabilities I could lend to the war effort in this war against infamy, I was pleased to do so. So Bascom and I did go to West Africa. (Edelman 1997:11)

In Africa, Harris worked as intelligence liaison between the British and Americans (Edelman 1997:11), then after a year in Washington recovering from malaria and receiving more espionage training, he was sent to South Africa and Mozambique.

At the war's end Harris spent time recuperating from schistosomiasis. Then, with Bunche's assistance, he received a Carnegie Foundation fellowship to write up his African materials. Harris refused a request to join the CIA, "partly because of promises which the US broke to certain of his contacts — people whom he owed a debt of gratitude for helping him out of some difficult situations [during the war]" (Melvern 1995:55). He taught again for a short time in Columbus, and then joined the University of Chicago's anthropology department. He taught at Chicago for two years, then left to accept Bunche's invitation to work for him at the United Nation's Division on Trusteeship Territories (Edelman 1997:12). It seems likely that had Harris stuck with the safety of his tenure-track position at the University of Chicago he could have avoided any clashes with McCarthyism and sat out the purging season of investigations of public employees, but instead he was caught up in the widespread security investigations of American employees of the United Nations led by the conservatives of the U.S. Senate.

Harris's work at the United Nations was aimed at improving the conditions of colonialized peoples around the world through increased self-rule. When his UN division received petitions asking for independence in East Africa, Harris accompanied the first UN mission investigating the requests. He spent July through September of 1948 visiting Tanganyika and Ruanda-Urundi as a UN observer (AAANB 1948 2[3]:43). Harris found this work to be fulfilling, describing it as having "wedded the best of academia and action" (Edelman 1997:12), but others found his recommendations troubling. Indeed, the British were displeased by the strong recommendations for accelerated African self-rule made by Harris and others on the UN mission. Harris's report condemned Great Britain for the widespread poverty of Tanganyika and called for a diamond export tax to keep some of the wealth in Tanganyika during the expropriation of its national resources. Harris's report was well written and cutting, but

Britain did not accept the right of the UN to tell her how to discharge her responsibilities. In London the UN's report was considered no more than mischievous political propaganda. At the time, the issue of colonialism was dominant in the UN as the East-West conflict and some countries were increasingly vociferous about how slowly the great powers were applying Charter principles. By the early fifties the member nations Egypt, India and Pakistan were busy organizing an increasingly effective anti-colonial bloc which was beginning to enjoy the support of the Soviets. The Americans were basically anti-colonial, but torn by their close alliance with Britain.

Washington worried about the radical nature of the Department of Trusteeship, and particularly the influence of certain Secretariat officials within it. Jack Harris did not concern himself with Washington. He was too wrapped up in his work. (Melvern 1995:51)

By this time Harris had met Anglican priest activist Michael Scott, who opposed the colonial destruction of native cultural traditions in southwestern Africa. The British and South African governments had successfully used their political clout to prevent Scott from addressing the United Nations, and the FBI and CIA used their investigations of Scott in a failed attempt to prevent him from addressing the UN in 1953 (Melvern 1995:53). But the British, South Africans, CIA, and FBI could not prevent Harris and the Division of Trusteeship from investigating Scott's claims of abuse, and Harris's thorough investigation was devastating to the British and South African interests (Melvern 1995:53–54). As Melvern noted, "Jack Harris was a natural ally for Michael Scott. Harris, with his outspoken anti-colonialist views cut quite a distinctive figure in the UN Secretariat: he was handsome, always self-assured, and had intimate knowledge of African nation[s] based on first-hand field studies" (1995:55). But Harris's abilities to conduct free and independent inquiries into the status of colonialism in Southern Africa ended when he was subpoenaed to appear first before a federal grand jury and then a senate committee investigating possible security violations at the UN.

During these appearances before the grand jury he was asked questions about his political associations as well as those of others. Harris remained silent because he "didn't feel it was proper for [him] to reply"—an act that only served to intensify suspicions that he was a dangerous subversive (Edelman 1997:12; U.S. Congress 1953a). Harris was placed on leave beginning October 22, 1952; he appeared before McCarran's Subcommittee on Internal Security two days later; and he was fired on December 5, 1952 (New York Times 1/2/53 p. 1; U.S. Congress 1952a:147–49).[1]

In 1953 the Senate Judiciary's Subcommittee on Internal Security subpoenaed Jack Harris to testify about the presence of American Communists working at the United Nations. The hearings opened with an explanatory prologue stating that Jack Harris had been subpoenaed the previous week but he had failed to appear. In truth, Harris had been out of town on business and had no knowledge of the subpoena until he'd read about it in the newspaper, wherein he contacted the committee and made arrangements to testify.

Harris's lawyer, Leonard Boudin, challenged the propriety of the committee calling Harris to testify because Harris was not then an employee of the United Nations. Boudin then entered a lengthy motion to vacate subpoena on several grounds, including the charge that the primary objective of the committee was to "harass the movant and to affect his economic livelihood in whatever fields he may work. The Committee has thus far been successful in destroying his career as an international civil servant. It has been successful, as a result of its earlier hearings and the headline publicity secured by it, in closing another field of employment—research and teaching in anthropology to which the movant has devoted most of his professional life" (U.S. Congress 1953a:646). Committee Chairman Johnson rejected Boudin's motion. Harris was then asked how much money he had received from the UN administrative tribunal as compensation for his discharge. Harris objected to the question on the grounds that under the UN statutes all judgments by the UN were final. After an objection and discussions between Chairman Johnson and Boudin, Johnson overruled the objection and directed Harris to answer the question. Harris stated that he was awarded his salary up to the date of the tribunal's judgment, as well as legal costs and an award of $40,000 "in lieu of reinstatement" (U.S. Congress 1953a:647).

When asked if he had joined the United Nations on the request of Ralph Bunche, Harris affirmed in the position, stipulating that he had previously stated this fact in an executive session of the committee. When further asked about the circumstances under which he joined the United Nations' staff, Harris's lawyer asked if Harris could read a statement itemizing the objections under which Harris would refuse to answer questions pertaining to this matter. Harris then read a detailed seven-point objection that in large part cited again the UN's mandate that matters under its purview be final and without appeal, but that also asserted the use of the Fifth Amendment. After numerous interruptions, as well as counterclaims brought by Boudin and Morris arguing that the goal of the committee was not to challenge a UN finding, Chairman Johnson overruled all objections with the exception of the use of the Fifth Amendment. Harris then refused to answer any question detailing how he came to join the UN at the special request of Ralph Bunche.

It appears that the committee was interested in unearthing any connection that could reflect negatively on Ralph Bunche, one of America's most prominent black leaders. Bunche was then the director of the United Nations Division of Trusteeship Territories, having already been awarded the Nobel

Peace Prize in 1950 for his work in the Middle East peace process, and eventually would become the UN's undersecretary general. Because Bunche had already been linked to Communist Party activities, the committee wanted to tie Harris to Bunche and establish a chain of guilt by association (see Bunche's FBI file, WF0138-14).

After much wrangling, the committee asked Harris if he belonged to the Communist Party when he began working for the United Nations. Harris reevoked his seven objections, and the committee sustained his objection of invoking the Fifth Amendment. Harris also refused to answer questions concerning his current party membership status. Morris next asked Harris if he had been born in Chicago on July 13, 1912. Harris confirmed this information. Morris stated that there was some confusion about the names that Harris had used in the past, and he asked if Harris was the son of Mr. and Mrs. Max Hersovitz. Harris confirmed that he was, and that he had legally changed his name in 1938. Morris then asked if he had used the alias Russell Sumner from 1931 to 1935, but Harris refused to answer this question as well as others concerning his work as a merchant seaman from 1931 to 1935, and he likewise refused to answer Morris's questions concerning past visits to Shanghai and Leningrad while working as a merchant marine.

After confirming that Harris had attended Northwestern University between 1932 and 1936, Morris asked a series of questions relating to the period between 1938 and 1940 when Harris studied anthropology at Columbia.

> MR. MORRIS. During that period of time did you know Dr. Franz Boaz (*sic*), who is the former dean of the School of Social Sciences.
>
> MR. HARRIS. Yes, I know Dr. Boaz (*sic*). I am not sure that your identification of him is correct, however, Mr. Morris.
>
> MR. BOUDIN. He is merely the head of the department of anthropology.
>
> MR. HARRIS. That is the way I knew him. He may have been dean.
>
> THE CHAIRMAN [Johnson]. However you can say you do know him, or you don't know him, or you can refuse to answer about these other men, and hide behind the Fifth Amendment.
>
> MR. HARRIS. Well, I must decline to answer that question on all the grounds stated.
>
> MR. MORRIS. Did you know a secretary of Dr. Franz Boaz (*sic*) named Mr. Moses I. Finkelstein?
>
> MR. HARRIS. As I did in the executive session, I do again. I have to refuse to answer that question on all the grounds stated, Mr. Morris.
>
> MR. MORRIS. Mr. Harris, were you at that period a member of the Communist Party, that is, the period 1936 to 1940?

MR. HARRIS. I must refuse to answer that question on the same grounds.

THE CHAIRMAN. We recognize the Fifth Amendment only.

MR. MORRIS. Mr. Chairman, Mr. Moses I. Finkelstein,[2] the last gentleman mentioned, has been a witness before the committee, and with respect to his Communist Party membership at the particular time I inquired, he refused to answer on the ground the answer might incriminate him. (U.S. Congress 1953a:653)

Four and a half decades later Harris recalled this testimony in his interview with Marc Edelman, saying that

I was confused, and I sought the help of a civil rights lawyer to know how I should deal with this. I was surprised. They brought up my activities as a sailor, they asked me questions about my colleagues at the UN, and also people I had known at Columbia. The civil rights lawyer then introduced me to the history of the Fifth Amendment, the amendment to the Constitution to protect one against this sort of kangaroo court. He explained to me that if I did reply to subsequent questions, then I could be held in contempt and jailed.

If I replied to the key question—"Are you or have you ever been a member of the Communist Party?"—then they could have asked me about all the other people I knew, some of whom I knew had been members or had been associated. If I refused to reply, then, in the temper of those times, I could be termed a traitor. In fact, later I was. *The Chicago Tribune* had a headline about me, saying that I had been called a traitor. Of course this disturbed me because my parents were in Chicago. In any case, it boiled down to this: did I want to become an informer? If I informed, there was no question I could keep my job. They told me that. (Edelman 1997:12)

The committee inquired about Harris's 1945 application for employment at the Department of State. Harris continued to assert his Fifth Amendment rights and refused to answer most questions, except to declare on record that he did not know nor did he ever meet Alger Hiss. Morris asked Harris if he had listed anthropologists Ruth Benedict or Willard Park as references when he applied for work at the State Department. Harris declined to answer under the Fifth Amendment, at which point Morris stated: "Mr. Chairman, I might point out Dr. Willard Park has been identified by one or more witnesses before this committee as one of the persons who had been involved in underground Communist activity" (U.S. Congress 1953a:656).[3] Once this committee established that a witness was going to assert his or her Fifth Amendment privileges, they often commenced asking increasingly accusatory and seemingly leading questions as an act of showmanship. Harris later recalled that "only in public did the Senators shout, wave their arms and call him a traitor. When hearings were held without the public in attendance the senators were civil" (quoted in Melvern 1995:57).

After inquiring about Harris's 1938 passport application, Morris asked Harris to list all the positions with the U.S. government he had held, and specifically with the OSS during the war. As in the executive session, Harris stated that he had signed secrecy agreements forbidding him from discussing these matters at any future time. The committee stated that these matters had been resolved and that Harris must answer questions on this topic. Morris pressed Harris to recount how he came to work for the OSS during the war. Harris recounted how after the bombing at Pearl Harbor he had gone to Washington, D.C., and offered his services to a variety of governmental agencies.

> Mr. MORRIS. Whom did you see in the Office of Strategic Services? Tell us who the people were whom you went to see.
>
> Mr. HARRIS. I wonder, Mr. Morris, if that isn't even more under this injunction to keep secret this information than other questions that you have asked me. I protest it, and point out to you as sincerely as I know how, if I do recall, I don't know whether it would be wise to have these names revealed, because I don't know whether these people continued in such employment or not.
>
> Mr. MORRIS. I take it you do recall now, since you have been talking you do recall some of the details about your obtaining this employment. I mean, that is a variation of your preceding answer, isn't it? You said you had no recollection.
>
> Mr. HARRIS. No it is not. You went on to ask me if I recall some of the people with whom I spoke in the agency at that time, and I can recall 1 or 2, but whether I was hired before that or not, I can't recall. That is the answer I have given. And Mr. Morris, if you will allow me, this letter that I and Mr. Boudin handed to you with this injunction does have a name on it which I would ask this committee not to reveal. (U.S. Congress 1953a:657)

Harris's lawyer stated that he had given this letter to the committee on October 24, 1952, and requested that this letter, without the names of the signatories, be added to the record of the hearing. Chairman Johnson responded to this request by making a speech concerning the importance of the committee's current work: "I think your statement will prove not only here in this case how much it is necessary, first, to have hearings and get evidence like this, because people that get in strategic places where they are not supposed even to tell where they work, how important it is then for us in the Senate to properly pass laws to make it more stringent and harder to get into those places, because after they once get in, this shows how they close up like a clam, and you can't get any information out of them" (U.S. Congress 1953a:658).

After more posturing by Boudin and Chairman Johnson concerning the propriety of disclosing information regarding the oss, Morris asked Harris if he had been a special consul general at Lagos, Nigeria, in 1942 and 1943 and a special assistant in Pretoria and Cape Town to the American counsel general during 1943 to 1945. Harris agreed he had, but he refused to answer questions concerning whether or not he had been a Communist during that period. Morris inquired into Harris's current employment, apparently as a means of endangering his current status.

> Mr. MORRIS. You are presently employed, are you not, Mr. Harris, with the Herrschaft Products, Inc., together with Mr. Sidney Glassman, and, until recently, Julia Older Bazer, who occupied the same position you did with respect to the dismissal and indemnity?
>
> Mr. HARRIS. Mr. Morris, I object to the question on all of the grounds mentioned.
>
> Mr. MORRIS. I might say this, Mr. Harris. Ordinarily the committee tries not to bring present employment in. But in this case, we have had it before in this committee with other witnesses, inasmuch as three witnesses, all working for the same employer, or had been working up until September 15, that is the fact that has to go in the record, just on the theory that he himself may not be involved. But in this case, 2 of your officials, 1 of them Sidney Glassman—he is treasurer of the organization?
>
> Mr. HARRIS. It seems to me, Mr. Morris, this is another form of harassment that you are trying to take away my economic livelihood to support my family. You blasted me as an international civil servant. You blasted my career.
>
> Mr. MORRIS. More than that, Mr. Harris, is your demeanor in invoking the fifth amendment. You are doing that. People have answered before this committee in executive session and it has not been brought out in public hearing.
>
> Mr. BOUDIN. Mr. Harris was upheld by the administrative tribunal. All Mr. Harris now is saying is that having eliminated him from two careers, the international civil service and the field of teaching of anthropology, why do you pursue him in the business field? You got the information in executive session as to where he worked. You had it

before. Why parade it in the public press? That is my point. You can't gain anything by it. All you can do is to be sure that people generally will know where he is employed, and it will affect his economic livelihood, and that, it seems to us is not fair. However what can we do? (U.S. Congress 1953a:659–60)

There was little they could do before this committee, but they had looked to the UN for some relief. On September 2, 1953, a UN administrative tribunal had found that the eleven Americans fired by the UN as a result of internal security investigations had been illegally fired. Senator McCarthy was outraged by this UN finding, and he denounced the ruling by stating, "if we can be forced to have Communists represent us in the United Nations, then we should very seriously consider the wisdom of remaining in that body" (*New York Times* 9/2/53 p. 1, 3). The World Court later considered Harris's wrongful dismissal case against the United Nations, and on July 14, 1954, the court found in favor of Harris and awarded him a sizable judgment of $40,000 because he would likely be unable to find work in his field after being fired from the United Nations (*New York Times* 7/14/54 p. 1). Harris later confirmed this speculation, saying, "of course, they were absolutely right. I couldn't find a university in the United States that would hire me" (Edelman 1997:13).

Harris later left the United States for Costa Rica, where he and a Costa Rican partner started a series of business ventures, including a small cement company, a newspaper, a brewery, a customs broker firm, and a taxi company (Edelman 1997:13).[4] Harris raised his family in Costa Rica and eventually became a Costa Rican citizen. While he enjoyed a productive and fulfilling life outside of anthropology, his quiet departure from the field left a gap. Even after the World Court confirmed Harris was wrongly fired, the AAA did not champion his cause. Indeed, they remained silent, apparently hoping that the havoc of McCarthyism would not notice them or their membership as the new victims of these bullying tribunals.

The Internal Security Subcommittee focused on Harris for a number of reasons beyond his Marxist associations and his connections to Bunche. There were general suspicions that UN programs advocating colonial liberation were linked to Communist organizations. Perhaps future research will shed light on questions surrounding the possible role played by the British government and American intelligence agencies in assisting the internal security subcommittee's purging of Harris. Many in the United States government were uncomfortable with Harris's radical anticolonial approach to the trusteeships his division investigated.

Mary Shepardson: Marxist Roots, Anthropological Leaves

Despite the persistent claims made by McCarran, McCarthy, Hoover, and others that Marxist or Communist scholars carried with them the blinders of class analysis, the dialectic, and a materialist framework as they engaged in scholarly work, there is little evidence of this in the writings of a variety of Marxist and Communist anthropologists. Indeed, the work of numerous such scholars bore none of the obvious signs of party or epistemological dogma (see the discussions on Paul Radin and Gene Weltfish in this volume). Mary Shepardson was an anthropologist steeped in the methodologies, dogmas, and traditions of Marxism and the Communist Party through her long-term membership in the party, but her anthropological writings reveal no analytical or topical indications of a Marxist or Communist perspective. Shepardson's journey from party faithful to ethnographer was a long and remarkable one that suggested a different sort of affinity between Marxism and anthropology. Whereas many anthropologists came to Marx through a political or epistemological reading of Marx, Shepardson was drawn to anthropology after decades of Marxist study and activism.

Mary Shepardson was born as Mary Thygeson in 1906 in St. Paul, Minnesota. Raised in a radical household, she attended Stanford at the age of sixteen, traveled in the USSR, and undertook a career as a social worker and activist in Harlem, joining the Communist Party in 1932. In 1940 she left Harlem for California where she helped raise the children of her recently deceased sister, and later married her sister's widow, Dwight Shepardson. She came to the FBI's attention in October 1941 due to her work with the San Francisco International Labor Defense group—a Communist front organization (WFO100-252442 11/27/43). In April 1942 an FBI informant reported that "he had recently learned that [Shepardson] had visited Russia and was interested in the work of Marx and Engels" (WFO100-252442-1). Throughout the 1940s the FBI monitored Shepardson's involvement in party activities and her work with various activist groups fighting for equal housing and equal rights for African Americans.

The FBI spent more time documenting her nonparty affiliated work fighting for racial equality than it did linking her to party activities. In the 1940s, the FBI cataloged Shepardson's work with various racial housing programs and listed the threatening attributes of these programs as striving to end sanctioned housing segregation areas; employ blacks at the war housing center; place members of local African American Communists on the board of the San Francisco Housing Authority; and end the serving of eviction notices until adequate housing could be found for the evictee (WFO100-252442-31:19 7/31/57).

In 1945 Shepardson was a delegate at the state Communist Party convention, where she was nominated for a position on the state committee of the Communist Party. As with most party functions of this size, the convention was packed with FBI agents and informants. At the convention the FBI recorded Shepardson saying, "the lack of Communist Party work among the Negroes was due to the lethargy of the California Communist Party rather than the National Committee" (SFI00-10824:2 10/1/45). Throughout the late 1940s and early 1950s the FBI continued to monitor Shepardson's association with numerous Communist-linked organizations working to establish equal rights for blacks.

On February 11, 1953, an FBI informant produced a photocopy of a letter between high-ranking California state Communist Party officials indicating that $6,000 was being held for the party in three separate accounts. One of these accounts belonged to Mary Shepardson, and the party noted that Shepardson's husband was "antagonistic and that she must be contacted without his knowledge." The informant provided a photocopy of a receipt signed by Mary Shepardson recording that she was holding $2,000 for an undisclosed third party. Although the FBI protects the identity of this informant, it seems likely that only a high-ranking individual in the party apparatus would have access to such a document (WFO100-252442-31:48 7/31/57).

In May 1954 an undisclosed informant reported that Mary Shepardson systematically monitored the legal testimony of "stool pigeons" testifying against Communist Party members. This informant advised the FBI "that Mary Shepardson, Former Organizational Secretary of the CP Professional Section in San Francisco, stated recently that some time ago she helped raise money to buy transcripts of the various CP trials. She stated that these transcripts have been carefully studied and have been classified and cross-referenced for the purpose of tripping up 'stool pigeons' in their testimony. She stated that the purchase of these transcripts was exceedingly expensive but was regarded as very worthwhile, particularly if at some time in the future it might become possible to have a perjury conviction of one of the government witnesses" (SFI00-25539 5/5/54). This report was forwarded to FBI Director Hoover.

Owing to some degree of well-founded paranoia about using a safe-deposit box, Shepardson kept large sums of party funds at her home in 1954. In a section of a September 29, 1954, report titled "Revolutionary Statements by Subject Showing Advocacy of the Overthrow of the Government by Force and Violence," the FBI reported that Mary Shepardson had argued that "peace is a broad issue—In the 1920's peace meant turning your guns on your own Government, which was what happened when Lenin took over." She reportedly quoted Stalin as saying, in effect, that peace means many things. Her interpretation of it, according to ███████████ was that peace means "victory" or "win by hook or by crook" (SF100-252442 9/29/54).

Shepardson resigned from the party after the arrest of Communist fugitives Robert Thompson, Sidney Steinberg, Sam Coleman, Carl E. Ross, and Shirley Keith Kerman. On August 27, 1953, the FBI raided a small cabin in the remote Sierra Nevada community of Twain Harte, California (WFO100-252442-29 12/12/56) and arrested these five members of the Communist Party on federal charges of escape, conspiracy, and Smith Act violations. The raid was national news: *Time* magazine said it had "ended the FBI's biggest manhunt in years" (*Time* 9/7/53, p. 20), and *Newsweek* reported that during the raid the FBI captured four top Communist leaders who were all "graduates of the Lenin School of sabotage and subversion in Moscow" (*Newsweek* 9/7/53, p. 19). *Newsweek* highlighted the dramatic moment of apprehension when "a posse of sixteen FBI agents, unshaven and dressed in dungarees, surrounded a cabin in the Sierra Nevada country in northern California. [Robert] Thompson and Sidney Steinberg . . . were sunning themselves outside the cabin. Two men and a woman were inside the well-appointed house. Thompson had dyed his dark hair a strawberry blond and grown a matching mustache. He had also put on 30 pounds. Steinberg was considerably thinner than his rogue's gallery description. Both were fully equipped with forged credentials and social security cards" (19).

The FBI found $2,000 in cash in their search of Thompson's car trunk, as well as a wealth of documents revealing the inner workings of the American Communist Party. Included with these materials was a cache of about five hundred dossiers and membership rosters containing a wealth of information on a variety of high-level members of CPUSA. Shepardson's name, address, and background information were included in these documents, but to the FBI, who had long monitored her activities, this was not new information (see *Time* 9/7/53 and 11/2/53; Bateman 1990a, 1990b).

In late 1956 the FBI learned that Mary Shepardson was amazed at the revelations concerning Stalin. She was reported saying "if you couldn't believe [the Russians] in the past, how can they be believed now?" (SF100-252442-28 12/12/56 p. 2). The FBI figured that Khrushchev's revelations might open the door for direct FBI contact with Shepardson, but their sudden appearance at her home only infuriated her.

In 1957 Mary Shepardson was subpoened to appear before HUAC's San Francisco hearings. Shepardson was forceful throughout her questioning (U.S. Congress 1957:1252–56), and she made powerful statements defending her rights of free association (Waite 1957a, 1957b). Her appearance before the HUAC hearings was overshadowed both by the suicide of one of the summoned witnesses and the H-bomb tests visible from San Francisco

(SFC 6/19/87:1), and the committee's authority was further seriously under-mined by three separate U.S. Supreme Court actions taken on June 17, which would come to be known as "Red Monday." In effect, the court ebbed the flow of McCarthyism by reversing a group of Smith Act convictions in Cali-fornia, leading to the release of five individuals and retrials for another nine. The court also found that John Stewart Service had been improperly fired from the State Department in the Amerasia case. Finally, in their most sig-nificant move, the Court reversed the contempt-of-Congress charge against labor leader John T. Watkins. The Court found HUAC's questions to be im-pertinent, thereby effectively undercutting HUAC's ability to engage in fish-ing expeditions and to intimidate witnesses with threats of being held in con-tempt of Congress. Shepardson's appearance before HUAC coincided with HUAC's neutering.

After leaving the party, Shepardson started work on a master's degree in anthropology at Stanford at the age of fifty. In the years after her appearance before HUAC, the FBI continued to monitor her, filing a short report each year verifying her whereabouts and known activities. This continued until May 5, 1960, when her name was finally removed from the Security Index (WFO100-252442-37). Her anthropology doctoral work at Berkeley focused on Navajo legal and governmental systems and culminated in her 1960 dis-sertation, "Navajo Ways in Government," which was published three years later as a memoir of the American Anthropological Association (Shepard-son 1963; see also 1965, 1983). On numerous occasions in the 1960s and 1970s Mary Shepardson collaborated with Boldwen Hammond (Shepardson and Hammond 1970; Babcock and Parezo 1986; Parezo 1993). During the 1960s Mary Shepardson obtained a position with the University of Chicago as a research associate (see Katz and Kemnitzer 1989:324), and in 1967 she began teaching at San Francisco State University, where five years later she became professor emeritus. Few anthropologists who worked with her knew of her past association with the Communist Party or her appearance before HUAC.

Disengaging Activism

Regardless of the willingness of the United Nations to act as an agent of American militaristic and economic interests in theaters of war ranging from the Persian Gulf to Bosnia, contemporary American conservatives still char-acterize the UN as an un-American organization complicit in an international conspiracy aimed at subverting American self-governance. But the purges of progressive Americans by the UN in the 1950s were part of a successful cam-paign to transform it into a body that would increasingly support the eco-nomic interests of the few against the many, and would no longer fight for the causes that attracted the bright minds and hopes of the likes of Jack Harris in the postwar period. Similarly, the purges in the State Department and in domestic federal programs silenced a generation of progressive intellectual would-be public servants and taught the surviving bureaucrats to not speak out, to refrain from having a private political life, to engage in doublethink when investigating questions of import to neocolonial powers, and to keep their eyes focused on the work in front of them.

Harris's critique of Africa's postwar neocolonial order made him a natural target for investigation and persecution. Had he stuck to more scholarly, less activist critiques of British colonialism's African legacy he could have established a comfortable and respectable career at one of America's better universities. Like Richard Morgan, Harris became another lost voice of American anthropology, but the public scrutiny of Harris's termination at least led to some compensation for the heavy-handed violations of his rights. The committee's efforts to damage his career were successful, and like Morris Swadesh, Harris left the United States.

Mary Shepardson's journey from activist to academic seems to reverse the pattern seen in the careers of Jack Harris or Richard Morgan. But one element of Shepardson's midlife career change is consistent with the experiences of others who were hauled before the loyalty tribunals of the 1950s: she left her life as an activist behind her and began a new life that compartmentalized her past.

Although Mary Shepardson apparently broke off all links with the Communist Party, this separation did not indicate a break with past convictions. Her compassion for the plight of minorities bridged her early years as a party activist and her later years as an anthropologist. Her Navajo writings contain nothing identifiable as a Marxist analysis, but they are marked with a compassionate understanding of those she studied. While Shepardson's ethnographic work among the Navajos is well known and well respected among scholars of the Southwest, her past involvement in the Communist Party and her appearance before the House Committee on Un-American Activities are facts that remain largely unknown to most anthropologists.

CHAPTER 9

Examining the FBI's Means and Methods

In 1952 I was sitting in my office, in Seattle,

When in came the F.B.I., truculent and bristling.

Did I know a poet named William Carlos Williams?

He had written a subversive poem called "The Pink Church"

In which he called the Russians comrades. Weren't they?

We were shoulder to shoulder in the war. I said he was

As good an American as they were or I was,

Investigate America, go back and read his poetry.

—Richard Eberhart

The public hearing to which Harris, Shepardson, Stern, and others were subjected was one of the most visible, powerful, and important tools of McCarthyism's inquisition. There were other techniques, however, that were used to identify, monitor, and frighten suspected radical and activist anthropologists. The techniques used by the FBI to collect information on anthropologists need to be considered here before examining how McCarthyism and the FBI marginalized activists outside the hearing rooms during the 1940s and 1950s.

The FBI frequently collected information on anthropologists through employment background investigations, reports by citizen-informers, reports by student-informers, unsolicited poison-pen letters, intercepted mail and telephone calls, press reports, and even casual statements made directly by anthropologists to FBI agents. The FBI also investigated anthropologists whose fieldwork in foreign countries might provide convenient cover for collecting intelligence information for U.S. intelligence agencies such as the CIA. In this chapter I present narrative summaries of several anthropologists' FBI files to examine the FBI's methods of gathering information on American anthropologists.

The FBI routinely conducted extensive background investigations on individuals appointed to federal positions of national importance. During the 1940s and 1950s background checks consisted of FBI agents interviewing applicants' neighbors, relatives, colleagues, and long-time acquaintances. The FBI consulted with a variety of other sources including credit bureaus, local and state police agencies, and pertinent newspaper indexes and clipping services. The FBI collected information on the subject, organized the raw information in reports, and then passed the information on to the requesting agency without recommendations. Ostensibly, the FBI's role in these background investigations was simply that of a designated collector and organizer of information, but in practice they routinely used the background checks as opportunities to collect information for their own ongoing free-floating hunt for Communists, Socialists, pacifists, subversives, and agitators for racial, gender, or economic justice. These "routine" background checks empowered Hoover's FBI to compile dossiers not only on individuals seeking high-level federal employment, but also on any individual they interviewed when gathering information on their primary investigatory subject. This allowed the FBI to build files on hundreds of anthropologists and tens of thousands of citizens that they would likely have had no other cause to investigate.

Hundreds of anthropologists who contributed to World War II were subjected to FBI background and security investigations. From the 1940s through the 1960s a wide variety of anthropologists were the focus of FBI background investigations initiated by employment applications and military and intelligence clearance procedures. Agents from the FBI interviewed anthropologists working for organizations such as the Department of State (e.g., Cora Du Bois, John Embree, etc.), or employed as American representatives in organizations such as UNESCO (e.g., Alfred Metraux [WFO 138-698], Marvin Harris [WFO138-3020], and Chuck Wagley [WFO105-HQ-109031; WFO138-HQ-3015]), or even the Smithsonian Institution (e.g., Kalervo Oberg [WFO123-1501]). In 1940, an unidentified person under the name "American Citizen" wrote the FBI with concerns that David Stout had been trying to obtain supposedly sensitive information on Panamanian Indians. As a result the FBI opened a file on Stout, although Stout's only activity in this area was his effort to acquire readily available maps (WFO61-7560). Hungarian-born anthropologist Bela Maday was investigated, and his citizenship application delayed, after the FBI received reports that he held pro-Communist views during the 1950s (WFO140-10547). The FBI generally followed up on any item of information they encountered: for example, when they learned in 1952 that anthropologist Sol Worth subscribed to the Communist Party's newspaper, the *Daily Worker*, they opened a file on him, although there was no further indication that he had any Communist ties (WFO62-60527-45990). When anthropologist Robert Redfield was appointed to a committee investigating the recuperation of "brainwashed" Korean War veterans, the FBI collected and consolidated information on him, noting a variety of progressive organizations to which he belonged as well as various statements he had made to the press over the years (WFO62-60527-42626). Employment background checks of anthropologists by the FBI were common, and although their presence was seldom noted in anthropologists' writings their appearances on campuses sent powerful messages that they were watching.

Investigating John Embree: Trolling the Hallways of Academia

The FBI's investigation of John Embree demonstrates how routine background investigations were commonly conducted as broad searches for damaging information relating to the subject as well as any individuals known to the subject. John Embree was a bright and complex individual devoted to using anthropology for public service, but he was also critical of the prospective danger of anthropology becoming a handmaiden to oppressive governmental or private interests (Embree 1943, 1945). When Embree suddenly died in 1950 he was being groomed for an appointment to help manage the European Recovery Program, more popularly known as the Marshall Plan. The FBI conducted an extensive background check on Embree as part of the process of clearing him for this position. They interviewed dozens of his colleagues, neighbors, and employers, as well as FBI informants, to gather information on his politics, lifestyle, habits, and character. Most of the information in the 157 released pages of Embree's FBI file is a compilation of information on his education and employment, but these materials readily illustrate how the FBI combed the halls of academia for information on applicants—or anyone of interest who crossed their path.

The FBI's first focus was on Embree's wartime service. In early 1942 Embree was a technician for the Office of Strategic Services, then in late 1942 and 1943 he became a Principal Community Analyst for the War Relocation Authority, and from 1943 to 1945 he was an associate professor and director of the Civilian Affairs Training School (CATS) Area Studies program at the University of Chicago. In 1945 Embree became a supervisor in the Psychological Warfare program at the Office of War Information in Washington, D.C. (WFOI24-5221). After the war he became, according to the AAA's *News Bulletin*, the State Department's "first cultural relations advisor to the United States Embassy in Siam" (AAANB 1947 1(1):8).

An FBI memo dated October 13, 1950 expressed concern over long passages in a newspaper article recording Embree's public call for a moderate U.S. policy approach to China's new government and advocating a swift U.S. recognition of China's new government. The article quoted Embree as saying, "The basic issue in Asian countries is not Communism . . . it is a complex of reactions against Western influences, political and economic, and a dire need for internal economic reforms." The article then added: "A realistic American policy, Mr. Embree states, would be to align ourselves with such leadership rather than with bankrupt regimes of colonialism, such as in Indochina[,] or of reactionary groups like that headed by the once revolutionary Chiang Kai-Shek in China" (NHI24-705).

The FBI learned that Embree went to Yale to conduct research in its program on Southeast Asia, but it had "become necessary for him to take on more teaching assignments because of the untimely death of one of the professors in the Sociology and Anthropology Departments."[1] A Yale informant declared that, "he has no doubt whatsoever as to [Embree's] high integrity, unimpeachable character, reputation or loyalty" (NHI24-705). Others at Yale provided similar testimonies of Embree's character and abilities.

The FBI analyzed summaries of a September 1948 speech Embree gave at the McAlpen Hotel in New York supporting Vietnamese independence. An October 1, 1948, FBI information bulletin

> carried an article which stated that the meeting was held at the McAlpen, as scheduled, and "Dr. John Embree[,] former Chief of the United States Information Service," was listed as one of the persons who made speeches.
>
> This article also stated that the gathering adopted the following resolution, copies of which were sent to various government officials: "We citizens of New York call upon the United States to cease giving political and economic support to France's War against the people of Vietnam. This policy of the United States is defeating the purpose of liberty and recovery of Asia for which so much blood has been shed. As citizens of

the United States oppose to totalitarianism of any kind, Fascist, Communist, or Imperialism, we call upon our government to support by all possible means the cause of freedom from colonial slavery in Southeastern Asia. (NY124-3039:5)

A general tone of free-floating suspicion permeates these files. In one passage a member of Yale's anthropology department indicated that "he is acquainted with the applicant's wife and although she is foreign born he knows of no connections whatever that she maintains in Europe or Asia. ██████████ explained that the applicant is presently writing various articles on Southeastern Asia and those articles fail to reflect any information which could be regarded as disloyal" (NH124-705). In another passage FBI agents seemed suspicious of Embree's marriage to Ella Lurip, a Siberian-born heiress who resided in Tokyo prior to their marriage. Agents from the FBI conducted extensive interviews in the Embrees' Connecticut neighborhood, questioning about a dozen of their acquaintances to collect gossip and observations about them. As was standard practice, the FBI tried to elicit reports of any political statements, actions, or behavior, such as heavy drinking, that would make the subjects stand apart from their neighbors.

Representatives at FBI headquarters expressed concerns that John Embree's father, Edwin Embree, was a member of the Common Council for American Unity, had connections to the American Soviet Friendship Council, was employed by the Rosenwald Foundation, and had attended a 1942 Institute of Pacific Relations conference (WF0124-5221 11/15/50). The FBI viewed the Rosenwald Foundation as a suspicious radical organization because it was devoted to fighting racism and discrimination in the United States. The FBI noted that the *Daily Worker* (7/5/43) reported that Edwin Embree had signed a statement issued by the National Council of American Soviet Friendship that criticized the controversy surrounding the film *Mission to Moscow*.

A radiogram from the Washington Field Office to the Honolulu SAC reported that an anthropologist who taught with John Embree at the University of Hawaii in the 1930s stated that Embree

> took entirely too "leftist" [a] view. . . . Embree's view too often ran parallel to communist objectives of the moment, but he was not unique among staff. ██████████ said that he and ██████████ received their Ph.D.'s from Yale in June ██████████ and then went to Univ. of Michigan the summer [of] ██████████ where he and ██████████ roomed together on ██████████ about a block from the Univ. That summer ██████████ received an offer to teach at Univ. of Hawaii. In accepting the position ██████████ insisted on being permitted to say what he

pleased. ▆▆▆▆▆▆ said he first met ▆▆▆▆▆▆ at the Univ. of Hawaii
the summer of thirty four when ▆▆▆▆▆▆ was a student in his class.
▆▆▆▆▆▆ said that at Yale he attended a cooperative with ▆▆▆▆▆▆
where the words of hymns were changed to suit communist doctrines.
. . . He thought ▆▆▆▆▆▆ got large doses of communism at Yale.
He said he believes with ▆▆▆▆▆▆ [that] communism is a religion.
▆▆▆▆▆▆ advises [that] Embree and ▆▆▆▆▆▆ were both on the
staff of the Dept. of Anthropology and Sociology at Univ. of Hawaii in
thirty seven and thirty eight, that the staff was small[,] not over five or
six, and necessarily Embree must have known ▆▆▆▆▆▆ but he does
not know the extent of their association. (WFO124-4657 11/16/50)

The identity of this left-leaning individual is not disclosed, but Alfred Hudson seems to be a likely candidate.[2]

Further communiqués from this period express concern over reports that Embree had taught with a Communist at Hawaii's anthropology department in the 1930s (WFO124-4651 11/17/50). A memo from the Honolulu SAC reported that an individual from the Counter Intelligence Corps told the FBI that he "recalled that the 401st CIC detachment in Honolulu, T. H., had a system of 3 x 5 filing cards, which . . . contained information on various individuals, and that on one such card the name of the Applicant appeared in the upper left-hand corner and the word 'Communist' in the upper right-hand corner" (WFO124-5221 11/22/50). Someone else reported seeing Embree's name on an index card labeled "Communist." Another version of this story reported that "this same card in the center thereof contained information indicating that during the Army censorship in Hawaii during World War II, there had been intercepted either a letter from the applicant to ▆▆▆▆▆▆ or from ▆▆▆▆▆▆ to the applicant, and the card contained a short excerpt regarding the content of this letter" (WFO124-5221-35 11/9/50). This rumor that Embree's name had appeared on an index card with the word "Communist" on it came to assume a worried importance in numerous FBI reports. As is common in FBI files, this one hazy report multiplied and took on a bureaucratic life of its own, as rumor became reified in the retelling.

The FBI's search of HUAC's files found a letter written by Embree in support of two teachers accused of being Communists. Although this report is redacted by FBI censors, the context and content of the passage suggests it was written in support of Aiko and John Reinecke (Holmes 1994). The Reineckes were public school teachers who were fired in Hawaii for alleged membership in the Communist Party (WFO124-4651:14–16 12/15/50). The letter is dated May 26, 1948, and was written by Embree on Yale University letterhead.

Dear Sirs:

I understand that there has been some question raised concerning the fitness and ability of ███████████ as teachers. Therefore, I should like to take this opportunity to write in favor of the good character of both persons concerned.

I have known ███████████ and his wife for a number of years, having first met ███████████ when we were both teaching Anthropology at the University of Hawaii in 1937. At that time he was an able instructor and was respected by his associates and students. In all my contacts with ███████████ and his wife since that time I have found them honest and reliable persons. The activities of the ███████████ as citizens of the Territory, as separate from university and school teaching functions, have always been, as far as I know, to oppose Japanese and other foreign aggression and, domestically, to favor the causes of labor and of minority groups. All thoughtful and loyal Americans were concerned with the rise of Japanese aggression in the Pacific in the 1930's which finally led to the terrible war which began on December 7, 1941. In regard to the activities of them in connection with organized labor and with problems of race relations and minority groups and the civic rights of individuals, in general, this concern, it seems to me is the prerogative, indeed the duty, of all citizens in a democratic state.

As a former resident of the Territory of Hawaii, I earnestly hope that the activities of teachers in carrying out their civic duties, as they see them, will not jeopardize their positions as teachers, (providing, of course, that they carry out their professional duties with ability and due attention to the internal regulations of the school system.) After all, a man should not abdicate his citizenship rights and duties on becoming a teacher any more than on becoming a medical doctor, businessman or a senator. (WFO124-4651:15 11/22/50)

Embree wrote a similar letter of support to the Commissioners of Public Instruction in Honolulu (HONI24-112-5 5/26/48).

As part of their employment background investigations of Embree, FBI agents visited the University of Chicago's registrar and met with members of the anthropology department. The registrar gave the FBI access to Embree's academic file and his admission application materials. Embree's application indicated that he "had written poetry for the "Troubadour Magazine" in May 1931 as well as short stories for issues of "Paradise of [the] Pacific" (CGI24-1079-3). The FBI considered these magazines to be Communist-infiltrated publications and noted their concern that Embree had published in these venues.

As the FBI agents trolled the corridors of Chicago's Haskell Hall they did not limit the scope of their inquiry to Embree. When FBI agents learned that one of Embree's contemporaries, John Murra (who taught with Embree at the University of Chicago's Civil Affairs Training School during WWII; see Rowe 1984), had been involved in political protests, they gathered information on Murra and included a subsection in Embree's report under the line "The following information is submitted concerning John Victor Murra."[3]

The FBI knew that Romanian-born Murra was a veteran of the 58th Battalion of the 15th International Brigade (aka the Abraham Lincoln Brigade) and that he had experienced difficulties in becoming an American citizen (although the FBI mistakenly identified Murra as Russian-born). The FBI reported that Murra had been arrested for protesting racial discrimination against blacks in Chicago and that he had an altercation with Drubin Roland who had filed an affidavit charging that Murra was "the Communist group leader of the University of Chicago."[4] The FBI report on Embree further states that an unnamed anthropologist at the University of Chicago reported to the FBI that "at the time Embree taught at the University of Chicago, another individual by the name of ▇▇▇▇▇▇▇▇ was also a colleague of Embree in the Anthropology Department at the University of Chicago. ▇▇▇▇▇▇▇▇ stated that ▇▇▇▇▇▇▇▇ was a Communist and that Embree's association with ▇▇▇▇▇▇▇▇ was only circumstance in that both were instructors in the Anthropology Department at the University of Chicago. It was ▇▇▇▇▇▇▇▇'s belief that Embree would never concur with ▇▇▇▇▇▇▇▇ any of the principles advocated by ▇▇▇▇▇▇▇▇ since Embree was an objective individual and would demand proof that a principle was correct before believing the principle" (CG124-1079:7). The report also stated that another anthropologist admitted that he had contributed to Murra's defense fund, adding that "he did not see anything wrong with ▇▇▇▇▇▇▇▇ other than the fact that he had fought in the Spain with the Communists, but did not consider him a Communist" (CG124-1079:8). The FBI ended this report with an account of an incident in 1945 when Communists had booed John Embree's father when he'd stated at a talk in Nashville that American Communist Party leader Earl Browder's stance on the "negro question" would create more problems than solutions.

Because Embree died suddenly in December 1950 at the age of forty-two, we do not know the outcome of this background investigation. It is not clear whether the government clearance Embree needed for his appointment to the European Recovery Program would have been affected by his record of independent, anticolonial views, his choice of marriage partners, his choice of associates in graduate school, and his father's work to end racial discrimination and segregation. Certainly other anthropologists' career paths were disrupted by less-significant findings.

Marshall Newman: A Casual Remark
Begets an Expensive Investigation

The FBI also investigated anthropologists during the Cold War because of casual remarks or even jokes made to agents or others who reported to the FBI. In one such incident, Marshall Newman, an otherwise brilliant scholar, apparently did not understand the dangers of joking about radical affiliations within earshot of the FBI.

Marshall Newman received both a B.A. and M.A. in anthropology at the University of Chicago in 1933 and 1935, respectively, and his Ph.D. degree at Harvard in 1941. During World War II he worked for the Institute of Andean Research in Lima, Peru, and later served in the navy. During the late 1940s and 1950s he occasionally worked for the FBI as a forensic anthropology consultant. A 1951 FBI report summarized a conversation between an agent and Newman "in connection with another matter," in which Newman remarked that in the course of his forensic work he had the opportunity to read FBI reports and he knew the sort of information that the FBI was interested in tracking down. Newman jocularly characterized his own political opinions to be a "shade left of center," and said that a number of his friends and neighbors in his community of Accokeek, Maryland, had been accused of being pro-Communist (WFO121-34169 10/25/51).

While Newman might not have expected the Spanish Inquisition (no one does), it seems odd that anyone who had read numerous FBI files would not have been aware of the FBI's predilection to investigate *anything* that appeared to have links to radical movements. As a result of this passing remark the FBI began an extensive investigation of Newman and his neighbors.

The initial report on Newman summarized a conversation recorded by "technical surveillance" between Marshall Newman and someone of interest to the FBI from the American Veterans Committee.[5] That the summary that follows comes from Newman's FBI file adds an air of intrigue or suspicion about this meeting, but the conversation was a normal, *legal* one between two citizens engaged in legal political strategizing. The conversation was summarized as follows: "She asked him about the meeting tomorrow night. He has the address and will be there. They plan to continue the pledge campaign. Newman said that he worked with the League of Women Voters in Shirlington. He mentioned a ▬▬▬▬ and ▬▬▬▬ who are active out there. Apparently, they got 5,000 signatures in that area. Newman told

her she could send press releases to ▆▆▆▆▆▆▆ of the North Virginia Sub-
urban City Citizen. ▆▆▆▆▆▆▆ mentioned ▆▆▆▆▆▆▆ and his wife who
organized Alexandria. They are leaving town. ▆▆▆▆▆▆▆ will probably take
their place this weekend at least, as Area Chairman" (WFO121-34169 10/25/51).
File notations indicate that FBI informants identified the individual speaking with Newman as a Communist. The FBI's search for records on Newman
"failed to disclose any derogatory information bearing on the loyalty to the
United States of Dr. Newman" (WFO121-34169). The matter might have been
dropped entirely if Hoover had not sent a memo to the director of Naval
Intelligence passing on this information and pointing out that Newman was
a member of the National Reserve, Inactive (WFO121-34169 12/19/51).

Newman's FBI file records that an Office of Naval Intelligence (ONI) investigator interviewed an employee of the Smithsonian's Social Anthropology Division who "knew Newman well," saying he'd just spent Thanksgiving
Day at his home in Accokeek. He characterized Newman as "a person who
lacked judgment," and then proceeded to tell the following story to substantiate this pronouncement. This anthropologist noticed that after Newman

> returned from Military Service, he has seemed always to take the side of
> the underdog, and is particularly interested in welfare movements. [The
> informant] cited a case whereby several years ago, a sailor married a girl
> in Norfolk, Virginia, and it was later developed that he had Negro blood.
> The girl's parents apparently decided to take criminal action against the
> husband for violating the state of Virginia's Miscegenation Statutes, and
> the National Association for the Advancement of Colored People took a
> deep interest in it and were looking for an Anthropologist to determine
> the amount of colored blood, if any, in the girl's husband.
>
> At this point [the informant] said that Dr. Newman became excited
> and went to the head of the Smithsonian Institution and asked if he
> could go to the boy's defense. This antagonized the head of the Smith-
> sonian Institution, who pointed out to Newman that they could not af-
> ford to have a representative of the Smithsonian Institution enter into a
> racial matter like that because it would reflect unfavorably on the organi-
> zation. He further said that an additional example of his bad judgment
> was that the case apparently was dropped and no one in the Institution
> was ever directly asked to appear in court as an expert to testify on the
> subject of the matter of blood, and [the informant] felt that Newman
> acted unwisely in crossing the bridge before he came to it in that he
> would not have aroused the heads of the Institution if he had been asked,
> but the bad judgment was his anticipating the call which, in fact never
> did occur. (WFO121-34169 11/30/51)

The Smithsonian thus shared the FBI's view that Newman's willingness to legally question the legitimacy of rules of hypodescent (maintaining that individuals of mixed racial ancestry are classified as belonging to the racial group of the lowest social status) was a scientific stance that had obvious political consequences and threatened America's mid-century system of racial hierarchy.

An investigator from the ONI interviewed T. Dale Stewart, Newman's supervisor at the Smithsonian, on August 20, 1952.[6] The subsequent report states that

> although he [Stewart] knows nothing unfavorable about Newman's loyalty or personal integrity, he is of the opinion that [Newman] does not always exercise the best judgment. He explained that [Newman] has developed the habit of "championing the underdog," and he cited as an example a recent incident in which one of the Philippine laborers at the Smithsonian had enlisted [Newman's] aid in requesting a six month's leave without pay in order to return to the Philippine Islands on personal business. [Stewart] indicated that such assistance could not be said to be even remotely connected with [Newman's] duties, yet he had undertaken to write memoranda and make all arrangements with the administration, which according to [Stewart] had only created an unfavorable impression of Newman. [Stewart] cited other similar examples of [Newman's] willingness to expose himself to criticism by defending anyone he felt was not receiving proper treatment, but he emphasized that he has never observed any situation in which [Newman] has defended a person by raising such issues as racial discrimination, discrimination against aliens, or other claims one would expect of a Communist sympathizer. (WFO121-34169-6:3–4)

Stewart stated that he did not believe that Newman was a Communist but added that he was "the type of individual who could be duped into following the Communist line" (WFO121-34169-6:4). Stewart then recounted various incidents he believed demonstrated that Newman was not an individual of sound judgment.

One such incident involved Newman's decision to build his home near Alice Ferguson. Alice and her husband Henry Ferguson purchased a property they called the Hard Bargain Farm in 1922, and during World War II they bought a neighboring spread of 850 acres that they subdivided into large housing lots to be sold to select individuals.[7] Stewart told the ONI that Ferguson was a wealthy amateur archaeologist who had located an ancient Indian village on her property at Accokeek. After Alice Ferguson died in 1951, Newman, along with a Smithsonian staff archaeologist and Robert Stevenson, excavated the site "in accordance with terms of her will." Marshall Newman built his home close to the Ferguson property, where according to Stewart all of the neighbors in the area "had been selected by Mrs. Ferguson for their intellectual and cultural interests in order to improve the standards of the community" (WFO121-34169-6:4).

Always eager to collect any stories of a sexual nature (apropos of nothing—but often useful at later dates), the FBI cataloged a secondhand story from a source in Knoxville regarding an unknown individual making unwanted homosexual advances toward Newman in the 1930s when he'd work for the Tennessee Valley Authority (WFO121-431169-11 5/11/53). This vague report took on a life of its own and its echoes were recycled for years in various FBI and ONI reports.

The ONI interviewed an associate curator in the Smithsonian's Division of Archaeology on August 26, 1952. Although the individual's identity is not disclosed, the information pertaining to his qualifications (e.g., "anthropologist hired by Smithsonian 10/30/50, 1948 Columbia Ph.D." [CIRA 1950:52], etc.) indicates that it was Clifford Evans. Evans reported that he knew Newman since 1948 and considered him "above reproach in his personal life and habits," adding that he "enjoys one of the finest reputations in the profession" (WFO121-34169-6:4). Evans described Newman in a positive light and discounted the suggestion that he was a Communist. The FBI indicated that their review of Evans's personnel file and of FBI records revealed nothing unfavorable about Evans's "associates or activities." However, their check of HUAC's files on August 19, 1952, indicated "that in the 2 February 1945 issue of PM (page 3) it was reported that one ▇▇▇▇▇▇▇▇ (not further identified) had been one of a number of persons who signed a statement sponsored by the American Committee for Spanish Freedom, Artists and Scientists Division, requesting the President to sever diplomatic relations with Franco Spain. The American Committee For Spanish Freedom has been cited as subversive by the Attorney General." (WFO121-34169-6:5). Notations in Newman's FBI file indicate the FBI may have begun investigations of Evans as a result of the background check on Newman, thus in such a manner potentially endless chains of investigations were launched (see Peace and Price 2001).

Chasing Newman: The Grand Accokeek Conspiracy

In a move that mixed bungling comedy with tragic absurdity, a naval intelligence agent decided there might be something communistic about Newman's neighbors bonding together to try to force their local government to improve the roads and schools. Thus, "it was deemed advisable to investigate the background of each of the so-called 'new residents' of Accokeek,

Maryland" (WFO121-34169:6). Naval intelligence checked police records, HUAC files, and FBI indexes of the Accokeek residents in question, and then compiled detailed dossiers on each of Newman's neighbors. Newman's neighbors were listed as belonging to such suspicious organizations as the Marian Anderson Citizens Committee (never cited as subversive by HUAC but deemed suspicious by the FBI because Communists were believed to be among its members and because its "sole interest is the advancement of the Negro race"); the American League for Peace and Democracy; the American Peace Mobilization; the American Veterans Committee; the Falls Church Community Theater Group, and other "subversive" groups (WFO121-34169-6:12).

Henry Gardiner Ferguson was identified in these files as a geologist who'd worked for the U.S. Geological Service since 1911. Ferguson's FBI file indicated that he reported on a 1952 personnel history questionnaire administered to federal employees that he was a member of the Washington Bookshop Association (listed by the attorney general as subversive) in 1935. Another ONI investigation determined that Henry Ferguson's wife Alice rented a house to various members of the Communist Party during the 1930s—including Charles Kramer, an individual of interest in the Alger Hiss case (Weinstein and Vassiliev 1999) and in Elizabeth Bentley's defection (Theoharis 2002:55).

Newman's Accokeek neighbors told the FBI that he mostly kept to himself and was a polite, good neighbor. One neighbor reported that, "two types of people lived at Accokeek: 'old residents' and 'new residents.' The latter had purchased their property from Mrs. Ferguson, and then later set themselves apart by forming a 'citizens association' that advocated for improvements for the area. These new residents were described as all being employed in Washington, and once the citizens association was successful in bringing improved schools and roads there was less friction between the old and new residents of Accokeek. One neighbor described one of the new residents as 'socialist' because he was 'continually advocating government health and welfare programs and other programs of a socialist nature'" (WFO121-34169-6:6). The depth of the FBI's and naval intelligence's interest in the Fergusons' unusual means of establishing a community of their own choosing exemplifies the FBI's unwillingness to leave private matters alone, as these individuals who countered the era's Levittown approach to mechanized, homogeneously designed communities became subjects of investigation.

Naval intelligence investigators questioned Henry Ferguson about Newman at his place of work. Ferguson told the investigator that he'd known Ferguson for several years and held him in high regard, and that he had no reason to doubt his loyalty. Ferguson recounted how he and his wife came to establish their community at Accokeek by attempting to intentionally "raise the cultural standards of the community" (WFO121-34169-6:8 12/1/52). Sales of Ferguson property were not advertised but were passed along by word of mouth, and most of the community had been introduced to the Fergusons through their neighbor Robert Strauss.

The FBI noted that Robert Ware Strauss was the vice president of "Presentation, Inc., an organization founded by Carl Marzani and others of Communist sympathies" (WFO121-34169-6:9). Strauss's brother Michael was assistant secretary of the Interior in the 1940s. In 1943 the ONI had investigated Strauss after he recommended two "known Communists" for positions at the Office of Emergency Management; this investigation revealed that Strauss reportedly attended a Communist Party meeting in Pennsylvania in 1942. The investigation also concluded that Strauss had numerous Communist friends, including the Washington, D.C., representative of the Soviet news agency TASS. Records from HUAC listed both Robert and Michael Strauss as belonging to the Southern Conference for Human Welfare, an organization devoted to advocating for racial equality classified as subversive by HUAC. Mrs. Lenore Thomas Strauss had been investigated by the FBI in 1952 and was identified as a member of "an underground Communist Party cell which operated in the Washington, D.C., area during the 1930s and early 1940s under the direction of Lee Pressman, Victor Perlo, and Charles Kramer." Information from FBI informants stated "that she was active in Party work from about 1934 to about 1949, but one informant expressed the opinion that her primary interest was in art and artists, and that her association with Communists was due to that interest" (WFO121-34169-6:9). Strauss's role in bringing Newman and many of the Accokeek community members together further raised the suspicions of the ONI and FBI that they had uncovered a nest of Communists.

Accokeek neighbor Max North signed the Truman loyalty oath at the Bureau of Labor Statistics in June 1952. In response to question 27, "Are you now, or have you ever been a member of the Communist Party, U.S.A., or any communist organization," he stated that in the past he "was associated with the Workers Alliance, the American Student Union, and the American Youth Congress. At the time I was associated with these organizations they were a part of the united front movement which attracted persons of a wide variety of political beliefs. In the case of the American Student Union I was a member of a group which resigned in protest of Communist domination" (WFO121-34169-6:10).

The Department of Commerce's Loyalty Board found nothing indicating disloyalty in North's answers. However, North belonged to the Rochdale Cooperative of Virginia, Inc., and local police records indicated "several persons of Communist sympathies are organizers" of the co-op. The ONI's suspicions were further raised when it learned his father had been the campus advisor for Ohio State University's chapter of the American Student Alliance.

The ONI also investigated Accokeek resident William Dewey Hanson. A lawyer by profession, Hanson had been a candidate for the Nebraska state legislature in 1936. He had also been involved in the defense of the "Loup City Riot" agitators, who had been arrested while fighting for labor's right to organize and strike, and for promoting a six-hour, five-day work week, freedom of speech and assembly, and the removal of ROTC from Omaha schools (WFO121-34169-6:13; DW 4/24/36).[8]

Accokeek resident Sally Ringe told the ONI in 1949 that she was a former member of the Communist Party, and that her friend Victor Perlo had been a frequent visitor at "Longview" (an Accokeek home) in the 1930s (WFO121-34169-6:12). The ONI also investigated Accokeek neighbor John Wharton Hazard, associate editor of *Changing Times* magazine, as well as Francis Robert Donohue, then president of the Accokeek Citizens Association. Donohue reported that Newman spent his free time with his family and working with the association, characterizing him as a good neighbor "in sympathy with the New Deal." Donohue discussed another Accokeek resident described as Jewish and having "earned the reputation of being 'pink'" (WFO121-34169-6:16). To give the ONI an example of the sort of views held by this individual, Donohue described a meeting of the Citizens Association where changes in the school bus system were being proposed: "When the point was made that to provide service in one particular area would require white and Negro students to ride the same busses, ▬▬▬▬ exclaimed that such an arrangement would be all right with him. Donohue explained that that remark in itself would not have been significant, but that it caused considerable consternation among the older residents of the country, who are known to ▬▬▬▬ to be traditionally Southern in their attitude towards Negroes" (WFO121-34169-6:16). Such comfort with "race mixing" indicated to the ONI that this subversive community needed further investigation.

The ONI noted that Newman listed Clyde Kluckhohn and Robert Redfield as references, and that E. A. Hooton had been a former supervisor. Kluckhohn's membership in the ACLU was noted with concern, as were Redfield's comments quoted in the *New York Times* and *Daily Worker* (see Redfield's FBI file, WFO62-60527). Files from HUAC (19/8/52) contained a letter dated March 23, 1948, from the Emergency Committee of Atomic Scientists indicating that Hooton sponsored a dinner for Edward Condon, the former director of the National Bureau of Standards, who had been characterized by HUAC "one of the weakest links in our atomic security" (WFO121-34169-6:21 11/3/53; cf. Hooton's file, WFO62-73410-1).

Newman was characterized as a loyal American during a May 1953 interview by the FBI with an anthropologist at the University of Kentucky who had worked with Newman in graduate school and on the Tennessee Valley Authority project during 1938 and 1939. An FBI informant of "known reliability," who'd known Newman fourteen years earlier, said that while Newman was a loyal American he would not hire him because of his "emotional instability." This same informant reported that he'd known Newman to get drunk "at least two times a week over a three-month period" (WFO121-34169:1 5/123/53). Dr. Richard Schaedel and Louis Stumer of the Institute of Andean Research both reported Newman was a loyal American (WFO 121-34169 9/18/53).

After compiling 137 pages of information on Newman and interviewing dozens of individuals, the FBI concluded that he did not represent an immediate security threat but that his ideas and associations might warrant future investigation. It did not matter that the FBI was unable to tie Newman to any radical cause or organization. His association with individuals challenging traditional ways of living was enough to launch a full-fledged investigation, and that he challenged the legal basis of racial classifications simply confirmed the FBI's suspicions that he might be an enemy of the state.

The FBI's Default Paranoia

The FBI's paranoia and lack of concern for privacy had few limits. Agents thought nothing of prying into the private life of anyone thought to be a subversive, all the while seemingly unable to detect most of the real foreign spies operating in America. The absurdity of these investigations is shown in the FBI's brief investigation of Charles F. Voegelin as a suspected Communist. In 1953 the FBI investigated Voegelin because of his involvement in a research "project in connection with claims made against the Government by Indians" (WFO105-23736-1). This project was likely a Justice Department study examining the "Indians of the Great Lakes–Ohio Valley Region," which was directed by Voegelin.[9] The FBI investigated Voegelin's loyalty because of his connections with a research project in which an anthropologist assisted a group bringing legal claims against the government.

The FBI's investigation determined that Voegelin attended a 1946 seminar at Indiana University with a "foreign Communist." One informant told the FBI that this individual "belonged to a group of Soviet sympathizers called the "Soviet Seminar," which included "a Professor Voegelin" (WFO105-23726-2). Shades of the FBI's xenophobia are apparent as they confused Voegelin with Thomas Sebeok and recorded with concern that Voegelin had studied Finnish folklore and the Finn-Ugric language (WFO105-23726-2). In 1951 an unidentified female anthropologist—apparently disgruntled after being passed over for a job at Indiana University—contacted the American Legion and apparently the FBI to report that Voegelin and others at Indiana were part of a vast Communist conspiracy. She charged Voegelin and others "with being communists, fellow travelers, sympathizers, or disloyal. The informant was interviewed concerning her allegations. She was reported to be emotionally unstable and had been in the hospital because of high blood pressure. Her statements concerning ▇▇▇▇▇▇▇▇ were nonspecific, and she stated that his staff 'must be disloyal because they are friends of ▇▇▇▇▇▇▇'" (WFO100-346896-7). FBI concerns intensified when their files indicated that when contacted by the FBI as part of a loyalty program investigation, Voegelin had "made his position clear that he was opposed to the loyalty program as conducted by the Department of Justice" (WFO100-346896-7).

While Voegelin's FBI file is a small one—only seven pages in length—it is one of hundreds maintained on anthropologists as a means of tracking those whose loyalties could not be taken for granted. Although Voegelin represented no threat to the FBI or its interests, the FBI collected, updated, and cross-referenced their information on him for use in the future.

Hail to the "Platypus Nincompoop"

Another technique used by the FBI to collect information on anthropologists in the 1950s relied on tips from students reporting "facts" such as that one of their professors was a bit odd, or had said something subversive, pacifistic, atheistic, or "unpatriotic" in class. Hoover's FBI regularly investigated professors reported as subversives by students, and in one chilling instance a former Miss America spied on her sociology professor, Howard Higman, and reported his comments to J. Edgar Hoover (Higman 1998). The files of Oscar Lewis, Bernard Stern, Gene Weltfish, Norman Humphrey, and other anthropologists document the FBI's reliance on student-informers.

On January 27, 1955, a Wayne University student contacted the FBI reporting that anthropologist Norman Humphrey had attacked "various groups such as churches, the Federal Administration, and various police agencies" during his lectures in his anthropology course (WFO100-14932 3/31/55). This student-informer thought it odd that Humphrey did not attack Jews or blacks, and further reported that Humphrey remarked that "President Eisenhower is just a platypus nincompoop and as for Nixon, well, he is just a vicious son of a b[itch]."

The student-informer recounted that on one occasion Humphrey entered the classroom and commented on a headline from the campus newspaper, the *Wayne Collegian*, reporting that professors Gerald Harrison and Irving

Stein had "been fired by Wayne University for taking refuge behind the Fifth Amendment during their appearance before the HUAC. Humphrey then attacked the 'Un-American Committee' and its investigations. After stating that he hated power and authority in general, Humphrey looked directly at ███████████ and stated, 'And especially I hate priests and FBI agents. Oh, I've talked to lots of them and I can smile and be friendly and normal in my actions, but deep down inside I hate their guts.'" (WFO100-14932 pp1 3/31/55). An informant from the Detroit FBI office identified Humphrey as being "a sponsor" of an upcoming conference of the Civil Rights Federation Institute on race relations (WFO100-417894 4/12/55). The FBI noted Humphrey's association with the NAACP, and a confidential source advised the FBI that Humphrey's name appeared in the files of the *Michigan Herald*, "a Communist weekly newspaper" (WFO100-14932:2 3/31/55).

The FBI learned that Humphrey canceled his classes during the last week of school due to an illness requiring treatment in Lakeside General Hospital. Even this hospitalization was cause for the FBI's paranoid scrutiny, as they noted, "this hospital is well known to this office due to the number of CP members and functionaries who have been patients there" (WFO100-14932:3 3/31/55). That being treated at a general hospital raised suspicions about communist affiliations—rather than assumptions about the class or wealth level of an individual patient—says much about the FBI's utter lack of perspective.

Two weeks after receiving this initial report, FBI headquarters replied that without further notice Humphrey should not be contacted by anyone working for the FBI. This was advised because previous reports "clearly reflect that Humphrey is not the type of individual who should be contacted in connection with official business of the Bureau" (WFO100-14932 4/14/55). The FBI instead decided to secretly interview officials at Wayne University to gather more information on "statements which Humphrey has made in the presence of students" (WFO100-14932 4/14/55). The agent, contacting an unnamed university official, was instructed to "not mention Humphrey's comments concerning President Eisenhower, Vice President Nixon or Senator McCarthy. Additionally, no mention should be made of Humphrey's sympathetic attitude for Negroes and Jewish people. In your contact with the Wayne University official, you should restrict your comments to statements made by Humphrey concerning priests, the FBI and the House Committee on Un-American Activities" (WFO100-14932 4/14/55). That the FBI did not want to disclose Humphrey's reported statements concerning the president and vice president or his "sympathetic" attitudes toward blacks and Jews, yet would reveal his anti-priest and anti-Catholic statements, reveals the bureau's interest in creating difficulties between Humphrey and campus administrators.

After checking files at FBI headquarters, the FBI discovered that Humphrey had mailed an advance copy of *Race Riot* (1943), his book on Detroit's 1943 race riots, to FBI director Hoover, "along with a request for his reaction to the book" (WFO100-14932:2 4/12/55). Internal memos by the FBI (10/20/43) "noted that the book referred in a critical manner to law enforcement" and that it "represents the viewpoint of crackpots and theorists" (WFO100-14932:3 4/12/55). Hoover did not send Humphrey or his publisher any reactions to the book.

The Detroit FBI office's records on Humphrey start in 1944 when Humphrey had "spoken at a meeting of the Twentieth Annual Forum at the YMCA concerning the general problems confronting the white and Negro races in the post-war world. He attacked the idea that a few whites in the world should control forever the much more numerous darker people. In response to a question, he opined that the Armed Forces were more prejudiced and discriminatory than the civilian population and other Government agencies. His audience was overwhelmingly Negro" (WFO100-135-15-171). The FBI also recorded that Humphrey was on the executive board of the NAACP in Detroit in 1946, and that he attended a 1946 Antioch College conference titled "Techniques for Good Race Relations in Community Living" (WFO100-135-10-111).

On April 21, 1955, a colleague of Humphrey's met with FBI agents. This individual, referred to as "Doctor," agreed to refrain from telling Humphrey about his meeting with the FBI. The FBI report on the interview stated that "Doctor" claimed that Humphrey was "a very valuable sociologist [who] has done some excellent work in this field throughout South America. [Doctor] advised that the man [Humphrey] is physically ill and that this, in addition to his observations of conditions in South America, has probably contributed to his present attitude. Doctor ██████████ stated, however, that regardless of Humphrey's physical condition, his statements are certainly not in accordance with the policies of Wayne University and are certainly those that should not be made to college students. He stated he would take care of the matter" (DE100-14932 4/12/55). The FBI determined it best not to activate a full investigation of Humphrey, but filed the information for future use.

Charles Hockett: Suspicions of a "Book-Worm Type"

For anthropologists with progressive political pasts, the FBI's broad background investigations from the period during World War II often determined the nature of their military careers. During the war the linguistic abilities of Charles Hockett led the army to initially consider him for cryptographic training. But when reports suggested that he was "disaffected" and that he held progressive views, the army decided instead that he should teach math, gunnery skills, and Chinese and Japanese to American troops (WFO100-130681 11/5/47).

The military could not figure out what to make of Hockett. His FBI and military intelligence files portrayed him as an unusual individual by army standards—as one report stated, he was "considered the 'book-worm' type" (WFO100-130681-1 6/10/42). Another report described him as "a near genius type, extremely brilliant, [who] has a varied opinion on the world in general, has rather liberal ideas and is a 'poetic dreamer'" (WFO100-130681-1 6/10/42).[10] Hockett did not get along well with the men in his division. His fellow enlistees reported behaviors they thought odd, such as his habit of walking "around the Battalion area to all of the trash and garbage cans, lift[ing] up their tops, peer[ing] intently into them, carefully [replacing] the tops, and walk[ing] away without comment to anyone. Corp. ████████ stated that Hockett's mind seemed to be a thousand miles away, and was hard to draw into conversation. He said that Hockett was not very popular with the rest of the men, and seemed to have a more or less negative personality. Corp. ████████ said that he knew [Hockett's] education far exceeded that of the other men in the platoon, and felt that his mental exertions along that line probably accounted for his peculiar actions" (WFO100-130681-1 6/10/42).

A June 16, 1942, Military Intelligence Division report recounts how Hockett walked into his colonel's office

> and told him that he had figured out a code system that would prove useful to the Army. Hockett then typed out this system, presented it to [the Colonel] who in turn gave it to [military intelligence].
>
> [The Colonel] concluded by saying that he would not recommend [Hockett] for assignment to the Counter Intelligence Corps, as he felt that Hockett was mentally unsuited for this type of work. This statement was qualified however, by the Colonel saying that he believed that [Hockett] would be valuable to the United States in some other line of work, such as cryptography" (WFO100-130681 6/16/42).

An initial recommendation for counter-intelligence training in 1942 was rejected after the Military Intelligence Division's (MID) investigation determined that Hockett held "Communistic leanings" (WFO100-130681 11/5/47). This investigation determined that "during his collegiate days at Ohio State University [Hockett] joined the National Student League and the American Student Union. It was also alleged he was a member of the Student League for Industrial Democracy. These organizations were Communist inspired but are presently defunct. In 1935 he was reported as active in the Young Communist League and attended Communist meetings in Columbus, Ohio" (WF0100-130681 11/5/47). The army was also concerned that Hockett's former father-in-law had "made speeches in favor of socialized medicine" (WF0100-130681-4 11/5/47).

Hockett's past involvement in progressive politics precluded the possibility of work in counter-intelligence or cryptography, and thus the War Department lost a brilliant and capable cryptographer who might have made significant contributions to ending the war. Instead, Hockett was assigned to language instruction, and after the war spent years teaching Japanese at the Presidio.

Demitri Shimkin: Foreign-Born on the Fourth of July

Foreign-born intellectuals, especially those whose ancestors came from regions occupied by the Soviet Union, were often subjected to extensive investigations, regardless of their commitment to American Cold War policies. Demitri "Jimmi" Shimkin was born on July 4, 1916, in Omsk, Siberia, although his family left Russia soon after the Revolution. Initially the family lived in Indonesia, but then moved to the Netherlands and then finally to the United States in 1923. Information gathered by the FBI in the 1950s indicates that the Shimkins came to the United States from Russia with a "price on their heads," and that they had "to leave Russia by stealth and were apparently being hunted by those forces which opposed the Czarist regime" (WF0121-43885-10).

Shimkin studied anthropology at the University of California at Berkeley, receiving a B.A. (1936) and Ph.D. (1939) there. His doctoral fieldwork was with the Wind River Shoshone and his dissertation was written under the tutelage of Robert Lowie. He became an American citizen in 1941 (Lehman 1992), and during World War II he worked for the Military Intelligence Division, rising to the rank of colonel (1941-1946). His intelligence work involved correlating "Russian intelligence information which was being obtained by the United States Army" (WF0121-43885-11). After the war he taught at the National War College, was a Social Science Research Council fellow at Princeton's Institute for Advanced Studies for a year, and then took a position at Harvard's Russian Research Center (RRC).

Shimkin's work for Clyde Kluckhohn at Harvard found him working with CIA personnel on a regular basis.[11] On August 3, 1948, Shimkin wrote to Kluckhohn that CIA representative Harrison G. Reynolds had "visited [Harvard's Russian Research Center] yesterday and desires information on the current operations and plans of the Center. I gave him a general oral survey but await your instructions before providing any written material. He is interested in receiving essentially the report of the Center's operations during the summer and the list of our staff members who would be capable of presenting materials and acting as consultants in fields of research in the USSR of significance to Reynolds' organization" (quoted in Diamond 1992:109). At the RRC Shimkin was surrounded by scholars doing intelligence work, and he himself worked on projects with military and intelligence applications (see Diamond 1992:97, 296, n. 8). After a few years at Harvard, he returned to the Institute for Advanced Studies in Princeton, where he analyzed intelligence data on the technological and geographic factors limiting the development of the Soviet economy, and reported on the capacities of the Soviet automotive and railroad industries.

In 1953 the FBI undertook a full field investigation of Shimkin after he applied for a position at the Bureau of Census in the Department of Commerce. The FBI's investigation in part grew from concerns that the name of Shimkin's thesis advisor, Robert Lowie, had appeared in a pamphlet in the FBI's files (as a sponsor of the California Labor School) and that Shimkin listed him as a reference in his application materials (WFO121-43885-1).[12] The FBI also learned that Shimkin's mother, the physician Dr. Lydia Shimkin, had helped the efforts of the Russian consulate in San Francisco to ship medical and technical books to Russia. Records from the FBI indicate that Dr. Lydia Shimkin subscribed to the *Daily People's World*, and that one of her patients told the FBI that Dr. Shimkin "had expressed herself favorably on the subject of Communism" (WFO121-43885-1). As the FBI intensified its investigation of Lydia Shimkin, an informant told the FBI that Demitri and his parents "used to pray every night for a revolution in France and Great Britain and hoped that this country would also have one because it would be good for the people" (WFO121-43885-10). Another informant reported that Lydia Shimkin told her about visiting a Communist children's home "'in the mountains' and had seen the American flag trampled in the dirt and the Red flag raised" (WFO121-43885-10). One informant reported that Lydia Shimkin said that Demitri remained in Berkeley after graduating "because he was organizing the Communist Party at the University of California" (WFO121-43885-10). In a November 1941 interview, Lydia Shimkin told the FBI that "America is my country now and I wish they would send everybody back to Europe who don't like America" (WFO121-43885-10).

Some of Demitri Shimkin's former neighbors told the FBI that he might hold Communist views; that he and his wife were "peculiar and critical of American institutions"; and that Shimkin was friends with another neighbor who "did not allow his child to celebrate VE-Day until the Russians had entered Berlin" (WFO121-43885-1). This initial report contains redacted references to friends of Shimkin who the FBI believed were pro-Soviet or Communists. A check with neighbors in May 1953 led the FBI to a former neighbor who reported that Demitri's wife, Edith Shimkin, had spoken approvingly of former Vice President Wallace, and was "very tolerant in regard to both Jews and Negroes." This informant also reported that Shimkin said that the Daughters of the American Revolution was a "ridiculous organization which would only be tolerated in the U.S.," and made statements that the inflationary period of the early 1950s would not culminate in another depression, but would bring a "revolution" (WFO121-43885-7).

Shimkin's Harvard colleagues reported that he was patriotic and loyal to the United States. A report on one colleague from Harvard's Graduate School of Public Administration stated that the colleague characterized Shimkin's writings and presentations at the RRC as revealing "a strong pro-American sentiment," and added that "nothing has come to his attention which would indicate any pro-Communist sentiments or beliefs on the part of Demitri Shimkin" (WFO121-43885-8). A report on another Harvard colleague stated that the colleague told the FBI that Shimkin's work demonstrated him to be pro-American, adding that Shimkin "has anti-Communist feelings because his family lost everything in Russia and fled from the Bolshevik terror. He said that Dimitri Shimkin presents absolutely no security risk as an employee of the United States Government" (WFO121-43885-8:4).

Despite the contradictory picture that emerged during the FBI's background investigation, Shimkin was hired to work for the Bureau of Census, where he worked in the Foreign Manpower Office from 1953 to 1960 as an analytical statistician studying (among other things) Soviet industry, and writing such papers as "The Soviet Mineral Fuels Industries 1927/1928–1958: A Statistical Survey."

On completing this 1953 investigation of Shimkin, the FBI showed no further interest in him until 1960 when the Los Angeles bureau received information from someone known to members of Shimkin's family who believed that Shimkin might have been engaged in espionage. This individual told the FBI that "Mr. Shimkin holds himself aloof from the rest of the family; that he apparently is engaged in some sort of espionage work because it has been indicated that his life has been put in danger on some occasion and since he speaks Russian, he is engaged in activities relating to Russia[.] ███████ has also advised . . . that since the Shimkins always live in the outskirt of the city [she] believed this would make it easier to transmit messages to a foreign country. ███████ refers to the Shimkins as 'intellectual snobs'" (WFO121-43885-33). This informant added that she had never met Shimkin, however, so we can assume that all of the information was derived from second- or third-hand sources.

In 1960 Shimkin took a leave of absence from the Department of Commerce to teach anthropology and geography at the University of Illinois. On

March 22, 1961, Shimkin informed military personnel at the Pentagon that he was concerned about "Communist Party (CP) infiltration at the University of Illinois" (WFO121-43885-35). When a Pentagon official interviewed Shimkin the following day, Shimkin elaborated on his worries about the Communist Party's campus infiltration and the direction of the pro-Castro movement on campus. He also stated that he did believe claims by groups like Fair Play for Cuba that they were not affiliated with the Communist Party.

Shimkin further stated that there were five individuals who were "the instigators of this pro-Castro activity"—three of which were described as townspeople and the other two were professors (with redacted identities). In a statement clearly referring to anthropologist Oscar Lewis (see chapter 12), Shimkin stated that "another specific involved was the fact that ███████████, who worked in Mexico for long periods of time, stated in conversation he had had contact with 'leftwing Marxists in Mexico' and further, he showed good acquaintance with technical Party terminology" (WFO121-43885-35).[13]

Portions of Shimkin's file remain closed due to the national security exemptions that the CIA and other agencies are allowed to evoke under FOIA. Thus, although it is difficult to know the extent of Shimkin's work for the CIA during the 1950s and 1960s, it is clear that he maintained a good working relationship with the CIA. In 1998 the CIA released to me one document (which had originally been processed for release to another party in October 1992) relating to Shimkin. This document consists of a cover letter dated June 27, 1961, from Director of Central Intelligence Allen Dulles to Major General T. W. Dunn, Commandant U.S. Army War College, in which Dulles thanked Dunn for passing on "two thoughtful questions posed by Professor Demitri B. Shimkin on 6 June" (CIA MORI ID: 30820). Dulles enclosed a four-page single-spaced report that provided answers to Shimkin's questions (CIA MORI ID 34176).

Shimkin died on December 22, 1992, in Urbana, Illinois and was buried with full military honors at Arlington National Cemetery. It is difficult to know what to make of the contradictory information collected on Shimkin: some suggests he was pro-Communist, some suggests he was anti-Communist. It seems likely that citizens who saw him as pro-Soviet simply lacked the sophistication to disentangle his strong Russian sentiments from pro-Soviet views, or to understand that one could have Russian heritage without being a Communist.

Window Shopping for Spies

In 1964 the FBI opened a small investigation on anthropologist Vera Rubin after she received a grant from the Marian Davis Scholarship Fund to travel to Mongolia. On December 7, 1964, a New York City FBI agent requested permission from headquarters to interview Rubin so that she could "furnish detailed information concerning her visit to Mongolia which would be of interest to other government agencies" (WF0105-133625). The FBI's New York bureau determined that Rubin was a self-employed scholar, and they established her area of academic expertise through "a pretext telephone call to subject's residence seeking a physician [a ploy that] determined that she is an anthropologist" (WF0105-133625). J. Edgar Hoover denied the New York SAC's (12/31/64) request to interview Vera Rubin, however, because FBI headquarters could not determine if Rubin was the same Vera Rubin, "who has contributed considerable amounts of money to various communist front and other subversive organizations in the past" and had been an "Executive Secretary for the American Labor Party in Westchester County, New York in the early 1940s" (WF0150-136424-1). Hoover ordered the case closed, as there were other scholars traveling to Mongolia who could be approached to conduct passive espionage for the United States.

Rubin was indeed the radical individual appearing in the FBI's files, although the FBI did not figure this out until their 1972 investigation of the Marian Davis Scholarship Fund (WF010-470269). Rubin was married to wealthy businessman Samuel Rubin, and she was very active in Westchester County progressive politics where she served as the chair of the county committee to reelect President Roosevelt (Saunders 1989:316). Rubin's work with the American Labor Party (ALP) is poorly documented, but the FBI did ascertain (in 1972) that she was the 1944 "Executive Secretary for the ALP in Westchester County" (WF0105-136424-1). In 1956 a confidential FBI informant reported that Vera Rubin "was an outspoken communist who admitted on several occasions her Communist Party affiliations" (WF0100-470269:6). The New York bureau searched its files for any information suggesting that the Marian Davis Scholarship Fund might have subversive connections, but no such information was located.

Monitoring Anthropologists' Ability to ▮▮▮▮▮▮▮▮
about ▮▮▮▮▮▮▮ *and* ▮▮▮▮▮▮▮

There are many examples of how the FBI's free reign of investigatory power while conducting background investigations led them to pry into the private politics and lives of anthropologists. For example, when Chuck Wagley applied for a UNESCO position in 1955, the FBI generated a 232-page report suggesting that he'd somehow held Communist tendencies, although it was unable to find any specific information to substantiate these fears.[14] In other instances, anthropologists conducting research in the Soviet Union (even those with firm, rich capitalist roots like Henry Field, the grandson of Marshall Field) were investigated by the FBI as potential Communists (WFO65-47510-26; WFO100-17007; WFO105-214558).[15] Even A. Irving Hallowell's name was added to the FBI's files when a letter from the Citizens Anti-Nazi Committee with his name listed on the letterhead was sent to J. Edgar Hoover prior to America's entry into the war (WFO61-7560-837). Similarly, Jules Henry first came to the FBI's attention when he mailed to them some anti-Semitic propaganda he had received, but the FBI eventually focused on his loyalty and that of his sister (WFO77-29387).

The FBI's methods and techniques described in this chapter illustrate how hundreds of American anthropologists came under the scrutiny of America's secret police. While it is to be expected that individuals such as John Embree or Charles Wagley who were applying for sensitive government positions would be investigated by the FBI, the extent to which secondary, or spur investigations, were undertaken is chilling. These secondary investigations were commonplace and produced mountains of FBI files. The propriety of the FBI's investigations of individuals like Marshall Newman and his lawful associations and activities must be questioned, and the full extent to which legitimate and legal political activities were repressed by the FBI has not adequately been studied by contemporary scholars, much less become part of our historical understanding of the FBI's role in spying on and subverting Americans' freedom of association, thought, and dissent. It is impossible to calculate the chill that these free-ranging investigations spread throughout academia as many scholars came to realize that their thoughts, actions, and associations were subject to surveillance.

The FBI relied on a wide range of techniques to gather information on anthropologists, the most basic of which involved interviewing the subject's friends, enemies, associates, neighbors, colleagues, students, campus administrators, and former professors. Moreover, what these interviewees often did not know was that in cooperating with the FBI they were opening the door for FBI investigations of themselves.

That the FBI undertook such extensive investigations of moderate anthropologists without producing any meaningful result is all the more interesting when one considers how many Marxist, Communist, and Socialist anthropologists lived through the 1940s and 1950s without being hounded by FBI investigators. As I show in the following chapters, activism—or in this case a lack of publicly identifiable activism—was generally of greater concern to the FBI than an individual's actual identifiable Communist affiliations.

CHAPTER 10

Known Shades of Red:

Marxist Anthropologists Who

Escaped Public Show Trials

"Thoughtcrime was not a thing that could be concealed

forever. You might dodge successfully for a while, even for

years, but sooner or later they were bound to get you."

—George Orwell

In this chapter I discuss the FBI files of some of the American anthropologists who were identified by the FBI as Marxists, Socialists, or Communists yet were not called before investigatory committees. In examining this issue I show how the FBI tracked the political and academic activities of certain individuals more than others, and how activism as opposed to mere party membership influenced the FBI's decision to investigate anthropologists.

During the 1940s and 1950s the FBI investigated numerous anthropologists who reportedly held memberships in Socialist and Communist parties yet who never were called to appear before security or loyalty committees. There are a variety of reasons why certain individuals were able to avoid appearing before committees—some maintained such low, nonactivist profiles that the FBI, HUAC, and other committees were not concerned with them; some put their ties to Communism behind them; and others, such as Roy Barton (Price 2001b), Ruth Benedict (Buhle 1994; Krook 1993),[1] Alexander Goldenwiser (Smith 1999), Franz Boas (Krook 1989) and Archie Phinney (Price 2003b; Willard 2000; NAPNR),[2] died before the age of McCarthyism.

Marvin Opler and Hoover's Dumpster Divers

Marvin Opler and his brother Morris were introduced to anthropology in classes taught by Leslie White at the University of Buffalo—Morris received a B.A. (1929) and an M.A. from Buffalo (1930), and Marvin studied there from 1931 to 1933. In the 1930s Marvin Opler was a leader of the University of Buffalo's National Student League (NSL), an organization later identified by HUAC as a Communist front organization (BU100-18367:13 7/15/64). One FBI informant stated that the Buffalo chapter of the NSL "was purportedly an organization of students designed to protect academic freedom and to prevent war, but that this chapter was actually controlled and dominated by the Communist Party in Buffalo" (BU100-18367:3 7/15/64). Morris later earned a Ph.D. in anthropology at the University of Chicago (1933) and Marvin received a Ph.D. from Columbia (1938) (see Price and Peace 2003). In 1938 Marvin Opler moved west to Portland, Oregon, where for five years he was the chair of anthropology at Reed College.

When Marvin Opler was appointed to the War Labor Board in 1943, the Seattle branch of the District Intelligence Office informed the FBI that two years earlier Opler had sponsored a local lecture by Anna Louise Strong. The FBI noted with concern that he had taught on the faculty at Reed College, had been secretary of the Medical Bureau to Aid Spanish Democracy, and had signed a petition protesting the Portland Censor Board's banning of the film *Professor Mamlock* (WFO101-6207-1 5/29/43). Marvin Opler soon was assigned to the position of the chief community analyst for the War Relocation Authority (WRA) at the Tule Lake center from 1943 to 1946.

The FBI routinely gathered information on organizations or individuals through an operation known as a "confidential trash cover," which is bureau-speak for the process of rummaging through garbage cans to collect documents to be read at FBI field offices. One such scrounging venture at the Portland Communist Party Headquarters in July 1943 located a handwritten letter referring to an individual known as "M," who the FBI believed was Marvin Opler. The letter began with an apology:

> Your letter finally got to us—signals being mixed on where of three or four places our mail should be delivered. Sorry to be late.

We think we've decided to stay here permanently, but don't tell this to anyone, because we have until Aug. 15 to let them know at school and it's always good to have two job possibilities. At any rate, we have found friends here, and made affiliations, so long-distance relationships with Portland are unnecessary.

You probably want our book numbers in order to transfer us. I'm ashamed to say it, but when we left Portland, M. decided to destroy them. We were subletting our house to strangers, and here we live under strict army rule, with sentries, surveillance and *censorship*.

The work is very fascinating & M. feels so useful and valuable for a change. He's within his power to improve the lot of these poor folk. There are 3 other couples here, also section heads like M., (and therefore in strategic, policy-making positions), who are our *friends*. So we work together. Naturally, this is much more satisfactory than the set-up in Portland, where little use of M's particular training & ability could be made.

I hope this is okay. Remember the censorship. We live behind barbed wire, and need a pass to get in or out.

Sincerely, ▆▆▆▆▆▆▆. (WFOIOI-6207-2 7/27/43)

An unfinished draft of a typed letter bearing the return address of the Portland Communist Party office, addressed to the California State Office of the Communist Party, was also mixed in with the Communist Party trash. This letter informed the California branch that three Multnomah County (Portland) Party members were transferring to Tule Lake, and that the Portland branch would send on the CP transfer numbers to the individuals at Tule Lake. The FBI concluded that this "letter by ▆▆▆▆▆▆ was never sent to the Tule Lake address, and it is believed that the letter in the handwriting signed ▆▆▆▆▆▆ mentioned in the forepart of this letter is undoubtedly ▆▆▆▆▆▆▆ and the person referred to in the body of the letter as "M" is believed to be Marvin Opler" (WFOIOI-6207-2 7/27/43).

This after-the-fact means of transferring branch memberships by way of mail went against standard Communist Party protocols. As laid out by Peters in *The Communist Party—A Manual for Organization*, "If a Party member moves from one place to another, he must secure a transfer from the Party organization before he moves. No Party member has the right to leave his unit without permission. The units must not accept any member without a transfer. A transfer card must be secured from the Section Committee in order to transfer from one Unit to another in the same Section; from one section to another in the same district, the transfer is issued by the District Committee; from one district to another; the Central Committee issues the transfer; from the Communist Party of the USA to a Communist Party in another country, the Central Committee issues the transfer" (1935:108). While it was not an unusual practice for party members or units in the 1940s to handle branch transfers with such carelessness, the sudden changes brought by World War II made such actions all the more common (Bob Patenaude to Price 11/02/98). An FBI informant later confirmed to the FBI that Marvin Opler had transferred his party membership from the Multnomah County branch to Tule Lake (WFO101-6207-9:3 9/12/44).

Two months later FBI Director Hoover instructed the San Francisco FBI field office to investigate Opler (WFO101-6207-2 9/20/43). FBI interviews with personnel at Tule Lake revealed that Opler was held in high regard both by his coworkers and by the interned Japanese Americans. One WRA employee told the FBI that "people in the WRA thought of Dr. Opler as a 'wobbly', a 'long hair' and a 'conscientious objector' but was unable to advise [the] Agent why, nor what the basis of such regard was" (WFO101-6207-5). The FBI noted that in the letter retrieved from the trash by the Portland branch, the individuals identified as "our friends" were employed as section heads at Tule Lake.

At Tule Lake on December 17, 1945, the FBI questioned Opler under oath regarding past or present membership in the Communist Party. He claimed that the only party affiliation he had ever had was as a registered Democrat, noting he'd been a Democrat precinct committeeman in Portland until leaving for Tule Lake. When asked seven different ways if he had ever belonged to the Communist Party or was involved in any organization advocating the overthrow of the U.S. government, he replied he had not. In the report of these questionings, the FBI characterized Opler as being "cooperative and courteous" (WFO101-6207-5). On July 10, 1944, a WRA supervisor wrote the Department of Justice's Interdepartmental Committee on Employee Investigations that inasmuch as it had not been determined that Opler had ever belonged to any subversive organizations they had no reason to take any action in this matter (WFO101-62070-8). This ended the FBI's interest in Opler for the next two decades.

In late 1963 the FBI again briefly became interested in Marvin Opler as they investigated an unidentified individual close to him (WFO101-6207-12). In early 1964 agents contacted eight informants in the Buffalo branches of the Communist Party, the Workers World Party, and the Progressive Labor Party and recorded that none of these informants knew either Marvin Opler or the unnamed primary subject of the investigation. Buffalo FBI agents learned that Marvin Opler would be presenting papers at "various anthropological meetings" in Europe as representative of the "American Anthropological Society [sic]" (WFO101-6207-20). After Opler's return from Europe, the FBI collected reports from security and police officials in Spain and France searching for information on him. The report from Spanish security officials is not released under FOIA exemptions b7c and b7d, and the Paris police reported that his activities did not come to their attention—as if the activities of an academic giving a paper at a conference might normally come to the attention of the police (WF0101-6207-26).

For unknown reasons the FBI undertook a background investigation of Marvin Opler's brother Morris on January 26, 1954.[3] Their chief finding was that Morris Opler had attended the India-America Conference in Delhi, India, in 1949, which was sponsored by the Institute of Pacific Relations.

Paul Radin: One Step Ahead of Hoover

Paul Radin was born into a Polish rabbinical family in Lodz, Poland, in 1883, the following year he and his family immigrated to the United States. At the age of fifteen Radin enrolled at City College (B.A. 1902), and later he studied zoology, then history, at Columbia. After studying anthropology in England for two years, Radin returned to the United States where he studied for his doctorate at Columbia under Boas (with a history emphasis under James Henry Robinson), receiving a Ph.D. in 1911 (Du Bois 1960:i). Radin conducted fieldwork with Ojibwa and Winnebago cultures in the Great Lakes region, where he brought a sense of detail and proportion to his fieldwork (see Radin 1949). Radin's ethnographic work concentrated on oral traditions and cultural structure; rarely did he focus on topics that might be expected of a Marxist or Communist theoretician, such as economic systems, political economy, or stratification (Radin 1932, 1933). This fact is a surprising one given his exposure to European Marxist traditions during his five years at Cambridge in the 1920s (Du Bois 1960:xiii). While Radin's ties to Marxism were not apparent to many anthropologists, as Laura Nader notes (1997a:112) they were sufficient to make him a target of investigation and harassment during the era of McCarthyism.

In 1945 the FBI learned that Paul Radin's brother, Max Radin—a law professor, legal philosopher, and popular novelist at the University of California—was close to "prominent Communist Party Association members and functionaries in the San Francisco and Bay Area" (WF0100-51471). Many members of Paul Radin's social circle in California were known by the FBI to be working for the party or for front organizations: his friends are recorded as working for the Communist Political Association in Alameda County, as editors of Communist publications, teaching at the California Labor School, working as Communist attorneys, and being veterans of the Abraham Lincoln Brigade (SF100-1876-1). One informant told the FBI that Radin had been a dues-paying party member since 1935, another indicated that Radin was a member of the Communist Party's professional section's unit, no. 107, a special professional section that consisted entirely of college professors (WFO100-51471-3). One report indicated that Radin sponsored a fund-raising party for the *People's World* (WFO100-51471-3:5). A Communist Party official from Alameda County told the FBI that Radin had "furnished financial support for the Communist Party in 1941 (WFO100-51471-47). Files from the FBI record Radin's membership in a variety of subversive groups dealing with issues of racial or economic equality, including the American League against War and Fascism, the Artists and Writers Union, the Joint Anti-Fascist Refugee Committee, and other progressive organizations (WFO100-51471).

Paul Radin began lecturing at the California Labor School in 1942 and, according to one FBI informant, by 1944 he was "practically a permanent lecturer" on the topic of race and social problems. Among the titles of his lectures at the Labor School were "Racism Refutation of the Race Theory of Hitler" and "Racial Problems and Social Problems." In 1945 the FBI concluded that "Radin is known to be a Communist and a prominent lecturer on the Racial Question at the California Labor School, San Francisco, in which school he has professed an extreme interest. He is reported to have gone to China in 1937 as a government emissary but his real purpose was for the Communist Party. Subject [Radin] is the author of a book entitled, 'Racial Myth,' which is believed to have been dedicated to [his father (see Radin 1934:iv)]. Radin has made several speeches at various Communist functions. Radin is known to have associated with ▆▆▆▆▆▆▆ in NYC in January 1944" (WFO100-51471 2/24/45).

In 1942 the California State Legislature organized a joint fact-finding committee investigating un-American activities in California. At these hearings one former party member reported knowing Radin, and that

> at some time in the Spring of 1937 Dr. Paul Radin, of the [University] of California, and one of the State Sponsors for the Historical Records Survey, dropped in at the Los Angeles Office; ▆▆▆▆▆▆▆ was present and introduced me to Dr. Radin as 'comrade'; Dr. Radin launched into a long discussion of the possibilities of the Historical Records Survey for doing useful work for the Communist Party, of which he was readily admitted himself to be a member; that Dr. Radin stated he was planning to leave very soon for China and other points in the Orient ostensibly to do anthropology research, but that he was going to attend [to] certain matters (which he did not elaborate on) for the Communist Party; at that time he made the statement there should be an Historical Records Survey Project in Manila, operated, of course, by the Communist Party members, in order to provide certain facilities for coordinating Commu-

nist Party work in the Orient with that in the United States. (WFO100-51471 2/24/45)

These hearings brought a chill to college campuses across the state of California. That Radin was identified as a Communist focused suspicious attention on Berkeley's anthropology department. Radin left California to teach in the Midwest and the South.

Black Mountain Days

Radin taught at Black Mountain College in North Carolina "intermittently from 1941 to 1944," and the FBI investigated his activities at the college from 1943 to 1944. Black Mountain was an alternative college established in 1933 by Theodore Dreier and John Andrew Rice (Harris 1987). The college sought to provide a unique environment where students and faculty lived, worked (several hours each day), and cooperatively studied together. Its radical approach to education attracted unorthodox students and faculty from across the United States and from Europe. In its twenty-four years of existence, Black Mountain brought renowned poets, artists, musicians, and other intellectuals including Josef and Anni Albers, John Cage, Buckminster Fuller, Charles Olson, Robert Creeley, Ben Shahn, Robert Duncan, (and anthropologists) Paul Leser and John Boman Adams (AAANB 1952:6(3)9).

An FBI informant—apparently a Black Mountain faculty member—provided the FBI with detailed information on Radin's views and activities at the college (WFO100-51471-9). Another Black Mountain FBI informant reported on Radin's performance and statements in the classroom. The FBI also collected records indicating Radin's professional views concerning the social construction of race, noting "in his classes on Anthropology [Radin] tended to ridicule the existing discriminations between the white and colored races, especially in the South[,] and expressed the opinion that such discrimination was undemocratic and should be abolished. Subject [Radin] admitted in informant's presence that he was a member of the Communist Party and it was informant's opinion that subject had probably been active in Communist Party functions in New York City prior to subject's residence at Black Mountain, N.C." (WFO100-51471-9:2).

One weekend in 1944 two female students from Black Mountain were arrested in Knoxville, Tennessee, on charges of prostitution after associating with several black residents of Knoxville. At a faculty meeting discussing the disciplinary action to be taken to punish these students, an informant reported that Radin defended the two coeds by stating that they "were victims of a bad class-conscious society"; The FBI reported that Radin's contract was not continued at Black Mountain as a result of his statements in defense of these students' actions.[4]

The FBI also noted Radin's statements in a lawsuit involving racial discrimination in which he "testified as expert witness on 1/26/45 for a negro in a case (Coleman v. Stewart) involving exclusion of [the] negro from a neighborhood on basis of a restrictive covenant running with the real estate. Radin is reported to have said that racial discrimination will not end in this country until economic and political changes occurred similar to those which took place in the Soviet Union" (WFO100-51471-11). The FBI recorded that Radin protested to the *People's World* after being misquoted in their write-up of his testimony in this trial.

During a visit to New York on January 13, 1944, the FBI tailed Radin as he had breakfast at a diner and met with various individuals for what the FBI interpreted as prearranged meetings. The FBI confirmed Radin's identity by the name on a "low three-figures" check a friend of his cashed at the Fiduciary Trust Company during the time of this surveillance. The check was drawn on the account of the Liverwright Publishing Corporation (WFO100-51471-5). The FBI was so suspicious of Radin and his acquaintances that they opened an investigation of Radin's friend after she had allowed him to cash this check (WFO100-51471-5).

In 1945 the FBI consulted State Department records to see what information was available pertaining to Radin's 1937 trip to China. In June 1945 Attorney General Biddle requested copies of Paul Radin's tax returns for the years 1938 to 1942 (WFO100-51471-6) in an effort to determine if Radin had been in contact with an unidentified individual mentioned by Radin in a conversation with an FBI informant. The FBI also investigated Radin's 1936 work for the WPA (WFO100-51471-7).

When the FBI contacted the Mellon Foundation for background information on Radin, it was recommended that agents speak with Fred Eggan or Robert Lowie (WFO100-51471-8). On July 5, 1945, Eggan provided the FBI with basic background information concerning Paul Radin's professional activities. When the FBI pressed for information on Radin's politics, Eggan said he did not believe him to be a Communist. Eggan further described Radin as loyal to the United States, adding that he was "of the opinion that his patriotism was qualified because of his international associations" (WFO100-51471-12). Eggan also told the FBI that he had seen Radin a half a year earlier and that Radin had told him that he was no longer teaching at any university but rather that his research was being financed by a patron from Pittsburgh, Pennsylvania. Eggan then said that Robert Lowie and another individual at Berkeley would know more about Radin.

In the months after interviewing Eggan, the FBI investigated the individual reportedly financing Radin's research. This individual is not identified in FBI records but is described as Radin's "sugar mama" (WFO100-51471-16) and as a woman of "considerable standing: living on an estate at Middleburg, Virginia" (WFO100-51471-19). Because of her social standing, the FBI decided not directly to interview her. It seems likely this patron was Mary Mellon, who resided on the Mellon estate in Middleburg (see Du Bois 1960:xv).

In March 1950 the San Francisco SAC sent FBI Director Hoover an updated summary of references made to Radin in the Communist press; a report of his presence at a Spanish refugee fundraising event; the results of a mail-watch investigation revealing Radin to be receiving Marxist literature; and a summary of his work at the California Labor School (WFO100-51471-28).

On January 5, 1951, Hoover sent a confidential four-page memo via special messenger to CIA Director of Central Intelligence Walter Bedell Smith with biographical and subversive information concerning Radin's status as a Communist security risk (WFO100-51471-29). The reasons for the CIA's interest in Radin at this point appear to be related to Radin's connection with Nathan Silvermaster.

Nathan Silvermaster ran a Soviet espionage network using American wartime governmental employees (known as the Silvermaster Group) to collect information of use to the Soviets during World War II (Weinstein and Vassiliev 1999:157–71). Although governmental investigations later determined that twenty-seven individuals had gathered intelligence for the Soviets under Silvermaster's direction, none of this group was ever indicted on espionage-related charges pertaining to these activities. The FBI suspected that Silvermaster was passing sensitive U.S. government documents to the Soviet Union through Earl Browder, Jacob Golos, and other party functionaries. Silvermaster ended his espionage in 1945, and by 1951 he and fellow Communist William Ludwig Ullman became "prosperous home builders on the New Jersey shore" (Weinstein and Vassiliev 1999:170), but the FBI investigated Silvermaster until the mid-1950s (see Silvermaster's FBI file, WFO65-56402).

It is not clear how Radin knew Silvermaster, but they may have met while Silvermaster was living in Berkeley in the 1920s and 1930s. In August 1951 the FBI determined that Radin had worked closely with Silvermaster in Communist Party matters and "was subsequent[ly] in contact with Silvermaster in Washington, D.C." (WFO101-786-158). The FBI also noted in a February 24, 1945, report that Radin stated in front of an FBI informant that he had seen a Washington, D.C., Treasury Department economist named "Greg." FBI agents believed "Greg" was Silvermaster, and they requested permission from Hoover to interview Radin concerning his contact with Silvermaster—noting that while Radin had been investigated over a long period of time he had never appeared on the Security Index and had not been the subject of investigation since 1946. Hoover instructed Cincinnati FBI agents to interview Radin about Silvermaster at his home in Gambier, Ohio, near Kenyon College (WFO100-51471 3/6/52). Four months later the Cincinnati SAC reported that Radin was no longer teaching at Kenyon College and had reportedly moved back to New York City. In December 1952 the FBI interviewed Kenyon College President Gordon Chalmers concerning Radin. Chalmers reported that Radin "left the University in good graces," and that the only problems he'd encountered with Radin related to Radin's complaints about the housing facilities. Chalmers said the college was pleased with Radin's performance and he knew of no reason to doubt his loyalty.

In February 1953 the FBI established that Radin was not living in New York but rather was traveling in Europe under a grant from the Bollinger Foundation (WFO100-51471-35). The following month the FBI determined that Radin's European address was listed as being in care of Thomas Cook and Sons, Lugano, Switzerland; however, this determination was likely more than just a cursory check because *another* Paul Radin was subpoenaed to appear before HUAC's Los Angeles hearings on March 12. This witness was Paul Benedict Radin, although almost half of his testimony was devoted to establishing that he was *not* Paul Radin the anthropologist; brother of Max; instructor at the California Labor School; member of the League of American Writers; contributor to *Science and Society*; and book reviewer for the *Western Worker* (U.S. Congress 1953c:965–66). The detailed persistence of this questioning indicates that HUAC (apparently with the illegal help of the FBI) was hot on the trail of Paul Radin the anthropologist, although his well-timed venture abroad prevented them from subpoenaing him.

An August 11, 1953, report from the Washington field office indicated that the FBI and State Department were undertaking a more aggressive investigation of Radin's ties to the Communist Party. The State Department instructed the American Consulate in Zurich to "take up and hold [Radin's] passport, and validate it only for return to [the] U.S. when travel arrangements [are] made" (WFO100-51471-34 5/8/53). The State Department advised that Radin "could be given the opportunity to execute an affidavit . . . covering past or present membership in the CP, and any other appropriate statement considered by [Radin] to be pertinent as to whether his case falls under . . . Passport Regulations limit[ing] [the] issuance of passports to persons supporting the Communist Movement" (WFO100-51471-34:2). When the Zurich consulate tried to notify Radin of this information with a registered letter, they learned he had left Switzerland for England. The consulate's letter was then forwarded to England, but there was no reply from Radin.

The following month the Cincinnati SAC reported that Radin was still abroad, but that he was expected soon to return to the United States. The Cincinnati bureau requested that FBI headquarters "place stops with the Collectors and Custom along the Atlantic Coast and with the Passport Division of the Department of State so that this office will be advised when the subject returns to this country" (WFO100-51471-40 9/8/53). However, Radin was in no hurry to return to the United States. The Bollinger Foundation advised the FBI on October 27, 1953, that Radin was not expected to return until approximately February 1954 (WFO100-51471-43).

On April 27, 1954, the Cincinnati SAC notified Hoover that Radin had made a phone call to inquire "as to what legal action would be taken if he (Radin) were to travel on the continent outside of Switzerland." Radin was informed that his passport would be taken and modified so that it was good only for return travel to the United States. Radin was reported as giving "no indication that he intended to return to the United States and/or give up his passport." The source of this information indicated he "would be surprised if Radin surrendered his passport to his office" (WFO100-51471-45). The passport and customs division placed Radin's pending alert on a "closed status" until they received reports that Radin would be returning to the United States.

On New Year's Eve 1956 the American embassy in Switzerland notified Hoover by teletype that Radin had come to the embassy to renew his passport and that they had renewed it for use until January 4, 1957. The FBI also learned that the Radins were scheduled to arrive in New York City on January 3 aboard the SS *United States*, and that Radin indicated his plans to lecture at Brandeis and possibly Harvard, Columbia, and Princeton—although it was noted that "his wife is opposed to that." The teletype also indicated that the "Passport Office will pick up Radin's passport upon his arrival in [the] U.S.," and it ended with the suggestion that New York FBI officials be present when Radin's bags were searched by customs officials (although the margin of the FBI's copy of the teletype bears a hand written "no" next to this scrawled suggestion) (WFO100-51471-48).

The Radins arrived in New York aboard the SS *United States* on January 3, 1957. They informed customs officials that they would be staying in New York at 272 Third Avenue, with no immediate plans to live anywhere else. A search of Radin's bags found "large amounts of books and papers concerning the study of American Indians." Radin told customs officials that he was "in semi-retirement and that his wife suffered a heart attack while in Europe and was not in good health" (WFO100-51471-51). Then after the Radins had cleared customs, the FBI or other intelligence agents followed them. The report notes that "subject and wife [were] met at pier by two middle aged women. Subject and wife accompanied by one of these women proceeded by taxi to 272 Third Ave, NYC where they entered with luggage (WFO100-51471-51). The "middle-aged" woman who met the Radins but did not live at 272 Third Avenue was identified by the FBI as having been a member of the Communist Party in 1944–1945, and as having been the national vice president of the American Association of Scientific Workers in 1954 (WFO100-51471-51).

Inquiries by the FBI at Columbia, Harvard, and Princeton did not reveal any plans for Radin to be hired as a lecturer in the foreseeable future (WFO100-51471-52, 53), although sources at Brandeis confirmed that he was to teach two classes beginning in February (WFO100-51471-55). The final pages of his FBI file show the Washington and Cincinnati bureaus informing the Boston bureau of their past interest in Radin. In 1957 Radin was appointed Samuel Rubin Professor at Brandeis as well as the chair of the Department of Anthropology. He died less than two years later on February 21, 1959 (Diamond 1960), having successfully avoided the worst of McCarthyism in part by prolonging his European travels.

Murray Wax: The Blacklist and the Freedom of Inquiry

In the late 1930s high school student Murray Wax joined the Revolutionary Socialist Party after being recruited by his sister's boyfriend, Abraham Kaplan. Wax was captivated by Kaplan's intellect and creativity, which he described as having "opened enchanting scholarly vistas" (Wax n.d.:4). Kaplan traveled in a circle of important intellectuals (including Saul Bellow, Bertrand Russell, Ithiel de Sola Poole, Rudolph Carnap, and Margaret Graham) who were part of a Chicago circle Wax described as "anti-Stalinist leftists, sympathetic to the Trotskyite cause, but only a few were politically active" (4).

In 1939 Wax entered the University of Chicago as a freshman math major, where he was under "great pressure" to maintain an A average in order to retain his scholarship. He recalls that "most of my fellow students were as radical as I, but diversely so, and few had read as much Bolshevik rhetoric. For a time, I followed the Leninist-Trotskyite political line that WW-II was a war of capitalist-imperialists, but my core identity was Jewish, and Hitler had targeted us as the supreme enemy" (Wax n.d.:5). After receiving his B.S. from Chicago in 1942, Wax turned down a job in a secretive "Metallurgy Laboratory" located at the University of Chicago, which later turned out to be the University of Chicago's contribution to the Manhattan Project. He instead worked for the Naval Research Laboratory (Wax n.d.:6). Wax joined the radical Zionist student organization Avukah, which brought him into contact with a great number of New York radicals (see Barsky 1997; WFO100-334514-

105; WFO100-362996; WFO101-786-351). During the war, Wax did not remain
actively involved in Avukah, but he did attend a meeting in upstate New
York after being "urgently solicited" by members he knew and respected.
Later Wax "discovered [that] a strong faction within Avukah was a political-
intellectual group . . . [centered on] Zellig Harris, an anthropological linguist
on the faculty of the University of Pennsylvania" (Wax n.d.:6). Harris was
interested in Wax's politics and impressed by his mathematical background,
and he made arrangements for Wax to leave the Naval Research Laboratory
to come work for him at the wartime Army Standardized Training Program.
Wax characterizes this move as undertaken primarily so that he could assist
Harris in political matters, but as Wax tried to balance his assignments dealing with Japanese, linguistics, Marxism, and anthropology, Harris grew increasingly dissatisfied with his relationship with Wax. When intelligence officers contacted Harris as part of Wax's security background check after he'd
declined to work on the Enigma project, Harris became "further displeased"
and he and Wax parted ways (Wax n.d. 6; cf. Bernard and Burns 1988).

After the war Wax taught philosophy at the University of Pennsylvania
and at Temple University, where he worked under Barrows Dunham. He
then taught in the social science program at the University of Chicago. One
of his fellow instructors there was anthropologist Rosalie A. Hankey, whom
he married in 1949. Both Murray and Rosalie Wax intended to earn doctorates in anthropology, but when the university announced its new "antinepotism" rule forbidding spouses to teach in the same department, Murray left
his teaching position because Rosalie was further along in the pursuit of her
degree. He then decided to pursue a doctorate in sociology rather than anthropology to avoid the antinepotism issue.

As a graduate student at the University of Chicago, Wax was an officer
of "the politics club" (a loose collection of leftist students with a core of
Trotskyites) that brought radical speakers to campus. In summer 1953 Wax
attended a Young People's Socialist League (YPSL) camp in rural Wisconsin.
In retrospect, he recalls "the active presence at the YPSL camp of a man who
simply did not fit the typical membership profile. In retrospect, [the camp]
might well have been infiltrated as an informer by the FBI" (Wax n.d.:9).
While the actual years of the camp differ from Wax's memory, there certainly
were FBI informants at the camp. In 1949 an informant gave the FBI a program for the Socialist Youth League (SYL) summer camp in Genoa City, Wisconsin, which indicated that Murray Wax would hold classes on "Dialectical
Materialism and the Scientific Method" and "The Marxian Concept of Class"
(CG100-23546:2).

Chicago FBI agents also filed an April 27, 1953, security report on Murray

Wax's involvement with the SYL (WFO105-20371-3). Robert Vernon Anderson had testified before HUAC at which time he named on July 14, 1952, Murray Wax as the "head of the Socialist Youth League at the University of Chicago" (WFO 105-20371-3). The FBI also investigated the political activities of his wife Rosalie, recording her involvement with the University of Chicago's chapter of the SYL during 1952 (WFO100-344527-1:15). The FBI recorded that Rosalie Wax had presented a program at the University of Chicago SYL on "The Rise of Fascism in the Japanese-American Relocation Camps" (April 9, 1950); "The Decline of Fascism in the Japanese-American Relocation Camps" (April 16, 1950); and "Americans Betrayed" (CG100-23546:12 1/13/52).

Wax taught sociology at Chicago's junior college branch of the University of Illinois while writing his doctoral dissertation. When Wax's teaching contract was not renewed following the 1953–1954 academic year, Peter Klassen, the social science section head, told Wax that his work was not in keeping with the style preferred by the University of Illinois. But another member of the faculty privately approached Wax to tell him that his contract had been dropped because of his radical views. As Wax recalls:

> Since I had not deliberately preached any political dogma in any of my classes, and Navy Pier had minimal campus activities, I found this hard to believe. Privately, I continued to blame the incomplete dissertation, although neither Klassen nor his superior stressed this. McCall was outraged by a criticism implicating our relationship, and he resigned his post. He was of southern extraction, and a man of honor. It was true that I disagreed with his sociological predilections—he being a disciple of W. Lloyd Warner, and I of Everett C. Hughes, Robert Redfield, Herbert Blumer—but we had managed to work cooperatively together on the joint survey course, and our intellectual disagreement would scarcely have been visible to a non-sociologist. (Wax n.d.:1)

Although Wax's wife Rosalie was by then an assistant professor of anthropology at the University of Chicago, they had recently purchased a home and needed the second income. Thus Wax applied for other teaching positions in the region, and he was offered a job at Wright Junior College. A few weeks after receiving notification that he'd been hired, however, he received a phone call from the Chicago superintendent of schools asking him to come to a meeting in his office. In private, the superintendent informed Wax that the job offer had been withdrawn. He stated that FBI agents had learned of his appointment and had shown him Wax's "thick dossier," which convinced the superintendent to reconsider his hiring. As Wax describes, these events caught him completely off guard: "[I] was stunned and asked, 'what should I do?' . . . [the superintendent] responded: 'Go to the FBI and make a clean breast of it.' I knew that would have meant narrating not only my own history but informing on others, and I could not do this, so I went to the offices of the [ACLU] and discussed my situation with a staff member" (Wax n.d.:2). The ACLU chose not to take legal action, but instead produced a leaflet outlining the facts of Wax's termination. Wax continued to search for teaching positions at institutions he "hoped would ignore a visit from FBI agents," but his search was without success (Wax n.d.:2).

In lieu of teaching, Wax worked in the private sector on various commercial market research projects in Chicago. He used his sociological training to design and administer surveys while working as a junior analyst at the survey division of Science Research Associates, and later in a senior-level position at the Gillette Corporation. Wax believes that the FBI never contacted either of these employers, and he surmised "that they did not do so, because the head of personnel at Gillette's Toni Personnel Division was I. Martin Lieberman, whom I had encountered years before as a "fellow traveler" of the Trotsky-ite group on campus. Marty would surely have informed me of such events" (Wax n.d.:2). Apparently Wax was not viewed as a threat while employed as a free-market capitalist, but as a teacher he was seen as a threat in the classroom.

Once Wax completed his doctorate at Chicago, several events precipitated a decision to leave the area in search of work. Principle among these events was the fact that Rosalie was denied tenure at the University of Chicago, as well as the growing dissatisfaction at Gillette that Rosalie did not fit the corporate model of an executive hostess spouse. In 1959 Rosalie and Murray Wax took teaching positions at the University of Miami at Coral Gables, and three years later they accepted positions at Emory University. As Murray Wax was preparing to leave the University of Miami he mentioned to departmental chair Bryce Ryan his past problems with blacklisting in Chicago. Wax describes his shock when Ryan told him "that the FBI had indeed called on the Dean of the College, presumably on my hiring in 1959. They had shown him a dossier, and he had examined it closely, and then responded that none of the items were recent, but from quite some time ago and when I was quite young. Whereupon he had shown them the door. As I write this, I feel a regret that, on hearing this story, I had not gone to the Dean to acknowledge his integrity, which one might not have expected of an administrator at a third class university (popularly dismissed and derided as 'Suntan U'). It was this same dean who had insisted to Bryce Ryan that Rosalie be paid, not as a part-time, but in proportion to a full-time faculty member of her stature" (Wax n.d.:2). There are no known indications that the FBI contacted anyone at Emory and other institutions concerning Wax's past political connections, and as the 1950s faded into the 1960s the FBI's interest in Wax decreased despite his continued interest in Marxism (Wax 1997).

Bernard Mishkin: The FBI Examines Scraps of a Radical Past

Bernard Eisenstadt Mishkin was born in Crimea in 1913. His family immigrated to the United States the following year, and he became a U.S. citizen a dozen years later. Navy Intelligence documents indicate that Mishkin's leftist sympathies were deeply rooted: while still in high school he reportedly "circulated a petition in behalf of Sacco and Vanzetti and was described as having Communist tendencies during his high school and college days" (WFO100-154696-3 9/3/49).

Mishkin studied anthropology at Columbia in the 1930s, where he often clashed with departmental views of the role of psychological factors in determining cultural configurations. He argued with Lowie's psychological explanations of warfare (which downplayed economic explanations); clashed with Benedict over her lack of interest in the economic features of other societies; and he "locked horns with Mead while working for her Cooperation and Competition seminar" (McMillan 1986:70).

During World War II Mishkin served in the U.S. Navy and entered the U.S. Naval Reserve as a lieutenant (WFO100-154696-3 9/13/49). His enlistment in the navy reserves triggered an FBI background investigation, which uncovered past ties with "subversive" organizations (WFO100-154696-3 9/3/49).

A December 19, 1947, memorandum to the secretary of state—apparently based on information gathered from the U.S. embassy in Lima, Peru—reported that "BERNARD MISHKIN, U.S. citizen, representative of UNESCO in Amazon Valley, lately in Peru, [is] reported [by] several sources as Communist. [On] account of this and [his] reputation in Peru this Embassy recommends against U.S. approval of his further promotion [in] UNESCO" (WFO100-154696-2 12/19/47). Later FBI investigations determined that this memo was authored by Prentice William Cooper Jr., the ambassador to Peru from 1947 to 1948. On October 13, 1953, an FBI agent interviewed Cooper, who had no memory of the memo, and who neither remembered Mishkin nor recognized him from a photograph provided by the FBI. Former Ambassador Cooper reported that he always signed his name in full—never just Cooper—except in instances of cablegrams requiring just the last name of the ambassador. Cooper stated that "he obtained all his information regarding Communism from the FBI and he specifically recalls he received no information concerning Communist activities of American

Citizens from the CIA while he served as Ambassador" (WFO100-154696-11 10/17/53).

In 1949 an FBI informant reported that an individual named Hyman Mishkin had been a member of the Communist Party during the 1930s in Lancaster, Pennsylvania, while working on an undergraduate degree at Franklin and Marshall College (AL100-13899-5). The informant reported that Mishkin was a member of the Communist Party on the basis that "Mishkin frequently used terms such as 'Fascist', 'Fascism', 'Reactionaries', 'Reactionary Press,' 'Bourgeoisie', and 'Wall Street Capitalists', and that he had handed out handbills that were reportedly Communistic in nature" (AL100-13899-6). Franklin and Marshall College's custodian of student records told the FBI that the only Mishkin to have attended the college was Bernard Mishkin of the class of 1933.

In 1949 Mishkin published an article on American foreign policy in South America in the *Nation*, which clarified the range of his neoliberal political views. There could be no confusing Mishkin's 1949 moderate views with those of a radical or a member of the Communist Party. He argued that the United States should infuse capital into South America under what might be called a model of "progressive colonialism" that thematically prefigures the Modernization Theory á la Rostow—a moderate position quite at odds with the Communist Party position. Mishkin wrote that

> the exploitation of South America by North American interests is a plain fact. Yet in considering American imperialism, or for that matter the other imperialisms in the area, the complementary fact should be recognized—that South America is made for exploitation, gets a living from it, precarious though that living may be, and is unprepared for another kind of existence. The exclusion of foreign imperialism at this point would bring disaster. A low standard of living would be driven even lower. A disorganized inefficient economy would collapse completely and end the hope that it would one day be able to serve the needs of the local population. The beginnings of a healthy economic system must be visible to the naked eye before the costly benefits of American investment can be dispensed with and the colonial economy scrapped. (1949:513)

FBI agents interviewed Mishkin at his home in November 1945. The FBI was interested in Mishkin's associations during World War II with an individual described only as a "former employee of the Department of Interior" (AL100-13899-3). Prior to the war this person had lived in Puerto Rico, where he determined there was a need for a "cold setting glue" that could be used in the manufacture of plywood. When Mishkin left the navy at the war's end, he, the individual, and Abraham Brothman entered into a contractual agreement under which Brothman would develop an appropriate glue and Mishkin would search out sources of finance for the operation. In accordance with this contract, Mishkin was to receive a 10 percent commission on the business deals he negotiated.

Abraham Brothman was already well known to the FBI as a chemical engineer who used contact names such as "Constructor," "Kron," etc. while working with American Communist Party officials on various projects (Weinstein and Vassiliev 1999:176, 218; Quigley 1966:920–23). Brothman had come to the FBI's attention in 1945 when NKVD (People's Commissariat of Internal Affairs) defector Elizabeth Bentley revealed Brothman's connections to the Communist Party and to the NKVD. His name was later linked to Klaus Fuchs and Julius Rosenberg through a network of party couriers including Harry Gold.

Mishkin failed to locate financial backers in the United States during the winter of 1946–1947. He then went to London where he found funding, although he later lost these backers when Brothman did not produce blueprints for the operation as specified under their agreement. In frustration, Mishkin went to work for the Nesco Company in Amazonia. When Mishkin returned from South America in September 1947 and discovered Brothman had nullified their contact, he severed all contacts with Brothman and brought suit against him (AL100-13899-5).[5]

Mishkin told the FBI he believed his former business partner was a Communist (WFO100-385191-2), and in a 1953 affidavit accompanying his passport renewal application he stated that he was a loyal American, had served in the Armed forces during World War II, and was neither a Communist nor Communist sympathizer. He also stated, however, that while never having

> been a member of the Communist Party or the Communist Political Association I was a member of the Young Communist League from 1933 to 1937. The membership began in 1933 when I was a graduate student in psychology at Columbia University. I joined the Young Communist League because it seemed at the time to represent a vehicle for attaining greater political, economic and free democracy for American youth. It also seemed to provide an effective vehicle for fighting the then growing world-wide Fascist movement. Like any other American I was interested and continued to be interested in the extension of Democracy and the obliteration of Fascism. My membership in the Young Communist League was a disappointing experience. I found my ideas of freedom and democracy in conflict and at odds with the discipline and monolithic character of the Young Communist League. After a series of episodes

which were cumulatively disillusioning in their exposition of the world democratic philosophy of the Young Communist League, I began to loose interest in the organization in sight of two years after joining, that is by 1935. Between 1935 and 1937 I attended but four or five meetings at the utmost. I left the Young Communist League definitely, permanently, and irrevocably in 1937. (WFO100-2841-6 9/25/53)

These admissions did not lessen the FBI's suspicions of Mishkin; instead they determined that it was "advisable to check thoroughly on this matter on complaints of his loyalty, especially in view of his present activity on behalf of the Alpine Tours Inc., which according to [Mishkin], necessitates a large amount of foreign travel" (WFO100-154696 11/17/53). The bureau reexamined their records on Mishkin and then learned that in 1932 he had written a letter to the *Daily Worker* as a representative of the Young People's Socialist League, urging increased cooperation between the Socialist Party and the Communist Party in their common struggle against fascism. The FBI also determined that Mishkin had been a speaker at a 1934 "open membership meeting" of the CP (WFO100-154696 11/17/53).

Mishkin's February 19, 1934 letter to the *Daily Worker* was written in reaction to the riot that had broken out at Madison Square Garden the previous week after five thousand Communists stormed into a Workers Party rally. In the resulting melee, chairs were thrown from the balconies with jeers and heckles from both sides (Ottanelli 1991:56–58). Mishkin told the assembly at Madison Square Garden on February 20 that he'd "been suspended from the Young People's Socialist League for the letter he had recently written to the *Daily Worker*" (DW 2/29/34, 2/22/34). The FBI noted he had addressed the group as "comrades" and his speech "criticized the Young People's Socialist League in general" (WFO100-154696 11/17/53:2). The front page of the February 22 *Daily Worker* carried the complete text of Mishkin's address to meeting of the open membership of the Communist Party two nights earlier. Reportedly to "thunderous applause," Mishkin stated:

> Another comrade and I have just returned from the general membership meeting of the Young Peoples Socialist League held in the Rand School tonight. We who are members of the Y.P.S.L. and members of the Socialist Party were not allowed to attend. When we arrived there we were met by members of the Executive Committee of the Y.P.S.L. and told we were suspended. The other comrade, Mietenen, was not given any reasons for his suspension. When I asked why I was suspended they told me I had written a letter to the Daily Worker, that I criticized the Party in a non-party organ. I told them I did not criticize the Socialist Party but gave my own personal impression of what had happened at the Garden.

They told me that well, I had labeled Algernon Lee a liar. I told them that I did call Algernon Lee a liar but that was not criticism, that was clarification. (Laughter.)

Comrades, the leadership of the Socialist Party has inaugurated a wholesale series of expulsions trying to stifle all United Front feeling, but the workers of the Socialist Party are realizing that now the United Front is more necessary than ever. They will continue to fight for the United Front. The leadership of the Socialist Party will not stifle or stamp out that feeling. (Applause.)

One more word comrades. At the door here there were passed out some very curious documents obviously by members of the Y.P.S.L. It is unnecessary to say that this document is a huge lie. It is signed—"rank and file socialist workers." The point is this. That not only was this document manufactured by Socialist leaders but it had to be passed out by Y.P.S.L. leaders (Thunderous Applause). (DW 2/19/34)

In 1954 FBI Director Hoover asked the CIA for any available information on Mishkin (WFO100-154696-12 1/6/54). Hoover wrote that Prentice Cooper, former U.S. ambassador to Peru, suggested that an undisclosed individual, then employed by U.S. Steel in Venezuela, might be contacted by the CIA about the embassy's report on Mishkin. It should be noted, however, that the CIA's action in this matter was not released in response to my FOIA requests (Price to CIA 6/12/99).

On March 24, 1954, the New York SAC requested that FBI headquarters downgrade the Mishkin investigation to a "pending inactive status" (WFO100-154696 3/24/54). Three months later the New York office instead compiled a comprehensive summary of Mishkin's links to Socialist and Communist organizations, complete with new information gathered from interviews with individuals who'd known Mishkin since his student days in the 1930s. According to an FBI report, an unidentified fellow graduate student at Columbia stated that Mishkin was "an individual with a Bohemian-type personality . . . [as well as] a very excitable person who was inclined to be an extremist in all phases of living. ▆▆▆▆▆▆ [the fellow student] felt that Mishkin was the type of person who could not be disciplined or regimented within any type of activity. He added that in his opinion, a man like Bernard Mishkin would not be inclined to follow the tenets of Communism as he would not abide by the rules laid down by the Party. He stated that he would not hire Mishkin at ▆▆▆▆▆▆ for the above reasons, nor would he recommend him for a position involving the security of the United States" (WFO100-385191:3 6/10/54).

On August 23, 1954, the New York FBI office closed Mishkin's FBI file after learning from the State Department that he had died in Germany (WFO 100-154696; cf. Wagley 1955).

The FBI's Noninvestigation of Leslie A. White

Leslie A. White's youthful experiences in World War I, his reading of Marx, and his years in the Socialist Labor Party helped to shape his distinct view of cultural evolution and his highly deterministic view of culture (Peace 2004). But references to Marx, Engels, or De Leon are all but completely missing in his professional writings; instead he credits Lewis Henry Morgan as the basis of his neoevolutionary theories. Thanks to the scholarship of William Peace, we now know that White's evolutionary anthropology was in fact directly derivative of Marx and, more specifically, of Socialist Labor Party (SLP) leader and Morgan enthusiast Daniel De Leon (Peace 1993).

Peace established that White joined the SLP in 1931, and that under the pseudonym of "John Steel" he secretly published numerous articles in Socialist publications between 1931 and 1943 (Peace 1993; Peace to Price 10/26/02). White also regularly traveled outside of his hometown of Ann Arbor to Detroit and Flint to give street-corner soapbox speeches advocating Socialism. White's speeches critiquing American capitalism were radical, with the showmanship and speaking skills that had made him a legendary classroom lecturer (see Carneiro 1981). As Peace recounts, "the church was . . . in White's opinion, the largest 'industry' in the United States, with more assets and income than Ford Motor Co., General Electric, Standard Oil, Anaconda Copper Co., Bethlehem Steel Co., Reynolds Tobacco, American Can and Proctor and Gamble combined! In addition, White held, much of the church's income was received from the rich 'in return for its efforts to keep the working class in subjection.' White argued that the church was like the state because it too was based upon the ownership of private property" (Peace 1993:139). But although White published political writing under a pseudonym and occasionally spoke out at speakers' forums, he shied away from public activism and rallies. In one sense, White's lack of activism was consistent with his theoretical view of culture: to White, individuals were without the agency needed to effect change. In White's world individuals were "like a pilotless aircraft controlled from the ground by radio waves," and thus activism would have little significance unless it occurred in a cultural milieu where such broadcasts were being received by a large portion of the culture (White 1949:157). Marshall Sahlins remembered White's professional view of culture as consistent with his political philosophy: "Leslie White always used to say that 'a liberal was just a human neutron in the political process,' somebody who ineffectively wanted a change that was no change—not to mention White's opinion, of which this was hardly the only expression, that individual action countered for naught in an all-determining culture" (2000:23).

White held Marxist political views, yet the extent of his party involvement and his Socialist politics were unknown to the FBI until 1956. Indeed, had he not been listed as a reference on a job application of another anthropologist, he might never have come to the attention of the FBI at all. He was listed as a reference was on anthropologist John B. Cornell's (WFO123-15303) application for a position at the Voice of America in 1955. As a result of Cornell's background check, the FBI's central office in Washington, D.C., discovered that White had a number of ties to subversive organizations. The FBI's records indicate that White had been identified by HUAC as belonging in 1938 to the atheist organization Free Thinkers of America. The FBI then contacted an undisclosed individual from the University of Michigan who "made available the faculty file on Dr. Leslie A. White" (WFO123-15303-8). The FBI then noted that White "was a leader of an anthropological party to tour the Soviet Union for the Open Road [based in] New York during the Summer of 1929, also of an extensive tour of the Far East and Indonesia in 1926" (WFO123-15303-8). The FBI reported the Open Road was a travel agency that had been determined to be a "Communist Front Organization" in 1948 by the California Committee on Un-American Activities. White's other suspicious affiliations included being on the mailing list of the American Russian Institute for Cultural Relations with the Soviet Union, a group cited by HUAC as a Communist organization supported by intellectuals. The FBI's records indicate that White subscribed to the Socialist Labor Party's publication, the *Weekly People*, and that he signed a petition in support of free speech at the University of Michigan. The FBI report also contains an interview with a second informant who stated that White was a Communist, although he further "stated that he had no definite proof of this fact and that he could not recall any specific statements which Dr. White had made which would indicate that Dr. White was a Communist, but he still felt that Dr. White had Communistic tendencies. ▨▨▨▨▨▨ advised that White had visited Russia on about three occasions in the early 1920s and that thereafter he frequently mentioned Russia and praised its system up until several years ago when he ceased this sort of talk entirely. ▨▨▨▨▨▨ stated that both Dr. White and his ▨▨▨▨▨▨ were atheists and this added to his belief that White was Communistically inclined" (DEI23-1402).

Because of this statement agents recontacted another known FBI informant who had provided information about White in the past. The FBI asked the informant if he or she would testify or sign a statement concerning White's subversive views, but the informant declined to do either. A still partially classified FBI document listing informants who had been contacted indicates that the person in question did so because he or she was related to White: "███████ [in] Pennsylvania, was recontacted, May 19 1955 by [Special Agent] ███████ are refused to have ███████ identity revealed; refused to testify; and refused to furnish a signed statement because of ███████ family relationship with Dr. White per Pittsburgh" (WFO123-15303-8:10 5/19/55). The identity of this individual is unknown but it is possible that he or she could be one of White's in-laws, who lived in Elkland, Pennsylvania (see Peace 2004).

It is not clear why the FBI did not further investigate White. That the FBI knew White subscribed to the *Weekly People* was more than enough reason for further investigation. It is possible that the relative lateness of the FBI's discoveries of White's radical politics led them to a decision not to not launch a full-scale investigation. It was one year earlier on May 30, 1954, that the so-called Army-McCarthy hearings had signaled the end of McCarthy's public power and presence. Locally, HUAC had been active on the University of Michigan's campus from spring 1952 until the end of the 1954 academic year; thus, had White come to the FBI's attention as early as 1952, it seems likely that he would have been brought before the committee (see Selcraig 1982; Pintzuke 1997).[6]

White's lack of progressive activism helped him avoid a prolonged FBI investigation: for the most part he was not engaged in political skirmishes on campus and was not involved in fights for racial equality. His highly deterministic view of culture and his theoretical insistence that individuals were ineffective instruments to instigate cultural change certainly predisposed him to avoid the sort of activism that brought the focus of the FBI and the show trials on other anthropologists. White's Marxist leanings had more to do with the theoretical interpretations of culture than they did issues of social justice, and the FBI was less worried about theory than they were about practice.

Elman Rogers Service: Anti-Communist Socialist

Elman Service's writings on cultural evolution show the influence of Marx, Engels and Leslie White. However, unlike Leslie White or other neoevolutionists, Service concentrated on classical Marxist themes, such as stratification and conflict, in his writings on the evolution of the state, and in explaining the progressive development of societies Service developed an evolutionary Marxist approach focusing on the mode of production.

In 1943, Service first came to the FBI's attention after he was inducted in the U.S. Army and placed in the 410th Infantry Regiment stationed at Camp Claiborne, Louisiana. The Military Intelligence Division (MID) also began an extensive investigation of Service in June 1943 (WFO100-212233-2) after they learned that from 1939 to 1941 he had been a University of Michigan leader of the Young Communist League and the American Student Union; had lived at "the Socialist House" (335 Ann Street, Ann Arbor); and signed a petition in 1940 to "retain the Communist Party on the State Ticket" (WFO100-212233-4). After searching their records in August 1943 the State Department notified the FBI that it was unaware of any record of Service's reentry into the United States after fighting in the Spanish Civil War in 1938.

Elman Service was issued a passport in June 1937 for the purpose of taking a "pleasure trip" to England, France, Germany, and Sweden. On December 13, 1938, Service traveled to Spain to join the Spanish loyalists as they fought the fascists in the Spanish Civil War. When the State Department learned that Service had joined the Abraham Lincoln Brigade they placed a "Refusal Notice" in his State Department file, and when the FBI became aware of this fact in 1943 they opened a "Custodial Detention-C [Communist]" file on Service (WFO100-212233-1 6/25/43).

Service was wounded while fighting in Spain. Years later when the MID interviewed members of Service's army platoon, one former soldier reported that Service had told him "about having been wounded while fighting with the Loyalists; that he recuperated in a hospital on the Riviera, that he was in Spain for about two years; and, that only about thirty six of his original group returned to the United States" (WFO100-21223-2:17). Once back in the United States, Service traveled around New York and the Midwest raising money in support of the Spanish loyalists. During World War II, he explained that his motivation for joining the fight was because "he thought that Franco was a [dupe] placed in Spain, by Hitler; and, that he thought the Spanish Revolution was only the start of this present war" (WFO100-21223-2:17).

One of Service's acquaintances told the FBI that Service had returned from Spain a changed man. The FBI noted that "his former friends would no longer associate with him due to his very definite ideas concerning Communism, which he had apparently attained during his tenure in the ALB" (WFO100-212233-20). The FBI received reports that as a student at the University of Michigan Service had attended a May Day peace rally held in Felch Park, where he gave a speech encouraging students to "organize and try to keep us out of [the] war" (WFO100-21223-20:9).

Members of Service's World War II platoon reported a great deal of admiration and respect for Service, much of which apparently was derived from his status as the only member of the platoon to have ever engaged in combat. Service's platoon members told the MID that he had been forthright about his service in the Abraham Lincoln Brigade. Service's superior officer told the MID that "Service is one of the best soldiers in his unit, and that this opinion is shared by other officers and non-commissioned officers who knew Service" (WFO100-21223-2:12). Service was approached by his superior officer and encouraged to apply to officer candidates' school, although Service had declined by stating that he would "prefer to remain a non-commissioned officer until his unit had engaged in combat, whereupon, he intended to apply for a direct commission" (WFO100-21223-2:12).

The MID interviewed a former college acquaintance also stationed at Camp Claiborne (WFO100-21223-2:14), along with his barrack mates and platoon sergeant (WFO100-21223-2:15), former professors, fellow anthropologists, and former neighbors and landlords. A composite picture of Service as a well-respected, hard-working individual emerges from these interviews. Throughout this investigation MID tracked and read Service's mail in an attempt to gather information on his loyalty and possible involvement in subversive organizations. In August 1943 one of Service's former neighbors reported that she had recently met a distant relative of Service at a "bridge party" who "mentioned something about [Service] being very much interested in Communist activities around the school" (WFO100-21223-2:76).

The FBI's investigation at the University of Michigan located two newspaper clippings relating to Service in the files of the campus alumni office; one (erroneously) reported his death while fighting with the Abraham Lincoln Brigade and the other reported his return to the United States after fighting in the Spanish Civil War (WFO100-212233-4). The FBI's investigation found nothing to disqualify Service from serving in the army, and he served with distinction. A few years after the war's end, however, he was again investigated when FBI Director Hoover notified the Detroit SAC that they should consider placing Service on the Security Index (WFO100-212233-8 10/22/48).[7]

In 1950 and again in 1954 the FBI reinvestigated Service's political activities, although these investigations mostly rehashed the first University of Michigan and FBI documents and reports. The 1954 investigation added a summary of Service's 1941 divorce from Alice Evelyn Reese, after two years of marriage (WFO100-212233-20). On November 16, 1954, the FBI interviewed Service and reported that he

> demonstrated a most co-operative attitude and indicated that he was most willing to discuss his past life and connections with "left-wing" groups.
>
> The information provided by the Subject agreed in the most part with that reflected in the Detroit files. He did, in fact, relate a rather thorough account of his progress in pro-Communist organizations and supplied the reporting Agents with some detailed background on these organizations. His answers and discussion, in the opinion of the interviewing Agents, were most forthright and to the point.

It was obvious that the Subject has changed his viewpoint concerning the organizations with which he was once affiliated although it was equally obvious that he was not ashamed of having had those affiliations. The Subject demonstrated an awareness of present day political issues and appeared to be well versed on political arguments. Many of his arguments could be misinterpreted, possibly explaining why some people continue to characterize him as pro-Communist. It was obvious from his statements and answers he gave to questions put to him by the Agents, that the Subject no longer holds sympathy for the Communist Party or any of its members. For this reason it is felt that the Subject does not presently pose a threat to the security of the U.S. and he is, therefore, not being recommended for the Security Index.

While the Subject named other individuals who were involved in the "left wing" movement with him, he declined to serve as a witness in the prosecution of any of the individuals he named because of the Subject's employment by a State university.

It appears evident that he would not wish to become involved with any subversive group and therefore would not prove suitable material as a potential informant.

The Subject advised that he is always available for contact by the Bureau should we wish to discuss further the individuals or activities in which he was engaged prior to 1942. (WFO100-212233 12/9/54)

Service explained to the FBI that when he first came to the University of Michigan in 1935 he was "fresh from the farm" and that he had never been "outside his home community." Service said he had been quite impressionable, and

in his eagerness to meet people and demonstrate his intellect he joined what was then called the University of Michigan Chapter of the National Student League. It was in this organization that he met and became influenced by individuals of the "popular front group". He further described these individuals, in retrospect, as Communists and pro-Communists. He did not recall just why it happened but the National Student League ceased to exist in the campus area in 1936.

Mr. Service stated he was a member of the Progressive Club. He described the membership as being the "liberal" or "left-wing" elements on the campus with definite pro-Communist sympathies. He stated that it was at this time that he began to realize the injustices that were present throughout the world and particularly this country. He stated things like racial intolerances, poverty and unemployment were ills which he desired to alleviate and it was his opinion this "left wing" or "liberal" faction had the answer. . . .

He stated he joined the YCL [Young Communist League] a few months prior to leaving Ann Arbor for Spain. He mentioned the names of individuals active in these groups but could not recall who it was that recruited him into the YCL. . . .

[Service] stated he was recruited into the International Brigade, destined to fight in the Spanish Civil War, by three individuals whom he named. He stated that it was a misnomer to refer to this group as the Abraham Lincoln Brigade. He says that the proper designation would be the Lincoln or Washington Brigade of the International Brigade.

[Service] stated that he does not recall what the circumstances were that resulted in his finally signing up with the International Brigade but he did recall that some individual came from Detroit and told the recruits where to go, who to see, etcetera. He stated he went to New York City in June 1937 and met with other volunteers there and then sailed for Spain. He stated he was assigned to the Fifteenth International Brigade which consisted of the Lincoln and Washington Brigades. He stated further that because of heavy losses within the Lincoln and Washington Brigades they were eventually combined into one battalion called the Lincoln Brigade. He stated he received three weeks [of] training and then was sent to the front.

Service stated that while only a small portion of the Brigade was composed of active CP members they did occupy most of the key positions. He was asked to join the CP after he had obtained the position of "cabol" or squad leader. He attended several CP meetings but stated he never became a member. He stated each battalion had what was called a "political commissar" and it was their job to orientate the volunteers regarding Communism. He added that at no time, however, was there any pressure applied to the volunteers to join the CP.

[Service] stated he was wounded and spent some time in the hospital in a small village in the outskirts of Barcelona, Spain. When he recovered he was returned to the front and drove an ambulance. He stated when the League of Nations offered to arbitrate the war, as a gesture of good faith, the Loyalist Army of Spain sent home what was left of the Brigade. [Service] stated he returned to his home in Tecumseh, Michigan, and then to the University of Michigan for further study. He stated that he continued his membership in the YCL and related the names of some of the other members during this time. He stated that he also became active in the American Student Union. . . .

[Service] stated that in November of 1942, he was inducted into the Army. [Service] stated that he has not been a member of any CP front group since that time. He stated that he realized that he has acquired the reputation of being a Communist or at least pro-Communist, but he states that this results from the fact that his ideas were new and because at times they parallel those of the CP.

The Subject stated that actually his actions in the "left wing" groups were precipitated by the events of the period within which they took place and that although at the present time he can see the fallacy of much of what he did, he believes that he would have reacted in much the same way should he have it all to do over again. He stated that he currently holds nothing but contempt for the CP and its members, but he does not believe that the solution to their peril lies in outlawing them as a party. (WFO100-212233-21 12/9/54)

At the end of his FBI interview, Service gushed support for the FBI's efforts to persecute Communists. The FBI report states that Service "has a great deal of respect for the Federal Bureau of Investigation and the work that it does combating Communism. He feels that the Smith Act is a potent weapon against the [individual party members] but that even a more powerful weapon is the education of the average American concerning the fallacies or inconsistencies of the Communist philosophy. He states that he 'does not hold with certain politicians who are making political hay by using the Communist threat to their own advantage'" (WFO100-212233-21 12/9/54).

Service's mixture of pro-Socialist, anti-Communist conviction and his sycophantic praise for the FBI and the Smith Act form an odd mixture of sentiments. While Service's anti-Communism seems to have fueled some of his comments to the FBI, his own fears of talking to the bureau may have led to his strong statements. This tact seems to have helped to keep the FBI at bay as their interest in him waned: the only activity in Service's file after 1955 is a minor reexamination when he was issued a new passport in 1961.

Thinking about Those Left Unpersecuted

That a number of American Marxist anthropologists were known to the FBI yet were never brought before the public tribunals of McCarthyism raises interesting questions about the nature of the FBI's inquiries. The FBI's reactions to their investigations' findings varied, and it is difficult to find consistent patterns of response or to know why they pursued some individuals over others. It is likely that in some cases the immense bureaucracy of the bureau accounts for the lack of further actions. Because of the piecemeal way that records are released we can only glimpse fragments of records elucidating the FBI's decision-making process.

The failure to bring Paul Radin before any local or national public hearing is intriguing. The FBI monitored Radin's radical political associations for years and their interest in him intensified during the 1950s, yet their investigation of him remained in the background rather than foreground of his life, while other anthropologists such as Harris, Jacobs, and Weltfish were made to appear before committees. Why this was the case, is unclear. It was not that Radin was somehow less of an activist than, say, Jacobs or Weltfish. Indeed, Radin's publications on race and racism were forceful scientific and humanitarian arguments for the equality of all peoples. Perhaps the inevitable disorganization of such a widespread suppressive campaign kept Radin on the back burner, or perhaps other individuals around him were of greater interest to the FBI, or perhaps his travels to Europe allowed him to escape what might have been more severe and direct scrutiny by the FBI or HUAC. It is difficult to discern how much his Communist-linked associations and activism contributed to his shifting about, but his prolonged European sojourn seems to have been at least in part motivated by a desire to avoid the domestic manifestations of McCarthyism.

While Elman Service's status as a veteran of the Lincoln Brigade brought the FBI's scrutiny to bear when he enlisted in the army, his openly anti-Communist beliefs and his cooperative approach to the FBI seem to have shielded him from persecution during the 1950s. Perhaps Service's apparently helpful anti-Communist remarks to the FBI were motivated by the anti-Stalinist views reported to the FBI, but the cheerful, willing (yet in the end nonhelpful) demeanor was affected by Service perhaps in an effort to be rid of the bureau's scrutiny. But while many American Socialists were hardening their opposition to Stalin's Soviet regime, few were welcoming the reckless hunt for Communists by the FBI and Congress. Service's decision to offer praise and words of support to the FBI's efforts in the attack on academic freedom is disturbing.

The timing of the FBI's discovery of an individual's Marxist ties often determined whether or not they were dragged before public committee hearings. Had the FBI learned earlier on of the Marxist connections of Vera Rubin and Leslie White it seems possible that Rubin and White would have been called to appear before public loyalty or security hearings, although White's general lack of activism—indeed his apparent epistemological opposition to the idea of activism—and his hesitant position on absolute racial equality may have contributed to the FBI's decision to not publicly humiliate or investigate him further. Likewise, had anthropologists Archie Phinney or Roy Barton lived into the 1950s they would likely have been subpoenaed to appear before national loyalty or security committees because of their years spent in the Soviet Union.

Murray Wax's firsthand account of his experiences as a mid-century Marxist allows us a rare personal view of the impact on a career of FBI surveillance and meddling. We know that other episodes of blacklisting occurred but that most cases lack clear paper trails. Such repressive acts by authorities generally were quietly accomplished through such means as remarks over a drink at a conference, a quick phone call, or the usual byways of the old-boy network. If not for the parting comment of an administrator, Murray Wax might not have been able to state with certainty that the FBI had undertaken the operation to blacklist him from teaching. We simply do not know how common such FBI slander campaigns were during this period, although the work of Sigmund Diamond (1992) suggests that such campaigns were widespread, successful, and seldom acknowledged.

CHAPTER 11

Red Diaper Babies, Suspect Agnates,

Cognates, and Affines

You have read many fairy tales, some of them very
beautiful and some that frightened you with their horrible
giants and goblins. But, never, I am sure, have you read
lovely stories about real everyday things. You see poor
people suffering around you every day; some of you have
yourselves felt how hard it is to be poor . . . All of us who
work must learn that we can make the world a better place
for workers and their children to live in if we help one
another . . . We must join together, we workers of the
world, and stop these wrongs. — Ida Dailes, *Fairy Tales for
Workers' Children*.

During the 1940s and 1950s the FBI investigated
some anthropologists because of the political activism or affiliations of their spouses, parents, or
siblings. The FBI's interest in radical relatives not
only brought anthropologists into the periphery
of investigations but also occasionally such inquiries prompted prolonged FBI investigations of
the anthropologists themselves. In instances where

anthropologists applying for high-level federal positions were discovered to have "subversive" relatives, this situation could seriously endanger their careers.[1]

Such free-roaming investigations of suspect relatives were common. When John Provinse joined the State Department in 1951, the FBI's background investigation focused on his wife Helen's activities in various progressive organizations in Washington, D.C. (WFO116-38798). The FBI had first monitored Helen Provinse after Maryland Governor Stassen received an anonymous letter reporting that Helen Provinse regularly read the *Daily Worker*. This investigation later complicated John Provinse's career advancement efforts as the State Department fretted over any suggestion that an employee might be married to someone reading a Communist publication (WFO128-2077-21). The FBI displayed similar concerns when Felix Keesing's wife Marie published a letter to the editor in the *San Francisco Chronicle* (9/23/46) supporting Henry Wallace's conciliatory views toward the Soviet Union (WFO121-23114-7 7/19/50).

The Army and FBI regarded Abe Halpern's decision to marry Japanese American Mary Fujii as grounds for suspicion and scrutiny. In a report dated June 30, 1948, the director of extensions and professor of education at George Washington University "stated he was under the impression that [Mary] was not Americanized to the extent that she should be" (WFO121-9532-2X4 6/30/48; cf. Eggan 1986). When Anthony Leeds applied to be an urban problems specialist at the Pan American Union in 1961 his mother's past membership in the Communist Party brought on a lengthy and intrusive FBI investigation (WFO138-3128; WFO138-4515). In another case, although Jules Henry described himself as a socialist it was his sister's involvement in radical political organizations that caused the FBI to investigate him (cf. WFO77-293871; WFO100-32678-55; Bernard and Burns 1988; Gould 1971). In these and other such instances the FBI seized on suggestions that family members had subversive tendencies to undertake or broaden investigations of anthropologists. The examples I offer below shed light on ways that the FBI monitored anthropologists' extended families.

Ruth Landes: Suspicious Academic from Radical Clan

Anthropologist Ruth Schlossberg Landes was the daughter of Socialist labor activist Joseph Schlossberg, a Russian native who came to the United States in 1888. As a clockmaker in New York City, he joined the Socialist Labor Party and participated in the 1890 clockmakers lockout strike, "the first Jewish labor strike of significance in the United States" (WFO77-11899-13:3). Later, Schlossberg edited Yiddish Socialist newspapers and studied political science at Columbia University. In 1914 he was elected general secretary of the Amalgamated Clothing Workers of America, with a membership of approximately one hundred thousand workers, and eventually was elected to the New York City Board of Higher Education. The FBI noted that Joseph Schlossberg was characterized as a radical in Elizabeth Dillings's muckraking books *Red Network* (1935) and *Roosevelt's Red Record* (1936), which were consulted by the FBI in its ongoing search for subversives. Schlossberg was arrested and briefly held by Canadian immigration authorities in 1919 when he tried to enter Canada with labor "literature of an inflammatory character" (WFO77-11899-13:4). He toured Europe at the end of World War I, writing about international labor conditions. At the time, "it was alleged that Schlossberg returned to this country following his foreign travel as an advance agent for Litvinoff and Reinstein, who in turn [were] agents for the Communist Lenin" (WFO77-11899-13:4). In the 1920s Schlossberg was active in organizations supporting Russia and American cooperation with Russia, as well as international labor organizations (WFO77-11899-13:5).

Ruth Landes was thus born into a household immersed in radical politics. In describing the formation of her personal outlook and academic background, she wrote that she was born and "lived in an environment highly charged with sociological interests. My father worked in a sweatshop and at 15 was active in the labor movement. He never spoke to me of high interests and prejudices; all that I knew came from intricate sources . . . I familiarized myself with the more prominent theories, social theories, descriptions of the individual order, with theories of political economy and the volumes on history, and I read fascinating books that dealt with Jewish legends, and literature and history and philosophy" (WFO77-1189-17:4 7/26/41). Landes received a B.A. in sociology from New York University at the age of twenty, followed by a master's degree in social work from Columbia University in 1929. After working as a caseworker for the Brooklyn Hebrew Orphan Asylum from 1929 to 1931, she returned to Columbia to study anthropology, where she earned a Ph.D. under Franz Boas and Ruth Benedict in 1937. Landes conducted fieldwork with Ojibwa, Santee Dakota, and Potawatomi between 1932 and 1936. She was a lecturer at the Rand School of Social Science (1936) and tutored philosophy at Brooklyn College (1937). As Robert McMillan notes, "Ruth Landes' interests were formed by the Harlem Renaissance, by a fascination with Black political leaders, poets and artists. (She was in the 'avant garde' as she later claimed, with her parents' encouragement, 'of those who had social relations with Negro peers')" (1986:61; see also Cole 2002).

In 1941 the FBI undertook a background check after Landes applied for an expert analyst position at the Justice Department, and when the FBI discovered her father was an outspoken socialist and labor activist the bureau intensified its investigation of her. It seems likely that had the FBI not uncovered her father's radical past they would not have investigated her to the depth they did.

B. E. Sackett, the New York SAC, expressed concerns to FBI Director Hoover that Landes had listed Franz Boas as a reference. Sackett wrote Hoover that

> Reference is made to the personal and confidential letters of this office to the Bureau April 11, 1940, et seq. regarding Dr. Franz Boas and to the teletype sent to the Bureau, this date, regarding Ruth Landes, Departmental Applicant, Expert Analyst. As indicated by this correspondence, Boas was the subject of considerable investigation by this office concerning his attacks on the Bureau and his communistic activity and membership.
>
> The Bureau's attention is called to the fact that the applicant gave Boas as a reference and that applicant studied and did research in his Department at Columbia University for approximately ten years. The extent and nature of this association will probably appear in the report of the Newark Office regarding its interview with Dr. Boas. (WFO77-11899-7)

A Marked Mentor

Agent Sackett's comments regarding Boas's attacks on the FBI refer to a campaign undertaken by the National Emergency Conference for Democratic Rights (NECDR), which was published in their *National Legislative Letter* on April 1, 1940.[2] Boas's FBI file indicates that the FBI was alerted to these anti-FBI statements when an unnamed informant wrote to FBI Director Hoover to notify the FBI of Boas and the NECDR's actions. The name of this informant's organization is obliterated by FOIA censors in the report, but the group's motto, "Vigilant Intelligence—Intelligent Vigilance," is legible at the bottom of the page (WFO62-12299-302). This informant enclosed a copy of a page from the April 1 *National Legislative Letter*, which showed the headline "The People of the U.S. vs. the FBI." The accompanying article highlighted half a dozen instances of the FBI abusing its power during the preceding two decades, including the FBI's infiltration of the U.S. labor movement, its illegal use of wiretaps, Felix Frankfurter's charge that the "legal murder" of Sacco and Vanzetti was part of a collusive effort between the district attorney and agents of the Department of Justice, and the examinations of the FBI, index of liberal and radical subversives (WFO77-11899-7). The article cites the sections of the U.S. Code that authorize the investigatory abilities of the FBI, and argues that the FBI engaged in illegal activities. The article then ends with a plea that concerned members write to President Roosevelt, Attorney General Jackson, and members of the U.S. Senate "asking for [a] full investigation of [the] FBI and public Destruction of [the FBI's] 'Blackmail' File" (WFO77-11899-7).

The piece in the *National Legislative Letter* was a scholarly but radical critique of the FBI's abuse of power. Hoover was concerned enough by the critique that on April 13 he sent a two-page letter via special messenger to Brigadier General Edwin M. Watson, secretary to President Roosevelt, informing him of Boas's complaint as well as the group's plans to meet with Roosevelt on April 15. In an effort to discredit Boas, Hoover wrote that "Professor Boas is not a member of the Communist Party, according to reports which I have received. He is over eighty years of age and is said to be paralyzed and seldom comes to his office. His name has been prominently linked with various organizations during the past several years. For instance, he has been a member of the American Committee for the Defense of Leon Trotsky . . . . [a list of eighteen other 'subversive organizations' follows]" (WFO61-7559-7564). There is no record of the response to Hoover by the office of the president.

Boas was a committed activist who lent his name to a large number of organizations fighting for social justice. While he suffered adverse consequences for taking antiracist, pacifist, and anti-imperialist stances throughout his life, he intensified these commitments during the final years of his life. As Susan Krook observes in her examination of Boas's FBI file, "from 1940 to 1942 alone, for instance, he wrote over 2800 letters, and interestingly enough, three-fourths of them pertained to what may be termed political and social issues" (1993:55; see also Boas's file, WFO100-153839).

The FBI used Landes's listing of Boas as a reference as a reason to gather more information on both of them. On June 6, 1941, the FBI interviewed Franz Boas at his home in Cliffside, New Jersey, concerning the reliability and character of Ruth Landes. The FBI described Boas (then a month away from his eighty-third birthday) as "a very old and feeble-minded person" (WFO77-11899-8). Boas spoke highly of Landes's research on social definitions of race in South America and of her work on the Potawatomi Indians, saying "he had always found her an energetic, loyal and trustworthy employee, and further that she had impressed him as a keen student, who had a good insight into social problems" (WFO77-11899-8; see also Krook 1989). Boas added that he did not have the impression that "she possessed any radical tendencies, or that she was in sympathy with a Communist or Fascist form of government" (WFO77-11899-8).

The FBI next interviewed one of Landes's former supervisors from Gunnar Myrdal's study examining social problems facing American Negroes, which was sponsored by the Carnegie Institute (Myrdal 1944). This supervisor told the FBI that she did not know Landes well enough to make any comments on her abilities, but then she freely told the FBI that "from her slight contact with Landes, she had gained the impression that she was Communistically inclined. When pressed for reasons why she had gained that impression, ███████████ stated that it was formed mainly from an observation of the applicant's dress and ideas. She could recall no statements or actions on the part of Landes, which might be a basis for such an impression" (WFO77-11899-8). No details were provided on how a "Communistically inclined" individual dresses, but this cavalier statement further encouraged the FBI to continue to investigate Landes. The former supervisor also recommended the FBI interview another individual at the University of North Carolina who had also worked on Myrdal's project.

Following this lead, the FBI interviewed an individual at the University of North Carolina whose identity is likely to be Guy Johnson.[3] Johnson's evaluation of Landes borders on slander; the report quotes him as saying that before coming to work on the Carnegie project, she had

> spent a year studying Negro Sociology. Her stay in Brazil was cut short by about three or four months by the Brazilian Government. [Johnson] did not know the exact facts as to why the government became involved, but he understood that they did not approve [of] the liberal ideology she was spreading in relation to the Negro problem.
>
> As far as her activities with the Carnegie Institute were concerned, [Johnson] advised she was very inaccurate in her work, and had the reputation of being rather morally loose. He also stated that she seemed to know the lunatic fringe of the most liberal, if not radical, set in New York.
>
> [Johnson] stated that he would not recommend her for a position with the department. (WFO77-11899-14 7/5/41)

It was fortunate for Landes that the FBI did not further pursue Johnson's comments regarding her exit from Brazil in 1939. Given the FBI's penchant for amplifying any information gathered relating to sex, her clearance would likely have been jeopardized had this been pursued further.

The events leading up to Landes's departure from Brazil were complicated, but in 1938–1939 she studied, with the assistance of Edison Carneiro, Brazilian homosexual-led "cults" known as *candomble*. George and Alice Park write that Landes's problems in Brazil were linked to the inherent difficulties of a female fieldworker attempting to study a topic such as male homosexuality in Brazil: "The field study became notorious in provincial, conservative circles and began to earn the two anthropologists open verbal abuse from the local military establishment. Landes found herself labeled 'communist' (by reason of ties with Columbia University), and at last the project succumbed to police espionage and provocative intervention. The team found refuge in Rio de Janeiro and with the advantage of influential friends there, broadened their work with a study of the macumba cults in this rather different region of Brazil. Then Boas and Benedict called Landes home for a research job with Gunnar Myrdal" (1989:210).

When Landes published her 1940 article "A Cult Matriarchate of Male Homosexuality" she found herself in the midst of a controversy that ended with her being "blacklisted in important sectors of the academic establishment" (Park and Park 1989:210; Landes 1940). Landes's article upset both Brazilian and American anthropologists, and it led Melville Herskovits and Artur Ramos to jointly write "a forty-odd page letter in 1939 to [Gunnar] Myrdal to the effect that his staff person had done research in Brazil by selling her sexual services to black informants" (Park and Park 1989:211). Myrdal showed the letter to Landes and expressed concern about the damage that would follow such accusations. His concerns were indeed well founded, because Landes found it increasingly difficult to secure academic employment after the attack by Herskovits and Ramos (Park and Park 1989:211).

The following summer an FBI agent interviewed an unidentified anthropologist at the Bureau of Ethnology who said he'd met Landes on several occasions and considered her to be "a capable person of pleasant temperament, but a bit aggressive," adding that he'd heard that people in Brazil did not like her "because of her aggressive attitude" (WFO77-11899-15 7/24/41). Such misogynistic comments are common in the FBI files of women anthropologists from this period. The FBI closed its employment background investigation of Landes on September 9, 1941, and she was hired as research director of the Office of the Coordinator for Inter-American Affairs.

On October 25, 1943, the New Orleans field office filed a Security Report on Landes and sent copies to Washington, New York, and Philadelphia. The FBI's suspicions were raised when Landes began gathering information on the Louisiana shrimping industry and the use of prisoners of war to harvest Louisiana sugar cane. She told police and shrimpers that she was on assignment for *Harper's Magazine* and the *Saturday Evening Post*, and that she was in Louisiana as a federal employee. Her interest in Louisiana's industry and her requests to interview POWs during wartime led the FBI to make inquiries at *Harper's* and at the *Saturday Evening Post* to confirm Landes's story (WFO100-241201-1).

The Louisiana State Department of Conservation indicated that Landes did not actually have much interest in the details of local industry. This employee reported that "from what he could understand she appeared to be merely interested in seeing the State of Louisiana and visiting its many industries without regard to research, and further she did not appear to possess the knowledge and experience which she claimed in connection with journalistic matters" (WFOI00-241201-2 12/11/43). On one trip to New Orleans a conservation department employee said "he had finally been able to force her to admit that she did not actually receive compensation from the *Harper's Magazine* or the *Saturday Evening Post*" (WFOI00-241201-2 12/11/43). These events increased the FBI's interest in Landes's activities in Louisiana, and they expanded their investigation. The *Saturday Evening Post* told the FBI that they had no record of a Ruth Landes ever having written for them, but suggested that she "might be attempting to gather information with the ultimate plan of selling an article to them" (WFOI00-241201-3 12/21/43). *Harper's* likewise indicated she had never been an employee.

The FBI finally closed its investigation of Landes on March 17, 1944, after determining that she was collecting ethnographic information for a book on the history of the Louisiana fishing and oyster industry. The FBI's concerns were allayed by the consistent reports that Landes "never asked for information on matters pertaining to the war effort or concerning military matters but that she always seemed to be interested only in the resources of the state as well as the people and customs of this particular section of the country" (WFOI00-241201-6:2). In December 1943 Landes published an article titled "Outside Looking In" in the *Louisiana Conservationist*, which gave an ethnographic view of Louisiana's bayou inhabitants (WFOI00-241201-6:3). While it is possible that Landes's unusual wartime behavior in Louisiana may have brought an FBI investigation regardless of her family's Marxist past, it is clear that the initial investigation of her would have progressed differently without such Marxist familial roots.

Harold Hickerson: Every Chip Has a Block

In 1923 Harold Hickerson was born in New York City to Ruth and George Harold Hickerson.[4] At the time of his birth both parents were active members of the Communist Party: his father was then the secretary of the party's X-Servicemen's League and a participant that year in the party's contributions to the Bonus March in Washington (WFOI00-354492). Later, his father ran for U.S. Congress as the Communist Party candidate in New York's 15th Congressional District.

Harold Hickerson enrolled at Columbia University before the war; after his military service he married Nancy Parrott and returned to Columbia on the GI bill, receiving his B.A. in 1947. Hickerson then moved to Indiana

University to earn an M.A. (1950) and Ph.D. (1954) under George Herzog. He first came to the FBI's attention on May 24, 1954, when the Indianapolis SAC informed FBI Director Hoover of communiqués from a confidential FBI informant living outside the United States containing information linking Hickerson with another member of the Communist Party of British Guiana (WFO100-411131-1:1). The FBI then examined Hickerson's academic records and determined that he was about a month away from receiving his doctorate in anthropology, which was based on research he conducted in British Guiana.

The FBI then decided to interview Hickerson's faculty advisor. While the identity of this "advisor" is unknown, it was likely anthropologist George Herzog, who was Hickerson's dissertation chair (Mark Mahoney to Price 8/9/00; see also BAAA 1951 5[3]:4). The FBI delayed the timing of this interview, however, waiting until after Harold Hickerson had been awarded his Ph.D. "in order that this interview . . . not prejudice his scholastic standing" (WFO100-411131 6/11/54).[5] In the interview, Hickerson's advisor stated that he had known Harold since about 1949. The FBI's report states that the advisor considered the Hickersons

> very liberal in their political theory but too engrossed in academic studies to be capable of serious political thought or action. He stated that since their return from a field trip to British Guiana, they have both spoken openly of friendship with "the known Communist leader" in British Guiana, whose name was unknown to ▆▆▆▆▆▆; both the subject and his wife treated this subject very lightly. ▆▆▆▆▆▆ further explained that he has never actually entered a serious political discussion with either the subject or his wife and, therefore, did not feel wholly competent to be able to judge the extent of their political ideologies. He gathered from his association with them over a period of years that their main interest in life is the study of anthropology and felt that they would not spare the time or effort away from their academic studies to indulge in any serious political act.
>
> ▆▆▆▆▆▆ stated that during his acquaintance, neither the subject or his wife has shown any indication by statements or action of any subversive tendencies. ▆▆▆▆▆▆ stated that although he felt incompetent to judge, it was his honest opinion that neither the subject or his wife constituted any security risk to the country. (1P100-10787:7)

It was during this 1954 investigation the FBI realized that Harold Hickerson's mother and father were known members of the Communist Party. New York bureau records indicated that Harold's mother, Ruth Hickerson, was listed in 1942 as a Russian-born member of the Eleventh Assembly District Club of the Communist Party, and had registered with the American Labor Party from 1943 to 1949 (WFO100-120271 8/10/54).

Earlier, in February 1952, the FBI had interviewed Ruth Hickerson at her home, and while she admitted her past membership in the Communist Party she refused to discuss either any of the party members she had known or any of the political activities of her former husband (Harold's father) George Hickerson. A confidential FBI informant previously provided information that Ruth Hickerson had worked for the Intourist, a Soviet travel bureau, in the 1930s. This same informant also claimed to have been "intimate" with her during this period, and stated that she had introduced him to a number of high-party functionaries, including Whittaker Chambers in 1931. The informant claimed that Chambers was Ruth's protégé (WFO100-120271 8/10/54). Ruth Hickerson later admitted to the FBI also that she had been employed by Amtorg (the exclusive buying and selling agent of the USSR), but denied ever meeting Whittaker Chambers or being "connected with an 'inner circle' at Amtorg" (WFO100-120271). The FBI learned that the American Legion's files indicated George Hickerson had been a party member in the 1930s, and had been elected president of the New York City James Connolly Branch of the Communist Party in 1946 (NYI00-120271:3; see also George Hickerson's file, WFO100-354492).

In late 1954 an FBI informant reported that while in British Guiana (between December 17, 1951 and March 15, 1952) Harold Hickerson had "[expressed] admiration and support for Dr. Cheddi Jagan, chairman of the People's Progressive Party in British Guiana" (1PI00-10788:2). According to one FBI informant, Hickerson "allegedly stated that the masses of British Guiana were struggling under a Capitalist dictatorship, and the only remedy was the return of Dr. Jagan and his party to power" (1PI00-10788:4). Hickerson was reportedly seen parading with Mrs. Jagan outside the Georgetown, British Guiana, council chamber in protest of a censorship bill that was being debated by the legislature. Hickerson was later seen at "People's Progressive Party Headquarters with what was described as a piece of alleged radio apparatus which was described as being similar to a portable transmitter. [Hickerson] carried a microphone" (1PI00-10788:4).

In February 1955 the Indianapolis FBI field office received permission from FBI Director Hoover to interview both Harold and Nancy Hickerson in order to "better formulate an idea as to the extent of [their] activities and associations with the Communist Party" (1PI00-10788 2/11/55). In this interview Nancy gave the FBI little information, telling them that she spoke with Mrs. Cheddi Jagan on half a dozen occasions and that she was aware of rumors concerning her husband's politics, but she did not know anything about this firsthand. She stated that "British Guiana was a very depressed country but [she] believed that it would be impossible for this country to try to either break [with] the British Empire or overthrow the current government by force" (IPI00-10788 5/4/55), and, finally, she told the FBI that she had never belonged to the Communist Party and could not identify any party members.

The FBI interviewed Harold Hickerson on the same day but gained little information. Hickerson told the FBI that an acquaintance he had made while sailing to British Guiana suggested that he and his wife meet Dr. and Mrs. Jagan once they arrived in Georgetown. They visited with Mrs. Jagan on several occasions, and after some time they met Mr. Jagan. Hickerson reported that he had never been a member of the Communist Party but that he had belonged to two Communist Party front organizations while an undergraduate at Columbia University. He reported he could not be sure about the names of these organizations, but he believed they were the American Students Union and Labor Youth League. He explained that he "joined these organizations because he thought [they] would enhance his social life" (IPI00-107787 5/4/55). Finally, he told the FBI that he "had no certain personal knowledge" of the identity of Communist Party members in either Indiana or New York, and he was not prepared to speculate on the possible party affiliations of any individuals he believed may have been affiliated with the party. The FBI decided to not list Harold Hickerson in the Security Index "because there is no indication of any membership or participation in the activities of a basic revolutionary organization within the past five years or membership or participation in any front organization within the past three years" (IPI00-107787 5/4/55).

Hickerson later taught at Arizona State, the University of Buffalo, and Simon Fraser University, and he conducted fieldwork in British Guiana and among the Chippewa Ojibway (Hickerson 1962, 1988). For nearly a decade (1954 to 1963) he conducted research for the Indian Claims Commission as part of Indiana University's Great Lakes–Ohio Valley Research Project (Hickerson 1967). In 1974 Hickerson was in an accident that left him hospitalized for the dozen years prior to his death in 1987.[6]

Red Redolence Redux

For a number of Marxist anthropologists like Ruth Landes and Harold Hickerson, a Marxist orientation was a natural outgrowth of an upbringing in a household where radical politics were part of the fabric of home life, and that they should adopt a Marxist approach is a logical extension of the enculturation process. But the FBI's interest in these individuals had other outcomes. It seems possible that Hickerson's knowledge of the FBI's investigation of him and his parents could have tempted him to engage in some level of self-censorship or to be cautious in becoming overtly involved in various political causes.

The FBI's files swelled in the 1950s as they expanded their listings of possible Communists, and building red family trees was a convenient way to enlarge their list of suspicious citizens. There were also bureaucratic rewards for agents capable of adding to Hoover's Security Index, his subversive master list. Agents who added names to the FBI's Communist and Security Indexes were seen as productive team players, and the vague criteria for inclusion on these lists made it easy to add the names of those with friends and family previously identified as subversive. Thus the FBI's lists grew until the mid-1950s when half a million names were given on their combined Communist and Security Indexes (see Swearingen 1995:42).

For individuals with Socialist or Communist parents or siblings there must have been a sense of grave unease when contacted directly by the FBI. Being questioned by the state about parents' or siblings' loyalties and activities is a distasteful prospect, and doubly so in a climate where one's noncooperation denotes disloyalty. When the FBI questioned anthropologists like Harold Hickerson about his politics and his contacts in the field they sent a chilling warning to him declaring the FBI was watching anthropologists at home and abroad, and any deviance or even contact with subversives would be noted.

But the FBI's interests went far beyond the family members of known Communists; indeed, they were keenly interested in the public and private lives of liberal activists who had no connections to Marxist, Communist, or Socialist organizations. Anyone—even anthropologists like Margaret Mead who supported various military applications of anthropology—who was aligned with progressive views on racial equality and other issues of social justice was fair game for extensive and intrusive FBI investigations.

CHAPTER 12

Culture, Equality, Poverty, and Paranoia:

The FBI, Oscar Lewis, and Margaret Mead

The FBI's war against Americans who were not criminals but who did not measure up to Director Hoover's idea of an acceptable citizen, is a blot on our claim to be a free society. —Congressman Don Edwards

Another measure of the FBI's commitment to hounding progressive activists rather than just individuals with ties to Marxist organizations is the degree to which moderate, liberal anthropologists working in governmental services were consistent targets of FBI investigations. In the next chapters I describe how anthropologists Oscar Lewis, Philleo Nash, Vilhjalmur Stefansson, Margaret Mead, Cora Du Bois, Ashley Montagu, and others became subjects of FBI investigations—initially because of their work as federal employees or their participation in federal research projects but later it was their beliefs in racial equality or internationalism and their activism that sparked the FBI's intensive investigations. These prolonged FBI investigations included mail-monitoring programs, constant location and fieldwork monitoring and compiling massive dossiers. None of the anthropologists I address here were ever shown to belong to any Communist or Socialist political organizations, and their work is not associated with Marxist theoretical underpinnings. That these law-abiding citizens became targets of extensive and expensive FBI investigations reveals the narrow latitude of tolerance for diversity of thought mandated by the Cold War's national security state.

It is noteworthy that the FBI thought these liberals were Communists. These moderates worked within the political structures of their time, and the bureau's surveillance of them reveals the FBI's central role as America's mid-century secret political police force devoted to spying on and repressing citizens working for progressive change. Most of these anthropologists were moderate New Dealers (some were Republicans) who worked in governmental service during or after World War II. As cultural anthropologists they all held progressive views supporting racial and cultural equality, and some of them worked in governmental agencies where they promoted cultural or racial equality—actions that fueled the FBI's suspicions. The actions that brought these otherwise dissimilar anthropologists under prolonged FBI surveillance included a diverse assortment of "thought crimes" ranging from reading subversive materials, speaking out against imperialism, not fearing the Soviet Union, studying the culture of poverty, acknowledging Soviet advancements in aviation and arctic exploration, establishing private, desegregated schools, mingling socially with blacks, and working for the establishment of civil rights legislation. To the FBI's crude sensibilities the politics of these liberal messengers could not be disarticulated from the more radical messages of Communism, so these anthropologists were hounded and placed under surveillance with the same vigor and perseverance as Communists and Marxists.

Political Surveillance and the Dangers
of Studying the Culture of Poverty

Oscar Lewis was born as Yehezkiel Lefkowitz at Manhattan's Jewish Maternity Hospital on December 25, 1914; at the age of twenty-four he anglicized his name to Oscar Lewis. According to Susan Rigdon, his family later bought a small farm near Liberty, New York, and converted a portion of the farm into a hotel. Lewis was educated in a one-room schoolhouse, where he was a bright student who began high school at the age of twelve (1988:10).

As an adolescent Lewis learned the basic tenants of Marxism through his friendship with a Communist Party member who vacationed in Liberty and occasionally worked at the Lefkowitz's hotel (the Balfour) during the summer months. This party member "shared with Lewis an interest in music and chess, as well as politics, and provided stimulating companionship in a community where people were concerned with farming and the resort industry. With his friend's encouragement Lewis began reading Marx and Lenin" (10). Lewis's reading of Marxist literature had an impact on his later social-science orientations, although it did not lead him to become a Marxist or a member of any Socialist or Communist organizations. As Rigdon clarifies: "Throughout his life Lewis remained a socialist by orientation and outlook, but he was not a joiner and he had neither the intellectual makeup nor the particular kind of discipline (or subservience) that it takes to sustain dogma" (16). At the City College of New York in the early 1930s Lewis studied under Marxist historian Philip Foner, who helped strengthen Lewis's critical view of social structure and social movements and instilled in him a capacity to view social systems from the bottom up (see Foner 1947).

Lewis entered Columbia in 1936 and studied anthropology under Ruth Benedict. Like others, his work did not show a strong influence from the culture and personality work that was being championed by Benedict and other scholars at Columbia. In 1936 he worked for a WPA project studying the effects of the African diaspora in American culture. His doctoral dissertation, "The Effects of White Contact upon Blackfoot Culture," was completed in 1940, and after graduation he taught night school at Brooklyn College. In 1942 he worked for George Murdock at the Institute of Human Relations's Strategic Index for Latin America, and he studied Spanish at a government language program in Philadelphia. In 1943 he analyzed the political orientations of Latin American press reports at the Organization and Propaganda Analysis Section of the Department of Justice's Special War Policies Unit, and then transferred to the Department of Interior. But it was after an odd encounter with U.S. Customs officials while on assignment for the Department of Interior that the FBI first identified him as a "subversive."

1943 Border Stop Alerts Hoover

While making an official trip as a wartime representative of the National Indian Institute with his wife Ruth Maslow Lewis, whom he married in 1937, and son Gene, Oscar Lewis's car and bags were searched as he drove across the U.S./Mexico border at Laredo, Texas. U.S. Customs censorship examiners found materials they believed were in violation of the Hatch Act, and described the incident in a report to J. Edgar Hoover:

> On the afternoon of Oct. 11, 1943, traveler presented himself to Customs, at Laredo, having with him a box of books and letters. Upon noticing that the Customs Inspector picked up from the box, two booklets concerning Communism, he remarked that the books had been placed

in the box by mistake, and that he did not want the censors to see these books for he did not wish to have his name connected with them. Traveler apparently became very nervous and excited. Upon being advised that all books and written matter would be subject to examination, traveler stated he had decided to return the same to his U.S. address and might even cancel his trip to Mexico. After reluctantly giving his name, he gathered his material and left, returning the next morning with the same box of material from which, however[,] the two Communistic booklets had been removed. He then apologized for the discourteous manner in which he had acted the previous day. Traveler's luggage also contained, scattered among his belongings, considerable written matter; classical music was found in a lady's bag, and other music and papers were found on the car floor between the front and back seats. Traveler remarked while waiting on the examination of his papers, that he wished he had burned all that Communistic stuff and not brought it, "they might think I'm one of them." (WFO101-6392-2)

Fifty-six years later Ruth Maslow Lewis recalled the incident at the Laredo border crossing, although at the time she remembered thinking that the customs officials seemed particularly interested in the German sheet music that was found in the car—apparently because of the war between the United States and Germany: "Since the FBI did not confide in us or ask us questions I never heard anything about them finding Marxist literature in our car or correspondence with suspected communists. The only thing we were aware of is that they found German operatic music among our things and questioned Oscar about it. My husband sang and planned to take voice lessons in Mexico" (Ruth Maslow Lewis to Price 7/25/99). The next month the FBI contacted Lewis's superiors at the Department of Interior. Abe Fortas, acting secretary of interior (and future Supreme Court justice), wrote J. Edgar Hoover of the details of Lewis's "problems" at the Mexico border and requested that the FBI investigate Lewis, writing that "Mr. Lewis is being recalled from Mexico and will report to the Office of Indian Affairs, either at their headquarters office at Chicago or at the liaison office in Washington" (WFO101-6392-3). Fortas sent Hoover a copy of the Office of Censorship's report on the October 15 Customs intercept, but Oscar Lewis was not recalled from Mexico as Fortas had initially indicated to Hoover (WFO101-6392-3). On December 2, 1943, Michael W. Strauss informed J. Edgar Hoover that the Department of Interior had "decided not to recall Mr. Lewis from his assignment in Mexico at this time, but if in connection with your investigation you desire his presence in the States at any time, the Department will direct him to return immediately" (WFO101-6392-2).

A few weeks later, FBI headquarters issued a report on Lewis titled "Internal Security—Hatch Act" (WFO100-11712 1/1/44), which included an inventory of items of interest that the FBI had found in Lewis's possession during the Laredo border stop. These items included:

— A Photostatic reproduction of his birth certificate (special note is made of his parents' last name being LEFKOWITZ, "natives of Russia") [WFO100-11712-2]. [Lewis's parents were from a region of Poland that is now the Republic of Belarus (Rigdon to Price 8/18/99).]
— Correspondence from the Hebrew Sheltering and Immigrant Aid Society of America addressed to Mrs. Bertha Lefkowitz.
— Paperwork indicating that Oscar Lewis worked as an "Organizations Analyst" for the U.S. Department of Justice which described his duties as including the "analysis of Propaganda and Organizations" [WFO100-11712-3].
— A full-page ad from the *New York Times* dated February 24, 1943 which had been purchased by the Communist Party. This advertisement consisted of the entire text of General Secretary of CPUSA Earl Browder's Lincoln Day address entitled "Hitler's Secret Weapon." The report states that someone had typed "Please save" at the top of this advertisement.[1]
— Multiple letters addressed to Oscar Lewis, signed by someone named "Arthur" in which Arthur reported on his first "party meeting," and later signs another letter, "Yours for the revolution!" The letter signed by "Arthur" dated August 31, 1932, said in part: "we attended our first Party meeting last night and have been given a load of work to do." And "I hope you will carry on in other things, the important matters, so that you can acquire some experience by the time you get down here for the real hard work" [see WFO101-6392-59 2/25/65 for these excerpts].
— Later reports noted that Lewis had in his possession the book, *Falange*, by Alan Chase [1943] [WFO100-11712-66; cf. SAI01-36-4].

Given Lewis's work at the Organization and Propaganda Analysis Section of the Department of Justice's Special War Policies Unit, *Falange* would not be unusual reading. Lewis described the nature of his assignment at this time as working toward becoming "an expert on the Falangist movement" (see Rigdon 1988:19).

On August 24, 1944, an FBI agent interviewed Lewis in Washington, D.C. Lewis told the FBI he was not, nor had he ever been, a member of the Communist Party or Communist Political Association. He told the agent that the only "organization, other than unions" he belonged to was the American Anthropological Association, explaining that he was "not an organization man" (WFOIOI-2939-6). Lewis "volunteered" an official statement denying any affiliation with a radical political organization that might be in violation of Public Law 252, which prohibited federal employees from membership in organizations advocating the overthrow of the U.S. government.

After the FBI agent told him that the interview was over, Lewis asked if "this is a routine examination and why [am I] being subjected to this investigation, although I have no objection whatsoever?" The agent replied that "the Federal Bureau of Investigation has been furnished with some confidential information in the nature of possibly a complaint, which we are either required to prove or disprove and the purpose of this statement was in connection with that information" (WFOIOI-2939-6).

Two months later Abe Fortas reported that the FBI's investigation concluded that there was "no evidence contained in the reports which warrants the [Department of Interior] taking any administrative action against Mr. Lewis. We are therefore, closing the case on that basis and are enclosing a copy of a self-explanatory letter which we are sending to Mr. Lewis" (WFOIOI-6392-19).

For the next five years Oscar Lewis's FBI file preserves no record of the FBI showing any interest in his politics, work, or private life. It seems likely that the FBI may not have had any further interest in Lewis if George Murdock had not taken it on himself to write a personal letter to J. Edgar Hoover informing Hoover of his suspicions that Lewis was part of his theorized secret Communist cabal trying to take over the American Anthropological Association (see chapter 4).

A Second FBI Informer Letter in as Many Weeks

Just ten days after Murdock sent his informer letter to Hoover a letter from another scholar informing the FBI of suspicions that Lewis was a Communist was sent to FBI headquarters. In this letter Lewis as well as another individual were accused of engaging in subversive activities. The first portion of the letter complained that the other individual held "suspect" pro-Russian beliefs during World War II, which was followed by details of various suspicions concerning Oscar Lewis's left-leaning politics. The writer stated that he knew Lewis through his capacity as a fellow member of Washington University's faculty. Like Murdock, this informer expressed some concerns about writing to the FBI, but after some brief hand-wringing he moved on to report on Lewis, writing:

I knew Oscar Lewis only slightly, as a colleague, for one academic year, 1947–48. The following several items made me wonder about his pro-Communist sympathies.

 a. The most definite was a heated argument which took place ███████ ████ one evening in which both Lewises ████████████ staunchly defended Russian policy in dominating and controlling Eastern European countries in the name of "democracy." This was shortly after the Petkov trial and liquidation, which both Lewises ███████ strongly defended, half justifying it and half dismissing it. Their main thesis in defense of Russia was the so-called "dirty hands" argument: Our hands are dirty from the various political past of United States, how can we now say anything about the U.S.S.R.? The reference was, of course, to past events of U.S. imperialism, especially in the Caribbean. At the same time feeling that our own imperialistic activity was deplorable, they used it to insist that Russia must similarly protect herself by infiltration and control of her western neighbors. Doubtless many non-Communists think or have thought similarly, so this item re Lewis can only be considered in its proper context.

 b. On another occasion, following the official public censure of Soviet musicians, Shostakovich *et al.*, in the U.S.S.R. Lewis remarked casually that he thought he saw some justification for it. These musicians had not been writing music that was close to the people. That, of course, was the basis of official censure of them. This statement may be seen in the light of the fact that Lewis is a person of musical pretensions, has had operatic training, and presumes to have a good voice and musical taste.

 c. On another occasion he expressed ambivalence, though possibly through lack of information, re the "official" Russian ███████████ ████████████. This last year, before the present public attention the matter has been receiving. As an anthropologist he would have at least a certain familiarity with ████████████ as a discipline.[2]

I readily agree that these items by themselves do not add up to a great deal. I am, of course, relying upon your judgment and fuller information to interpret them correctly. I do not know whether Lewis is a Communist, pro-Communist, or what. I believe he has been acquainted with Communists in Cuba and Mexico where he has studied (as an anthropologist), but that, too, would scarcely be significant alone. I hope, however, that the foregoing may be of some use to you in your work. (WFO 101-6392 1/11/49)

The Springfield, Illinois, FBI field office produced a Security Report evaluating Lewis on February 28, 1949, which apparently was precipitated by the FBI's receipt of the two separate informant letters. The report consisted largely of summaries of the 1943 Laredo border incident along with information collected by the FBI during World War II background checks. The report also contained an interview with a female identified as being associated with Columbia University's Department of Anthropology, wherein she discusses Lewis and his participation in a 1939 ethnographic field research project she had supervised. Although FOIA censors withhold the identity of this individual, Ruth Benedict hired Lewis to conduct fieldwork on the Blackfoot Reservation research project she had organized and led during summer 1939. The interview report includes the information that Lewis had worked on the

> special research project ████████ for a period of five months, from June until October of 1939. She stated that this project was a study of the various Indian Reservations throughout the West. She described his [Lewis's] work as being excellent, showing a thorough knowledge of the Anthropology field. He is mentally alert and intellectually rates high. . . . She stated that the applicant is thoroughly patriotic, and has no reason to believe he possesses any radical tendencies. He is intensely interested in history and politics, but from the historical viewpoint, rather than an active association. She has heard him express his opinion concerning his feelings against the Fascists, and has also heard him speak highly of the Russian people, but not in such a way that would lead one to believe he is a Communist. She stated that she would not hesitate to employ him, if she could offer him a permanent job. She felt he was completely reliable and qualified to be employed by the government. (WFO101-6392-22-2)

Interviews with individuals associated with the Department of Anthropology at Brooklyn College during the war were also reproduced in the Springfield report. These interviews likewise reflected favorably on Lewis and his abilities.

Another confidential informant familiar with Lewis's anthropological work commented that "he felt sure [that] the applicant had no radical tendencies, and that he was absolutely loyal and patriotic, but, at the same time, he would question his employment in any field other than teaching" (S1100-7573-5). The reports of various neighbors contacted in Brooklyn and New Haven as part of his wartime background check were also included, and each gave a positive report on Lewis and his family.

The conclusion of the report identified two leads to be followed by the Springfield division. First, the Springfield office was instructed to use "regularly established informants and sources of information" at the University of

Illinois to gather more information on Lewis (SI100-7573-13). Second, the field unit was instructed to undertake and "report the results of a thirty-day mail cover placed on the subject's residence at Temporary Building F39, Stadium Terrace, Champaign, Illinois" (SI100-7573-13).

The FBI found little of interest in these investigations. One Security Report indicated that confidential informants "of known reliability, who are generally familiar with disloyal activities on the University of Illinois campus at Urbana, Illinois, advised they were not cognizant of any Communist activities of [Lewis]" (SI100-7573-1 5/4/50). The results of the FBI's mail-cover operation were also included in the report, although the dates of the report indicate the mail surveillance stretched far beyond the initially requested period of thirty days. Indeed, Lewis's mail was monitored from (at least) April 1949 until February 1950.[3]

After this flurry of interest in 1949 the FBI appears to be uninterested in Lewis for most of the 1950s. This record gap is puzzling for a number of reasons given the bureau's expanded interest throughout the early 1950s in identifying and monitoring the activities of suspected Communists. There are also indications that the FBI began several avenues of inquiry concerning Lewis that seem to be unresolved. For example, one memo from the Springfield SAC to Hoover requested that files from HUAC be consulted for information relating to Oscar Lewis (WFO101-6392-22 3/29/49). Five weeks later Hoover authorized the Springfield office to follow this line of investigation, but the results of the inquiry are unknown.

The Culture of Poverty and a Controversy in Mexico

While it is not known why the FBI did not more actively monitor Lewis during the 1950s, its renewed interest in him during the 1960s coincided with his rise in prominence as a popular anthropologist and visible social activist. With the publication of his widely read *Five Families: Mexican Case Studies in the Culture of Poverty* in 1959 and his popular *The Children of Sanchez: Autobiography of a Mexican Family* in 1961 he became an important spokesperson for issues of poverty and underdevelopment.

Although the concept of the "culture of poverty" was inconsistently applied in Lewis's work, the very notion that an underclass was in some way an endemic feature of mid-century America was a threatening proposition to the economic interests that Hoover's FBI served to protect.[4] The culture of poverty became an important catchphrase among academics, policy makers, and activists, although it meant different things to different people. Spokespersons from the American left—ranging from American socialist Michael Harrington to Daniel Patrick Moynihan—adopted and popularized the notion of a culture of poverty, incorporating it as a dimension of the programs of the Great Society (Moynihan 1968). For Lewis, studying poverty was not just an academic pursuit but rather part of a larger activist strategy to improve the lot of a large segment of humanity. As Susan Rigdon observes: "Lewis wanted to use his work to attack poverty. He thought his ethnographic realism would allow him to do this by conveying to the reading public graphic depictions of poverty, implicit in which, he seemed to suggest, would be messages about its causes and consequences, and perhaps about its solutions as well" (1988:63). It was this activist attack on poverty that brough Lewis again to the attention of the FBI.

After the Mexico City publication in 1964 of the Spanish translation of *The Children of Sánchez*, Lewis came under attack at the annual meeting of the Mexican Society of Geography and Statistics. The chief complaint was that Lewis used excessive vulgarities in the text, creating a negative impression of Mexico and its people (see Velasco 1965). Lewis and his press were censured by a vote of the society, and a suit was filed by the Mexican attorney general claiming that Lewis slandered the Mexican people and government— although these charges were dropped two months later (Beals 1969:12–15). Rumors circulated that Lewis had taped his informants using hidden microphones, or that he had invented the Sanchez family. Ironically, according to Ralph Beals, "more than once it was charged that Lewis had collected the data while serving as an FBI agent in Mexico. One letter charged that *The Children of Sánchez* was part of a plot of the wealthy of the world to discredit the Mexican Revolution; others charged that it attempted to show the incompetence of the Mexicans to govern themselves" (1969:12). Lewis's FBI file establishes the falsity of claims that Lewis worked for the FBI, and oddly enough in a violation of FBI policies J. Edgar Hoover publicly denied that Lewis was an FBI operative.[5]

A number of scholars complained that the books suffered from various deficiencies, including (as summarized by Lewis in a 1965 letter to Vera Rubin):

(1) The book was obscene beyond all limits of human decency;

(2) The Sánchez family did not exist. I made it up;

(3) The book was defamatory of Mexican institutions and of the Mexican way of life;

(4) The book was subversive and anti-revolutionary and violated Article 145 of the Mexican Constitution and was, therefore, punishable with a twenty-year jail sentence because it incited to social dissolution;

(5) The Fondo de Cultura Económica, the author, and the book were

all cited for action by the Geography and Statistics Society to the Mexican Attorney General's office; and

(6) Oscar Lewis was an FBI spy attempting to destroy Mexican institutions. (Rigdon 1988:289–90)

The FBI was interested in an article by Manuel Velasco published in 1965 in the Mexican bulletin *Foro Politico* claiming that *The Children of Sánchez* was "pornographic and progressive" (WFO101-6392-60). The FBI's translation division translated the article, and a summary report was prepared for Hoover. The report stated:

> The quotations by Mr. Manuel Larenos Velasco of the aforementioned book are extremely obscene and derogatory to the Mexican people and politics.
>
> Mr. Manuel Larenos Velasco indicates that the book is being used by the "progressives" (pro-communists) to support their argument against the existing social problems in Mexico. The "progressives" do this in an effort to show that a "blood revolution" is inevitable and imminent. Also Mr. Manuel Larenos Velasco says that the "progressives claim that the author, Mr. Oscar Lewis, is an agent of the FBI in an effort to give credence to their argument. In this manner, the proverbial "whipping boy" of the communists and pro-communists—the FBI—"serves for a kiss as well as a kick."
>
> Besides criticizing the author, Mr. Lewis; Mr. Manuel Larenos Velasco criticizes the Economic Cultural Fund of Mexico, which company published the book. Mr. Larenos Velasco says that it would be difficult to take an action against Mr. Lewis because he is not within Mexican legal jurisdiction. Mr. Manuel Larenos Velasco states, however, that something can be done with respect to the publisher, the Economic Cultural Fund. (WFO101-6392-60)

A December 1959 memo from the legal attaché at the American embassy in Mexico to Hoover records that the FBI monitored Lewis's presence, fieldwork, and movements in Mexico—a troubling finding for ethnographers past and present. The memo reported that "ticklers for an annual report and periodic residence and employment checks are being maintained in the Mexico City office" (MC100-1849-2), and the FBI thus tracked Lewis's movements in Mexico during summer 1960 (WFO101-6392-30).

A 1966 report from the San Juan SAC (SJ100-6666-D 12/13/66) discussed Lewis's efforts to convince the Mexican government to allow him to film a cinematic version of *The Children of Sánchez*. Lewis was in contact with Albert Maltz and other individuals described as being "more or less prominently associated with the American Communist Group in Mexico." The San Juan report concluded that the FBI should not interview Lewis because he was "known to be conceited, aggressive, and very argumentative. His manner and bearing are such that it is considered likely that any approach by a Bureau Agent for interview would be resented by subject as an invasion of his right of academic freedom. It is felt that such an approach would present a real possibility of embarrassment to the Bureau" (SJ100-6666-F). The FBI noted Lewis's travel to Cuba for the 1961 July 26 celebration, and reported that a University of Illinois associate identified him as "an outspoken exponent of the Castro regime" (SJ100-666-F). The FBI then listed Lewis on its Security Index as "Pro-Cuban."

Postrevolutionary Cuba: Lewis Monitored by
Socialist and Capitalist Secret Police

Lewis first visited Cuba in 1946 under State Department sponsorship as a visiting professor at the University of Havana. His research concentrated on the conditions found at the Melena del Sur sugar plantation, and he conducted a "reconnaissance survey of the lower-class slum settlements in Havana" (Rigdon 1988:275). Fifteen years later, following the CIA's botched Bay of Pigs invasion, Lewis returned to Cuba and located some of the individuals he had interviewed earlier in 1946. He also noted that Havana's slums looked fundamentally the same, but that there was a pervasive postrevolution spirit of optimism (Lewis et al. 1977).

In 1961 the FBI drafted a report titled "Alleged Communist Party Pro-Castro Activities at University of Illinois."[6] Released portions of this report indicate broad FBI surveillance of Lewis in Illinois. The report includes the comments of a University of Illinois informant who reported that

> the essential problem at the University of Illinois is alleged CP infiltration. He [the informant] made this statement on the basis of his own observation, plus conversations with ███████████. It is their joint interpretation that the pro-Castro demonstrations at the University of Illinois this spring were "a fully Party line job" with a high degree of prior preparation and organization. The group sponsoring these demonstrations, advertisement and fund-raising activities were very careful to give the impression that they were affiliated with no organization; that they were simply a group having mutual interest in fair play for Cuba, which was in no way connected with the Fair Play for Cuba Committee. Their disclaimers about lack of ties with the CP and Fair Play for Cuba Committee "are not credible." Direct evidence of their activities and the party

line nature of their activities and the "party line["] nature thereof is available in advertisements of theirs and articles which appeared on the campus and in the Champaign, Illinois newspaper, the "Courier" and the "News-Gazette." [The informant] stated he was informed that the group initiating the above activities had, for a year previous thereto, been maintaining a Marxist study group.

[The informant] related that he was referring to five people who were the initiators of the pro-Castro activity. Two of the group are townspeople and the other three are professors at the University of Illinois. [The informant] could not recall the names of the townspeople but identified the professors as OSCAR LEWIS, ▆▆▆▆▆▆ the later name being phonetic.

[The informant] stated another specific involved was the fact that OSCAR LEWIS, who worked in Mexico for long periods of time, stated in conversation he had had contact with "left wing Marxists in Mexico" and further, he shared good acquaintance with technical Party terminology. (WFO101-6392, with a stamp stating "not recorded" 6/29/61)

FBI censors inadvertently missed redacting the name of an informant, "Zellmer," in processing an August 18, 1961, memo from Mexico City to FBI Director Hoover. Zellmer reported Lewis's address while conducting research in Mexico in summer 1961: "On July 21, 1961, the American Embassy, Mexico City advised that subject had visited the Embassy on that date requesting authority for travel to Cuba for five or six days on an assignment for Harper's Magazine.[7] According to subject the magazine had asked him to do a piece on the July 26 celebration and he was also interested in updating a study he did in 1946 of communal life on a Cuban sugar plantation" (SI100-7573-3).

A November 21, 1961, Springfield, Illinois, FBI report filed as a "Security Matter-C[ommunist]" stated that Lewis said that "he visited Cuba for five days on an assignment for Harper's Magazine and while there learned that Cuba has been completely misrepresented in the United States. Subject asserted that the Cuban people are not being oppressed; that conditions there were excellent; that Castro is not a Communist, and that claims that Cuba is controlled by Communists are greatly exaggerated if not completely untrue. Statements to the contrary offered by his colleagues immediately evoke a response from subject in which he accuses the United States of ill faith, militarism, and as having provoked not only Cuba but the Soviet Union by threats both direct and implied" (SI100-7573-4 11/21/61; cf. WFO100-6392-59-3).

One FBI informer at the University of Illinois on November 16, 1961 remarked that Lewis was poorly disciplined and, in his judgment, would make a poor Marxist. He stated, however, that subject is capable of converting his views into action and, in this regard fulfills all the requirements of being a Leninist. [Informant] said that subject has "tremendous vanity" and, due to this fact, could be easily used. He advised that subject's current efforts are being directed to the achieving of peace between the United States and the Soviet Union. [Informant] reported that subject has taken the position that official statements relating to nuclear war, fallout and construction of fallout shelters have been made to incite fear. Subject insists that unilateral disarmament and cessation of nuclear testing is the only answer as the situation has become so hopeless that peace at any cost is the only answer. [Informant] related that subject's view[s] on Cuba and international peace are entirely in accordance with the current thinking of the Soviet Union but that he does not know subject to be a Communist or to be engaged in open subversive activities. [Informant] concluded, however, that his assessment of subject as a security risk is that he is "quite dangerous" from the standpoint that subject has an opportunity to influence the thinking of students with what [informant] considers false doctrines. (SI100-7573-4)

Another informant reported that Lewis "was among those at the University of Illinois who had engaged in pro-Castro demonstrations and [he] indicated a sympathy for the Cuban government" (WFO100-6392-59-3; cf. SI100-7573-4).

After FBI agents read an Urbana, Illinois, newspaper article indicating that Lewis would be going to Puerto Rico, an alert was forwarded to the SAC in Puerto Rico. The FBI monitored Lewis during his 1963 field research in Puerto Rico and even interviewed a research subject who had seen the questionnaire Lewis was using to collect information on Puerto Rican voting habits (SJ100-6666-5). Using this information, the FBI reconstructed their own list of interview questions used by Lewis in his research. A memo from the San Juan SAC to Hoover then requested permission to undertake another "mail cover" for Lewis. The envelopes of all mail sent to Lewis were inspected and the addresses and names of senders were recorded in order "to determine associates in Puerto Rico." The FBI believed Lewis associated with many members of the Communist Party, and there was a hope that "a mail cover would develop additional Communist contacts that [Lewis] might have in Puerto Rico" (WFO101-6392-52). The FBI continued to monitor Lewis's movements in Puerto Rico during 1964 (see WFO101-6392-54), and they transcribed and filed the complete text of a June 28, 1964, article on Lewis that appeared in the Champaign, Illinois, *Courier* concerning Lewis's research in Puerto Rico. The FBI noted that Ruth Maslow Lewis stated in the article that her husband planned to travel to England and Moscow later that summer, although he did not complete the planned trip to Russia [SJ100-666-2]. FBI agents frequently used false pretexts to call the Lewis's listed residences in Champaign, Puerto Rico, and New York City trying to establish the whereabouts of Lewis and his family.

In February 1968 Lewis briefly visited Cuba by invitation from a Cuban publishing house (Instituto del Librio) interested in publishing editions of his books. During this trip Lewis met with a number of university professors and party officials as well as President Fidel Castro. Over dinner with Rolando Rodriguez (head of the Instituto del Libro) and Dr. Rene Vallejo (Castro's friend and physician) at one of President Castro's rural homes, "Castro told Oscar he had read *The Children of Sánchez* and said it was a revolutionary book, 'worth more than 50,000 political pamphlets'" (Lewis et al. 1977:x). Castro suggested that Lewis do research in Cuba because "Cuba did not have the time or personnel for such a study and he was convinced Oscar would do an honest job" (Lewis et al 1977:ix).

Castro agreed to give Lewis complete freedom of investigation. He provided assurances that informants would not be penalized for expressing any views to Lewis and he guaranteed that Lewis could freely bring research materials and equipment in and out of Cuba. As Ruth Maslow Lewis later wrote, "why Castro was interested in having this research done in Cuba and agreed to the guarantees requested is a matter for speculation. We believed it was a genuine, if impulsive, gesture on his part, to show that his government had no fear of revealing internal problems, and that unlike other socialist countries, Cuba had a certain climate of free inquiry" (Lewis et al. 1977:xi).

An FBI document dated April 15, 1968 from Miami reported on a March 5, 1968, article from the Cuban daily *El Mundo* in which Lewis had "praised Cuba." Under the headline (translated as) "Cuba Praised by American Author," the text of the article by Enrique Gonzalea Manet was translated and reproduced in full. The article quotes:

> "From my experiences in Cuba, which I visited in 1947 [*sic*; should read 1946] and 1951, [*sic*; should read 1961] I am inclined to believe that the culture of poverty does not exist in Socialist countries," said the famous anthropologist and American writer, Oscar Lewis, whose work "The Sons of Sanchez," created a sensation in Mexico.
>
> Lewis gave a lecture on his latest work "Life" [*La Vida* (1966)] at the Casa de las Americas . . . He spoke of his experiences in the barrio of Las Yaguas in the pre- and post-revolutionary periods, stating the difference is that Marx, Engels and Castro and the Revolutionary Government feel

these people should be developed and brought into the process of social change. (WFO101-6392-70-1)

The FBI also mentioned an article that appeared the same week in the University of Illinois's campus newspaper, the *Daily Illini*, with comments made by Lewis at a public symposium on contemporary urban problems. The FBI report notes that Lewis

> reported that he had recently discovered that slums, which existed in Havana, Cuba, during his visits there in 1949 and 1961, have now disappeared. According to the above article, Lewis noticed this change while doing research for a study of family poverty in a socialist country. He observed that reports from Cuba relating vast changes in social and economic life have not received credibility in this country. Lewis reported that Havana has cleared slum areas and replaced substandard housing with public dwelling units. He offered this example as part of an argument for greater Federal spending on domestic issues. In this regard he was quoted as stating "When you spend $30 billion a year in Vietnam and only $1 billion on model cities, there seems to be a moral problem. (WFO101-6392-67; article dated 3/8/68)

Lewis submitted a proposal to the Ford Foundation in 1968 requesting $294,903 for a three-year ethnographic study of postrevolutionary Cuba. In a letter to Harry E. Wilhelm of the Ford Foundation Lewis described his recent meeting with Castro and Castro's invitation to undertake unrestricted research in Cuba:

> I was surprised and pleased to hear that [Castro] was thoroughly familiar with my book [*The Children of Sánchez*], which he had read in the Spanish version, and which we discussed at some length. He had his favorite characters and made astute comments on the reliability of the accounts of the various informants . . .
>
> When Fidel Castro invited me to undertake similar studies of poor families in Cuba, I explained in some detail the conditions that would have to be met for my work, namely, complete freedom of investigation, including my selection of sample families without interference and, above all, assurances from the government that the subjects that I selected for study would not be investigated or otherwise harassed. In this connection I recalled that during my study of a village in Spain in 1949, the peasants were called up for questioning by the local police, at which point I left the village and terminated my study. I also explained that I would have to be able to assure the people who cooperated in the study that they would remain anonymous and that my taped interviews with

them would not be subject to examination or seizure. Finally, I said I would want to bring my own secretary and research assistants.

Mr. Castro agreed to these conditions. He said that he and his government were not interested in the particular individual families that I studied but rather in the general results of the study. He went on to say that there was nothing to hide, that Cubans were the most talkative people in the world and there were probably no complaints or grievances that people would tell me which he hadn't already heard from counter-revolutionaries. (quoted in Rigdon 1988:276–77)

Lewis's approach to Ford used the neutral language of impartial science appropriate to the Cold War period to state his research objectives. Rather than telling Ford that he wanted to see if Socialist Cuba had no culture of poverty, he instead wrote that his work would "provide us with comparative data on the culture of poverty in another Latin American country" (Rigdon 1988: 277). This description was accurate but contained no mention of testing the progress of Cuba's Socialist experiment or the beneficial outcomes of the revolution. As Ruth Lewis later described, as a goal of the Cuban project they "hoped to observe the mass organizations and revolutionary institutions as they functioned at the local level and to evaluate, albeit tentatively, the degree of success or failure in achieving some of the goals of the Revolution" (Lewis et al. 1977:xi).

Lewis received three years of funding from the Ford Foundation, and after working out the logistics with Cuban governmental officials the Lewises arrived in Cuba in February 1969 (Lewis et al. 1977:xi). The Cuban government was notified of the Ford Foundation's sponsorship soon after the grant was awarded, but when the Lewises arrived in Havana, the Cuban government made public new policies opposing its cooperation with "organizations such as the Ford Foundation, which they considered an agency of the CIA and of North American imperialism" (Lewis et al. 1977:xii).

After a year and a half in Cuba the Lewises were preparing to return to Urbana in summer 1970, when suddenly the Cuban government seized most of their records and research materials and terminated their project. The sensitive nature of some of the informants' critiques of the Cuban regime made the government's seizure of records extremely troubling. One informant, an individual highly critical of some aspects of the Cuban Revolution, was arrested, imprisoned, and spent years working on a Cuban prison farm (Rigdon 1988:167).

Castro was not simply being reactionary in his suspicions of the Ford Foundation's interest in funding Lewis's research. There is some truth in the logic that even though Lewis was not a spy his sponsor was. Lewis *was* being spied on by the FBI, and (unwittingly on Lewis's part) his research was of interest to American intelligence agencies. This is not to accuse Lewis of wrongdoing but rather only to highlight a seldom-discussed feature of academic research funding. The ties between Ford and the State Department have been well established for this period, and Ford's interest in assisting an independent scholar in his efforts to live and study in Cuba fits the model of Ford and other funding agencies helping independent scholars gather information on their own, which would then be of use to America's national security braintrust (see Fisher 1983; Gough 1968; Huizer 1979; Kleinman and Solovey 1995; Montague 1991; Saunders 1999; Scott 1975; Price 2003d; cf. Stocking 1985). Ford and the state were very interested in having such a competent fieldworker as Lewis get his finger on the pulse of America's southern enemy, regardless of Lewis's divergent interests and motivations.

After his 1970 expulsion from Cuba, some anthropologists accused Lewis of carelessly endangering his informants while other critics accused him of working for the CIA or FBI (Rigdon 1988:169). Lewis certainly did not protect the identities of his research subjects as well as he could have. As Rigdon notes, Lewis "knew that Cuba had a secret police network that could further jeopardize every informant and that his field materials, which contained highly sensitive personal information, could fall into government hands" (1988:167).

Oscar Lewis died suddenly of a heart attack in December 1970 at the age of fifty-five, leaving behind a large corpus of published and unpublished work. The FBI closed their file on Lewis on learning of his death.

Hunting Mead: The FBI's Inability to Distinguish a Liberal from a Radical

Margaret Mead is undoubtedly the publically best-known anthropologist of the twentieth century. Her *Coming of Age in Samoa* (1928) helped chaperone a sexual revolution in the United States and was instrumental in bringing anthropology into America's consciousness. Mead was a highly visible intellectual, bringing anthropology to the masses, where she popularized the tenets of cultural relativism and sent critical messages of gender and racial equality.

While many individuals from the 1960s' counterculture identified Mead with leftist notions of progressive action, Mead's politics were complex and cannot be reduced to simplistic caricatures. Mead had little involvement in political activities until the outbreak of World War II; indeed, she rarely even voted during the 1920s and 1930s (Yans-McLaughlin 1986a:193). Mead contributed to America's World War II efforts by serving on the National Research Council's Committee on Food Habits from 1942 to 1954, and as the postwar era transformed the world she contributed her anthropological skills to the Cold War. Thus, at the same time that Mead was advocating for a broad cultural relativist stance recognizing that all cultures and all people are created equal she was supporting America's Cold War hard-line military stances. As Lenora Foerstel and Angela Gilliam observe, "Perhaps no other aspect of Mead's intellectual life is more fraught with contradictions than her relationship to the U.S. armed forces and the military goals of her country" (1992:117). Mead worked on numerous government-sponsored projects that had direct war-related applications (Yans-McLaughlin 1986b), including her involvement in the Culture at a Distance project, her work on military-linked projects at the Institute for Intercultural Studies,[8] her conservative stance on the Vietnam War,[9] and her work on the Rand Corporation–sponsored study of Soviet personality types (Mead 1951). Mead regularly corresponded with political figures—such as Vice President Nixon, to whom she suggested means of dealing with Krushchev during his U.S. visit (MM: C43, RN/MM 9/7/59)—or with personnel at the State Department on various issues (e.g., MM: C37 2/15/57 or MM: E154 5/5/75). Despite a consistent record of Mead's service contributing to America's Cold War military status quo, the FBI investigated her as a possible Communist or subversive largely because she articulated and advocated anthropological views regarding the equality of all peoples.

There are a number of problems involved in working with Margaret Mead's FBI and CIA files. The FBI has only released approximately half of her 992-page file. The contents of the unreleased 497 pages are unknown, although the 495 released pages reveal information on what is *not* in the unreleased pages. The unreleased pages do not contain any significant derogatory information on Mead. This may safely be inferred from the numerous background reports on Mead that repeatedly rehash the same narrative materials. These reports contain no additional information on Mead otherwise summaries of this new information would appear in the released documents. All researchers must confront problems of missing data, but Freedom of Information Act researchers must perpetually address fundamental issues of withheld or missing data that are different because this data is *intentionally* withheld by governmental censors intending to mystify the researcher. In a case such as Mead's where more than half of the available data is withheld by the FBI for undisclosed reasons it is vital that any consideration of released data be cautiously and tentatively examined as being only part of narrative that is selectively released.

Most of Mead's released FBI file pertains to background investigations for employment on a variety of governmental projects, although a seventy-four-page section of her file documents an FBI investigation of her as a possible

Communist security risk. This report speaks volumes about the FBI's bizarre paranoia and its penchant for seeing all who threaten even portions of the economic and cultural status quo as needing monitoring.

Buttle : Tuttle | Meade : Mead

In 1941 the FBI initially placed Margaret Mead on the custodial detention index because of a clerical error. On March 31, 1941, J. Edgar Hoover sent a memo to L. M. C. Smith, chief of the Special Defense Unit, informing him "Margaret Meade" was to be "considered for custodial detention in the event of a national emergency" (WFO100-386818-X). This was because the August 13, 1933 issue of the *Daily Worker* indicated that one "Margaret Meade" of New York City was a Communist and was the secretary of the League of Homeless Women (WFO77-28804-3). Later attempts by the FBI to determine if Margaret Meade was anthropologist Margaret Mead, and to learn anything about the "League of Homeless Women" were inconclusive; individuals associated with the building listed in the 1933 *Daily Worker* knew nothing of this organization (WFO77-288041-10 8/28/43). Eight years later the FBI determined that their files contained "information concerning one Margaret *Meade*, born in Oklahoma, who is not identical to [the anthropologist Mead]. However, it is to be noted there is no information pertaining to any Communist activity on Margaret Meade's part" (WFO121-14450-20).[10]

In 1949 the FBI conducted an extensive background investigation on Mead when she applied for a job with the World Health Organization. The FBI interviewed her colleagues at Harvard, Columbia, Rutgers, Vassar, the Community Service Society, the Social Science Research Council, and the American Museum of Natural History. These dozens of interviews generated a consensus that Mead was a brilliant, hardworking scholar with nothing in her background or character indicating she was anything but a loyal American. The FBI noted that Mead belonged to a number of organizations deemed subversive, such as United Service to China, Inc., East and West Association, Foster Parents' Plan for War Children, and United China Relief (WFO121-14450-20), and that the *Daily Worker* had reported on Mead's talk at the Conference of Young Women (WFO121-14450-20).

Mead's file contains dozens of newspaper articles reporting on her statements to the press and on her work presented at international conferences. Most of the pieces have headlines like "Social Work Is Seen as Aid to Democracy: Dr. Margaret Mead Stresses the Need of New Institutions" (*New York Times* 1/18/41); "Our Young People Aren't Conformists" (*New York Journal American* 1/31/57); "Are Spinsters Singular? Dr. Mead Draws a Bead" (*Washington Daily News* 10/17/63); and "Mom, Poor Mom" (*Evening Star* 10/22/63).

Mead's work in 1952 on a project funded by the Office of Naval Intelligence and administered by the University of Minnesota initiated another FBI investigation (WFO100-386818-2 1/18/52). Files from the ONI indicate that Mead had published a book review in the Institute of Pacific Relations' *Pacific Affairs* journal and belonged to the following supposedly "radical or subversive" organizations: ACLU, American Association for the Advancement of Science[!], Council for Democracy, Committee for National Morale, Common Council for American Unity, Downtown Community School, East and West Association, and National Council of American-Soviet Friendship (WFO100-386818-5).

In 1953 Mead joined the Human Relations and Moral Advisory Panel, a group consisting of nine scientists who met quarterly under contract with the Office of Naval Intelligence and the University of Minnesota (WFO100-386818-2 1/18/52; see also WFO100-386818-11). Because of Mead's membership on this panel, the New York bureau requested permission to interview her concerning her "present sympathies with the CP or related organizations," but Hoover rejected the request and recommended that the case be closed unless new information came to light (WFO100-386818-12 4/15/53). Susan Krook reports that the FBI used a wiretap on Margaret Mead at the American Museum of Natural History in 1954 (Krook 1993:113).

In 1954 the FBI interviewed an individual at the Rand Corporation concerning Mead's loyalty. He told the FBI that Mead's work with Rand led to her writing the book *Soviet Attitudes Towards Authority* which Rand published in 1951. The informant described this as a book, "critical of the Soviet system, is testimony to Dr. Mead's anti-Communist attitude" (WFO138-2729 8/4/54). In *Soviet Attitudes* Mead reduced numerous complex cultural traits to simple cultural caricatures designed to highlight the lack of freedom in Soviet society. Had the FBI bothered to read the book they would have found Mead's crude personality and culture generalizations of Soviet society to be closely aligned with the American government's anti-Soviet stance.

Mead's FBI file contains a report dated August 17, 1954, that is based on information gathered by an unidentified "governmental investigative agency." The identity of this organization is unknown, although the categorization as such is generally used to identify organizations such as the CIA or the Military Intelligence Division.[11] An unidentified source from this unnamed governmental agency stated that

> at Columbia University, Dr. Mead had Communist Party members working for her. . . . This was with her knowledge and also the full knowledge and approval of the University inasmuch as the job she was doing for the Navy Department involved comprehensive and intimate

studies which, to be successful, required the services of Communist Party members.

███████████ said he also had knowledge of the fact that ███████████ had failed to clear the applicant for certain jobs and that he believed this was due to her early organizational affiliations. He commented, however, that she has delivered top secret lectures at the National War College and in his opinion she is completely loyal to the United States. (WFO138-2729 9/17/54)

Neither Mead's FBI file nor her resume provide further information on the top-secret lectures Mead gave at the National War College, but it is possible that she delivered such lectures during World War II.

In 1954 the FBI investigated Mead's involvement in the Downtown Community School. She told the FBI how her daughter came to enroll in the school and how as a concerned and involved parent she had helped with a night school program for parents and at one time had been a member of the board. She reported that,

> there were all sorts of peculiar elements represented among the parents, people alleged to be Communist Party members, people said to be Trotskyites, etc., but they formed a small section of the entire group . . . Whether any of them were Communists or not I never knew for sure, but [I] had continually to deal with accusations and counter accusation, with attempts to use the mailing list of parents for all sorts of causes etc. . . . This was my first experience with working with an organization in which there was suspected Communist membership, and I learned a good deal about Communist tactics, and lost a good deal of sleep staying up till 2 o'clock in the morning to be sure nothing was put over at the end of a meeting. (WFO138-2729 8/4/54)

Mead also gave the FBI detailed explanations for the association of her name with organizations such as the East and West Association, United China Relief (she joined at the invitation of Pearl Buck), Foster Parents' Plan, and National Committee for People's Rights—the latter of which she reported she had never been a member. Perhaps it was inquiries from the FBI such as this that led her to instruct her assistant to write to labor publications and ask to be removed from their mailing lists (MM: C37 Crane/*Labor World* 6/12/57).

The FBI noted that on January 14, 1962, the *Worker* mentioned Mead's participation in the November 1961 U.S./Soviet Peace and Disarmament Conference, which was sponsored by the Woman's Intentional League for Peace and Freedom and the Jane Adams Peace Association (WFO121-14450-

39). On July 17, 1962, the *Daily Worker* likewise mentioned Mead in an article titled "Scientists of 30 Nations to Meet" (WFO121-14450-47).

As part of a 1963 FBI background check Mead again provided detailed explanations for the association of her name with a large number of organizations deemed subversive by HUAC and the U.S. attorney general. She volunteered this information because "during the last twenty years, I have been involved in a great many security enquiries as well as having been cleared a good many times myself" (WFO121-14450-48). She explained that she had been listed as a member of the American Russian Institute (ARI) in 1947, when in fact she had merely taken out a subscription of ARI publications as part of an Office of Naval Research contract with Columbia University's Research in Contemporary Cultures Project. Likewise, her receipt of the USSR *Information Bulletin* was explained as a one-year subscription in 1949 for a Rand Corporation contract she had worked on at the American Museum of Natural History (WFO121-14450-48:3). In explaining her presence at the 1940 Conference of Young Women (as reported in the *Daily Worker* on December 16, 1940) Mead stated that she had only attended the meeting to detract from the attempts of the Communist Party to take control of the meeting: "I attended this meeting, after having been consulted by a recent Vassar graduate on how to attract a cross-section of young women; I was instrumental in instructing a representative of the Junior League, who was sufficiently impressed by the dangers exposed at this meeting to help organize a Young Republican Group. I attended the meeting because I was worried about the emphasis which I thought might be developed there" (WFO121-14450-48:4). Finally, Mead furnished a list of eighty-eight organizations with which her name was associated with her approval.

Mead's family was also subjected to FBI investigation. In November 1963 the bureau investigated Mead's daughter and son-in-law (Mary Catherine and J. Barker Mihram Kassarjian) as part of their inquiries into Mead's background. The investigation determined that they were "unknown to some Boston informants familiar with some phases of communist activity in Massachusetts" (WFO121-14450-45).

Mead's FBI file indicates the bureau maintained interest in her from the late 1960s until mid-1970s. In 1969 a letter was forwarded to Hoover regarding an appearance by Mead on an NBC television program where she made comments supporting the use of marijuana. While the identity of the individual forwarding the letter to the FBI is redacted in the file, it seems likely that they were affiliated with NBC (WFO121-14450 10/29/69). In 1975 Jane Dannenhauer, White House staff assistant, requested that a background investigation be conducted on Mead (WFO77-28804-14). On April 25, 1975,

A. B. Fulton wrote a book review for the FBI of Mead's *Soviet Attitudes towards Authority* (WFO77-28804-13). The review offered a two-paragraph synopsis, a paragraph about the author, and then a four-page summary of the book's main points, including the Soviet reliance on force, the subordination of the individual, and the direct coercion by the KGB to maintain control over individual citizens.

Susan Krook comments on the differences in the makeup of Mead's FBI files and those of Boas (1993:114). There are many significant differences between the two, but most can be accounted for by the reasons *why* the files were compiled by the FBI. Boas's file was compiled because of his activism while Mead's file was compiled primarily as a result of her willingness to work for agencies with which the FBI co-operated. Margaret Mead was a complicated individual. While her progressive views regarding gender and racial equality raised the FBI's concern, her willingness to work within the system for a variety of governmental and military agencies found Mead working for rather than against the push and pull of the military industrial status quo.

Margaret Mead helped Russian social scientist Mark Zborowski secure funding and work after he came to the United States from the Soviet Union. Zborowski was later tried, convicted and imprisoned for lying about his links to Soviet espionage organizations and the assassination of Leon Trotsky (see Krook 1993:125–27; Dallin 1956a, 1956b; Deutscher 1963; Price 1998b). It is likely that the FBI investigated Mead's contact with Zborowski, and it is possible that these reports are among those currently withheld by the FBI.

Untangling Lewis and Mead

It is not surprising that the FBI monitored and tracked radical Marxist anthropologists, but the extent to which mainstream liberal anthropologists like Oscar Lewis and Margaret Mead were monitored and hounded by the FBI raises questions concerning basic civil liberties and the monitoring of intellectuals in a "free" society. Given Mead's support for various military programs, it is especially odd that she was the target of ongoing FBI investigations.

The fact that Mead's progressive public-education campaigns against racism and for gender equity raised FBI suspicions is indicative of the FBI's intent to monitor activists regardless of the activists' commitment to values that could be compared to those of mainstream American values. That Mead had every indication of supporting the governmental programs to which she contributed clearly did not diminish the FBI's concern.

But the Cold War bred paranoia everywhere. Lewis's FBI file illustrates the difficulties faced by nonaligned anthropologists during a period when those who did not proclaim alignment were assigned it through the suspicions of others—both at home and abroad. If Oscar Lewis were not being spied on by Hoover's FBI as a threat to capitalism, then he was being spied on by Castro's secret police as a threat to the Socialist revolution. It mattered not at all that Lewis was neither a Marxist nor an agent of northern imperialism—his interest in documenting and describing the culture of poverty presented him as a threat. While it was the border patrol's discovery of his subversive reading material that first brought him to the FBI's attention, it was his interest in civil liberties (in protecting Richard Morgan's), internationalism, inequality, and his refusal to interpret political events from a jingoistic/American stance that held the FBI's interest for decades. This interest in Lewis was kept active both by informer letters from anthropologists and Lewis's own public work on poverty. Indeed, the paper trail left by the FBI indicates that it was Lewis's popular writings on poverty and his public statements questioning U.S. policy on Cuba that kept the FBI's interest—certainly they found no evidence of Lewis breaking any laws. Although Lewis's role as a public activist for the poor was in many ways less confrontational than the activities of Jacobs, Stern, Weltfish, Morgan, and Swadesh, it was similar in that it posed a threat to normative understandings of poverty.

Without the assistance of anthropologists and other academics who were willing to become FBI informants and sources, the FBI would not have focused its attentions in the ways it did. Had George Murdock and the unidentified informer not written to Hoover in 1949 voicing concerns that Oscar Lewis was a Communist, the FBI's monitoring of Lewis would have been quite different. Likewise, Lewis's FBI file records numerous comments by university employees voicing suspicions relating to Lewis's political beliefs, which fits the overall pattern of behavior by academics in the FBI files of other anthropologists. We do not have a systemic examination of the extent to which fellow anthropologists and other academics have been FBI informers, and although numerous scholars of Cold War academia have documented instances of academics informing on their fellow colleagues (see Diamond 1992; Schrecker 1986), we still do not know the extent of this practice nor how it changed the career paths of those who pitched anthropology's diverse paradigms.

Lewis's story should also remind all anthropologists that their fieldwork may endanger their informants, and that they should adopt practices of protecting both informants and the subjects of study. As Lewis's case clarifies, anthropologists not only need to be concerned about protecting informants from retaliation by their own governments but also aware of the possible interest of Western intelligence agencies (see Price 2002d, 2003d). All anthropologists should note with concern that the FBI was able to spy on Lewis in the field and to "reverse engineer" his 1963 research instrument by interviewing some of his Puerto Rico research subjects.

In 1999 I presented a paper on the FBI's surveillance of Oscar Lewis at an annual meeting of the American Anthropological Association. At the end of my presentation one member of the audience asked me what harm was done to Lewis if he remained unaware of the FBI's surveillance of him and his work (which his widow, Ruth Maslow Lewis, assured me was the case). This question is an interesting one because it concerns the basic issue of the rights of privacy: the very asking of this question suggests that no harm is done to an individual if they do not know they are being watched. The FBI's surveillance of anthropologists during the Cold War era was a totalitarian act of suppression, regardless of the subject's limited knowledge of the FBI's actions. An individual or group need not know that they are under surveillance to be violated, in much the same way that victims of sexual voyeurism are violated even without knowledge of the voyeur. This point is a fundamental one that many scholars examining the FBI records of social scientists working in earlier periods have failed to adequately address. For example, in *Stalking the Sociological Imagination* (1999) Mike Keen struggles to find any significant impact resulting from the FBI's extensive surveillance of dozens of prominent American sociologists. Keen suggests that these surveillance campaigns may have slightly altered the development of sociology through the adoption of self-censorship, and perhaps fostered the growth of more objectifiable quantitative methods. The weakness of Keen's conclusion betrays a widespread lack of appreciation of the ease with which the ebb and flow of academic research can be manipulated, redirected, and constrained.

Although difficult to document, there have also been instances of social scientists losing federal research funding due to FBI intervention and surveillance. One documented example of this is the case of sociologist Joel Montague who used the Freedom of Information Act to document how his radical affiliations during the Depression came back to haunt him in the 1950s when a Fulbright scholarship offered to him to conduct research in Japan was inexplicably withdrawn (Montague 1991:201–50). Montague established how the FBI used their knowledge that scholars had radical associations in order to sabotage their Fulbright funding. It is remarkable that there are not more documented instances of the FBI interfering with the funding of radical social scientists—but this is an area where scholarly research is scarce. Indeed, we can only speculate the extent to which the FBI must have been party to withdrawals of federal funding opportunities. Perhaps evidence of such instances are routinely redacted by FBI censors under current FOIA guidelines that allow the FBI to keep their methods and techniques private.[12]

CHAPTER 13

Crusading Liberals Advocating for Racial

Justice: Philleo Nash and Ashley Montagu

It was always a struggle for anthropology to be politically

relevant to the needs of the poor and powerless. But, the

ease with which the Cold War dampened even a casual

interest in meaningful social change exceeded the most

cynical expectations. —Eric B. Ross

Philleo Nash came from a prominent Wisconsin family. His grandfather, Thomas E. Nash, was
the first president of the Nekoosa-Edwards Paper
Company and later served President Grover Cleveland as director of rail service. Philleo's father, Guy
Nash, channeled the family money into an expan-
sive cranberry farm, the Biron Cranberry Company, located north of Wisconsin Rapids. Philleo
worked the farm in his youth, during which he
came to embrace the family's commitment to politics.

As an undergraduate in the late 1920s Philleo
Nash studied anthropology under Ralph Linton
at the University of Wisconsin, and in 1932 he
began graduate work in anthropology at the University of Chicago (McMillan 1986:146–70). Nash
later recounted that he found himself "in sixth—

if not seventh—heaven" while learning functionalism from Radcliffe-Brown; community studies techniques from Robert Redfield; an activist approach to applied anthropology from Redfield and Manuel Gamio; and fieldwork techniques from Leslie Spier on the Klamath Indian reservation in southern Oregon (Nash 1986:189).

After the United States entered World War II one of Nash's former professors, Harold Lasswell, recommended him for an appointment as a specialist in the Office of Facts and Figures (OFF), a domestic intelligence agency monitoring racial tensions throughout the United States. At OFF Nash monitored rumors pertaining to American minority groups, the analysis of which, according to Nash, "led to close examination of the tensions between groups, and the geographic pinpointing of tensions. Among the prime tension centers were Washington, D.C., and Detroit, Michigan. Numerous memoranda went out from OFF to all the War Agencies naming these and other cities where sporadic violence was occurring and where it seemed likely to grow" (Nash 1986:191; see also Nash 1980).

Charley Cherokee and the "National Grapevine"

Nash's FBI file indicates that in November 1944 "the Military Division in Washington suspected Philleo Nash was using the pen name, CHARLEY CHEROKEE, to write articles for the *Chicago Defender*, a Chicago Negro newspaper" (WFO121-12261-18).[1] Charley Cherokee's "National Grapevine" column in the *Chicago Defender* covered a variety of topics, with an ongoing focus on race in the military. The column's tone was folksy, often written in a colloquial black dialect, but there were frequent comments that suggested that Charley Cherokee had contacts with sources within the ranks of the Washington establishment. Charley Cherokee consistently argued for the equality of all races in the military, making statements such as "if Army rules are so damned hard and fast, why aren't white privates compelled to salute Negro officers? Rules say all privates salute all officers, and until they do, and until a lot of things change, Charley will continue to put ants in the shiny pant seats" (*Chicago Defender* 7/22/44:13). Column topics often mirrored those of Nash's White House work, including race riots, inequality in the military, attacks on Governor Dewey, complaints about the army's refusal to release pictures of black soldiers storming the beaches of Normandy, and changing views on the acceptance of "darkling" nurses in the military.

One 1944 column mentioned Nash by name, writing "F.D.R. won't make a move on race without consulting Jonathan Daniels, Jonathan won't budge without seeing Philio [*sic*] Nash, Philio Nash won't talk until he sees Ted

[Poston]. This is unfair to Ted as it puts him in a spot and when something goes wrong, he's going to catch it. But so far it's working very nicely, thank you" (Chicago Defender 10/7/44:13).

Philleo Nash may have been a logical suspect as the true identity of Charley Cherokee because of his access to the latest information circulating in Washington on race and the armed forces. Because Charley Cherokee favored Communists (or perhaps more accurately, to use the double-negative doublethink of the era that would follow, he was anti-anti-Communism) he drew the concerned attention of the FBI. In his July 29, 1944, column, Charley Cherokee wrote,

> Communists scare the pants off our white folks, chum. It's funny. Y'see, the "Commie" creed calls for relentless "struggle" against national oppression of Negro people, for complete equality of Negroes in all American life, and for uniting white-skin and dark-skin workers.
>
> "Conservative" whites hysterically lump "Communists," "Radicals," and "liberals," so that now if you so much as read a liberal book or paper, or disagree with a northern capitalist or southern white-supremacist, you're a Commie. For example — everybody who believes in public housing projects or fights the poll tax is a "Commie." A Congressional Committee denounced the pamphlet "Races of Mankind" as communistic and refused to let Army distribute it. And if you like Henry Wallace, you're throwing over "Americanism" for "Communism."
>
> Now here's the part that ain't funny. We darklings are scared of Communists. Average Negro leader seems to think — "rich northern whites and poor southern peckerwoods running from "Commies," what the hell am I waiting for?" Wide-eyed Negro mass noting frantic whites and its own leaders, steers clear of "them Bolshiviks."
>
> When even the otherwise emancipated Capital Press club (D.C. darkling newsmen) is afraid to have colored Communist Doxey Wilkerson as a luncheon guest, it leaves the foolish stage and becomes a damn shame.[2]
>
> The now-rotting Dies gang said the Communist Party, or as it is now called, the Communist Political Association, seeks overthrow of U.S. Government. Maybe so, but to us it has always seemed it merely wanted to throw out of government those things hurting democracy. This happens to be what we try to do. One thing is certain, the "Commies" fight for workers and the underprivileged, and from here darklings still look like underprivileged workers.
>
> Personally, Charley carries no blazing torch for the "Commies," realizing that like the Republicans and Democrats, some of them are good and some bad. But let's stop being damn fools, because if it's a choice

between conservatives who can't forget white supremacy, and radicals
who can't forget democracy, the way seems clear. (And if that be treason,
Pfui!) (*Chicago Defender* 7/29/44:13).

Note here that Cherokee comments on Congress's decision not to let the
army distribute Benedict and Weltfish's "The Races of Mankind," yet he does
not mention either the authors' names or their positions as anthropologists.
It was very rare for Cherokee to not mention such credentials, affiliations,
and names; perhaps this lack of attribution was done to divert attention to the
possibility of Nash's contribution to the column. In the end, the FBI never
was able to definitively establish whether or not Nash was Charley Cherokee.

Postwar Nash: Crusading Liberal in Racist America

Nash's progressive activism was moderated by his practical commitment to
work within existing power structures. His general political approach can be
seen in his postwar support for the Americans for Democratic Action, which
tried to find middle ground for the schism within the Democratic Party between supporters of Henry Wallace and President Truman. Likewise, Nash
helped found the American Council on Race Relations in 1944—not with
the support of radical Marxist groups but with the funds of America's philan-
thropist families (Nash 1986:191; Hess 1973). Nash also worked on President
Truman's Commission on Civil Rights and within the confines of the federal bureaucracy to push for greater racial equality. But Nash's commitment
to moderation did not shield him from McCarthy's witch-hunt, or Hoover's
investigation.

As a result of his work for the Truman Administration, Nash became the
subject of a 1948 "full-field loyalty investigation" (WFO100-414572-10) because of his alleged contacts with a number of suspected Communists. In
their investigations for the case the FBI interviewed David K. Niles, who
during the war had worked with Nash at the Office of War Information. In
the report Niles described Nash as "a 'crusading liberal' but believed him to
be entirely loyal to the United States. Niles said that Nash served as one of
his assistants handling matters relating to the Negro race. Niles further indicated that he had not hired Nash but had 'inherited him somewhere along
the line.' Niles said that Nash, during his employment at the White House,
had approached him and asked if he might employ a Negro secretary. Niles
said that he discouraged the idea. Niles concluded the interview by saying
that he realized that Nash was a 'little liberal' and had on various occasions
come up with some rather radical ideas" (WFO100-414572-11). It is sobering
to see that Nash's suggestion that a person of color should be hired to work

in an office devoted to the study of racial tensions was seen as radical and inappropriate.

The FBI identified Nash as being associated with the Inter-racial Day Nursery School and the Sidwell Friends' School,[3] and stated their belief that "the Directors, Officers and Board of Trustees of these institutions are, with two exceptions, members of the Communist Party or Communist front organizations" (WFO121-12261-7). The FBI was convinced that Communists had infiltrated a variety of educational institutions where they abused their positions of authority to promote racial integration.

The New York City field office sent FBI headquarters an "urgent" communiqué reporting the existence of a pamphlet "listing Dr. Philleo Nash and others as connected with a course entitled 'Race, Race Theories and Politics' offered by [the] School for Democracy, Fall Term nineteen forty two" (WFO121-12261 11/4/48). The School for Democracy (later the Jefferson School of Social Science) was a Marxist school founded by Communists who had been fired from City College (Gettleman 2001). Nash's FBI file includes a copy of this fall 1942 course listing, which includes the following anthropology instructors: Sula Benet, Manet Fowler, Lottie Hu, Marian Minus, M. F. Ashley Montagu, Philleo Nash, Gitel Poznanski, Dr. Margaret Schlauch, Bernhard Stern, Vilhjalmur Stefansson, and Gene Weltfish. The FBI was unable, however, to establish any concrete links between the School for Democracy and Nash.

The FBI interviewed a variety of sources for Nash's file, including some of his high school teachers, staff members at the University of Wisconsin, several former classmates, archaeologists at the Milwaukee Public Museum, and a fraternity brother (Theta Delta Chi), but with few results. One of his former classmates did comment to the FBI that Nash had been "advanced in his thinking," but when pressed by the FBI he clarified this meant "that many of the changes in the economic and social life of the United States that have taken place in the past twenty years were changes that Nash advocated twenty years ago" (WFO121-12261-9).

In 1948 agents in New Haven, Connecticut, interviewed an anthropologist who appears to have been Ralph Linton, although the name has been deleted in the report. The report states: "███████ Yale University, advised that he had Nash as a student at the University of Wisconsin from approximately ███████. During that time Nash did not by word, action, or association give reason to question his loyalty to this country. ███████ further stated that based upon his knowledge of Nash both as a student and casual contacts with him since, he would judge Nash to be a 100% loyal American in all respects" (WFO121-12261-8, 11/5/48). After interviewing an unidentified female (perhaps a departmental secretary) who had access to anthropology department records at the University of Chicago, an unnamed anthropology professor reported that Nash had been an excellent student who married Edith Rosenfels—also a former student in the department of anthropology. Aside from this, the professor reported that Nash "was considered by him . . . to be a 'liberal' and that he meant by 'liberal' that [Nash] was very interested in improving racial relations in the United States and was in sympathy with minority groups" (WF0121-12261-10). Other departmental professors at Chicago passed on similar words of academic praise and political caution (WF0121-12261-10).

Wittfogel the Informer

Throughout the 1940s and 1950s the FBI continued to compile reports on Nash. One night in 1946 FBI agents on a stakeout observed Nash's car dropping off two individuals at a party where suspects in the Silvermaster spy ring were in attendance. One FBI source noted that Nash was "extremely liberal on the racial question and it is possible that some people may have mistaken this for disloyalty, also because he is a professional expert on Negro matters, and that he's thrown into social contact with persons whose loyalty may be questionable" (WF0121-12261-24). In June 1951 the New York SAC reported that an informant had supplied information on Nash. Although the name of the informant is not given, background information clearly indicates it was Karl A. Wittfogel.[4] Wittfogel told the FBI that "he and his wife [anthropologist Esther Goldfrank] have always been suspicious of the political leanings of Nash and have drawn the opinion that he has Communist leanings and sympathies.[5] [Wittfogel] advised that their opinion comes from their associations in the educational field together and from the limited personal and social associations they had while ▮▮▮▮▮▮ was associated with the University of Wisconsin. He advised that he has no other information to substantiate his own personal opinion" (WF0121-12261-40). The final report on this interview states that "[Wittfogel] explained that he had formerly been a member of the Communist Party but that he dropped out of the Communist Party in 1933. However, because of this connection he is acquainted with various Communists, and is well versed in the doctrines of Marx and Lenin. Some time after he met Nash, during the course of a social evening, [Wittfogel] advised, he told Nash and his wife of his analysis of Marx and Lenin, which was highly critical. On this occasion Nash evinced a sullen reaction and refused to discuss the analysis, although he had previously indicated some knowledge of the subject" (WF0121-12261-47). Wittfogel also commented that during numerous visits "Nash had always tried to be very friendly, but that both he and his wife felt that Nash was concealing his inner feelings" (WF0121-12261-47). Wittfogel reported that when Nash came to New York he stayed with someone described by Wittfogel as an individual "who has always been sympathetic to Communism and Communist causes" (WF0121-12261-47). Although the name of this individual is redacted, one paragraph documents the individual's ties to the Communist Party.

Although at the time of this interview Wittfogel was a staunch anti-Communist, he had once been a member of the famed Marxist Frankfurt School (Taylor 1985). After his release from a Nazi concentration camp in 1934, Wittfogel immigrated to the United States (via China) where he became a naturalized citizen in 1941. He appeared in front of McCarran's Internal Security Subcommittee as a friendly witness identifying a number of former friends as current and former Communist Party members. During these hearings anthropologist David Aberle was identified as one of Owen Lattimore's research associates (U.S. Congress 1951:327). Ironically, Wittfogel's writings on hydraulic societies were instrumental in bringing overt materialist analyses back to anthropology during the 1950s, when only a fervent anti-Communist like Wittfogel could selectively use and praise the methods of Marxist historical materialism (Wittfogel 1955, 1957).

Wittfogel was instrumental in assisting Senator McCarran's Internal Security Subcommittee's efforts to establish links between the Institute for Public Relations (IPR), American high-level policy makers, and the Communist Party. As McCarran himself put it, his goal was no less than to uncover "to what extent the IPR was infiltrated and influenced by agents of the communist world conspiracy [and] to what extent these agents and their dupes worked through the Institute into the United States Government to the point where they exerted an influence on United States Far Eastern policy" (quoted in Schrecker 1986:164). By connecting an assortment of supposed Communist and Communist dupes (including Alger Hiss and Owen Lattimore) with the IPR and U.S. policy makers who were even distantly affiliated with IPR, McCarran connected a chain of names with an unseen, imagined communist plot.

After his arrival at Columbia University in the 1930s Wittfogel met regularly with a group of graduate students who were reading and discussing Marxist materials (Ulmen 1978). In his appearance before McCarran's judiciary committee Wittfogel did not hesitate to identify these students, and one of the students named committed suicide as a result of Wittfogel's testimony (U.S. Congress 1951:273–342). The students identified by Wittfogel included Lawrence Rosinger, M. I. Finley, and Daniel Thorner—all of whom refused to testify by invoking the Fifth Amendment (Schrecker 1986:165). But this former student discussion group was not the main target of Wittfogel's testimony; his intended victim was his colleague Owen Lattimore, with whom he'd had personal, intellectual, and political differences for years (Lewis 1993). As Schrecker points out, Wittfogel never in so many words testified that Lattimore was a Communist Party member. Instead he found a general "pro-Soviet" slant throughout Lattimore's analysis (1986:165). Wittfogel's lengthy testimony against Lattimore (and others) before McCarran's committee concluded with the submission of statements supporting Wittfogel's scholarship from numerous scholars, including the anthropologists C. Martin Wilbur, George P. Murdock, Clyde Kluckhohn, and Fred Eggan (U.S. Congress 1951:341–42).

In 1952 Lattimore appeared before the Internal Security Subcommittee as a combative witness confronting McCarran with evidence that the hearings were little more than show trials without any real evidence. As a reward for this bold display before the subcommittee, McCarran had Roy Cohn issue a perjury indictment against him. This indictment and a similar second attempt were both thrown out of court, but despite the baselessness of Lattimore's persecution and prosecution the damage was done. According to Schrecker, "Lattimore and his friends and family had spent years on the case. His lawyers, Abe Fortas and Thurman Arnold, contributed for free what one scholar estimates was $2.5 million (in 1950 dollars) worth of legal services. Since he had tenure, Lattimore kept his job, but his reputation and influence within the academic world suffered, especially after Johns Hopkins abolished the Walter Hines Page School of International Affairs and with it Lattimore's position as director. He had to curtail his public speaking engagements. His graduate students and even his former secretaries had trouble getting jobs. And he had trouble getting published" (1986:166). Anthropologists such as David Aberle who had worked with Lattimore, as well as those who had any remote connection with the IPR, began to worry about the impact of such associations (Aberle interview with Price 1/6/2000).

Given Wittfogel's role in identifying Lattimore and the IPR's links to Communism, the FBI took Wittfogel's information regarding Nash very seriously and conducted follow-up interviews of New York residents regarding Nash. A 1951 New York City bureau report commented on an interview with a woman who had known Nash since 1941. This informant reported that someone with Communist ties helped Nash receive his wartime assignment. She also recounted an exchange from either 1943 or 1944 wherein her husband had dined at the Nash's home along with a third party (from Yale) who "made an anti-Semitic remark which enraged Nash, and Nash spoke out quite strongly on the subject" (WFO121-12261-53). This incident was then contrasted by the informant with another episode that occurred when Nash had last visited her in New York. The report states that she said that "Nash had absolutely nothing to say when [someone] tried to discuss the violent anti-Semitism in Russia. She claimed that this was an indication that no matter what his reaction to anti-Semitism was, he would not discuss anything derogatory to the Soviet Union" (WFO121-12261-53). Finally, with a quote that seems to capture the nonaligned political position of Nash, she told the FBI that she had once heard Nash say that although some people "thought he was a Communist sympathizer, whenever he was among Communists, the Communists were furious at his attitude" (WFO121-12261-53). As Nash would soon learn from Senator McCarthy, this was not a time when any such ambiguous stances were charitably interpreted.

Paranoia Strikes Deep in the Heartland:
Senator McCarthy on the Attack

As Senator Joseph McCarthy rose to national prominence, many of his Democratic opponents in his home state of Wisconsin became increasingly vocal in their opposition to him and all he stood for. In early January 1952, Philleo Nash's sister Jean and a dozen other Wisconsin Democratic activists paid for a large anti-McCarthy advertisement in the *Wisconsin Rapids Daily Tribune* (WFO121-12261-57 1/30/52). McCarthy was not amused. A few weeks later, on January 29, 1952, Senator McCarthy publicly charged that the FBI had given him information proving that Philleo Nash—then President Truman's special assistant on minority problems—was a Communist. McCarthy stated that the FBI evidence proved that Nash "had been in close contact with the Communist underground in Washington and in the early 1940s permitted his home in Toronto to be used by members of a Canadian spy ring." McCarthy stated that the FBI files proved that in the early 1940s Philleo Nash "was attending Communist meetings and had officially joined the Communist Party" (*Washington Post* 1/29/52).

Nash denied McCarthy's charges. In a statement to the press he declared that McCarthy's "accusation that I am or ever have been a member of the Communist Party or have had anything to do with the Communist Party or have had anything to do with the Communist movement is a contemptible lie" (*Washington Star* 1/30/52). The FBI records one unidentified newspaper reporting that when asked about his Communist connections, Nash referred to his own business dealing with cranberries by saying, "Cranberries are red, aren't they?" (WFO121–12261). McCarthy claimed that individuals within the FBI gave him files, which was an action violating FBI records policies. The press had a field day with McCarthy's attacks on Nash, as well as with Truman's counterattacks on McCarthy. At a White House press conference the next day Truman attacked McCarthy for his claim that Nash was a Communist, denouncing him as "the pathological Mr. McCarthy." In an editorial titled "Truman Pot, McCarthy Kettle: It's Time We Had the Facts," T. O. Thackrey traced back the witch-hunt tactics used by McCarthy to Truman's own federal loyalty oath. Thackrey noted that Nash had been seriously harmed by McCarthy's charges, and then observed that

> the President, in defending his own aides COULD not have given the simple and direct answer as to the truth or falsity of McCarthy's claims without being called upon to make whatever was in the file public, so that it could be traced to its source.
>
> The excuse for secrecy, which originally was persuasive to me, was that the mere accusation, publicly, of a government servant, would be enough to harm his reputation . . . and that if "cleared" in secret hearings, evil and misleading half-truths or falsehoods in the charges against him would not be unfairly exposed to the public gaze. The FBI made a further plea that to reveal the identity of its "informants" and the nature of the "investigation" would "destroy the usefulness of informers."
>
> Neither reason can any longer be taken as valid. Innuendo—by the McCarthys and others—often goes far beyond the actual "evidence" from the "mysterious" files: The identity of the employee in question is public, despite a half-hearted attempt at secrecy. And men's whole lives are being destroyed on the excuse that [the] "FBI informant" must be protected. In heaven's name, why? The whole "loyalty" procedure is worse than a mess; it is a menace. Let us have security, by all means—but let us have some for the citizen who ISN'T a Presidential aide. (WFO121-12261A; editorial in the *Daily Compass*, 2/4/52)

McCarthy's claim launched an FBI internal investigation to determine if and how he had gained access to Nash's FBI file. A memo from Hoover to Hiram Bingham, chairman of the Civil Service Loyalty Review Board, indicates that the FBI dusted for fingerprints the loyalty board's file on Nash to see what latent prints could be detected on the file. The results were inconclusive. The FBI's inquiry determined that "Senator McCarthy did, in fact, obtain the information contained in his speech from FBI reports" (WFO121-12261-56). The FBI then decided to take no further action in this matter, and McCarthy succeeded in tarnishing Nash's reputation without ever producing any evidence that he was in any way linked to the Communist Party.

The White House issued statements clearing Nash of any wrongdoing, but McCarthy continued to attack Nash from the Senate floor claiming that the FBI had established "nine points" indicating Nash was a Communist. McCarthy did not publicly cite each of these supposed nine points, but his "evidence" included claims that Nash had Communist friends, supported Canadian Communists, and had attended Communist Party meetings in the early 1940s (Hess 1973:772).

A January 30, 1952, FBI memo from C. H. Stanley to A. H. Belmont that assesses McCarthy's claims against Nash clarifies that there were only three aspects of the investigation into Nash's background that indicated any "possible disloyal information" concerning Nash; these include Nash's name appearing in the School for Democracy's 1942 catalog (although Stanley notes that "a photograph of Nash was displayed to informants who have previously furnished reliable information regarding this school, and they were unable to identify Nash as being connected therewith"); Nash's contact with a former member of the Communist Party during September of 1947; and Nash's work on the Board of the Georgetown Day School in 1948 (WFO121-12261-57; see also E. Nash 1989).[6]

After McCarthy began attacking Nash, letters from concerned citizens poured into the White House and FBI headquarters. In one letter to McCarthy and Truman, a citizen urged that Nash—the "World Citizen with a pink taint"—be removed from his position. This letter typified the logic of guilt by association that pervaded America during this period, as well as the extent to which average citizens were without much provocation willing to join the public pillorying. This letter writer noted that

> as far as we are concerned Senator McCarthy seems to have the upper hand, in that he always proves his case and has the data to show it. Many people, probably the weaker element and I don't mean the female sex, think Senator McCarthy talks too much. [Well], there we go right back to one of the fundamentals of our constitution[,] "free speech" and our [honorable] Senator is entitled to the floor, if he can prove that one of our so-called Americans is playing cards so that they benefit someone else. . . .
>
> If we are Americans, let us work together for the right. Let us clean out political rats and others who cannot possibly understand what loyalty means.
>
> As a Loyalty Board, we feel you should cooperate fully with the FBI and if not—WHY NOT: Has there been a "mink coat deal" on in your Department, too?
>
> Show us your colors for 1952—and don't let a pink ribbon bind the diploma. (WFO121-12261-66)

The public illusion that Senator McCarthy "always proves his case and has the data to show it" was extremely powerful and prevailing. As long as the media and FBI failed to challenge his claims, many citizens believed his bluffs and lies. For its part, the FBI always replied to such hackneyed attack letters with brief statements declaring that it was not the FBI's policy to provide access to the results of their investigations, thus leaving a lingering suggestion that such accusations might be true.

Although McCarthy was certainly reckless, frequently drunk, and often callous, he was not stupid. He knew he could legally say any damaging lie with impunity as long as he hid behind the unique immunity of Senate privilege. In the week following his original accusations about Nash, McCarthy repeated his allegations while speaking to the Wisconsin Seed Dealers' Association in Milwaukee. Because Nash had threatened to sue McCarthy for slander if he ever repeated the charges outside of the Senate floor's protection of immunity, McCarthy carefully read from a transcript of the Congressional Record when making his accusation (*Milwaukee Journal* 2/5/52). Later news reports (*Times-Herald* 3/4/52:4; WF0121-12261A) indicated that despite Nash's efforts to bring a damage suit against Senator McCarthy, no suit would likely be forthcoming because it appeared that McCarthy was still protected by senatorial immunity if he was only quoting his own comments from the Senate floor rather than making original statements. To gain the maximum political capital from this situation, McCarthy told the Milwaukee crowd that he was making a tape recording of his statements for Nash's benefit so that he could begin his lawsuit that afternoon—all the while knowing that he was protected from litigation. This was one of McCarthy's standard tricks, and despite several months of efforts Nash was not able to obtain a copy of McCarthy's tape (Reeves 1982:397).

According to columnist William T. Evjue of the Madison *Capitol Times*, the source of McCarthy's information on Philleo Nash's Communist connections could be traced back to Wisconsin. Evjue asserted that Nash was "about as much of a Communist as McCarthy [was] a statesman," and he further stated that

a wealthy Republican in Wisconsin Rapids picked up some gossip that Philleo Nash, while living in Canada, was fraternizing with people of left wing tendencies. This Wisconsin Rapids Republican is reported to have relayed this rumor and gossip about Nash's Canadian affiliations to the FBI at Washington. In due course, two FBI investigators appeared in Wisconsin Rapids. They interviewed a number of Wisconsin Rapids people including Mr. Nash's father who is now dead. All investigations which they made and the rumors, gossip and charges which they hear are placed in the FBI files. It is because so much of the information, rumor and gossip collected by FBI agents is of the rumor and gossip variety that the FBI department all through the years, has followed the policy of holding this unsupported material strictly private as a matter of justice to people who are being unjustly accused. (*Capitol Times* 5/22/52)

Evjue also stated that McCarthy's comments were based on nothing more than the raw, unevaluated data collected by the FBI some previous year, writing, "the whole case against Nash apparently rests on the gossip and rumor furnished to the FBI by a wealthy Wisconsin Rapids Republican who hates Nash because he undoubtedly thinks that Nash is a traitor to his class in identifying himself with the communistic philosophies of Pres. Roosevelt and Truman" (*Capitol Times* 5/22/52).

In May 1952 FBI agents interviewed an anthropologist friend of Nash's, who reported that Nash and he "had tacitly agreed between them not to discuss politics when they were together" due to political differences. This anthropologist added that he felt that Nash was "imbued" with what he characterized as "Communist ideologies," although he knew of no proof connecting Nash with either Communism or the Soviet Union. He added that Nash did not obey the social norms requiring that blacks and whites keep distance from each other, and in the FBI report he mentions "one occasion in 1942 or 1943 while . . . in Washington, he spent the night at Nash's apartment. He recalled that the address was on the fringe of a white/black neighborhood and that the occupants of the apartment house where he stayed consisted of members of both races. During the evening, while he was there, a young man introduced to him by Nash as a veteran of the Abraham Lincoln Brigade [*sic*] had also been present" (WFO100-414572-1).

On May 11, 1953, Philleo Nash testified at an executive session of the Senate Subcommittee on Internal Security (the Jenner committee), answering questions that Senator McCarthy had raised in his attack the previous year. Because it was an executive session the records are not available, but notes in Nash's FBI file indicate that the FBI illegally acquired access to the testimony "on a confidential basis for review and the original [was] returned to the Committee" (WFO121-12261-70). During his testimony Nash reported that "his association with the School for Democracy . . . consisted of one lecture in 1942," and he also testified that his contact with Communist Party members was limited to people associated with the Georgetown Day School. Nash acknowledged that he had once subscribed to the *Canadian Tribune* (an "official organ of the Communist Party in Canada"), but he denied knowing that party members used his property (WFO121-12261-73).

Years later the FBI interviewed an unidentified government employee who had known Nash since 1938 or 1940 (WFO161-153:12/9/21/61). This individual reported to the FBI Nash's version of why Senator McCarthy had targeted him for attack. He stated that while Nash "was an instructor at the University of Toronto, [Nash] had rented a room in his house in Toronto to two young men students who were students at the University. ▄▄▄▄▄▄▄ said that Nash told him that he knew nothing of the background of these two individuals and that following their departure from his home, a check of their room had revealed quantities of Communist Party (CP) literature. ▄▄▄▄▄▄ stated that Mr. Nash told him that he had no knowledge how this material got into this room and that he was not aware that the two young students had had any connection or anything to do with communists" (WFO 121-7939-3).

There are no indications that Nash was ever a member of the Communist Party. The FBI failed to find even a single one of its many party informants who had ever heard of Nash. One FBI informant in Milwaukee who had been a member of the Communist Party in Wisconsin from 1935 to 1940, and who "was familiar with the various members of the Communist Party during that time," said he had never heard of Nash (MI161-131-20). Three other former Communist Party members in the early 1960s likewise informed the FBI that they had no knowledge of Nash having any association with the Communist Party (MI161-131-22).

Philleo Nash had a brief career in public office when he became the lieutenant governor of Wisconsin in 1957. As lieutenant governor his primary responsibility was to perform the duties of president of the Wisconsin State Senate. Nash left office in early 1961 after losing the seat in a tight election (Nash 1989:3), and the campaign resurrected all of McCarthy's accusations and rumors. Indeed, a leaflet claiming that Nash was a known Communist was circulated throughout Wisconsin—some of these leaflets were posted and scattered throughout Wisconsin, some were even dropped from an airplane by a group calling itself the National Action Movement (WFO121-12261-80).[7]

During Nash's campaign the FBI received letters from housewives, concerned citizens, war veterans, and civil servants wanting to know the "truth" about Nash's reported links to Communism. The FBI read and answered each of these letters, often transcribing them on bureau typewriters from jumbled cursive script. In accordance with bureau procedure the FBI's extensive files were checked to see if they contained any information on a given letter's author. J. Edgar Hoover personally signed each reply and usually remarked that "the FBI is a fact-finding agency and does not grant or deny clearances to Government employees" (WFO121-12261-75). In other letters Hoover assured citizens that "the files of this Bureau are confidential and that no reports of the FBI were furnished to the late Senator McCarthy by any employee of this Bureau" (WFO121-12261-76). This latter point, however, overlooked the

FBI's finding that McCarthy had obtained the information he misrepresented from the FBI's own files.

Although the National Action Movement leaflet contained numerous points of misinformation—many of which directly related to the FBI and their role in Nash's investigation as well as the alleged disappearance of Nash's FBI records—the FBI kept its distance and neither confirmed nor denied any of the allegations. In a memo about the increased number of queries that the FBI received concerning the National Action Movement leaflet, C. D. De-Loach wrote that several "individuals have written in to us concerning this matter, and the Director has approved replies stating the confidential nature of FBI files. *Such answers will avoid implication of the* FBI *in the political campaign in Wisconsin*" (WFO121-12261-77; emphasis added). This silence when faced with such inaccuracies added to the perception of wrongdoing on the part of Nash. The FBI's practice of not correcting such misinformation embedded the FBI in Nash's political campaign, and their silence helped unseat Nash from the position of lieutenant governor.

In 1961 President Kennedy appointed Philleo Nash to be the U.S. commissioner of Indian affairs, where he fought for native rights until his removal in 1966 (Nash 1986:195). Nash served as advocate for indigenous peoples, although his approach to controversial issues seemed more reserved than that of his pre-McCarthy encounters. Nash later taught at American University from 1971 to 1977, and he was long an active force in the Society of Applied Anthropology. He returned to Wisconsin for the decade preceding his death in 1987.

Ashley Montagu: The Radical Threat of the Nonexistence of Race

Ashley Montagu studied at the London School of Economics and at Kings College, London, before leaving for the United States in 1927. In the United States he studied anthropology with Franz Boas, receiving a Ph.D. from Columbia in 1937.[8] Montagu was a prolific writer on a variety of topics, and he was well regarded for his popularization of anthropology. He published over sixty books on topics ranging from racism, evolution, the biases in the notion of IQ, the natural superiority of women, and the nature of human aggression. He wrote hundreds of articles for popular publications, such as *Redbook*, and he became an influential voice of reason on pressing social issues.

A common thread linking much of Montagu's life's work was his patient commitment to rationally examining how cultural differences were often misinterpreted as "natural" differences—whether these were differences in gender, race, or ethnicity. Perhaps more than any other twentieth-century anthropologist, Montagu threatened American notions of the biological realities of race. His contributions to the United Nation's 1949 "Statement on Race," a document affirming the biological equality of all peoples, was an important milestone for applied anthropology (see Montagu 1972). Given the FBI's suspicious obsessions concerning those who advocated for racial equality it is not surprising to find that he was the subject of a prolonged investigation.

The FBI began a security investigation of Montagu apparently as a tangential outcome of a 1953 investigation of the state of Communist infiltrations in higher education and in the Institute for Advanced Study. Records from the FBI linked Montagu with a 1946 movement protesting Harold Ickes's hardline anti-Communist remarks (WFO100-40292-1), and they recorded him contributing funds to abolish the poll tax and, in 1946, to assist the Southern Conference for Human Welfare. Records further indicated that Montagu published a letter opposing the "Mundt-Nixon Police State Bill," and that he belonged to the New Jersey Committee for Peaceful Alternatives (WFO100-40292). In spite of these actions, however, Montagu was unknown to all Communist Party informants contacted in the New Jersey area.

Many of the peace and racial equality groups to which Montagu belonged were considered by the FBI to be Communist front organizations, and the FBI cataloged summaries of these groups as well as Montagu's known involvement with each (NY100-402992-2 10/30/53). FBI records, obtained through interviews with informers as well as "Trash-Cover" and garbage-rummaging operations, indicate that Montagu belonged to or served in the following organizations: the Interim Committee of the Civil Rights Congress (1946), Independent Citizens Committee of the Arts, Sciences, and Professions (1948), American Committee for Spanish Freedom (1946), Joint Anti-Fascist Refugee Committee (1948), National Federation for Constitutional Liberties (1948), Russian War Relief, Inc. (1942), Philadelphia Council of American Soviet Friendship (1947), American Council for a Democratic Greece (1947), American Jewish Congress (1948), Association of Interns and Medical Students (1948), Teachers Union of Philadelphia (1951), American Association of Scientific Workers (1947), and Philadelphia Council of the Arts, Sciences, and Professions (1949) (WFO100-402992-3 11/10/53).

The FBI's collection of reviews and newspaper clippings is a testimony to Montagu's importance as a popular spokesman for anthropological notions of equality and moderation. One of the largest files of clippings relates to the public impact of Montagu's 1942 *Man's Most Dangerous Myth: The Fallacy of Race* (WFO100-402992-7 1/29/54). In this work—a magnum opus still in print over six decades later—Montagu critically examines the cultural construction of race; effectively arguing against the racist typologies then prevalent in American, or even Nazi, society. *Man's Most Dangerous Myth* had a dramatic effect on American anthropology, as well as on both intellectual and general audiences. The F B I's interest in reactions to this work reflects their bias that racial activism was part of a vast Communist conspiracy rather than a natural outgrowth of America's self-evident principles that all people are created equal. In order to gather information on Montagu the F B I interviewed New York University's vice chancellor (WFO100-402992-4 12/31/53), consulted INS records, and examined the details of Montagu's coming to America and name change (WFO100-402992-5).

A photocopy of the 1942 New York School for Democracy academic catalog listed Montagu as an anthropology instructor, but Montagu later explained that the catalog was in error:

> Poznonski, Weltfish and Bernhard Stern were all communists. There was another grad student named [Jack] Harris who had to escape to Cuba [*sic*, actually Costa Rica] whose communism had run him into trouble. I was never a communist and have always been what was called a liberal— even [though] Walter Winchell called me a communist in one of his columns. On another occasion Einstein and I were bracketed as comrades in the press and [by Russell] Maguire–I think that this Catholic guru owned the American Mercury, which he purchased from Alfred Knopf. As for the School of Democracy, I did give them a lecture at which time I discovered they were a communist organization at which time I wrote them a furious letter of protest.
>
> Einstein roared with laughter when I told him of the libel that had been uttered by the Catholic idiot. (Montagu to Price 12/28/98)

One informant reported that "many of the officers and faculty members of [the School for Democracy] were known to him during 1943 as Communist Party members and sympathizers," adding that "he did not know [Montagu] as a Communist Party member or sympathizer, furthermore, he did not have any knowledge as to the degree of association [Montagu] may have had with officers or faculty members of this school who were Communist Party members or sympathizers" (WFO100-402992-6 1/27/54).

In 1953 former chief research director for HUAC, J. B. Matthews, published in the *American Mercury* an article titled "Communism and the Colleges," which named Montagu as a sponsor of the Mid-Century Conference for Peace held in Chicago in 1950 (WFO100-402992-7; Matthews 1953). Matthews claimed that Montagu held a "socialist view on American society," and the FBI recorded in their files Matthews's quotation of Montagu's statement that "a profit-motive, economic-struggle-for-existence society is a predatory society, a class-and-caste society, a divisive society, in which each person is an isolate preying upon and preyed upon by others" (WFO100-402992-7 1/29/54).

Montagu Sacked from Rutgers

A memo from SAC Newark to Hoover reported that the Newark "office has not developed any information indicating recent activity by [Montagu] on behalf of the CP in New Jersey" (WFO100-402992-9 2/12/54). Because Montagu was chair of Rutgers's anthropology department it was decided that they would not interview individuals on campus until their background investigation was completed. The FBI also determined that Montagu's wife, Helen Marjorie Peakes, was unknown to informants with knowledge of Boston-area Communist Party members (WFO100-402992-10 3/11/54).

The Newark SAC recommended that the investigation of Montagu be closed due to the lack of information on the possibility of ties to any Communist organization (WFO100-402992-13 4/26/54), and the Washington field office compiled some final reports and temporarily suspended its investigation (WFO100-402992-14 4/30/54). After "all outstanding leads" concerning Montagu had been closed, the investigation was officially closed on August 5, 1954 (WFO100-402992-17).

In 1954 Ashley Montagu was fired from Rutgers University one year after a letter was sent to university president Lewis W. Jones "recounting remarks made about Montagu by an important alumnus, the vice president of the Hanover Bank. Referring to a presentation made by Montagu to the Women's Club of Milwaukee, he stated: 'One of the prominent Milwaukee ladies who attended the meeting told me that the audience was shocked and highly insulted when Dr. Montagu, in his closing remarks, suddenly shifted to a blistering attack on Senator McCarthy. It was quite apparent that Dr. Montagu's position coincided with the usual Communistic theme song'" (Sperling 2000:585). After being fired from Rutgers, Montagu focused on writing popular books and articles on anthropological topics.

Two years after Montagu was fired, the Norfolk SAC notified Hoover that Montagu had been invited to deliver a public talk at the inauguration of Grellet Simpson as chancellor of Mary Washington College. This Norfolk agent wrote that Colgate Darden (former Virginia governor and president of the University of Virginia) was asked "why Montagu should be asked to come to Virginia to speak at the inauguration of the Chancellor of Mary Washington College when the state officials of Virginia were endeavoring to resist integration and Montagu was in favor of integration. ▮▮▮▮▮▮▮▮

stated that he also contacted ██████████ [at] Mary Washington College, [and] advised him of the background of Ashley Montagu. ██████████ stated that he was interested in Montagu's appearance in Virginia and that he intended to 'smear' Montagu in a coming issue of *The Virginian* which is the official publication of the Virginia League, an organization which resisted integration in the State of Virginia" (WFO100-402992-17X 10/15/56). The FBI reported that an agitator planned to question Montagu regarding his views on integration at the Mary Washington College inauguration. Records from the FBI do not clarify whether or not this agitator was an agent provocateur, but their advance knowledge of these plans and their general deployment of such tactics suggests this possibility.

Montagu resigned from the American Association of Physical Anthropologists in 1953 and from the American Anthropological Association in 1955, "because," he states, "of their inactivity in rising up against the House Un-American Activities Committee and similar organizations. I had protested this at the American Anthropological Association annual meeting, and also at the American Association of Physical Anthropologists—I remember [Ales] Hrdlička getting riled up and exclaiming 'we don't want to irritate those who are already sufficiently irritated'" (Montagu to Price 12/28/98).

The FBI showed a renewed interest in Montagu in 1968 and generated a detailed thirty-six page "Correlation Summary" report, the impetus for which is not clear. The report summarized all the information collected on Montagu, including professional, political, and personal information and a detailed dossier of all political and social organizations to which he was known to belong. The listing was extremely detailed and included itemized reports of petitions he'd signed advocating the abolition of HUAC and promoting various movements for racial equality; notes of his work being mentioned in publications such as the *Daily Worker*; and lists of the numerous public talks he had given on racial equality or peace. The report contained a quote from a February 2, 1957, Walter Winchell broadcast and newspaper column where Winchell commented on Ashley Montagu's appearance on the television program "The $64,000 Question." In this column Winchell wrote that Montagu "was the signer for a brief before the U.S. Supreme Court on behalf of the Communist Party" (WFO100-402992-18 2/13/68).

This report clarifies that although the Washington field office closed its investigation of Montagu in 1956, other FBI offices continued to collect information: the New York bureau recorded that it checked on Montagu in 1964, and the U.S. Customs Foreign Propaganda Unit reported that Montagu had received a publication titled "No More Hiroshima" described as "foreign communist political propaganda" (WF0100-402992-18:33 2/13/68), and they described Montagu's involvement with an anti–Vietnam War "Conscientious Resistance" group (1967) and various other antiwar protests.

Several reports from 1967 and 1968 list Montagu's anti-war actions. There is a curious, highly redacted, report from a Washington, D.C. based FBI agent sent to FBI Director William Webster labeled "Classified by 8960, Exempt from GDS, Categories 2 and 3, Date of Declassification Indefinite" (WF0100-402992 4/18/78). The final entry in Montagu's released FBI file is dated April 18, 1978, and provides a summary of the FBI's interest in Montagu and his affiliations and states that "no information is available to indicate Montagu had been or is in a position to provide information which might be harmful to the national security" (WF0100-402992 4/18/78). We are thus left to wonder how many tens of thousands of dollars were spent by the FBI to reach such an obvious conclusion about this compassionate, principled, and gentle man.

The Hazards of Publicly Fighting Racism

The FBI's interest in Nash and Montagu was at first piqued and later prolonged by their advocacy for racial equality. Nash strove to change federal policies and attitudes from within the federal bureaucracy, while Montagu conducted original research and argued his case to the masses as a critical popularizer and developer of vital critiques of race and racism. As the FBI imagined traces of Communist ideology in Nash's and Montagu's work, they intensified their surveillance and investigations—even though they found no evidence of connections to Communism or wrongdoing of any sort. But the lack of evidence was not important. The FBI was so paranoid that a lack of evidence seemed to suggest the presence of broad and deep conspiracies.

Karl Wittfogel's willingness to inform on Nash to the FBI raises questions about the extent and impact of such practices. The FBI's tendency to protect informers from the FOIA process leaves us to speculate on the extent to which other anthropologists informed on their colleagues. But collecting Wittfogel's speculations padded the FBI's files and helped exaggerate the significance of Nash and Montagu's names appearing in the catalog of the School for Democracy.

The American Anthropological Association's silence during the public persecutions of Nash and Montagu is remarkable. By this time the AAA had quit commenting on such incidents, and the organization made no effort to defend these anthropologists as their reputations came under fire. Their silence not only reassured the red-baiters but also facilitated their attacks.

That liberal/moderates like Montagu and Nash could be even thought of as Communists highlights the threat that the issue of racial equality brought to mid-century America, and it illustrates how the pervasive climate of fear silenced those who might otherwise have questioned these drastic condemnations. Perhaps the only thing that fanned the FBI's paranoia more than the advocacy of racial equality was the advancement of international political positions that either ignored or ridiculed American Cold War positions as set forth in the Truman Doctrine. Anthropologists and other scholars who questioned America's Cold War commitment to containing Communism around the world frequently found themselves accused of engaging in un-American activities simply for questioning American foreign policies about regions known to them through fieldwork. In the following chapter I examine instances where anthropologists' loyalties were questioned when they questioned Cold War policies, strategies, and constructs.

CHAPTER 14

The Suspicions of Internationalists

One may be completely innocent but if one's actions
invite suspicions then one might as well be guilty. To be
trustworthy is not more important than to seem to be
trustworthy. — Julius O'Hara (Peter Lorre) in *Beat the Devil*

.

Vilhjalmur Stefansson was one of the twentieth-
century's best-known maverick explorers of the
Arctic — he was both a showman and a natural field
researcher. Born to Icelandic-Canadian immigrant
parents, as an infant his family moved to North
Dakota. As a student at Harvard Divinity School
Stefansson took a class in anthropology in 1904,
and he soon transferred to the anthropology department to begin work on a doctoral degree that
he never completed.

Under the tutelage of Frederic Putnam, Stefansson conducted his first fieldwork in Iceland where
he examined the relationship between the introduction of cereal-based foods and increased rates
of tooth decay (Stefansson 1964:48). He was influenced by Putnam in many ways, not the least
of which was Putnam's own bias against the bureaucratic wrangling of academia. Putnam's views
had a deep impact on Stefansson, who then chose

to master his field without completing a program for advanced degrees or bothering with the standards of academic posturing (see Stefansson 1964:55). Stefansson's linguistic fluency and general knowledge of Iceland and the Arctic made him an invaluable research companion. He participated in the University of Chicago's 1906–1907 polar expedition, and after its failure he procured funds from the American Museum of Natural History for prolonged research among various Inuit groups. He later accompanied Diamond Jenness on the 1915–1918 Canadian Arctic expedition, and he became a minor celebrity after publishing popular accounts of his fieldwork in books and articles (Stefansson 1913, 1921).

In 1921 Stefansson coordinated a controversial expedition to Wrangel Island—a two-thousand-square-mile island in the Arctic Ocean, one hundred miles north of Siberia.[1] Arguing that claims of Wrangel Island's ownership were in dispute, Stefansson sent an expedition of four men (Allan Crawford, Fred Maurer, Lorne Knight, and Milton Galle) and an Inuit woman (Ada Blackjack) to establish a permanent base of residence based on the local game food sources. It is likely that the expedition would have succeeded had they followed Stefansson's original plan to buy *umiaks* (traditional Inuit open boats) while stocking up on supplies in Nome, but the crew changed plans at the last minute. Alaskans were outraged to learn that the party had first raised a British flag claiming the island for Canada, and ill feelings intensified when Harold Noice and the rescue ship the *Donaldson* returned two years later to find that Ada Blackjack was the only survivor. Crawford, Galle, and Maurer had disappeared heading over the ice to Siberia the previous year, and Knight had died of scurvy shortly before the arrival of the ship.

The news of the expedition's tragic outcome shocked the world, and Ada Blackjack's rescuer, Harold Noice—for reasons unknown, but perhaps in order to attract sensationalistic attention—altered Lorne Knight's notebooks in a manner suggesting that details of a sexual nature had been erased. Noice told the *New York World* "that Ada killed Galle after he spurned her" (Hunt 1986:202). Stefansson was subjected to severe criticism in the international press for his role in mounting such an ill-prepared expedition for what appeared to be personal reasons of fame and glory. When Noice's reports claimed that Stefansson had sent a youthful and inexperienced party to their death, criticism of Stefansson intensified even though the party members were in their late twenties and well experienced in arctic travel and survival (Stefansson 1964:260–63). Noice later confessed to Stefansson that he had exaggerated his press reports due to "a serious nervous condition," and later he publicly apologized for his conduct in the matter (Hunt 1986:202; Stefansson 1964:263).

The Wrangel Island expedition first brought Stefansson to the FBI's attention. A January 17, 1922, summary report from New York City, titled "In Re: Vilhjalmur Stefansson," reads as follows:

> While interviewing ▇▇▇▇▇▇ that the above explorer had sent out an expedition in September, 1921, consisting of four men, this expedition being designated as the Stefansson Advance Polar Expedition, and it is understood to be headed by a man by the name of Knight. This expedition was placed on Wrangel Island by the Ship "Silver Wave," commanded by Captain Jake Hammer. Captain Hammer stated to ▇▇▇▇▇▇ that upon arriving at Wrangel Island the first act of this expedition was to raise the British flag and take possession of the Island in the name of the British Government, this, according to ▇▇▇▇▇▇ in violation of the international Law, as Wrangel Island was taken by the United States in 1881. The expedition to Wrangel Island, in so far as it was transported by Captain Hammer, was financed by Carl Lohman, a friend of Stefansson who guaranteed Captain Hammer's pay for the trip. ▇▇▇▇▇▇ states that when these four men sailed on the "Silver Wave" their port of departure was Nome, Alaska, which is Captain Hammer's home port, and they took with them a young Eskimo girl considered handsome, who was an attractive woman as Eskimo go. This woman was taken by them ostensibly as a seamstress. ▇▇▇▇▇▇ states that there undoubtedly will be jealousy and trouble among the four men on Wrangel Island before the winter is over, which may even result in one or more of them splitting with the rest of the crowd. Agent would suggest that in the event of this occurring, any one of the disgruntled members of the expedition might be a good informant regarding the alleged seizure of the Island for the British government and any other activities of Stefansson or his expedition. (WF062-1219)

Fifteen years later Stefansson asked the FBI for help interpreting alterations made to Lorne Knight's Wrangel Island journal. On December 21, 1939, J. Edgar Hoover wrote Stefansson to inform him of the results of the FBI's forensic tests and examinations of the Wrangel Island diary. After several pages of detailed analysis Hoover concluded that "it is apparent that the deletions are of a character which would occur if a person reading hastily through the diary and failing to observe in detail all of the entries, desires to create the impression of some sensational information being suppressed and hastily erases portions at places which because of the erasures will appear significant but which actually contain no more information than other portions which remain unchanged" (WF062-1219-14). A week later Stefansson replied to Hoover, writing: "You have deciphered enough so that, when your work is taken with that of the two others, it is now clear, as indeed your letter explicitly states, that the reasons given by Mr. Noice for his mutilation of the Knight diary are not the true reasons. He said he did it to hide proof of immorality. But you have shown (a) that no immorality is involved in the erased passages and (b) that the content of the erased passages is only more of the same information as contained in the diary part that were not erased" (WF062-1219-15 12/27/39). With this exchange, Stefansson's contact with the FBI concerning the Wrangel Island affair ended, but once the Cold War got underway the FBI's interest in Stefansson intensified.

Black, White, and Red All Over: Encyclopedia Arctica

In the 1930s and 1940s the FBI monitored Stefansson's membership in dozens of progressive groups such as the Committee of Fair Play for Puerto Rico, the American Russian Institute, and the Committee for the Protection of the Foreign Born (WF0100-7513-2 12/26/40). The FBI tracked an "undated press release" from the magazine *Soviet Russia Today* in which Stefansson supported the "Friendly North Doctrine," saying, "there is no reason to fear Soviet invasion through Alaska," and that he believed that "the Soviets are not an aggressive people" (WF0100-7513-1 12/26/40). In HUAC's files the FBI identified over thirty subversive organizations to which Stefansson belonged.

Because of his neutral approach to the Soviet Union, stories quoting Stefansson frequently appeared in the Communist Party's *Daily Worker* newspaper. One story from the December 3, 1940, edition, under the headline "Stefansson Urges U.S. Friendship with Soviets after Alaska Tour," reported him as saying that Alaskans "had no fear of Russian expansion or aggression but rather were uneasy about Japanese penetration via the Bering Sea fishing waters." Other *Daily Worker* articles reported his talks on Soviet-U.S. friendship (12/19/40), his opposition to legislation such as the Mundt Bill (6/6/48) and the Anti-Alien Dempsey Bill (4/29/40), and his opposition to the inclusion of Argentina in regional security talks (5/7/45).

Stefansson had little concern for the paranoia and posturing of the Cold War, but in the end he was not allowed to operate outside of the realm of these political realities. Stefansson's career suffered two direct Cold War setbacks. The first derived from his involvement with the doomed *Encyclopedia Arctica* and the second involved Senator McCarthy's interest in his work and politics.

At the end of World War II the Office of Naval Intelligence asked Stefansson to oversee the compilation of an encyclopedic survey of scientific knowledge on the Arctic and sub-Arctic. His wartime work and his international reputation as one of the most knowledgeable scholars of the Arctic made him a natural choice for this position. In 1946 Stefansson agreed to be the Encyclopedia's editor-in-chief, writing much of the copy and taking on the responsibility of identifying source materials and locating suitable experts and translators from a pool of scholars around the world. He later recalled: "When I signed the encyclopedia contract with the United States Navy, I counted on Soviet help almost as much as I counted on British or Canadian. I hoped that Russian cooperation would give us as good coverage for the northern USSR as we could get for any other parts of the world that I had not myself visited" (Stefansson 1964:361–62).

Stefansson's collection of international polyglots compiled a wealth of materials for translation and incorporation into the encyclopedia, but soon the Cold War context of this enterprise became overwhelmingly apparent. Stefansson states that during "the beginning of the encyclopedia's second year [the staff] began ruefully to realize the many disadvantages . . . of a cold war with the Soviets" (1964:362). Air travel (and eventually ICBMs) in the Cold War context transformed the great frozen north from a barren desert of little interest to the quickest route for the Soviets and the United States to exchange a sudden and final volley of atomic weapons. Not only did the Soviets control about half of the Arctic region, but as tensions between Washington and Moscow increased, geography and ethnology became increasingly politicized. What Stefansson hoped would have been openly accessible scientific data became potential intelligence data. Individuals with detailed knowledge of anything Soviet automatically became suspect in the United States where political neutrality, or the luxury of rolling one's eyes at the absurd logic of McCarthyism, became a thing of the past. When Stefansson hired an American-born translator of Russian who had studied Russian in Moscow, his naval intelligence sponsors reacted with horror, concluding that "such a man . . . must have had some communistic leanings, if he was not actually a Communist stooge" (Stefansson 1964:364). As military personnel increasingly found themselves under fire from the attacks of Senator McCarthy, Stefansson's admiration for advances in Soviet aviation further damaged his credibility within the Pentagon.

Despite these problems the first two volumes of *Encyclopedia Arctica* were shipped out to Johns Hopkins University Press for publication in 1948, with arrangements made for other volumes to follow at a projected rate of four per year until the projected twenty volumes all appeared in print (Stefansson 1964:365; cf. Hunt 1986:260). But Stefansson was abruptly notified that the navy was withdrawing their support and that the volumes would not appear in print (Stefansson 1964:365; Hunt 1986:260; cf AAANB 1951 5[3]:14).

Stefansson was never given a straightforward explanation for the navy's behavior, but over the years he developed his own theory. In the early 1960s Stefansson mused that

> after more than a decade of listening to theories, hunches, and supported conclusions, I am increasingly in favor of a view of my own that developed while McCarthyism was collapsing and the fires it started were cooling off. I feel that at first the Navy higher-ups did not take McCarthyism much more seriously than I did at the outset. Yet, when they saw McCarthy, in Senate committee hearings, riding roughshod over the Army, they got the idea that it would be wiser to sever connections with me, as one of McCarthy's possible targets, before they were accused of having anything to do with me. They could then admit ruefully, if accused, that they had at first been taken in but that they had fired me before I had had a chance to do any harm. They might then pride themselves on their performance of the noble task of preventing, by having stopped the publication of the encyclopedia, the spread of arctic knowledge potentially helpful to the Soviets. (1964:366)

McCarthy had requested "information from the Department of Navy regarding the type of work that Stefanssen was doing for the Navy either under his own name or under any other name or organization." On November 28, 1950, the secretary of the Navy informed McCarthy "that specific instructions had been issued and that no classified information was to be disclosed to Stefansson nor was Stefansson authorized to enter any Naval installation; further the Navy had never sponsored any trip into the Arctic by Stefansson" (WFO100-7513-50). Thus as political concerns obliterated even the simple collection of data by declaring entire geopolitical regions to be sensitive; the abilities of anthropologists to conduct fieldwork became increasingly limited. Anthropologists were thus forced to limit their geographic arena of inquiry while concurrently avoiding the application of overtly Marxist analyses.

New Hampshire Politics, Land, and Lattimore

Stefansson's next encounter with Cold War politics, which even brought more scrutiny to him and his wife, resulted from his friendship with Owen Lattimore. Lattimore, Stefansson, and their wives had been friends for some time. In the 1940s Stefansson sold the Lattimores a joint ownership on a large homestead adjoining the Stefansson's home in rural Vermont. After Senator McCarthy accused Lattimore of being a high-level Soviet agent, the Lattimores were forced to sell their interest in this property to raise funds for his legal defense. The Stefanssons acted as the Lattimores' sales agents for the property, and they sold it to Ordway Southard who had answered their advertisement in the *Saturday Review of Literature*. But when Southard turned out to have once run for governor of Alabama on the Communist Party ticket, the FBI decided that Stefansson must have been an important link between Lattimore and Southard (Stefansson 1964:370). This random link fueled further speculations by Lucille Miller (a key figure in accusations that Alger Hiss was a Communist) who accused Ordway Southard of having ties to Soviet Communism.

The locations of the Stefanssons' property holdings further complicated matters. Because of his political support for Vermont senators Aiken and Flanders, Stefansson was a registered voter in Vermont (the location of their farm), although he also owned property and was employed in New Hampshire. His wife, Evelyn, however, had decided that these conditions meant she should register to vote in New Hampshire.[2] One day Stefansson received a phone call from New Hampshire's attorney general asking him to come to his office to submit to an interview concerning all he knew about Communism. Stefansson replied that he would be happy to do so "to the proper officer and in the right office. Since I was a Vermont resident, however, he must give me time to decide whether a Vermonter ought to accept this kind of invitation from Concord or await one from Montpelier" (1964:372). Later that day Stefansson was served a summons to appear at the New Hampshire attorney general's office. After consulting his attorney, it was decided that he should appear at Attorney General Wyman's office the following day: "When we appeared at the attorney general's the next morning, Wyman seemed surprised that my attorney was about the best, legally or socially, that Concord could produce. The examination began. Did I know much about Communists? Of course I did, for I was an alumnus of the Harvard Divinity School, where they considered Jesus a Communist, and we knew a lot about Jesus. That was not what he meant. Did I know anything about American Communists? I replied that I had lived for years with the North American Eskimos, who were all formerly communist, though some were now becoming quite capitalistic" (1964:373).

Wyman was perturbed by Stefansson's playful response and told him to stop "play-acting" and tell him about American Communists known to him. Stefansson then recounted how some time earlier he'd seen an interview in the *New York Times* with a Harvard classmate of his named Crosbie in which Crosbie admitted he was a Communist; after reading the article Stefansson telephoned Crosbie and made a lunch appointment. Stefansson informed the attorney general that "if the attorney general cared for hearsay evidence, I would be glad to report what Crosbie had told me" (1964:373). Instead,

Wyman asked detailed questions about his wife, Evelyn, relating to when she had left Hungary and what contacts she maintained with Hungarians. When Stefansson informed them of Evelyn's age and that she had been born in New York, Wyman exhibited confusion and disappointment. Stefansson was then excused while his attorney conferred with the attorney general in private.

In this private meeting it was revealed that the attorney general was not after him—they had thought that Stefansson was "an elderly fool who had been hoodwinked by a scheming wife" (Stefansson 1964:373). Wyman showed Stefansson's attorney a letter from an informer claiming that "Evelyn had been a high-ranking communist functionary before she left Hungary and that she was now indoctrinating Dartmouth students and misleading me while masquerading as a teacher of the Russian language" (1964:374). Although Evelyn learned Russian in New York and at Middlebury College, and, further, she had never been employed by Dartmouth to teach Russian, she too was summoned to appear for an interview with attorney general Wyman's staff.

Accusations Fly: "Joiner of Red Fascist Groups"

A sensationalistic article published in the *Journal American* on January 12, 1948, claimed to have uncovered efforts by Stefansson the Communist to warp the thinking of the Boy Scouts by allowing them to camp on his property. Under the headline "Reds to Train 30 Scout Executives" reporter Howard Rushmore wrote:

> Thirty Boy Scout executives, representing one of the most actively anti-Communist youth organizations in America, will take a training course under a veteran joiner of Red Fascist groups, it was learned today.
>
> These Scout executives from the Jersey area will spend a [week] in "Operation Snowdrift," starting Jan. 25 at the Bethel, Vt, home of Vilhjalmur Sefansson.
>
> According to the House Committee on un-American Activities, Stefansson is a member or sponsor of 76 Communist front organizations, including a number labeled subversive by the U.S. Attorney General. . . .
>
> The Scout leaders, all full-time members of the national staff will have Winter camping, testing of equipment and other Winter exercises at the Stefansson farm. They also will hear lectures by Stefansson, widely known as an Arctic explorer.
>
> A Scout spokesman said Stefansson "offered the use of his farm" and in no way is connected with the Scouts. He admitted that "no check was made of Stefansson's political activities.

Many of these executives will later teach in the national Scouts training schools throughout the United States. . . .

Stefansson's articles have appeared in such Red Fascist publications
as the New Masses. He was a member of the Citizens Committee to Free
Earl Browder, a group set up to win a pardon for the one-time Communist leader convicted of passport evasion.

The explorer also sponsored the American Committee for the Protection of Foreign Born, a front group named as subversive by the U.S.
Attorney General. (WFOIOO-7513-A)

More accusations of Communist affiliations were to follow. A 1951 FBI
security briefing in New York City reported that an unidentified individual
"furnished records during 1947 which reflected that the subject was reported
to be a Communist Party member and that most of his employees were Communist Party members" (NYIOO-9953-4 6/5/51). The report noted concerns
that Stefansson had worked with Soviets in the Arctic back in 1937–1938, and
that in May 1950 an unnamed individual reported he heard Stefansson say
"that Russia is winning the cold war, therefore the United States would start
the next war because it is losing the cold war. [Stefansson] also indicated that
the United States would start the next war because it would be fought elsewhere and the people do not know the horrors of war. [Stefansson] stated
that Russia had ten to twenty thousand airplanes, which could destroy the
East and West Coast cities of the United States. Russia also has the best me-
chanics and the people are better fit and they have freedom to eat, according
to Stefansson. He said that 'wise man Stalin says it is more important to have
food than freedom of speech'" (NYIOO-9953-5). Such reports intensified FBI
interest in Stefansson, and it was only a matter of time before he became a
person of interest to Senator Joseph McCarthy.

On August 22, 1951, Louis Budenz told the Senate Subcommittee on Internal Security that he had firsthand information from "official reports" indicating that Stefansson was a Communist. The FBI reported that two days
later the New York *Herald Tribune* carried an article reporting that Stefansson
remarked that "he was 'a little surprised' at Louis Budenz, former Communist, listing him as a Communist. 'What an honor,' Mr. Stefansson said. 'I
would hate to be called a Communist by almost any one else, but I don't mind
it much from Budenz. If Gen. Marshall and Mrs. Roosevelt can be listed as
Communists by Sen. Jenner, I don't know why I can't be called one.' He said
he knew of 'no basis' for Mr. Budenz's charge" (WFOIOO-7513-55). Needless
to say, the FBI was not amused by Stefansson's lighthearted approach to Budenz's accusations.

Stefansson's unusual position outside of academia in addition to his personal wealth allowed him to sidestep some of the discomforts and humiliations of McCarthyism. With this independence came a measure of freedom not afforded those whose employment depended on a reputation free from accusations of thought-crimes or wrongdoing. This independence also brought a level of free speech not allowed to those who lived under the contingencies of employment on conditions of respectability. Had anthropologists such as Weltfish, Morgan, and Jacobs had such conditions of relative independence one can imagine different exchanges between them and their accusers. It is not that Stefansson did not suffer adverse consequences for speaking his mind. One need look no further than the military's cancellation of his *Encyclopedia Arctica*—a project that would have been a crowning achievement of his life's work—to observe part of the price he paid for his independence during this time of war.

Cora Du Bois and the Limits of Protest, Free Inquiry, and Academic Freedom

Cora Du Bois was born in 1903 into the Swiss-American family of Jean Jules and Mattie Schrieber Du Bois in Brooklyn, New York. As a child she enjoyed the benefits of a mixed continental and American upbringing, being schooled both in the United States and Europe. She received a B.A. in history from Barnard in 1927, and an M.A. in medieval history and culture the following year. Her studies at Barnard and Columbia brought her into contact with Ruth Benedict and Franz Boas, which sparked her interest in anthropology. With Benedict's recommendation and assistance Du Bois studied anthropology under Alfred Kroeber and Robert Lowie at Berkeley, where she received a Ph.D. in 1932. She worked as a research associate at Berkeley and then studied "types of psychiatric training suitable for professional anthropology" under a National Research Council Fellowship (Seymour 1989:73).

Du Bois's work used psychological techniques and theories to examine culture and personality. Unlike many other anthropologists drawn to the culture and personality movement, Du Bois's approach was grounded in the techniques and measurements of psychological examinations through her work with Abram Kardiner at the New York Psychoanalytic Society and Harry Murray at Harvard's Psychological Clinic. Her book *The People of Alor* (1944) is a sophisticated application of Western psychological models and measurements of personality development ranging from the Rorschach and Maze tests to the construction of pre-Eriksonian psychobiographies.

Like other women scholars of this period, Du Bois experienced difficulties securing viable academic employment. After encountering problems finding a full-time academic position in the 1930s, she became an instructor at Hunter and at Sarah Lawrence College, and in 1937 thru 1939 she received SSRC funding for Indonesian field research. Du Bois conducted intelligence and policy work during World War II, first as the chief of the Indonesian section of the OSS from 1942 to 1944 and later as the chief of the OSS's research branch in Ceylon from 1944 to 1945 (Rossiter 1995:4). She worked in the State Department until 1949 when she became a consultant at the World Health Organization (WHO) and elsewhere, eventually receiving an appointment to Harvard's prestigious Zemurray Stone-Radcliffe Professorship.

The FBI's 218-page file on Du Bois illustrates some of the ways that federal agencies such as the State Department or WHO restricted discussions through the machinations of McCarthyism. While Du Bois's politics were progressive, they were far from radical, and thus it was perhaps her insistence on examining policy issues from nonnationalistic, unethnocentric perspectives that brought on her decades of FBI surveillance. As an analyst who recognized both the power and justice of anticolonialist movements in the postwar world, Du Bois attracted the scrutiny of Hoover's FBI.

On June 25, 1948, J. Edgar Hoover wrote Samuel D. Boykin (acting director of the Office of Controls at the Department of State) reporting on a "preliminary inquiry" concerning Cora Du Bois. Hoover indicated that HUAC records stated that Du Bois's name appeared in a letter published in the *New Masses* (WFO121-8030-4 6/25/48). Also included in Du Bois's file is an open letter to Brazil's President Getulio Vargas, which was published as an advertisement in the *New Masses* (12/3/40). The letter includes as cosignatories anthropologists such as Ruth Benedict, Franz Boas, A. F. Montagu, Bernhard Stern, as well as other individuals including Thorton Wilder, Rockwell Kent, Hugo Black, and Horace Grenell and Anita Marburg from Sarah Lawrence. The letter calls for the release of Luis Carlos Prestes from Brazil's prison system, where he had been held for five years. The letter also argues that the principles of freedom, democracy, and dissent would be upheld with his release. Du Bois's letter concerned Hoover, and he asked Boykin to "institute appropriate investigations at Alor, Netherlands East Indies, and Kandy, Ceylon, to determine if [Du Bois] adheres to the doctrines of the Communist Party or is a member of any organization declared by the Attorney General to be within the purview of Executive Order #9835. In the event substantive information is developed reflecting disloyalty on the part of . . . [Du Bois], it will be appreciated if you will endeavor to secure signed statements from individuals furnishing disloyal information" (WFO121-8030-4 6/25/48).

When the FBI interviewed Du Bois later in 1948 they asked if she had ever signed a Communist-sponsored petition. She replied:

To my knowledge no. However, in searching my memory I recall that the only petition I have ever signed which might have political implications involved the following situation:

From 1939–1942 I taught at Sarah Lawrence College in Bronxville, New York. At that time ███████████ was on the staff. Occasionally we met at the 125th Street station of New York Central on our way to classes at Bronxville. Since anthropological interests were our only common ground, we frequently discussed problems and personalities in that field. In 1940 or 1941 I remember that we shared a train seat. . . . ███████████ said that Vargas had arrested Prestes. Both names were vaguely familiar to me as associated with Brazil but I had no further knowledge of the personalities. To the best of my memory I asked who Vargas and Prestes were. Again, to the best of my memory ███████████ said that Prestes was a liberal intellectual; that Vargas was a Fascist dictator; that intellectuals should take a stand on the matter and would sign a petition. I believe that he held out a green sheet of paper and I know that I hastily signed it with a pen I had in hand while working on my class notes. . . . Aside from the occasional contacts while commuting, my relations with ███████████ were limited to rare lunches at faculty tables in the Sarah Lawrence dining room. I have not seen ███████████ since 1942 when he asked me to dinner at his home to meet his wife.[3] (WFO138-1830-17 11/17/48)

The FBI also inquired about an individual who had worked for the State Department until she resigned after her name appeared on New York primary records as having registered as a member of the Communist Party, and it became known she had signed a Communist petition in the 1940s. Du Bois described her relationship to this individual and then asserted that the individual had been railroaded into resigning, stating "my association with [her] convinces me that she is not a Communist and never has been a Communist and that she lacks real political interest or knowledge in either domestic or foreign affairs and finally that the evidence leading to her forced resignation were actions of an idealistic but immature person trying to assert her personal independence" (WFO138-183017:9 11/17/48).

In the following months the FBI interviewed Du Bois's acquaintances, neighbors, former neighbors, colleagues, former instructors, and friends in six cities across the United States. Although the FBI collected no specific information suggesting that Du Bois was anything other than a loyal, hardworking, patriotic scholar, one source told the FBI "she was of the opinion that Du Bois was a Communist, although she had no tangible proof" (WFO21-8038-10).

This investigation of Du Bois came during a period of widespread purges at the State Department's Asian Division. The anti-Communist hysteria shaped not just American containment policy—decisions of who could advise the state had long-term policy implications, including launching America toward its future wars in Southeast Asia. Eventually, a generation of America's best China analysts, including John Paton Davis Jr., John Service, Fulton Freeman (Ruth Benedict's nephew), John Carter Vincent, and dozens of others were fired for their lack of support for Chiang Kai-shek (see Kahn 1975). Like many of her liberal colleagues at the State Department, Cora Du Bois sought work outside of the government when in the new Cold War the oppressive climate curtailed her scope of analysis.

On April 18, 1950, J. Edgar Hoover wrote Seth Richardson (name redacted, but title included in released materials), chairman of the Loyalty Review Board of the U.S. Civil Service Commission, responding to a request for information on Du Bois's loyalty. Hoover indicated that Senator McCarthy had informed the Senate in February that a State Department employee simply identified as "case number 60"

> was employed by oss in the Division of Research, from June 1942 to September 1945, at which time he [*sic*] was transferred to the State Department. He [*sic*] is now branch chief in Research and Intelligence. One of his former supervisors stated that he was a Communist.
>
> For some Time he [*sic*] has resided with another State Department employee, previously mentioned herein whose investigation was requested because of communistic activities. Nevertheless, this individual has been cleared and is still working in an important position where he [*sic*] handles top-secret material in the State Department. (WFO121-8038-31)

Hoover identified Du Bois as the individual referred to as "case number 60." Hoover noted with suspicion that Owen Lattimore had offered Du Bois a job in 1949 as part of a research project on Mongolia (WFO 121-8038-31-2). The FBI was also interested in Du Bois's domestic arrangements. Significant portions of her FBI files remain withheld by FOIA censors, and even after appeals it is not known if the FBI collected information on her sexual orientation, but there are portions of released records indicating the FBI was investigating a longtime housemate of Du Bois. Although the identity of this individual is not known, it is possible that these records pertain to Du Bois's longtime companion, Jeanne Taylor. Given the FBI's penchant for compiling extensive dossiers (at times used to blackmail or manipulate individuals) on individuals believed to be homosexual, this remains a possibility (Charns and Green 1998; Powers 1987; Summers 1993; Theoharris 1991, 1995).

An employee of the State Department's Far-East Southern Areas branch approached the FBI on February 6, 1953, reporting that the branch "had been infested with persons she believed were Communists or pro-Communists" (WFO138-1830-2). This informant indicated that because Du Bois directed the branch, she must be in part responsible for its Communist leanings. The informant added that Du Bois's refusal to sign the California loyalty oath was further proof of her commitment to radical politics. According to the FBI report, the informant's "suspicions of some of those in the branch were aroused when she found them [to be] staunch supporters of Ho Chi Minh a Moscow trained Communist who organized and heads the Viet Minh Movement, a nationalistic group opposed to colonial rule" (WFO138-1830-2). Articles critical of Ho Chi Minh were reportedly degraded in the Far-East branch as being "French inspired, while those supporting Ho Chi Minh were viewed favorably by Du Bois." The informant asked Du Bois if she believed Ho Chi Minh to be a Communist, and Du Bois reportedly replied that, "it's hard to draw the line where Nationalism ends and Communism begins" (WFO138-1830-2). The informant also said she clashed with Du Bois many times and that Du Bois threatened her opportunities for career advancement—although it is difficult to imagine anything more threatening to a State Department employee's career than a coworker secretly making damaging accusations to an FBI agent.

Du Bois's Resistance of the California Loyalty Oath

When Du Bois applied for a position at the World Health Organization in 1953, J. Edgar Hoover ordered the Washington SAC to conduct a full field investigation on her. The FBI was concerned with reports that Du Bois refused a prestigious position at the University of California at Berkeley because she was unwilling to sign the California loyalty oath (WFO138-1830-1).

Although Communists were banned in 1940 from teaching in the University of California system, on March 25, 1949, the Regents of the University of California adopted a loyalty oath for all employees. This action was taken in part as a preemptive means of preventing the California legislature from enacting similar legislation—thus positioning the regents to take a public stance declaring the university system to be hard on Communism (Schrecker 1986:117). The anti-Communist, or loyalty, oath was instituted with little notice until May when faculty found the document attached to their yearly contracts. Throughout summer 1949 faculty senates within the University of California system met and debated the oath. When only half of the university system's faculty returned signed oaths, the professors who refused to sign were paid but did not receive signed contracts. During the 1949–1950 academic year a series of maneuvers by the regents wore down the faculty's resolve and the majority of the faculty signed the oath.

Only thirty-one professors refused to sign the oath. Those refusing to sign were liberal defenders of civil rights, indeed, it is generally believed that not a single Communist refused to sign. As a testimony to the idiocy and ineffectuality of such oaths, it should be noted that several dozen members of the Communist Party did falsely sign the oath without penalty. In character with its cowardice during this period, the American Association of University Professors sat on the sidelines until 1956 before censuring the administration of the University of California for its mistreatment of professors who would not sign the oath (Schrecker 1986:123).

The California loyalty oath did, however, function as a wake-up call to many liberals and conservatives in the association. Even conservative George Murdock was outraged by this course of action. Murdock paid his own way to the 1950 association meetings in Berkeley with the proclaimed primary purpose of organizing an opposition to the California loyalty oath situation (RAAA: 5, GM/RB 12/11/50). Given his actions as an FBI informant it is appropriate to wonder if these stated motivations and proclaimed positions represented his true positions. Certainly Murdock's contemporaries were surprised to see him take such action. When President Beals wrote Murdock expressing some surprise that Murdock was campaigning to oppose the oath, Murdock replied, "you intimate that my own standing has been changed from that of a year ago. I do not think that this is the case. We were then faced with a bogus issue, not a genuine one. This year it is a genuine issue threatening the very foundation of academic freedom and the freedom of scientific inquiry. I feel that a scientific association should not take a stand on political issues unless they seriously threaten the social foundations of science and teaching as I am convinced the present one does" (RAAA: 5, GM/RB 12/18/50). This was a very different public Murdock than the one who had attacked Bernhard Stern as a Communist just a few months earlier at the American Ethnology Society meetings, and who just a year earlier had secretly identified a dozen colleagues and "friends" to the FBI.

The 1949 retirement of Robert Lowie as chair of Berkeley's anthropology department brought a nationwide search for a qualified individual to continue to guide Berkeley as a premiere anthropology department.[4] After a careful consideration of the candidates, Cora Du Bois was approached and offered the position of chair, and had she accepted she would have been the first female chair of a major anthropology department in the nation, and one of the few woman chairs of any department at a nationally recognized flagship university. But Du Bois's concerns that the California loyalty oath damaged academic freedom led her to decline this prestigious offer.

When San Francisco FBI agents interviewed anthropologists and others at the Berkeley campus in late July 1953, someone provided the FBI with a copy of the letter that Du Bois wrote to Berkeley President Robert Sproul explaining the impact of the California loyalty oath on her consideration of this position. The complete text of her letter is as follows:

Geneva,
Switzerland
27 September 1950

President Robert G. Sproul
University of California
Berkeley, California

Dear President Sproul:

On my return from a prolonged trip to South Asia, I found waiting for me the announcement of my appointment as professor of anthropology dated 21 July 1950. With it were the forms for the constitutional oath and the contract with the Communist Party clause. In the same mail I found letters from friends enclosing clippings from the New York Times on the deplorable difficulties which the University is facing these days on the issue of signing these contracts. I was particularly disturbed by news of the action taken against the University of California by the American Psychological Association.

To you, personally, I need scarcely reiterate my devotion to the University of California and my interest in seeing it resume its distinguished academic reputation. My loyalty to my country is also unquestioned. It is based on a profound faith in the traditional values expressed in its founding documents. I am deeply concerned by attacks on those traditions from radicals of the extreme right and extreme left. I recall my distress at the supine role of many intellectuals when Germany was coming under the influence of the Nazi Party. The miserable moral position of intellectuals in the US is too well known to need comment. I should not like to be counted among those who will justify any means for ends that may be laudable. However futile gestures against such means may sometimes be, not to make them is the beginning of personal and social degradation. In all conscience I cannot feel that I would be loyal to our country if I abet the adoption of methods used by ideological systems antipathetic to those of our democracy.

I have served for the last five years in a sensitive agency of our government. I know how demoralizing suspicions and repeated questioning of motives, thoughts and actions can be, and I also know that the nation is ill served when such demoralization attacks its employees. Whereas such scrutiny may be justified in sensitive agencies of the government it seems unpardonable in academic institutions, one of whose important functions is to foster the spirit of free and fearless inquiry. I would therefore have no hesitancy in signing the contract were the first 2-1/2 lines of the "Communist clause" deleted. The statement would then read: "I have no commitments in conflict with my responsibilities with respect to impartial scholarship and the free pursuit of truth. . . ."

Therefore, before signing the papers sent me, may I ask you to forward a full statement of the facts in this complicated and unfortunate case? I realize the undesirable position my hesitancy places the Department of Anthropology and that my hesitancy is only a very trivial factor in the many more serious difficulties facing you as a result of decisions by the Board of Regents.

Please accept my personal regards and my apologies for adding to your burdens at this time.

Yours sincerely,
Cora Du Bois (WFO138-1830-11)

The FBI did not collect President Sproul's reply, although Du Bois's letter explaining her decision to decline the appointment is included in her file.

July 30, 1951

President Robert Gordon Sproul
University of California
Berkeley, California

Dear President Sproul:

I regret that a negative decision on our "gentlemen's agreement" had to be reached early in July when you were absent from the campus. Since I still should have had to sign the new contract required by the Regents, your hope of last September that the situation might improve had not yet been realized. I was told that the State Supreme Court's review of the faculty case could not be expected before October. This is obviously too late for an appointment. The Department of Anthropology has long suffered from inadequate staffing and already had waited too long to make satisfactory plans for the coming semester.

In addition, since our last exchange of letters, a more trouble-some development has occurred. The State Loyalty Oath has been added to the requirements placed on the faculty. As you must realize, I had not intended to be blanketed into the California Civil Defense regulations when I contemplated joining the faculty. If I am to serve under a series of regulations appropriate to the defense activities of my country, there are undoubtedly more pertinent efforts than teaching anthropology. In accepting an appointment, I had even less expected to be asked to sign an oath whose meaning is obscured by vague drafting and that appears to have retroactive implications.

Today no reasonable person can believe that oaths are an assurance of loyalty. The cause does not lie exclusively in subversive ideologies. When oaths are multiplied and loosely drafted, they can and do engender cynicism in even the most upright people who are forced by personal considerations to sign them. The function of an oath, with all of its important implications for the maintenance of our social and legal system, is thereby jeopardized. Instead of being an affirmation of personal integrity, the oath is being used increasingly as a device intended to provide legal sanctions against communists and suspected communists. But many oaths including the California State loyalty oath, are so phrased that they can be used to serve against anyone holding certain kinds of opinions and joining types of organizations that are unpopular with a majority or even a powerful minority. The extension of such sanctions over a larger and larger portion of our population, even if not flagrantly abused, cannot fail to inhibit that free discussion and inquiry basic to the strength of our democracy. As I said to you in an earlier letter, I recognize the need for strict security controls in sensitive agencies of our government. But I believe also that the fundamental interests of our national security require us to guard jealously against the useless and unwarranted extensions of such controls and their loose application. You will surely agree that we cannot scrutinize too carefully every method suggested to safeguard our internal security lest in the process we forge tools that willful men or even well-intentioned but short-sighted ones can use to intimidate their less powerful but equally loyal fellow citizens. Intimidation is an insidious disease, like cancer it can develop undetected until it is too late to cure it. I feel sure that you join me in hoping that this disease will never gain headway among the California faculty despite the infection to which they are exposed.

I am told that the faculty of the Berkeley campus acquiesced to the state loyalty oath without protest on two main grounds: first, that in contradistinction to the Regents' oath it was non-discriminatory; and second, that it was the duty of the citizens of the state to abide by state laws. The first position must seem to you as it does to me a narrow "trade union" interpretation that evades the larger issue of academic freedom. The second position is incontrovertible but does not make employment in a state institution desirable to a non-resident. Fortunately, state laws are not irrevocable. When, however, they are to be submitted to referendum as a state constitutional amendment the question of state politics becomes urgent. Since state politics are thus brought into University affairs, any new faculty appointee is forced to consider them. I do not find reassuring the need to consider state politics in accepting an academic position. When the political forces at work in California are further scrutinized, the cause for concern seems even greater.

One cannot resist speculating upon other attitudes underlying the faculty acquiescence to the state loyalty oath. Had their still unresolved quarrel with the Regents over the more temperate, but still deplorable, University oath robbed them of insight by centering their attention on a narrower immediate issue? Were the emotions of the situation such that it seemed "wiser to cede the larger issue while fighting the smaller"? Were the preceding months of dispute so disheartening and distracting that an "ostrich" position seemed preferable to men interested in getting on with their work? Had the most courageous and farsighted members of the faculty already left the campus? These questions are not answerable, but the story of universities in the development of totalitarian states suggests such speculations.

During my five days on the Berkeley campus in July I had the privilege of talking to a relatively wide range of the faculty. The judgments on these issues varied greatly. However, the people I saw were, without exception, dedicated to maintaining the tradition of academic freedom and scholarly achievement for which the University has been noted. It was difficult not to join them in this undertaking. A refusal could be interpreted as too pessimistic a judgment on their efforts. On the other hand, acceptance could be interpreted as too optimistic a judgment on the situation as it existed early in July 1951. Clearly neither decision could be faultless.

For better or worse, the situation on the Berkeley campus has acquired symbolic proportions in the academic world and what will occur there will be proportionally magnified. Every success you and the faculty may achieve in maintaining your traditional standards will be heartening to all of us. If at any time I can be of assistance within the framework of views I have expressed, I shall be honored to have you call on me.

Please accept my warmest regards and my appreciation for the generous stand you personally, the faculty and the Department of Anthropology have taken in respect to the troublesome decision that faced me.

Yours sincerely,

Cora Du Bois (WF0138-1830-11)

Du Bois's decision to refuse the appointment must be considered without the hindsight that a few years later she would be appointed to one of academia's most prestigious positions at Harvard. When she declined the chair at Berkeley she did so without comparable offers from other institutions, and as such hers was a courageous act with negative consequences.

In November, 1951, the AAA's *News Bulletin* reported Du Bois's decision to decline Berkeley's offer, writing that her decision "to accept the directorship of a resources research program with the Institute of International Education rather than a position on the faculty of U. of Calif. points up the fact that the U.S. regents oath program is still, in spite of one adverse court decision, actively tearing away at the foundation of a great academic institution" (AAANB 1951 5(4):5).

As part of her employee background investigation for the World Health Organization the FBI interviewed a former coworker at the State Department's Office of Intelligence Research. Du Bois was described as a hardworking, loyal American posing no security risks, who believed, this individual felt, "in self-determination on the part of all peoples and that this appears to be her ideological make-up. . . . She believes that independence must be granted to all subjugated people and that independence will be obtained sooner or later" (WFO138-1830-17:5).

Kenneth Colegrove, a pro-McCarthy political scientist from Northwestern University, testified before the Judiciary Committee that Cora Du Bois had presented pro-Communist views at State Department roundtable discussions concerning American policy in Asia (see Wormser 1993). He summarized a lengthy statement made by Du Bois in which she said "one should remember in dealing with Southeast Asia that not all disorders are necessarily revolutionary. For the United States to interpret the Southeast Asian scene solely in terms of its own preoccupations with anti-Communism is to run the risk of seriously misunderstanding the forces at work in Southeast Asia and thereby of alienating the all-important leadership of the area" (WFO138-1830-17:12).

In 1947 United Fruit tycoon Samuel Zemurray donated a quarter of a million dollars to Harvard for the establishment of the Zemurray Stone-Radcliffe professorship for a distinguished female scholar from any academic discipline (Rossiter 1995:38). In 1954, on the retirement of historian Helen Maud Cam, the first Zemurray professor, Cora Du Bois became the second woman to hold a named chair at Harvard. Du Bois's appointment to this high-status position was the crowning jewel of a career that consistently pressed the limits of engendered access to positions of power and prestige. Her accomplishments were both large and small, and while many of the small accomplishments were of the type that are not generally listed on one's curriculum vitae they were nonetheless important.[5]

In February 1958 J. Edgar Hoover reconsidered his authorization for an interview with Du Bois regarding an unidentified espionage suspect. Hoover wrote that during an FBI interview (not included in her released FBI file) conducted in Honolulu on March 1, 1957, Du Bois had been "ostensibly cooperative" with the FBI but had "indicated that she was becoming 'tired' of repeated interviews regarding [the unidentified subject of the FBI's espionage investigation], emphasizing that she had been interviewed several times since 1944" (WFO100-35543 2/7/58). Hoover recommended that this reinterview of Du Bois "emphasize that the purpose of the interview is to develop information regarding the associates of ■■■■■■■ as well as to determine if she recalls any additional information regarding her" (WFO100-35543 2/7/58). No record of such an interview is included in the materials released by the Washington, Honolulu, and Boston FBI offices.

A Mixed-Up Confusion: Binds that Tie Lewis, Stefansson, Nash, Du Bois, and Montagu

Racial activism was not the only reason the FBI undertook investigations of American anthropologists — indeed, Hoover's suspicions were also raised by commitments to internationalist political agendas. Regardless of how supportive anthropologists were of various appendages of the Cold War's national security state, if there were suspicious indications that they made public statements in support of internationalist foreign policy, they were often subjected to FBI surveillance and investigations. Like liberal anthropologists Mead, Lewis, Montagu, Nash, and others, the FBI investigated Stefansson and Du Bois because their personal political views appeared to be outside of the narrow range of acceptable beliefs.

Many anthropologists worked with military and intelligence organizations during the Cold War. Some taught military courses in language, area studies, or cultural sensitivity, some worked as spies, and others worked as consultants on specific topics or geographic areas of interest (Price 1998a, 2002d). Regardless of an anthropologist's commitment to supporting the Cold War, however, their personal and professional views were scrutinized for traces of latent or manifest Communism.

There are some common themes found in the records of the FBI's pursuit of Du Bois and Stefansson, principal among which is that although they were devoted to establishing careers in public policy, the rigid institutional Cold War biases they encountered within government led them to shift their career paths. Du Bois left the State Department for work at other federal agencies, and eventually returned to finish her career in academia. Similarly, Stefansson was forced to abandon his massive encyclopedia project and was marginalized from policy matters.

The documents available on the FBI's surveillance of Lewis, Nash, Stefansson, Montagu, and Du Bois raise more questions than they answer. While we have some records of this monitoring, we know very little about how it impacted the personal and professional lives of these individuals. Although we do know that it was common practice during this period for J. Edgar Hoover to instruct FBI agents to leak information that appeared to be damaging to individuals it deemed subversive, we simply do not know if and how the FBI may have chosen to disseminate the information they gathered.

The FBI's practices during this period helped create and maintain the climate of fear that led to the cancellation of various research opportunities, and made the pursuit of governmental employment an unattractive or even impossible option for independent thinkers like Oscar Lewis, Philleo Nash, Vilhjalmur Stefansson, and Cora Du Bois. The FBI's investigation of these law abiding, non-Communist, non-Socialist, liberal anthropologists instructs us about the ever-present narrow boundaries of intellectual freedom. McCarthyism was more about identifying and penalizing subversives (in Spitzer's sense of the word) than it was about hunting Socialists and Communists. But none of this ended with the passing of the 1950s: while McCarthyism as an identifiable American trope fell out of fashion in the 1950s, anthropologist activists in the decades following continued to draw the attentions and interference of the FBI.

CHAPTER 15

A Glimpse of Post-McCarthyism: FBI Surveillance and Consequences for Activism

what a waste of thumbs that are opposable

to make machines that are disposable

and sell them to seagulls flying

circles around one big right wing

yes, the left wing was broken long ago

by the sling shot of COINTELPRO

and now it's so hard to have faith in anything

—ani difranco

The compartmentalization of history contributes to a false impression that the oppressive techniques of McCarthyism neatly ended with the 1950s and that Hoover's FBI went back to law-abiding responsibility. The truth, however, is that this is far from the case. While the prominence of congressional hearings and loyalty boards did give way to increased free speech and to the civil rights movements in the 1960s, there continued to be adverse consequences for anthropologists and others challenging the dominant views of America's stratified social order.

Even though HUAC continued to operate until 1975 its influence and that of other congressional committees waned in the 1960s (Criley 1990:77). Penalties for anthropologists working as social-justice activists continued in the decades to come. While their stories are beyond the temporal (though not the thematic) scope of this book, it must be noted that in the 1960s and 1970s large numbers of anthropologist activists suffered adverse professional consequences for their activism and for taking radical analytical stances in publications. The late 1960s brought a florescence of Marxist and materialist anthropology in the United States in an academic climate that still penalized activist anthropologists.

In this chapter I examine three episodes from the late 1950s and early 1960s in which anthropologist activists garnered the attentions of the FBI because they worked for greater equality and informed democratic consent or because they opposed the United States's suicidal policy of mutually assured destruction. In each of these episodes anthropologists were drawn into activist stances through their academic concerns with anthropology as well as through outside political influences. These examples are meant to suggest that the oppressions of McCarthyism have continued to threaten the prospect of academic freedom and applied anthropological activism.

Kathleen Gough Aberle: Academia Eschews a Radical Appreciation of Imperialism

Kathleen Gough was born in York, England, in 1925. Her father was a working-class radical who exposed her to Marxist critiques at an early age. She studied anthropology at Cambridge, where she received her doctorate in 1950. Her work in Kerala, India, began in the late 1940s, and she continued this research into the 1950s and 1960s. Kathleen Gough married anthropologist David Aberle, a radical kindred spirit with a strong background in ecological anthropology and a developing interest in Marxist critiques.[1] In many ways Aberle and Gough's marriage conjoined two critical scholars with radical views and secrets to be withheld from a society that did not tolerate deviance.

Gough's membership in the Johnson Forest Tendency (known to the FBI as the Johnson Forest Group, or JFG) first brought her to the FBI's attention in 1960. The Johnson Forest Tendency was a small organization of Trotskyites inspired by the writings of C. L. R. James and Raya Dunayveskaya. The group took their name from James's and Dunayveskaya's Socialist Workers Party pseudonyms, which were, respectively, J. R. Johnson and F. F. Forest (see Boggs et al. 1978; Boggs 1998; BS100-4336-7).

C. L. R. James was born in Port of Spain, Trinidad, in 1901, and grew up in rural Trinidad where he developed both a passion for literature and the skills of a gifted cricket player. James worked as a schoolteacher in Trinidad, and along with Alfred Mendes, Albert Gomes, and Ralph de Boissiere he helped found two Trinidadian literary journals. In the early 1930s he moved to England to work as a sports writer, eventually writing for the *Manchester Guardian* and the *Glasgow Herald*. In England James became a Trotskyite after reading Trotsky's *History of the Russian Revolution* and Oswald Spengler's *The Decline of the West*. In 1938 James moved to the United States and joined the newly formed Socialist Workers Party (SWP)—the Trotskyite party organized by Max Shachtman and James Cannon. James's work within the SWP brought issues of race to the fore, examining the "Negro problem" and developing an innovative critique of race and class issues (McLemee 1996; McLemee and Le Blanc 1994). His 1938 *Black Jacobians* is an important Marxist critique of the European and American refusal to acknowledge the legacy of slavery and racism. After James was expelled from the United States for passport violations he lived in England for five years, then returned to Trinidad where he was an instrumental figure in the Trinidadian independence movement.

Kathleen Gough was not the only American anthropologist to be deeply influenced by James's writings. Eric Wolf first encountered James's writings after he fled Sudetenland in 1938 for England, and he later credited James with teaching him to "think of Marxian methods to understand colonialism and global inequalities . . . [because James's writings] gave me an entry into the so-called underdeveloped world" (quoted in Baumann 1998). James's work similarly marked Gough's theoretical considerations of imperialism and the developing world.

An FBI informant reported on July 11, 1960, that Gough had left Detroit and traveled with members of the JFG to Trinidad. A memo to Hoover from the New York SAC ten days later indicated that the FBI had received intelligence information specifying the dates of the group's return from Trinidad. Grace Boggs later recalled that during this trip when Kathleen Gough met James "for the first time, she found him so overbearing and self-centered that she moved out of the house the very next morning" (Boggs 1998:112).

Gough published numerous articles and essays in JFG publications, such as her 1962 pamphlet "The Decline of the State and the Coming of World Society." This essay uses cultural evolutionary theory to analyze the development of the state and a Marxist approach to imperialism to speculate on the state's future (cf. Boggs 1998:282; Boggs et al. 1978:100–2),[2] and it draws heavily on the acknowledged anthropological writings of Marshall Sahlins and Leslie White. The essay's opening is essentially a Whiteian analysis of cultural evolution focusing on the harnessing of energy as human societies evolved from bands, tribes, and chiefdoms to the state. But unlike White, Gough overtly uses Marxist theory to address the needs of praxis, and she begins her discussion of the state by focusing on its monopoly on violence.

Whereas White focuses on the evolution of the state in neutral terms, Gough stresses the coercive foundation of the state and she elucidates the inherent stratification of state systems. She sees colonialism as inalterably transforming the developed and underdeveloped worlds, and she notes that goods and energy flow in a pattern in which the energy of "colonial regions was then devoted to production of raw materials for the use of the mechanized conquering states" (1962:10). This analysis moves beyond White's neutral narrative where culture changes through sterile intensifications of energy without mention of the impact of industrialization on human subjects. For Gough, the development of political managerial systems derives from relationships of dominance and extraction. Historically, "for the colonies [this] meant that the most oppressed layers of the ruled classes of the industrial state lay outside its own borders, and were thus excluded from its home-polity. The more fortunate layers, living inside the mother country, profited enough from imperialism and from industrial technology to be trusted to vote—although they often created trouble and incidentally won most of *their* rights (votes for women, organization of labor unions, etc.) through civil disobedience outside of the electoral system" (Gough 1962:10; emphasis in original).

Gough saw this pattern repeated around the globe in different manifestations. In analyzing the evolution of the United States, she argues that unlike most imperialist powers, its chief colony lay within its own geopolitical borders. She observes that historically the American South, "has been a kind of colony for the North since the industrial revolution. Southern Negroes have thus in some respects played economic, social and political roles comparable to those of Africans in white-occupied Africa. Southern whites have played roles in many ways comparable to those of white settlers—both in relation to the Negroes and also in their ambivalent relationship to whites of the 'mother country'—in many detailed parallels, for example, the recent migration of southern Negroes to the industrial north, paralleled by that of West Indians to Britain or of Algerians to France" (Gough 1962:13).

As a Trotskyite Gough saw that the imperialist West was no better than the Soviet East, and she observes that both superpowers needed the other "as bogeys" (1962:16). Gough saw the world's future as tied to the acceptance of a negotiated anarchist confederation of statelessness, and she believed "we must either break into stateless, world society, or we must perish" (1962:17). The FBI was troubled by Gough's focus on issues of socialism, peace, and equality (see Gough 1961), and in June 1962 the bureau filed a report, titled "Women's Strike for Peace," which identified Gough as a member of the "subversive" group protesting warfare and the Cold War's escalating state of military preparedness (WFO100-433636-2). Her real public troubles, however, would come later that year as she spoke out against President Kennedy's dangerous nuclear showdown during the Cuban nuclear missile crisis.

Speaking Out Against American Policy in Cuba

The FBI tracked Gough and Aberle's move to Boston when Aberle was hired to chair the department of anthropology at Brandeis University, where Kathleen was also offered a professorship. Gough's troubles at Brandeis began after she gave a speech at a student meeting protesting U.S. actions toward Cuba on October 21, 1962. The FBI obtained a copy of her speech, which is reproduced here in full. It provides a rare view of a critical, dissenting, public analysis of President Kennedy's threat to use nuclear weapons in a first-strike attack. This speech assumed a central importance in shaping Gough's career-path, and documents the complexity and courageousness of Gough's analysis, while the resulting consequences of such an analysis clarify the limits of free speech and academic freedom in the post-McCarthyism era. The speech reads as follows:

AT THE HEIGHT OF THE CUBAN CRISIS
Speech at the Brandeis University Students Protest Meeting, Oct. 21, 1962

When I was asked to speak at this meeting I was at first reluctant for I am a foreigner in the United States. My views are different, more extreme than most American liberals and I did not want to impose them upon you. For I feel that in many ways the Cuban Crisis is your American Suez. Unhappily however you seem to lack at this time wise allies who would restrain your government from a hasty and most dangerous course of action.

Second thoughts tell me that I am also an internationalist, and that this crisis threatens the whole world with nuclear war. Everybody therefore has full right to speak out in, and to, the United States of America. So I am glad to tell you my views and try to join with you in some course of action.

Let me say first that I am one of those who strongly supports Fidel Castro and his revolutionary government. If I had been in London yesterday I would have joined those two thousand who streamed through police lines to the American Embassy, shouting "Viva Fidel! Kennedy to hell!" I don't like the poetry, but this is how I feel. I admire Castro very deeply as a great American hero of the mid-twentieth century, and I feel pity and sorrow for him and for his government and people in this terrible crisis. I wish them success and safety with all my heart. If there is to be a war, I hope first that it will not erupt into a nuclear war in which all of us, north and south, east and west, will be ruined. One would of course rather anything, any outcome than that. But I also hope, second, that if it is a limited war Cuba will win and the United States will be shamed before all the world and its imperialistic hegemony ended forever in Latin America.

THE MIGHTY AND THE MEEK

Some of the reasons why I support Castro's government are, first, that it ended the torture, corruption and bloody tyranny of Batista, which the United States had upheld. Second, the Castro government brought about agrarian reform. It attempted to diversify agricultural production, to remove the stranglehold of large corporations and of a mono-crop economy, and to industrialize and modernize the country. It spread literacy and built roads, schools, and hospitals. It cleaned out corruption and prostitution in Havana, emptied big hotels and filled them with poor women from the countryside who were trained to cook and use sewing machines. I admire Castro because he put down the mighty from their seat and exalted the humble and meek. He filled the hungry with good things and the rich he sent empty away to Miami.

For me also a profound reason for admiration of the Cuban government is that as I understand it, it has given equality—social in law and economically to its Negro population. Between one-third and one-quarter of the people in Cuba are Negro and today Negroes occupy many high positions and receive justice in everyday life. When I think of the history and movement of colored races and of colonial peoples and of white "spheres of influence" over the past hundred years, it seems to me no accident that this difference exists today in the position of the Negro in Cuba and in the U.S.A. To me it is no accident that Robert Williams a brave American Negro leader who fought against the Ku Klux Klan in North Carolina should today be in exile in Cuba, hounded by the FBI on an erroneous charge of kidnapping. It is no accident that William Worthy faces a prison sentence for illegal entry into the United States after having had the courage to visit and report on conditions in Cuba. And it is no accident that Ross Barnett, who so recently encouraged violent revolt against the government and laws of the United States, should be among the first to congratulate President Kennedy on his blockade of shipping in Cuba Waters.

MISGIVINGS

I admit the unpleasant features of the Castro regime and admit that there is much that I do not know about Cuba. I know from eye witnesses that after the revolution there were many public executions of men who had committed crimes as former Batista agents carried out amid howls of applause from vengeful mobs of Cubans. This is the horrible side of revolutions and I do not like it. There have been other executions since, some of them seemingly inexplicable, I do not know whether all of them were essential to assure the safety of a regime which, I do believe, retains the support of a majority of the people. There has also apparently been inefficiency and mismanagement, and especially this past year, attempts to modernize agriculture and to increase industrial production too rapidly and with too little technical skill. Cuba has been declared a Communist nation, a phrase which is ominous to us with our memories of Stalinism. And now finally, Cuba has received from the Soviet Union missile bases with which, in the last resort, she would be able and presumably willing to retaliate against the United States if she was driven to extremity by the invasion of North American forces.

CUBA AND ANGOLA

I believe, however, that the worst features of the Cuban situation, which we now so deplore, have been brought on us by the folly of the United States government. Since a few months after the 1959 revolution, it has pursued the policy of an arrogant imperialist power toward a wayward and rebellious small nation. The United States rejected the Cuban Revolution as soon as American property was threatened, and before Cuba turned to Russia. This being so, where else could Cuba turn? And since Cuba turned, the United States has ended trade and travel, maintained offensive propaganda, sponsored an invasion, and carried on repeated military harassment. And now the United States in true imperialist fashion is saying in effect that Cuba has no claim to sovereignty at all. She may not defend herself, pursue her interests, or create her own social system, Cuban missiles are automatically bad and offensive while American missiles are automatically good and defensive. Cuba has no right to bases on her own lands, but America has the right to keep Guantanamo base on Cuban land, not to mention the hundred-odd bases in some thirty-five foreign countries which ring the Soviet bloc. I do not accept this imposition and I believe it must be rejected by every internationalist who is at all inspired by the modern ideas of equality and justice between peoples. If we would support Angola against Portugal, Algeria against France, Kenya against Britain, we must surely support Cuba against the United States. For Cuba's struggle for emancipation from American imperialism was not obliterated by the fact that she had only the Soviet Union to turn to. Nor can we exactly blame her for making every effort to win a struggle in which the odds were so heavily against her.

I wish to make clear that I do not support or praise Castro for equipping Cuba with nuclear weapons. For me as for most people who are active in any disarmament movement, nuclear weapons are in themselves a greater evil than any social system or any political policy, because they threaten man's annihilation. This is true whether they are Communist or Capitalist. For me there are no "good" nuclear weapons, no matter what revolution they are defending.

But I must also say that I think from where we sit, here on the Eastern seaboard where our economy is very largely sustained by arms production, cannot single them out for condemnation. We cannot do this any more than we can, for example condemn the Black Muslims for saying that they intend to defend themselves against White oppression. The beam is in our eye and only the mote in theirs. We have here more bases, more stockpiles, than any other nation and we are the only nation ever to have used nuclear weapons. We are reaping the whirlwind of that subsequent event today.

So it does mean that we are really on the brink of a nuclear war. It is hard to believe—for although the morning papers warn us that we may all be ashes by tomorrow, they also still keep an eye on the effects this supposed conflagration will have on the November 6th elections. I must admit to a curious sense of unreality, and in fact, I do not believe that either the U.S. or the Soviet Union will purposefully initiate a nuclear war. I hope only that if they are pushed to the last extremity, the Cubans will not forget their humanity and send their missiles in a last desperate retaliation. I hope that if invasion comes to them they will be able to repel it as bravely and gloriously as they did the last one and that they will never be pushed to that last extreme.

In my view the blockade, this war, that the U.S. government has so hastily initiated, [is of] the gravest tyranny against the American people as well, not to mention the Europeans the Latin Americans and the Canadians. A Gallup Poll of 10 days ago showed that only 10% of Americans wanted an invasion of Cuba, but the government ignored the rest of us and did not ask our consent. It did not ask our little children if they were willing to be incinerated. It did not ask the Europeans or the Latin Americans whether they wanted their cities to rise in smoke. That the government of these nations have now servilely fallen into line with

America's rash action does not alter the case for me. For I believe no government, with or without adult consent, has the right to threaten to initiate human extermination on so vast a scale.

HONORABLE WAY OUT

I have expressed my views frankly, because although my family is American and I have never seen Cuba, I believe they have more to fear from us at this moment than we have from them, and so today my mind is with them and I wish them well. Finally, however, I wish to say to all of you, even those who disagree with me most strongly, that there is another and honorable way out for the U.S. which would save us from the danger of nuclear war while admitting nothing to Cuba and redounding only to the safety and international credit of the U.S.

Last night 40 delegates of neutral states in the United Nations led by Ghana, Cyprus and the United Arab Republic, agreed to ask Secretary General U Thant to intervene in the Cuban crisis and to appeal to the United States, Cuba and the Soviet Union to halt equally their war preparations. If reason prevails in Washington, I believe that the government will heed this appeal and will stop its blockade and delay any invasion of Cuba which may be planned. I think that we should appeal to the government to do this, and to request, in the United Nations, that a special commission be set up to inquire into the Cuban military build-up. At the same time, to avert further conflict, I think it is necessary for us to urge willingness to accept also a UN enquiry into the equipment and potentialities of the U.S. base at Guantanamo. I hope that before we leave this meeting some such resolution may be adopted. (BSI00-34577:6 4/29/63)

Gough's speech was well received by the students and faculty at the rally: Herbert Marcuse, who also spoke at the event, remarked to Gough before the crowd, "you have more courage than I" (Lee and Sacks 1993:187). But Brandeis's administration worried that trouble would follow if it did not disassociate itself from these views. Speaking out against Kennedy's "reckless" nuclear gambit, or suggesting that Cuba's revolutionary role in fighting imperialism was laudable, were notions that the administration viewed as wildly irresponsible.

As Brandeis's administrators worried about the fallout from Gough's statements, the FBI tracked summaries of Gough's talk in the JFGs publication *Correspondence* (WFO100-433636-2, 1/23/63; file is stamped "Subv. Control"). Brandeis President Abraham Sachar felt that Gough exhibited poor judgment by speaking at this student rally, and he felt she exceeded the limits of academic freedom by critiquing American military policy. In the week following her public statements, Gough was summoned to President Sachar's office and chastised for her critiques. When contracts for the following year were issued, Kathleen Gough did not receive a recommended raise and she was informally told that her upcoming tenure application would not be approved (Gough 1993:282).

Fallout and Resignation

J. Edgar Hoover informed the Boston SAC that a story in the *Washington Post* stated that Gough "and her husband had resigned from their positions at Brandeis University after a dispute with the president of the school over a speech in which [Gough] was critical of the United States policy during the Cuban Crisis" (WFO100-433636-3 3/29/63). Aberle's FBI file contains newspaper clippings from the *Boston Globe* on March 28, 1963, covering the events leading up to their resignations, as well as the Brandeis faculty senate's actions in this matter.

President Sachar issued a formal statement in the campus newspaper designed to counter Gough's remarks claiming she suffered from discrimination for engaging in political speech at a public forum. In the article President Sachar states that Gough's remarks were "dangerous, reckless and undisciplined" (*Boston Globe* 3/28/63). In later years Sachar denied that Gough had been discriminated against or that her academic freedoms had been limited, but he would not discuss the reasons for denying Gough her raise or the reports that her tenure hopes were doomed (see Sachar 1976).

Gough and Aberle's resignations led the Brandeis faculty senate to meet in a closed session to discuss a motion declaring that Sachar had infringed Gough's academic freedom (*Boston Globe* 3/29/63). On March 30, 1963, the *Boston Herald* published an editorial criticizing Sachar's handling of the controversy, stating that "Dr. Sachar has not lived up to his own high standards in his handling of the case of Mrs. Kathleen Gough Aberle, the left-leaning anthropologist who spoke out for Castro last October at the height of the international crisis over Russian missiles in Cuba." It is not known if members of the Brandeis administration consulted with the FBI prior to Kathleen Gough's provoked resignation, but a few anomalies in her file seem to indicate this possibility.[3]

In President Sachar's memoir he portrays himself as a champion of academic freedom and integrity by offering anecdotes such as his efforts to fend off strings-attached inquiries from deep-pocketed financiers interested in the staffing of Brandeis's department of economics; his hiring of Earl Browder's mathematician son, Felix, in 1956; and his hiring of Marxist Herbert Marcuse in 1954. Sachar estimated that during the twenty years of his tenure his "administration's record on the principle of faculty freedom of expression was challenged" only by his treatment of Kathleen Gough (1976:197–98). Sachar reflected that he was "bewildered when the ACLU's judgment was announced that I had 'blemished the reputation of a highly respected institution' and a good record of protecting academic freedom by an unwarranted reprimand of Miss Gough and a discriminatory denial of an appropriate salary increase for her. My bewilderment came because the executive committee of the Massachusetts ACLU reached its decision in my absence abroad, without offering me any opportunity to present my interpretation of the circumstances or to defend my action. Further, I was the president of a university whose dedication to academic freedom had never been questioned, and I had played no small part in creating this climate of freedom" (199). Sachar was convinced that the only reason why the ACLU had found against him was because an economist who had been rejected for a teaching position at Brandeis was on the ACLU committee, and she "had apparently nursed her resentment through the years and when the Aberle case came up she had pressed for an immediate judgment" (200). It is noteworthy that Sachar's regrets were not for the actions he took but rather that he had not adequately bureaucratically insulated himself from the decision to punish Kathleen Gough for expressing her dissent.[4]

Traveling to Oregon in Search of Academic Freedom

In April 1963 the Boston FBI office informed the office in Portland, Oregon, that Kathleen Gough and David Aberle would be moving to Eugene, where Aberle would teach anthropology at the University of Oregon. The memo containing this information also provided the Portland office with a summary of Gough's subversive activities (WFO100-43363 4/29/63). The FBI also continued to monitor Gough's public talks and publications in radical journals and newspapers. A memo dated February 8, 1963, recounts a letter to the editor of the Manchester *Guardian* written on August 6, 1962 by Kathleen Gough in protest of the assassination of a Black Muslim in Los Angeles on April 27. In the June 1963 issue of the JFG's *Correspondence* Gough published an article titled "Student Movement in the South," where she critiqued race relations in the southern United States. In the article, she states: "Southern Negroes are a colonial population. The chief difference between them and Africans of the Congo is that white men brought the Negroes to America to slave for them instead of conquering them in their native land" (Gough 1963:1).

The Boston SAC sent the Portland FBI office copies of Kathleen Gough's Security Index Cards, as well as an extensive collection of newspaper clippings and memos regarding Gough and her problems at Brandeis. The FBI also had a University of Oregon employee check payroll records to ascertain that the department of anthropology employed David Aberle (WFO100-43363-12 12/26/63). On January 31, 1964, the FBI filed a report concerning journalist William Worthy Jr. of the Freedom Now Party (FNP) (WFO100-433636). The FBI was concerned that Worthy was affiliated with the Uhuru Black Liberation Movement. In 1956 Worthy had defied the State Department's ban on travel to China, and in 1961 he again defied the media blockade and went to Cuba to cover the revolution. After a number of Cuban reporting trips in the early 1960s, the State Department sentenced Worthy to prison for his defiance (the sentence was later overturned by a federal appeals court). A black graduate student from Eugene contacted the Portland FBI office reporting that Gough "had gotten Worthy to come to Eugene so that she could learn about the FNP and the reason whites were barred from it. Subsequently, Worthy came to Eugene, stayed at the Aberle home and spoke on racial integration, both in Eugene and on campus, University of Oregon" (WFO100-43363 1/30/64).

Another informant reported a statement from Worthy that the reason why whites were not allowed in the FNP was because "they would take it over." The informant also added that Worthy stated that "Martin Luther King is a dupe of the nation's press, that he has no real leadership and that the true leaders are militant young Negroes located throughout the [country]. He scorned the Congress of Racial Equality (CORE), the Urban League and the NAACP all as being ineffectual. Not once did he have anything derogatory to say concerning the Black Muslims" (WFO105-20110-389 1/30/64). One FBI informant reported that Worthy planned on determining which blacks in the Eugene area owned firearms, and that Worthy said he wanted to interview these individuals for an NBC broadcast on the topic of America's growing "Black Militia" (WFO105-20110 1/30/64).

In the March 1964 issue of *Correspondence* Kathleen Gough criticized America's fledgling peace movement, writing that she did not think "that the mere suppression or avoidance of conflict can be our aim. Conflict is endemic in human society. If we are to progress, some conflict must be fought and won" (Gough 1964a:6). After differentiating between different types of violent movements in the twentieth century, Gough wrote that "revolts against capitalist imperialism on the part of colonial peoples and people living in capitalist spheres of influence" and "struggles inside independent nation, on the part of oppressed classes or races, for a reorganization of the national political economy to give them a just and dignified place within it" are "desirable and inevitable" (1964a:6). Gough wanted Western industrial powers to withdraw from localized conflicts so that peoples around the world could determine their own political and economic destinies. She advocated that the United Nations take on the role of "promulgator of world law," as well as help poor nations with long-range economic planning: "Inside the rich industrial nation, most of the people now form a kind of 'upper class of the world.' Although they have long enjoyed the fruits of other nations' labor, they do not usually realize this and their horizons are bounded by the class and nation in which they live. We in the industrial nations need to expand our view of the world so that we may meet the challenges and demands which will shortly be made upon us" (Gough 1964b:6).

On May 4, 1964, J. Edgar Hoover notified the Department of State's Bureau of Intelligence and Research and the CIA's Director of Central Intelligence, that Kathleen Gough was planning to travel to India. A report on Gough accompanied this memo, as did a request to acquire "any pertinent information [the State Department] or the CIA receive concerning subject while she is traveling in India" (WFO100-433636-14 5/4/64). The FBI modified Gough's Security Index Card to specify that she was outside the country (PD100-10430 5/21/64) and tracked her May 1965 return to Eugene from India.

The FBI recorded a letter by Gough published in the *Eugene Register Guard* on December 21, 1965, in which she wrote she was "deeply ashamed of those of my countrymen who support the American outrage in Viet Nam, and also of Harold Wilson who, while purporting to favor peace negotiations, toadies to Lyndon Johnson and acquiesces in America's crimes. Fortunately, however, the British are still not quite as brainwashed on certain subjects as the Americans and there are millions, if not a majority, who will refuse to lift a finger to provide material aid for American genocide in Viet Nam."

In early 1967, with the assistance of one of her acquaintances, the FBI tracked Kathleen Gough's movements as she returned to England to see her seriously ill elderly father. On August 7, 1966, two FBI agents observed Gough speaking at a demonstration on the steps of the state capitol in Salem, Oregon, with the Citizens Coordinating Committee to End the War in Vietnam. The FBI also recorded that she participated in a Marxist seminar discussion group at the University of Oregon in Fall 1966 as one of two faculty participants. The FBI further monitored Gough and Aberle's involvement with the End War Group and indexed the occurrence of her name appearing on anti-Vietnam War leaflets (WFO100-433636-29 5/16/67).

In one report the FBI reprinted a letter dated May 24, 1967, from Aberle to the editor of the University of Oregon's campus newspaper, the *Oregon Daily Emerald*, explaining why he and his wife had decided to leave the United States for Canada (see also Gough 1993:282). The letter is as follows:

Emerald Editor:

Before long, I expect to leave the University to join the University of British Columbia in Vancouver, B.C. I am leaving in spite of my great respect for President Flemming, my pleasant relationships with the members of my department, and the friends I have found among students, faculty, and townspeople. The reasons for my departure center about the war in Viet Nam and its effects on this country and its universities.

I have said many times that the war is immoral, illegal and inhuman, that it is killing and maiming civilians in Viet Nam in uncounted numbers, and killing American soldiers, who are asked to die in a bad cause. There is no point in repeating those arguments here. But I might have stayed to protest the war, were it not that academic life involves me in complicity in the war. Indeed, perhaps almost all of us who are not in jail for opposing it are involved in some complicity.

Specifically, at present I am required to grade for the draft board. I am unwilling to continue to be an unpaid and involuntary servant of the Selective Service System in a war to which I never assented, and to which I believe the American people did not assent when they elected Johnson president. Nor do I wish to have the responsibility of deciding what bad student is to go to Viet Nam and what good one to be reserved for other purposes. It is not to do this that I became an anthropologist and a teacher.

My wife, Kathleen Aberle, also feels very strongly about this; so much so that she resigned a part-time teaching post in November, rather than grade her students. Unfortunately we do not find that most American university student or faculty bodies are willing to face up to what the Selective Service does to the university. Nor, indeed, are most faculties willing to face up to the consequences of receiving major financial support from the Department of Defense.

I am willing neither to abandon my role as anthropologist and teacher in order to make my protest fully effective, nor to continue to work for the draft board and to work for institutions that serve the present military purposes of this nation. Faced with this conflict, and after painful thought, I have decided to go to Canada. There perhaps, I can think through my obligations as anthropologist and teacher and, at the cost of losing my opportunity to protest within this country, free myself somewhat from complicity with its war machinery. This is by no means the only valid solution for academic protesters: it is, however, the one that seems best for me in my present circumstances.

It is two years since I led the all-night protest against the war at this university. I cannot go without mentioning one heartening and unexpected byproduct of that event. Through that and other protest activities I entered into new relationships with students that have meant a tremendous amount to me. It has changed my entire view of students, of the teacher-student relationship, and indeed of the proper role of the university.

I hope that I can absorb and use that experience in years to come. My wife and I will never forget the students and staff we have worked with in protest against this war.

David F. Aberle

Professor of Anthropology

(WFO100-433636-35)

In summer 1967 David Aberle and Kathleen Gough left Eugene for Vancouver, where David had found a job at the University of British Columbia and Kathleen had been hired at nearby Simon Frazer University. Several months later on October 30, 1967, the Portland FBI office sent a memo to Hoover recommending that Gough's name be removed from the Security Index due to her "alien status . . . and her voluntary residence outside the United States." However, shortly thereafter FBI headquarters decided that without further evidence that Gough and Aberle had permanently settled in Canada it would be premature to remove her name from the Security Index.

Land of the Lost: Academic Freedom at Simon Frazer University

Gough was finally removed from the Domestic Security Index on December 8, 1967 (WFO100-433636-35). This was little more than a formality because a memo was simultaneously sent by the attorney general's office to the Portland SAC declaring that under the "Emergency Detention Program" Kathleen Aberle was to be added to the international Security Index by the Internal Security Division. This same month David Aberle presented a motion at the annual AAA business meeting condemning the United States' use of weapons such as napalm and agent orange in Vietnam. According to Gough, the motion was "ruled out of order by the then chairperson, Frederica de Laguna, and vehemently opposed by Margaret Mead, who argued that political resolutions 'were not in the professional interests of anthropologists.' There was a commotion on the floor. David Aberle, Gerald Berreman and others argued against the chair, but the day was won when Michael Harner rose and stated: 'Genocide is not in the professional interests of anthropologists.' Against the chair's ruling, the resolution was then passed by a large majority" (1993:280). This resolution unleashed a provocative debate in the pages of the association's newsletter and was an important landmark on the way to the AAA's confrontational meeting four years later, when years of bitter contention came to a head and divided the association in ways that are still visible today (see Wakin 1992).

The final released entry in Gough's FBI file is dated June 24, 1968, and records an Ottawa FBI contact notifying Hoover of ongoing student unrest on the campus of Simon Fraser University (SFU). The campus troubles mentioned in this FBI report eventually led to the firing of eight SFU faculty members, including Kathleen Gough. Many of the events leading up to Gough's firing are still in dispute, but the basic facts are described by Gough in a letter she sent to over a hundred of her colleagues in an effort to enlist their assistance:

> In the academic year 1968–69 the P.S.A. [Political Science, Sociology and Anthropology] Department made two experimental changes in policy. It began to associate students in departmental decision-making, and it moved to establish links with property-less groups in Vancouver— people displaced by urban renewal, people on welfare, Indians, and some labour unions.
>
> In a department of twenty-one faculty, about fourteen were of left-liberal or "radical" orientation. Some of these teachers began to use modern Marxist-influenced works in the classroom by such authors as Baran, Sweezy, Hinton, Frank and Marcuse, in addition to orthodox social science literature.
>
> In May, 1969 the Simon Fraser administration refused to consider the department's recommendations on tenure, renewals and promotions on the grounds that a student committee had helped to make them. In July the elected chairman was removed and replaced by an administrative trusteeship of six professors from outside the department. In August the Dean of Arts appointed a new P.S.A. Tenure Committee containing only one member of the P.S.A. Department, (a political scientist), the rest being from [other departments]. This committee made recommendations about P.S.A. faculty to a University Tenure Committee composed of two scientists, two Education professors, a geographer and an economist.
>
> As a result of these committees' efforts, Kathleen Gough Aberle (a full professor) and John C. Leggett (an associate professor) were denied tenure or further appointments at the end of the present contracts. In the case of Kathleen Gough, a member of the Department Tenure Committee later indicated, in a meeting called by students, that the two committees had read only one article of hers, "New Proposals for Anthro-

pologists" [published in *Monthly Review* April 1969, and republished in *Current Anthropology*, December 1968]. . . . It was found "controversial" and she was refused tenure on the grounds of "serious doubts about her scholarly objectivity." One other associate professor was denied tenure with the possibility, though not certainty, of a further appointment. Two assistant professors were denied further appointments. Three assistant professors received the unusual one-year renewals with further consideration dependent on Ph.D.s or publications. An instructor and an assistant professor were denied promotions which the department considered overdue. *Out of 16 P.S.A. candidates for renewal, only six received the contracts for which the Department had originally recommended them. Five of them had been either unassociated with the department's radical programs and experiments with student committees or were actively opposed to them.* (ST 47,10 11/5/59; emphasis added)

Gough thus accused the university of violating its own tenure policies and the fourteen faculty members demanded the reinstatement of their duly elected departmental chairman. When this demand was not met, they and over two thousand students went on strike, with a number of students engaging in a prolonged hunger strike. Nine days into the strike, SFU President Strand fired the eight departmental faculty who had joined the strike.[5] During the next year North American anthropologists contributed $5,000 to the legal defense fund to assist these eight faculty members (ST 16,4, KGA/ST 1/18/71; see also *Peak* 11/12/69, *Georgia Straight* 11/5–12/69).

On November 15, 1969, Gough wrote to the AAA's president and executive board requesting assistance for herself and the other seven colleagues who had been dismissed from SFU. After reviewing supporting documents submitted by Gough, AAA President Cora Du Bois and the executive board appointed an ad hoc committee, consisting of Peter Carstens and Laura Nader, to investigate Gough's accusations of improper dismissal (Carstens and Nader 1971:1). On December 1, 1969, the executive board presented Carstens and Nader with three charges. First, they were to determine if SFU had followed its customary procedures in terminating Gough and other members of the department. Second, they were to ascertain if the procedures in place were observed and were in accordance with those of other Canadian universities. Finally, they were to see if SFU "correctly and objectively evaluated all pertinent evidence in making its decision about Dr. [Gough]" (Carstens and Nader 1971:7).

Carstens and Nader interviewed most of those involved in the dispute, including "President Strand, Dean Sullivan, 30 professors and lecturers at SFU, 65 students, as well as 10 professors from other Canadian Universities"

(Carstens and Nader 1971:2). President Strand argued that the university had only followed standard procedures in this matter—although he conceded that the procedures were new and had not actually been used much before this episode. Strand admitted that these were indeed unusual procedures for a Canadian university, but he argued that this was because under SFU's alternative approach to education deans and other administrators had less power while faculty were more empowered. Nader and Carstens found that despite Strand's claim that faculty had increased decision-making power, the Canadian Association of University Teachers (CAUT) had found the exact opposite to be true in their determination that "power centralized in the President's office and the Dean's offices was directly related to a long history of faculty grievances" (7).

One outcome of SFU's alternative approach to education was that the lines of power and authority were vaguely defined. In theory, SFU had an administrative structure that left decision-making power in the hands of faculty members, while the power of deans and other administrators was curtailed. But SFU's ill-defined protocol for advancement, grievances, and other vital aspects of academic life empowered the presidency and left few avenues to administratively appeal disagreements. Carstens and Nader observed that the 1960's "social architects of SFU planned an administrative structure which could not cope with internal problems as they arose" (3). The final report of the ad hoc committee saw these structural weaknesses as a significant factor leading to the crises:

> This conclusion is no conjectural fantasy of two social anthropologists. For only after two years of the University's existence the SFU Faculty Association resolved "to call in the CAUT to investigate the breakdown in communications between the Faculty Association and the President". The CAUT made a highly commendable and thorough investigation and published its findings in an official Report. The Report we regard as crucial to the case under consideration because it enables the members of the academic community in general to see Dr. Kathleen [Gough's] predicament in a wider context than the micropolitics of the PSA Department.
>
> As our investigation into the case of Dr. Kathleen [Gough] progressed it became evident that the probability that a faculty member at Simon Fraser would file a complaint against the University could have been predicted from earlier courses of events. For not only had the decisions of the office of the President been questioned by members of the faculty through the Faculty Association, but also there had been expressions of grievance relating to salaries, appointment and tenure procedures, contract renewals, and the like. (3)

Carstens and Nader concurred with CAUT that SFU's unusual administrative configuration of a single president and twenty-five heads predisposed the institution to such episodic crises. Some of the structural changes occurring since 1968 had disempowered deans, leaving their function to being "analogous to children errand-runners in peasant communities" (4).

Simon Fraser had a scattered approach to awarding promotion and tenure. The ad hoc committee final report argued that tenure is an important protection for the academic freedom of all professors, but also argued that is especially important for those in the social sciences and humanities because, "controversy is their stock-in-trade. If they are to enjoy academic freedom they must not live in fear of the reaction of their Department Head to their contrary views. Yet as long as their appointment is subject to review they are in a state of dependency. Heads of Departments and Deans, as well as Presidents and Boards of Governors, are human and susceptible to the universal temptation to resist those who disagree with us. To establish a procedure that caters to this human weakness is to invite frequent disputes, masquerading under some false front, pretending to be disputes about teaching, scholarly interests, or contributions to the University" (6).

In July 1970 an external committee appointed by the chief justice of British Columbia convened to evaluate the causes and procedures involved in the firing of the professors. E. E. Palmer, a highly regarded Ontario lawyer, chaired the committee. President Strand refused to cooperate with the committee's investigation, so the committee conducted its investigation without Strand's assistance. The Palmer committee issued a unanimous decision on July 24, 1970, holding that "there is no cause for dismissal of the faculty members involved and that, therefore, the President may not recommend dismissal to the Board of Governors" (ST: 16, 4, Palmer Report p. 4). President Strand angrily refused to accept the committee's decision, arguing that the committee had not heard the relevant evidence in this matter.

On August 19, 1970, the AAA's ad hoc committee submitted its final report to the executive board summarizing their findings and making four specific recommendations concerning Kathleen Gough. First, they recommended that all dismissal procedures against Gough be withdrawn, and that SFU be censured for ignoring the Palmer committee's findings. Second, they recommended that an investigation be undertaken into the ongoing structural problems at SFU that contributed to similar ongoing problems. The third recommendation pertained to the issues raised by having the professional association "identified with one country reviewing the academic cases arising in another" (Carstens and Nader 1971:13). The ad hoc committee recommended that in such instances in the future an international anthropological committee be appointed for investigations. The final recommendation was that "ethnographic and comparative study of universities be treated as urgent research by anthropologists" (13). This research would focus on articulations of power relations within the university structure, and would be used to discover new ways of dealing with the controversies that arise at institutions of higher learning.

Two days after the report was submitted to the executive board, SFU's board of governors notified Kathleen Gough that she was fired as of that moment. Her official comment made upon the receipt of this news was, "As I was exonerated by a duly constituted Hearing Committee, I can only conclude that the University authorities have fired me because I was found innocent, and they were found guilty. This simply rounds out the arbitrary administrative actions of the past two years. Our struggle has, of course, throughout been against precisely such violations of due process" (quoted in Carstens and Nader 1971:13).

Peter Carstens and Laura Nader had been asked to undertake a difficult and controversial task and despite the obvious risks of being labeled as troublemakers, they produced an accurate report that was well researched and carefully written. It calmly and clearly exposed President Strand, the SFU administration, and the board of governors as acting vindictively and outside the standard practices of academia. The report stands as a model for future inquiries into accusations of violations of academic freedom or improper dismissal. There were mixed outcomes from the investigation for both Gough and the university; as Gough wrote years later, as a result of these events SFU "was censured and boycotted for 15 years by most professional associations in the social sciences worldwide. The result for me, however, was that I could not find a regular teaching position locally until 1984" (283).

After being fired by SFU, Kathleen Gough remained in the Vancouver area because her husband continued to teach at the University of British Columbia. From 1974 until 1990 Gough held the position of honorary research associate in the university's department of anthropology. She continued her academic research and writing even without a full-time position, publishing dozens of articles on a variety of anthropological subjects (Lee and Sacks 1993; Singh 1993). In 1978 she published *Ten Times More Beautiful: The Rebuilding of Vietnam* and later wrote *Political Economy in Vietnam* (1990). In these books she examines the impact of Vietnam's battles with the West as well as its efforts to establish a viable socialist society.

Kathleen Gough Aberle died of cancer in 1990. She left innumerable contributions to anthropology's ethnographic literature as well as substantive contributions to anthropologists' understanding of imperialism, polyandry, gender issues, and the role of women in agriculture. Her activist work and political writings were in many ways inseparable from her academic work, and both her work and writing continue to influence a new generation of anthropologists. The consequences of her commitment to activism illustrate the flimsiness of the supposed advancements in the protection of academic freedom in the post-McCarthy period. But her scholarship and activism left an impact on those who knew her and her work: as Richard Lee and Karen Sacks conclude, Kathleen Gough's life and work was "in the tradition of the indigenous English radicalism of Gerard Winstanley, William Blake, Tom Paine and Robert Owen. The moral strength touched all who had the good fortune to know her personally, and many more through her voluminous writings" (1993:192).

One of the unfortunate lessons of Kathleen Gough's ongoing troubles is that as news of these events traveled through both official channels and as gossip, a wide sweep of anthropologists and graduate students were educated in the lessons of disassociation with activism. It is impossible to measure the impact of these events. Other anthropologists, such as Earle Reynolds, who were linked to antiwar activist movements did not even bother pursuing work within academia after having devoted significant portions of their lives to activist protest movements.

Earle Reynolds: An Informed Protester of Conscience

Earle Schoene was born October 18, 1910, to German parents who came to America to perform as trapeze artists in the Ringling Brothers Circus. Earle's father (William Schoene) died in a trapeze accident when Earle was eight, and he later changed his last name to Reynolds, the name of his stepfather. In college he studied anthropology at the University of Chicago (A.M. 1943) and the University of Wisconsin (Ph.D. 1944). After World War II Reynolds taught at Antioch College in Yellow Springs, Ohio, and then went to work as a physical anthropologist for the Atomic Energy Commission, studying the effects of radiation on the survivors of the atomic bombing of Hiroshima. Reynolds and his family moved to Tokyo in 1951 where he spent three years as a biostatistician for the Atomic Bomb Casualty Commission's Pediatrics Department, studying Hiroshima survivors. In 1953 he wrote a detailed report titled "Growth and Development of Hiroshima Children Exposed to the Atomic Bomb," which established the long-term effects of nuclear weapons on children and documented the devastation brought to Hiroshima survivors and their offspring. This research had a deep impact on Reynolds and his politics (Reynolds 1961; Reynolds and Reynolds 1962; BAAA 1954 [3]:6). The development of Reynolds's radical antinuclear weapon activism was nurtured from his years of working with survivors of the Hiroshima and Nagasaki atomic blasts. Although his radical activism grew out of his anthropological research, his actions left him at the margins of employability in his field.

While living in Hiroshima Reynolds built the *Phoenix*, a fifty-foot ketch. After leaving Japan in 1956, Reynolds and a crew of five (including his family) spent almost two years sailing around the globe. When the *Phoenix* arrived in Honolulu in 1958 Reynolds learned of the arrest of George Bigelow and his crew for sailing their ship, the *Golden Rule*, into the atomic testing site in the waters off of the Marshall Islands as an act of protest. Reynolds was intrigued by this act of civil disobedience.

On Valentine's Day 1958 the U.S. Atomic Energy Commission issued public notices prohibiting watercraft from approaching the Eniwetok Proving Grounds in the Marshall Islands due to the upcoming Hardtack nuclear tests. On June 4, 1958, George Bigelow, captain of the *Golden Rule*, was arrested on charges of conspiring to violate a district court injunction prohibiting vessels from entering the area near the Marshall Islands where nuclear tests were being conducted. After Bigelow was given the option of being released on his own recognizance or being jailed, he chose jail. Later that afternoon, the *Golden Rule* again set sail, with William Huntington at the helm. Huntington and his crew were returned to port under escort, and the following day they were sentenced to sixty days in jail. But Reynolds was willing to take up where Huntington and his crew had left off. A UPI story, dated June 4, reported that "Earle L. Reynolds, Skipper of the yacht "Phoenix" and a former member of the Atomic Energy Commission,⁶ called President Eisenhower and the AEC urging them to lift the ban that prohibits entering of the nuclear testing area. Reynolds then added, 'The Phoenix will sail from Honolulu in the near future, clearing for the high seas'. He indicated that the high seas he mentioned were the waters surrounding Marshall Islands" (USDOE Box 2929, Folder MRA 7 Hardtack v3). In the week following Huntington's arrest, Reynolds, his wife and two children, and a Japanese national, Niichi Mikami, left Honolulu for the test area. Documents from the Department of Energy record contingencies being made to arrest those on board as Reynolds's *Phoenix* set sail (USDOE Box 2929, Folder MRA 7 Hardtack v3). They undertook this action with the full knowledge that they risked exposing themselves to the horrors of radiation and the painful degeneration and death that would follow.

On June 30, 1958, the *Phoenix* was hailed by a U.S. coast guard vessel and notified that its position was within the one hundred mile "off-limits" area around the nuclear testing site. Reynolds responded that it was his intention to enter the test area, indicating, "he understood that by so sailing he was endangering his crew and his vessel" (USDOE 61A1524 Box 36). Navy communication documents record that on July 1, CINPAC laid a plan wherein the *Phoenix* would be cautioned again at a distance of five miles "outside the danger area," and if they failed to stop the Navy would then "Hail, stop and board the vessel, place Master under arrest for indicated violations and remove vessel from the danger area, towing vessel if master unwilling to comply with your order to sail his vessel clear" (USDOE 61A1524 Box 33). In the days prior to the *Phoenix*'s entry into the test area, the navy sent dozens of communiques detailing all of the maneuvers that the coast guard should prepare to undertake to board and seize control of the *Phoenix*. After three pages of detailed contingency plans for boarding and halting the *Phoenix*, navy personnel dryly noted that,

> the above proposal does not fully cover all possible maneuvers. For example, the Phoenix may make a right angle turn at the Danger Area Border and continue to voyage legally but in a swaggering little-boy fashion. In such event we may have to make further refinements in our proposed plan. At any rate the proposal has the advantage of preventing a recurrence of the original phoenix incident in which the fabled bird phoenix was consumed by fire and rose again from the ashes. Dr. Reynolds may perhaps fancy himself as a 20th Century Phoenix capable of duplicating both portions of the fable. Despite natural curiosity as to the outcome we must deny him the opportunity. (USDOE WNRC 61A1524 Box 36 p. 11, 6/30/58)

Statements in some of these transmissions indicate some members of the navy would have been satisfied to observe the Darwinian implications of allowing protesters such as the crew of the *Phoenix* or the *Golden Rule* to enter into the detonation area, but they had orders to prevent such acts of atomic martyrdom.

On July 1, 1958, the *Phoenix* was hailed and warned by navy vessels but it continued on its way. The *Phoenix* was boarded the following morning by the coast guard. Earle Reynolds was arrested but was allowed to stay on board with the arresting officer as the *Phoenix* was forced to sail to Kwajalein. At Kwajalein, Reynolds was placed on a military aircraft and flown on July 8 to Honolulu, where he was taken into federal custody. On September 26, 1958, he was convicted in a Honolulu federal court of "interfering with violation of the Atomic Energy Commission's order forbidding nationals from entering [a nuclear] test area" (WFO117-2236-3). Reynolds received a prison sentence of two years (eighteen months suspended), but his conviction was later overturned by the U.S. court of appeals on December 29, 1960 (WFO100-437334-47:2; classified "Secret"). This experience only furthered Earle Reynolds's resolve to oppose U.S. military policies through dramatic acts of civil disobedience (see Reynolds 1960). Reynolds's arrest and trial marked him as a marginal, dangerously unpredictable academic. His later legal vindication by the U.S. court of appeals did not restore his status in academia, however — his commitment to activism marked him in ways that a court ruling could not erase, and he would remain an outcast from mainstream academia for the rest of his days (Price 1998c, 2003c; Wittman 1987).

Attempts to Sail to the Soviet Union

In 1959 Reynolds briefly taught anthropology at Methodist Hiroshima Women's College, then in September 1961 he wrote a letter to the Soviet ambassador to Japan asking permission to sail to Vladivostok. Reynolds wrote the Soviet ambassador that he had once "sailed into the United States testing area in the Pacific in 1958 to protest the testing of nuclear weapons . . . [and he now] . . . desired permission to enter the Soviet port to protest a new Russian series" of nuclear weapons tests (WFO100-437334-47:3 4/28/67). Reynolds, his wife, son, daughter, and a friend, Thomas Yonea, set sail for Vladivostok a few weeks later on September 24. The FBI's classified "Secret" summary of Reynolds's 1961 trip to the Soviet Union reports that "prior to departure a Department of State representative telephoned Reynolds to make certain he fully understood the risks of sailing into the territory of a foreign government without [an] appropriate visa or other permission. Reynolds expressed appreciation for the interest shown; said he was aware of the risks; and intended to issue a statement that the venture was entirely a private one and that he had no desire to create an international incident or embarrassment to the American Government. He relieved the American Government of a duty or responsibility with regard to protection or assistance" (WFO100-437334-47:3 4/28/67). On October 21, 1961, three Soviet patrol boats near the Soviet port city of Nakhodka confronted the *Phoenix*. The Soviets boarded the boat and then spoke with Reynolds and the crew for two hours. Japanese newspapers reported that Reynolds and his crew were politely refused when they tried to give the Soviets petitions protesting their testing of atomic weapons. Reynolds bragged to the press that "he was arrested by American authorities at Eniwetok, but merely turned back by the Soviets" (WFO100-437334-47:4 4/28/67).

A year later, in October 1962, Reynolds was a crew member aboard the *Everyman III*, an old fishing cutter covered in peace slogans. The *Everyman III* was to sail from the U.K. to Leningrad, with the crew planning to travel to Moscow to distribute antinuclear testing information. Reynolds's FBI files contain a ten-page, detailed report of Reynolds's trip aboard the *Everyman III* — it appears that the information for this report was provided by an informant who had tape-recorded one of Reynolds's public talks back in the United States. Reynolds described the *Everyman III* as barely sea-worthy, but he sailed it from Wales to London and then, with a cargo of 50,000 antinuclear Russian language leaflets, to Belgium, the Netherlands, and Stockholm, where they unsuccessfully tried to acquire Soviet visas. On September 17, without visas, they left for the Gulf of Finland, where they encountered Soviet patrol boats that escorted them to Leningrad Harbor.

At Leningrad Harbor they were boarded, vaccinated, and kept under guard by Soviet authorities. After some failed negotiations to acquire visas, the *Everyman III* was towed away from the port, at which point some of the younger members of the crew dove into the water and attempted (without success) to swim for shore. Next, some crew members "knocked out some of the sea cocks so that water came into the hull" (WFO100-437334-13:6). The Soviets then boarded the ship and tied up the crew, while four guards tried to stop the leaks from the sea cocks. The ship moved to five different anchorages over the next week, during which Reynolds reports that the crew was "pleasant but noncooperative." Eventually they were escorted out of Soviet waters (WFO100-437334-13:6).

Sailing to North Vietnam and China

In March 1967 Reynolds, his second wife, Akie, and five other Americans departed on the *Phoenix* from Hiroshima with the intent to deliver needed, but banned, medical supplies to North Vietnam. The U.S. State Department learned of Reynolds's plans and announced that anyone delivering medical supplies to North Vietnam would be subject to ten years' imprisonment and a fine of $10,000. An American newspaper reported that Reynolds and the crew of the *Phoenix* were planning to sail medical supplies to North Vietnam as part of an organization known as "A Quaker Action Group" (*Philadelphia Inquirer* 2/25/67:2). The FBI compiled and sorted this and dozens of other newspaper clippings about the trip, and they archived petitions calling on President Johnson to let the *Phoenix* travel without interference (WFO100-437334-41).

On March 20, 1967, after reaching Hong Kong where they purchased $20,000 of medical supplies, Reynolds informed the American consulate of his intentions to travel to North Vietnam. In this communication he confirmed that although their actions were in violation of U.S. laws they felt directed "by a religious sense of the oneness of mankind" (WFO100-437334-42:7). On March 30, 1967, the *Phoenix* arrived in Haiphong, North Vietnam, and delivered medical supplies. The American press coverage was limited and relied on foreign, predominantly Soviet, sources for information on the trip. The *Sunday Bulletin* of Philadelphia passed on reports from the TASS News

Agency of the crew's statements of peace and brotherhood: "TASS quoted [crew member Karl] Zietlow as saying that the Quakers, being pacifists, believe the responsibility for the continued bloodshed in Vietnam lies with the U.S. Government for violating the 1954 Geneva agreements on Indochina" (WFO100-437334-42:6). The U.S. State Department revoked the passports of five of the *Phoenix*'s crew, and instructed Reynolds to turn in his passport to the Tokyo embassy and sail back to the United States (*Washington Post* 4/25/67).

A great deal of publicity followed the *Phoenix*'s journey; *Look*, for example, ran a pictorial spread along with a sympathetic account of their trip (Massar and Hedgepeth 1967). On their return to the United States the FBI collected reports from the *Phoenix* crew's speaking appearances before Quaker groups and other progressive organizations (e.g., WFO100-437334-48).

In August 1968 Reynolds departed Japan on the *Phoenix* on a "goodwill visit" to China (WFO100-437334-69). He and Akie traveled without visas or sanctioned approval from either the United States or Japan, but this time they were stopped by Japanese authorities while under sail. The authorities forced the *Phoenix* to return to Japan where Akie was arrested for violations of the Immigration Control Law, and Reynolds was charged with being an accessory to this charge. The FBI's report of the incident noted "Dr. Reynolds has objected strenuously to the Japanese authorities, but without avail, as they were escorted back to Nagasaki and are currently restrained from leaving the boat. They have since both been indicted and must stand trial for the offense" (WFO100-437334-71). Reynolds sought assistance from the American embassy, but he was met with a cool response while the FBI used his enquiries to gather more information on Reynolds and his activities. The FBI noted that Reynolds had responded with an angry outburst when he was informed that the American embassy would offer him no assistance in this matter (WFO100-437334-76).

The next summer Reynolds and five other Americans sailed from Nagasaki with the goal of undertaking another "people to people goodwill visit" to China (WFO100-437334-81). The FBI monitored news reports from the Kyodo news agency in Nagasaki that,

> the Phoenix arrived in Shanghai June 16th and Chinese patrol ships were requested on June 16, 18, 19 and 20 to grant entry permits to Reynolds and the other members of the group, but the Chinese replied that no Americans may enter China so long as U.S. continues its present policy toward Taiwan. The Chinese then gave the Phoenix a drum of fuel for its return journey to Japan.
>
> According to press reports, the entire group is now in [the] custody

of Japanese Immigration officials, who have refused them permission to land because they did not posses entry permits. (WFO100-437334-87)

A lengthy account in the *Washington Post* on August 17, 1969, of the *Phoenix's* encounter with a Chinese gunboat detailed the dialogue between the two crews. The *Phoenix* stated their wish to visit China to bring messages of peace from the West, but the Chinese crew ordered them to return to Japan. The *Phoenix's* crew asked the soldiers to come to the *Phoenix* in a dinghy so that they could present them with flags and greetings. The Chinese solider replied that

> Chairman Mao has said many times that the people of China and the U.S. are friends. You should go back and resolutely struggle with the American people against the imperialists. Chairman Mao orders you to leave these waters.
>
> [*Phoenix* crew member and Dartmouth China specialist, Jonathan Mirsky, replied:] If we leave it will be a great blow to the American peace movement. Our movement is stronger every day, but this would be a serious failure.
>
> [Chinese Soldier]: You are imperialists from an imperialist country. Down with imperialism! (*Washington Post*, cited inWFO100-437334-93)

An extended dialogue then ensued in which the *Phoenix's* crew told the Chinese that they were "in serious need of oil" and requested permission to go to Shanghai to refuel. The Chinese, however, held up signs in Chinese saying "you must go away." Despite the *Phoenix* crew's uses of quotes from Mao stating that the Chinese and American people are friends, as well as statements of disagreement with U.S. policy and an expressed desire to witness the revolutionary changes of Chinese society for themselves, the Chinese crew continued to insist that the *Phoenix* leave. After some extended dialogue (and a heated exchange after a *Phoenix* crew member took a photograph of the Chinese vessel) the *Phoenix* headed out to sea accompanied by the Chinese gunboat. Once they had traveled farther out to sea, the *Phoenix* stopped its engines and continued a (somewhat more friendly) dialogue with the Chinese. The *Phoenix* was eventually given oil by the Chinese gunboat crew and told to "go back and join in the American struggle" (WFO100-437334-93).

The ships departed but five hours later the *Phoenix* returned to the same area and again told the gunboat's crew that they wished to sail through to Shanghai. One member of the *Phoenix's* crew stated that he alone wanted to go to China "and do some kind of collective work" (WFO100-437334-93). This offer was made several times, but was met with silence then eventually refused. Shortly thereafter the *Phoenix* began its return voyage to Japan.

In 1970 Reynolds, along with his wife (who had not been granted a U.S. visa), sailed the *Phoenix* back to the United States. The FBI monitored Reynolds's statements at a peace rally the day prior to his departure, where the report claims he told the crowd that "he was being forced to leave Japan because of his 'peace' activities, but pledged he would continue his anti-Vietnam War" work in the United States (WFO100-437334-97). On July 10, 1970, the Tokyo FBI legal attaché sent a memo to Hoover regarding Reynolds and the "Japan Peace for Vietnam Committee," with material enclosed for the FBI's laboratory. The report is currently heavily redacted and the content is not decipherable (WFO100-437334 7/10/70). The FBI continued to monitor Reynolds after his return to the United States, as he and Akie settled into a Quaker community in Ben Lomond, California (WFO100-437334-99).

Reynolds's work to bring medical supplies to Hanoi during the Vietnam War, as well as his friendship voyage to Leningrad, were documented in the Canadian Film Board documentary "The Voyage of the Phoenix." Reynolds became a dignified leader and spokesperson of the movement to end the war in Southeast Asia. In his later life he and Akie worked as caretakers at a Quaker retreat center and he occasionally taught college courses. After Akie's death in 1994, Reynolds moved near his daughter's home in Southern California, where he lived until his death in 1998.

Grassroots Anthropological Activism: Inventing the Teach-In

It is fitting to conclude here with a brief examination of the FBI's interest in anthropologists involved in the antiwar movement's teach-ins of the 1960s.[7] Anthropologists were instrumental in the creation both of the first antiwar teach-in at the University of Michigan and of the first national teach-in, and they were key actors in the diffusion of the teach-in movement to campuses across the United States.

After President Johnson authorized bombing campaigns in North Vietnam in February 1965, a group of mostly untenured faculty at the University of Michigan began planning a faculty protest response. In early March groups of faculty began discussing how this response might be organized. According to Matthew Newman, "sociologist William Gamson proposed a one-day strike or "moratorium" during which faculty protesters would refuse to teach classes and instead devote the day to teaching interested students about US involvement in Vietnam" (1995:11). Needless to say, these plans came under fire by Michigan Governor George Romney and university officials, and the plan was changed so that instead of holding a strike, faculty and students would have an all-night teach-in on the war on March 24. With these changes faculty and administration support for the teach-in escalated.

As Marshall Sahlins observed, when the idea was brought forth at a small organizational meeting:

> the assent in the room was instantaneous, immediately the idea popped out, so many strategic virtues and political resonances did this simple symbolic inversion convey. (Structural inversions were in the intellectual air: this was the time of the first American publication of major works of Claude Levi-Strauss.) A form of free speech of its own, devoted to momentous national issues, the teach-in was at least as good as, and different from, any of the current university politics. Rather than shirking our own responsibilities as teachers by not holding classes, we were multiplying them by going on to teach through the night: making the university a source of greater enlightenment—a double entendre that seemed palpable during the event—instead of shutting it down. (2000:24)

An estimated three thousand students and faculty attended the teach-in, and despite three bomb threats there were eight hundred students still in attendance at 8:00 A.M. the next morning (Newman 1995). The first teach-in had three speakers and a series of workshops and discussion sessions on the war, imperialism, and the political history of Southeast Asia. The three speakers were Fairleigh Dickinson University economist Robert Browne, Michigan State University anthropologist John Donahue, and Arthur Waskow from the Michigan's Institute for Policy Studies. John Donahue spoke of his firsthand ethnographic knowledge of Vietnamese culture and the long struggle of the Vietnamese against foreign imperialism. Untenured University of Michigan anthropologists Marshall Sahlins and Eric Wolf were active participants in organizing this first teach-in (Baumann 1998; Thomas 1999: 15; Wolf 1969:ix–x).

In the days and weeks that followed, similar teach-ins spread to Columbia University, University of Chicago, Wayne State University, and University of Pennsylvania. On May 15, 1965, there was a nationwide teach-in held in Washington, D.C., which was broadcast to college and university campuses across the United States. As an outgrowth of the teach-in movement, a variety of antiwar sessions were organized at the annual meetings of the AAA. The group Anthropologists for Radical Political Action organized some sessions, while others were organized within the usual academic framework of the meetings. Morton Fried, Marvin Harris, and Robert Murphy held an antiwar symposium at the 1966 annual meetings of the AAA and "sponsored a resolution protesting inhumane U.S. actions in Vietnam and urging a rapid peaceful settlement" (Sanjek 1995:45; see also Fried et al. 1968). While the sort of purge that befell Gene Weltfish after speaking out against American military actions in South Korea did not befall anthropologists participating in these teach-ins, the FBI did begin tracking the movements and politics of anthropologists associated with these early teach-ins.

Marshall Sahlins, Eric Wolf, Morton Fried, and the National Teach-Ins

Marshall Sahlins's participation in the March 24, 1965, teach-in led him to take on a central organizing role in the national teach-in held just seven weeks later on May 15. Sahlins and Michigan philosophy professor Arnold Kauffman "set up the teach-in from a room in Washington's Mayfair Hotel which eventually had three phones constantly ringing off the hook with calls from virtually every major press, radio, and television office" (Sahlins 2000:205). Sahlins saw teach-ins as part of a new democratic social movement where citizens and intellectuals with pertinent knowledge could discuss vital policy decisions without the blinders of governmental policy makers. He observed that governmental policy in Southeast Asia was still being shaped by the legacy of McCarthyism: "One could reasonably speculate that an effect of the Teach-In was to clear some air in Washington. Part of the legacy of the China lobby and McCarthy era is well known: the flow of informed, outstanding scholars to government service was seriously curtailed. About another effect one can only guess: a lingering disinclination to raise certain issues, discuss certain possibilities, to the extent that internal dialogue in policy bureaus is constrained, options are reduced, and some people [are] perhaps even forced to compromise their judgment, their intelligence, and their morality" (215).

The teach-in used (politely negotiated) guerrilla tactics and public unfiltered discourse to challenge the limited range of military and diplomatic policy discussions that resulted from McCarthyism's purges. The State Department, Pentagon, and other decision-making governmental bodies had purged the left from their ranks, and the teach-in brought back the views of the ranks that had been purged. Informed voices with different values, knowledge bases, and theoretical understandings of the nature of power and imperialism were brought to the public without the filters or sanctions of the government.

Because of anthropologist Eric Wolf's involvement in the first Michigan teach-in and the national teach-in, the Detroit FBI field office notified J. Edgar Hoover that Wolf and approximately eight other individuals were affiliated with the Inter-University Committee for Debate on Foreign Policy (IUCDFP) (WFO100-444509-1). The Detroit field office notified headquarters that although it had information on a number of the individuals affiliated with this group it had only basic information on Wolf, and a request was made to "initiate a limited investigation" of Wolf and other individuals associated with IUCDFP.

FBI headquarters then sent a "Security Matter-C" report to the Detroit bureau, much of which is currently withheld by FBI censors.[8] The FBI's background investigation on Wolf outlined his personal history (birth, marriage, etc.) military experience, academic training, and employment history (WFO100-444509-3). The FBI combed through Wolf's immigration and military records and established that he was born in Vienna 1923, had become an American citizen in 1943, and was a decorated veteran of World War II. Officials and colleagues at institutions where Wolf had studied and taught were contacted, and all reported that Wolf was a bright, hard-working individual.

In April 1966 the New York SAC sent Hoover a memo on Wolf that contained a five-hundred-word summary of the Independent Socialist League (ISL), formerly known as the Workers Party (WP), indicating the FBI believed Wolf was involved with the ISL (WFO100-444509-13). One partially released document indicates the FBI used 1965 records from Queens College to determine if Wolf's mailing address was the same as that identified from the ISL publication's "Labor Actions" mailing list (WFO100-444509-16:13 6/16/66).

The FBI noted that Wolf was the faculty coadvisor for the University of Michigan chapter of the W. E. B. DuBois Club (WFO 100-444509-14). The FBI also recorded Wolf's involvement in the University of Michigan's June 5–6, 1965, Inter-University Committee for a Public Hearing on Vietnam conference (WFO100-444509-16). Further the FBI located a summary of an FBI interview with Wolf conducted in 1954:

> [Eric Wolf], during 1954 while employed as a visiting Assistant Professor of Sociology and Anthropology at the University of Illinois, Urbana, Illinois, was interviewed by Special Agents of the FBI in connection with another matter. He advised that he had met Angel Palerm in Mexico City, Mexico, during December 1951, while he was in Mexico on anthropological fieldwork. He advised that he had been referred to Palerm who introduced him to various people in Mexico during the first several months of his stay. He advised that he maintained professional contacts with Palerm since that time in view of their common anthropological interests and their anticipation of a joint project anticipated for summer 1954, studying an Indian community in Mexico. He described Palerm as in his opinion, extremely anti-communist. He advised that from conversations with Palerm, he understood that Palerm had fought with the Spanish Republic Army and had come to Mexico after the termination of the Spanish Civil War as a refugee from Spain.[9] (WFO100-444509-16)

On June 16, 1966, the Detroit bureau recommended against Eric Wolf's name being placed on the Security Index, "inasmuch as available information does not qualify him under existing criteria." The bureau did, however, maintain a record on Wolf in their Reserve Index "Section A" (WFO100-444509-16).

On March 11, 1968, a "Security Flash" requesting that information on Wolf be forwarded to the Subversion Control Section of the Domestic Intelligence Division was issued by the FBI (WFO100-444509-13). This appears to be a standard governmental employment background check, however, and a file from this same date notes an identical request being made by the U.S. Department of Heath Education and Welfare.

Anthropologist Morton Fried's involvement in antiwar teach-ins also was monitored by the FBI, but their interest in Fried predated his antiwar actions. Fried's name first appeared in an FBI espionage file because he had published a book review in the June 1954 edition of the Institute of Pacific Relations's journal *Far Eastern Survey* (vol. 23, no. 6; WFO100-64700).[10] A decade later Fried's name appeared in FBI files monitoring the Teach-In movement of the 1960s. The FBI documents on the April 1966 University of Michigan teach-in on China appear to indicate that a Students for a Democratic Society insider at Michigan was an FBI informant, providing confirmation of Morton Fried's and Owen Lattimore's early confirmation on their participation in the teach-in. The FBI recorded that Michigan anthropologists Norma Diamond, Marshall Sahlins, and Eric Wolf were speakers at the teach-in. The FBI described Fried's talk as "a rather academic and apologetic lecture on China today" (DE100-30957:66). A file on the teach-in describes Fried's afternoon talk as follows:

> ██████████ advised that Morton Fried, described as an anthropologist from Columbia University, said that he had done some two or three years field work in China before the Communists took over power in that country. He spoke briefly on the fact that Voltaire's ideas were the model for the China culture of yesterday and that that philosophy was unsuccessful and a failure because it was too authoritarian. He said that the Communist historians give much concentration on the idea of why the "Taipei" society failed and have concluded that it was because of the authoritarian family culture which did not permit the individual to contribute to society. He noted that this condition has completely changed in China today and that in the prevailing Chinese philosophy all individuals can and must contribute. (WFO105-151582-8:17)

Fried's evening address is also summarized in his file, although most of the information appears to have come from the *Michigan Daily* newspaper for April 5, 1966. The FBI reported that Fried said the United States needed to admit it was involved in another nation's civil war, and that "the entire concept of containment is a myth" (DE105-11627:20–21). As was too often the case, much of the FBI's information concerning Fried and the teach-in was wrong. After reviewing the FBI's notes on Fried and the conference, Norma Diamond remarked that, "whoever 'advised' about Fried's comments on the afternoon panel obviously never had a course on modern Chinese history or a course from me on Chinese society and culture. Surely Fried would have been referring to the Taiping Rebellion . . . and not to 'Taipei' society. And there is no way he would have said that Voltaire's ideas were the model for China. Au contraire, the Jesuit explication of Confucianism was seized on by the French Enlightenment philosophers as a model: they loved the idea of a state governed by the best and brightest of the intelligentsia rather than an inbred aristocracy" (N. Diamond to Price 7/20/00).

The FBI noted Fried's membership on the national board of the Inter-University Committee, along with anthropologists David Aberle, Stanley Diamond, Lawrence Krader, Anthony Leeds, and Marshall Sahlins (DE105-11627:19). The New York FBI office also mentioned Fried in a May 31, 1968, file on the SDS's role on the morning of April 30, 1968, in the five-day student occupation of the Columbia University's campus. The report contained twenty-seven photographs relating to the student occupation action (WFO 100-439048-34-208x), and the accompanying narrative discussed the role of factionalism in the events leading up to the student takeover of the campus (see Harris 1968b; Roberts 1968; Sanjek 1995:45–46). In characterizing these divisions the FBI observed that they "seemed to be dictated by age, as the younger faculty members tended to support the students and the older ones tended to support the administration. Support for the students was most pronounced in the Liberal Arts Division. The most outspoken and openly in support of the students were ▬▬▬▬▬, ▬▬▬▬▬, ▬▬▬▬▬, Morton Fried and ▬▬▬▬▬. One group of faculty members who supported the students, regardless of age, was composed of faculty members who felt that their talents had not been recognized by the university and that they had not advanced as rapidly as they felt they should" (WFO100-439048-34-208x:29). Although heavily censored (despite a reprocessing after an appeal arguing that the document should be released in full in compliance with Executive Order 12958) the report indicates that the FBI determined that some members of the faculty were advising students of the administration's plans to disrupt student sit-ins. The FBI reported that "as a result, the sit-ins were being advised of plans by the university to cope with the situation and could take counter measures" (WFO100-439048-34-208x:29).

In Activism Begins Responsibility

While social-justice activism became increasingly popular in the 1960s and 1970s, the FBI continued to investigate activist anthropologists. Although an examination of these campaigns are beyond the scope of this book, the actions in post-1950s America continued to have negative impacts on the careers of individuals both inside and outside the academy. For every Wolf or Sahlins whose career advanced despite their involvement in radical political actions, there were numerous anthropologists such as Earle Reynolds and Kathleen Gough whose careers suffered for such actions. The history of activist anthropology in the 1960s and 1970s still needs to be written. It is a rich history that finds the FBI investigating the AAA's radical anthropology caucus Anthropologists for Radical Political Action (ARPA), while a generation of young anthropologists came of age during the Vietnam War protests.[11]

Kathleen Gough's experiences at Brandeis and Simon Frazer map out some of the limits imposed on anthropologists who examined the evolution of imperialist relations relative to current events and extrapolated conclusions at odds with U.S. foreign policy and with campus conditions. The AAA's decision to actively investigate Kathleen Gough's dismissal from Simon Fraser indicates a measurable but limited change in political climate and suggests an acknowledgement that such advocacy is an important function of the association—a significant change from the position of silence during the late 1940s and throughout the 1950s. But it is not clear that the association would engage in such aggressive advocacy today, when its timidity to investigate (much less clearly define) ethical improprieties finds it increasingly avoiding the controversies of its day.

The FBI's monitoring of anthropologists at teach-ins shows the links between the 1960s activist anthropologists and their predecessors in the 1930s through 1950s. The AAA's radical caucus, ARPA, used grassroots activism to educate and organize anthropologists who opposed American military actions in Southeast Asia. And these actions drew the attentions not only of the FBI but the CIA as well, as CIA spies monitored both anthropologists and the annual AAA meetings (Price 1998a:418).

Earle Reynolds's story shows how anthropological research can move beyond the clinical study of people and issues to a compassionate understanding that we are a part of the world we study and that inaction can be a form of action contributing to the problems we study. Reynolds's physical anthropological research on Hiroshima survivors moved him to take actions beyond his academic analysis—actions of protest against the development of inhumane weapons. Like Lisa Kalvelage, Reynolds understood inaction to be guilt. That few contemporary anthropologists know of him is part of the lesson of Earle Reynolds: his acts of heroism sent him to the margins. His message of danger was itself dangerous and demanded that he be kept at a distance from the halls of academia. It does not matter that Reynolds operated outside of the theater of mainstream anthropology because he would not have been welcomed back to the academy after his acts of civil disobedience.

One senior anthropologist told me that Earle Reynolds stopped being an anthropologist when he began his peace work. This is the wrong view: Reynolds was a radical applied anthropologist who used the principles of activism, cultural relativism, and an anthropological view of cultural and historical processes to advance the cause of human survival. But his applied work was not funded in the normal sense. It is instructive to consider the lack of funding that would have been available to Reynolds for his peace work had he chosen to work within academia or governmental service. His refusal to limit his travel to nations approved by the State Department surely would have led to his dismissal from any U.S. university, because no mainstream research foundations would have funded the study of issues of concern to Reynolds (much less his humanitarian supply missions). But we must likewise consider the types of funding that *were* made available to anthropologists who were ready, willing, and able to apply their anthropological craft to the questions of human survival after a nuclear holocaust; applying linguistic skills to Cold War cryptographers at the NSA; studying levels of radiation on remote populations; designing anthropogenic seats for aircraft designed to deliver doomsday bombs; or applying ethnographic skills to assist the U.S. war efforts in Southeast Asia (Nader 1987a, 1987b; Price 2002b, 2002d).

But these issues are not only issues of the past, they are with us today. In the same way that Reynolds, Gough, Wolf, and Sahlins's activism is directly linked to the anthropological activism of the 1940s and 1950s, so too is today's anthropological activism in opposition to various military and domestic policies. And the present is also bridged to the past by the continuity of opposition and surveillance by American intelligence agencies viewing the actions of activist anthropologists as a threat to American national security.

CHAPTER 16

Through a Fog Darkly: The Cold War's

Impact on Free Inquiry

If they can get you asking the wrong questions, they don't

have to worry about answers. — Thomas Pynchon

American anthropology has been slow to acknowledge — much less honor — its disciplinary victims of McCarthyism. The reasons for this are multiple and complex and reveal McCarthyism's success in stifling debate and activism in America's body politic. That these victims of assaults on academic and political freedom were often members of Marxist organizations still blemishes the legitimacy of their struggles. Thus, there remains a hesitancy in acknowledging American anthropology's historic links to Communist and Socialist political organizations.

Historians of anthropology study the discipline's links to colonialism, but critical examinations of the impact of other political or economic forces are limited. The tendency to disavow the influence of Marxist activism and epistemology, or even the active role of political economy, has weakened the interpretative power of twentieth-century U. S. anthropology to a point where the political motivations of actors are squeezed from the discipline's canonical historical narratives.[1]

Laura Nader reminds us that anthropologists' depoliticization of their own history is not accidental and has significant implications for the development and practice of the field. She reflects that her own contact with McCarthyism as a student was as a background phenomenon that was not to be noticed or commented on: "The foreground was to come later, but the issues for anthropology were all there in the 1950s: academic freedom and academic fear, temptation, the funding carrot, red baiting and the McCarthy repression, nuclear power uses for war or peace, and concern for those we study. It was as if we lived in a fog; we saw such happenings as extraneous to the student of anthropology" (1997a:114). Nader notes how anthropology's intersection with politics is made invisible through processes of "mind colonization," whereby anthropologists learn to dissociate their past and present actions from embedded political events (1997a:141).

Historian George Stocking's (1982) criticism of presentist histories, (which view the past through the judgmental lens of the present and lead to the construction of Whiggish morality tales) helped establish a dominant American historicist school (marked by its goal of understanding the past only in terms of the past) of the history of anthropology.[2] But despite the contributions of this school, its inattentiveness to political economy has led to sizable blind spots in anthropology's understanding of itself. As a result, the field is overdue for a reevaluation of its past and present relations to political forces. We need to build a new history of the discipline that mixes the concerns of historicism with the justifications of presentism. Even Stocking concedes that presentism can direct "attention to problems which are historically significant, but which were not likely to be raised so long as one tried to work from within the perspective of the historical actors" (1982:xvii).[3] We should not abandon historicism's relativistic appreciation of time and place, but we can benefit from a more presentist interpretation of past dilemmas—not to rebuke those from a past age but to cast new light on our current predicaments. For what would the point of history be if not to critically learn from the past?

Anthropologists must shrug off the negative connotations of radical political associations and reexamine the historic political actions that anthropology's collective colonized mind learned to not see. This requires understanding, for example, that the racist attitudes that prevailed throughout the United States from the 1930s through the 1950s contrasted sharply with the far more progressive positions held by the Communist Party, which, more importantly, took far more effective action in the cause of racial equality than did either of the dominant political parties. Although for many the ravages of Stalinism continue to discredit the Soviet legacy, the individuals of the American Communist Party worked for a particularly American form of Communism that was largely rooted in an American experience. But McCarthyism succeeded in linking all American Communists with Stalin under contingencies of doublethink, where all Communists shared the international guilt of one nation while the atrocities of capitalist nations were not transferred to those who praised capitalism. The American dialogue on alternatives to laissez-faire capitalism was thus channeled away from considerations of middle-range socialist alternatives, as the failures of the Soviet Union were claimed to negate even considerations of the forms of social democracy being developed in Scandinavia and other parts of Europe.

It is difficult to assess the toll of McCarthyism on America and American anthropology. We do not know how widespread was the surveillance of anthropologists, nor do we know the depth of the F B I's activities. As Natalie Robins observed in her examination of the F B I's surveillance on American writers, "most of the damage was invisible" (1992:398).

After the red scares spread to campuses, progressives wondered if their politics secretly influenced the outcomes of job interviews, submissions for publications, and promotions and tenure decisions. Fears on American campuses created plenty to wonder about when seemingly straightforward advancement opportunities were rejected without explanation. In reflecting on questions raised by Harvard's rejection of his tenure application in the late 1950s, anthropologist Dell Hymes, without regrets, wonders if Cold War politics might have played a role:

> I came up for tenure five years later (1959–60). The department recommended me, and the next higher level did also. The chair of the department, a social psychologist, Robert White, called to tell me and congratulate me. He then called a week later to say that the President, Nathan Pusey, had overruled the recommendation. No explanation was forthcoming.
>
> I have heard two explanations. One was that a member of the outside committee, on returning home, changed his mind, and wrote a letter saying so. (If that happened, as it may have, I can infer who it was.)
>
> The other was that it was connected to the Cold War atmosphere. In those years I continued to subscribe to *The Nation*, *Monthly Review*, *Science and Society*, and Morris Swadesh came to visit us, and gave a talk I arranged (on linguistics, actually featuring acquisition of language, because he had a new young child). But none of that was ever noted, so far as I know. Kluckhohn indeed was interested to some degree in Swadesh's efforts to mount coordinated surveys of Native American languages.
>
> The two public activities which I can recall were attending a debate between Irving Howe and Paul Sweezy (small audiences)—we became

friends with Paul, who was living in Cambridge, at that time. And attending a rather large public meeting, sponsored by H. Stuart Hughes and others, devoted to what could be done to revive the left (that's how I recall it at least). I got up and said something, not much about the importance of working together. That would have made my presence known, if someone was attending to such things.

The reason I think this might have had something to do with the tenure decision was that after it had been made, walking on Boylston Street, I passed Hughes, whose face took on a look of chagrin. It's the only thing connecting us of which I can think to cause such a look. But of course it may have been rumor, not knowledge.

All this is indirect and conjectural. Perhaps Pusey disliked linguistics, or had been appealed to by Joshua Whatmough, then chair of the Linguistics Department, whose magnum opus, *Language*, I had reviewed favorably, to his appreciation, but then criticized somewhat in a second review in another context. A small thing, perhaps, but he had a very large ego. Kluckhohn took it [as] directed against himself, at least in brief remarks to me one day. Perhaps all these things had a part. In any case it was quite unexpected.

I should add that one step of the process was an interview with McGeorge Bundy, then Dean (later a member of John F. Kennedy's cabinet). I feel sure that I disappointed him, because when, asking me about an offer from Berkeley, I answered that I'd like to able to choose. Which was true, but in retrospect, not what a Harvard man may have wanted to hear. (Hymes to Price 8/27/96)

While concerns and speculations such as Hymes's were widespread, gossip about such decisions spread messages of fear that contributed to an environment that encouraged and even rewarded self-censorship.

When presenting papers on anthropology and McCarthyism at conferences, I have heard anthropologists argue that no anthropologists were really harmed by McCarthyism, or, as one put it, "things were rough for a few years but everyone who had troubles still kept their teaching jobs." It is true that most anthropologists were able to work in some, more often than not, reduced, academic capacity. But Weltfish left Columbia and Stern was left to night school despite stellar careers in the classroom and in print, while anthropologists like Richard Morgan and Jack Harris left the field permanently and Morris Swadesh and Robert Armstrong left the country. Not only did people lose their jobs, but the careers of prominent scholars such as George Murdock or Ralph Linton advanced as they covertly attacked the reputations of scholars they believed to be un-American.

McCarthyism's impact on anthropology is not measured in the numbers of individuals who lost their jobs; more accurately, it is measured in the extent it broadcast messages of fear and self-censorship to those who might otherwise have generated radical critiques or taken action for social justice. To use anthropology's analytical metaphor of cultural evolutionism, McCarthyism could be described as a highly adaptive social innovation. It was an ideological component of the infrastructural strategy of America's geopolitical expansion, which supported not the interests of the society as a whole, but the interests of America's business elites. Those who opposed the expansion of American hegemony, or the racial divisions that are an intrinsic component of the dominant relations of production, were demonized as enemies of the state and effectively disempowered. The efficiency of this adaptation was remarkable: it allowed the bulk of American society to willingly and fervently act in concert against their own economic and judicial best interests. Like other cultural adaptations in highly stratified societies, the strategies of McCarthyism were not selected because they best served the interests of most of the culture's members but rather because they served the interests of *some*. In this instance, those served were not only elites profiting from the expanded national security state, but also included all who benefited from America's racial segregation or antilabor policies and laws.

Anthropologists during the early Cold War were keenly aware of the dangers of openly applying Marxist analysis in their work, and many altered their work accordingly. For both radical and moderate anthropologists self-censorship became a standard practice and the tone and focus of theoretical inquiries of the period demonstrate the power of McCarthyism. Some anthropologists adopted a crypto-Marxist approach wherein Marx and openly Marxist scholars were never cited but Marxist analyses were employed in research. As Joan Vincent observed, HUAC led to "a certain 'laundering' of dissertations [that] took place when their authors later published their work" (1990:228). Other anthropologists simply avoided considering Marxist approaches to social phenomena altogether. The extent to which this was a conscious choice is unanswerable because scholars seldom leave records of punches pulled.

Functionally, the public humiliation rituals of the hearings advertised the painful consequences of engaging in activism and highlighted the message that scholars were being watched or, better yet, announced that any anthropologist who wished to receive private or governmental grants or employment should avoid anything that could be interpreted as a subversive analysis. The costs of such deviance were easily contrasted with the virtue of compliance.

Embodying the Academically Disappeared: To Publish and Perish

McCarthyism's most significant impact on anthropology was perhaps its ability to limit and shape anthropological research and critiques. It is difficult to quantify the extent to which anthropologists who insisted on engaging in radical critiques in the 1950s were pushed out of academic anthropology. This book has not told the stories of those who quietly left anthropology without a trace because it is difficult to track that for which there is little or no record, and those who were led out of the field for political reasons seldom left records indicating why. As the experiences of Murray Wax indicate, blacklisted scholars were at times unaware of their fate. It is likely that many of anthropology's victims of McCarthyism suffered in ways not easily established, or in instances where these anthropologists were graduate students they disappeared leaving little trace of influence on the discipline.

The late Jerome Rauch's experiences during the 1950s illustrate the sort of troubles that befell anthropologists who critiqued disciplinary connections to the national security state. Rauch's experiences are worth recounting, first, to acknowledge that there are many more victims of McCarthyism than could ever be established through a search of archives or record systems and, second, to stress how the fears of McCarthyism repressed the development of specific voices.

In the late 1940s Rauch began studying anthropology at Columbia University where he undertook fieldwork in the Mortlock Islands (AAANB 1947 1[2]:16). Rauch took graduate courses with Kardiner, Strong, Benedict, Wagley, Weltfish, and Steward. He was active in the Columbia chapter of the American Veterans Committee, the Henry Wallace campaign, and the campus Marxist Club (Julie Rauch to Price 7/7/01). Things went well for Rauch until 1955 when he published an essay in the *Journal of Negro Education*, titled "Area Institute Programs and African Studies." This article developed a sophisticated, radical critique of the social sciences' ties with governmental agencies. Rauch critically analyzed how increased funding for area study centers caused these centers to think in specific ways and to ask questions with applications to the military and diplomatic interests of the Cold War. With frankness and detail Rauch argued that relationships between funding patrons and client anthropologists "transformed academic research into applied science, and reconfigured social research into ideology" (Rauch to Price 2/22/01). Rauch observed that there was a "configuration of government and business interest[s]" that could be seen in the mixture of governmental policy agencies (e.g., State Department, Foreign Service Institute, etc.), intelligence agencies (e.g., Office of Intelligence Research, Office of Naval Intelligence, etc.), military (e.g., National War College, U.S. Air Force, etc.), private foundations (e.g., Viking Fund, Rockefeller Foundation, etc.), and private industry (e.g., Standard Oil, etc.) directing research funding opportunities and research agendas for anthropology (Rauch 1955:415–16).

Rauch directly experienced negative consequences for his analysis of the "subordination of area research to government and business policy" (1955: 415). After publishing this critique, Rauch was given a Cold War cold shoulder by many in Columbia's anthropology department. Decades later he recalled that after publishing his impolite study he was taken aside by "Julian Steward, [who] told me that I was unemployable, and trying to face reality, I enrolled in library school" (Rauch to Price 12/13/00).[4]

Rauch was not bitter about this unwanted career change. He lived a productive life outside of anthropology working with W. E. B. Du Bois on the Council on African American Affairs, researching the history of the Caribbean slave trade, assisting the Maryland Legislative Black Caucus, and working as an applications programmer at the Oncology Institute of Johns Hopkins Hospital (Rauch to Price 12/13/00). But the culling of Rauch from anthropology not only curtailed the development of his line of critical research, it limited the audience who would encounter his critique and it sent a message to other anthropologists that such frank analyses could detrimentally affect one's career.

The anthropologists whose encounters with McCarthyism and the FBI are described in this book differ from each other in many ways. These individuals came from different schools of anthropology and had diverse professional careers and backgrounds, but many of them shared a common bond of FBI scrutiny because of their commitments to activism. Many came to the FBI's attention because they were *applied anthropologists*—not in the sense that the term has come to be used in the last few decades (meaning anthropologists hired by private or public organizations for work on specific projects),[5] but applied in the sense that they used anthropology's understanding of the inherent equality of all peoples, the myth of race, and theories of stratification as a foundation for their work for social justice.

To attract the attentions of the FBI or McCarthyism it was not enough that anthropologists recognized that race was a social construction. Knowledge was important but action was paramount. Many anthropologists publishing antiracist technical works in academic books and journals were not subjected to extensive, prolonged FBI surveillance; rather, it was when they wrote antiracist materials for a more general audience or took action by joining protest movements that the FBI considered them of interest. Although conducting research on inequality and publishing findings for an academic audience is important, it did not become *threatening* in the eyes of the FBI and other agents of McCarthyism until it reached a general audience, either through public actions and publications or presentations aimed at the general public.

The FBI did not view anthropologists siding with prevalent racist attitudes as a threat. In 1943 when FBI agents read a newspaper account of a proposal made by anthropologist Earnest Hooton of Harvard for a national governmental supervised human breeding program, FBI agents noted that the plan was devised by "a first rate fool," but they did not further investigate Hooton (see Price 2002b:20).[6] One explanation for the FBI's dismissal of Hooton's work is that because eugenics was not considered threatening to the existing racial, social, and economic hierarchy (indeed, his plan would have intensified the extant economic and racial stratification system) it did not threaten the interests the FBI protected. Eugenics represented continuity, not change.

The Hand that Mocked Them

One measure of McCarthyism's awareness that activism was a threat was the extent that known Marxist anthropologists (such as Socialist Labor Party member Leslie White) who were not actively engaged in public activism were rarely brought before loyalty boards or investigated by the FBI in any depth, whereas those who engaged in public acts of either scholarly advocacy or protest, either with (Melville Jacobs, Paul Radin, Mary Shepardson) or without (Oscar Lewis, Philleo Nash) documented party affiliations, were subjected to scrutiny by the FBI and by loyalty boards. Vague reports of supposed Communist-related activities led the FBI to maintain long-term investigations of anthropologists like Philleo Nash, Vilhjalmur Stefansson, Cora Du Bois, Margaret Mead, and Oscar Lewis, even though the bureau consistently failed to find anything other than thirdhand or fourthhand rumors that these individuals had any Communist ties. Given Senator McCarthy's belief that the best proof that someone is a Communist is that they say they aren't, it is difficult to imagine just how the FBI could ever determine that an individual was *not* a Communist.

Today there are those on the right who employ neo-McCarthyist tactics in contemporary culture wars. As Micaela di Leonardo observes, these battles evoke the names of past anthropologists such as Ruth Benedict, Franz Boas, Melville Herskovits, or Margaret Mead as the intellectual demons responsible for the release of the germ of cultural relativism into the world. In di Leonardo's view, the right's attack on cultural relativism is a "hypocritical attempt to rewrite the American morality play, to lay claim to virtue through focusing on the mote in Others' eyes while ignoring the beam in one's own" (1996:28–29). To these critics, anthropologists have undermined the power of patriotic jingoism by accepting the premise that other voices and other views have legitimacy.

Today, few American anthropologists engage in activities designed to threaten the status quo of American or international patterns of inequality on the level of past anthropologists like Jacobs, Morgan, Swadesh, or Weltfish.[7] Instead, the discipline is awash with postmodern reflectionists, many of whom skillfully critique the manifestations of hegemonic power in subjects both ideographic and universal but few of whom actually confront the political-economic power bases that generate and support these structural exhaust features of the contemporary world.

Theory without action is only theory. Activism is important because it is action. The current doldrums of postmodern anthropology are bogged down in Foucault's fallacy that theory "does not express, translate, or serve to apply practice: it is practice" (1977:206; cf. Foucault 2000). While some postmodernists cut their teeth on the premise that science is embedded in the society of the scientific practitioners, their approach to this premise explicitly ignores Marx's recognition of the primacy of the materialistic features of society. Many postmodernists have grown comfortable in the saddle, riding a one-trick pony following a well-worn path that explains the interpretable world through a rendering process that boils down all that can be known to the self. This narcissistic obsession with the self increasingly focuses on the emotive whims of salon-bound academics to the neglect of examining the expanding manifestation of a new stage of capitalism that is increasingly mobile, global, and aggressive.

One measure of the serious limits of postmodernism is found in the absence of political action and activism on the part of its practitioners. It is significant that this methodological approach first flourished during Reagan's America. As America's rich got richer, entitlement programs were dismantled wholesale, child poverty rates climbed, and America's postmodern anthropologists shunned activism to colorfully pontificate about agency, the Other, and various tropes of inaction. The extent that such criticisms ignore the economic and demographic underpinnings of American inequality and stratification belies the avowed political commitments of these "thought-itioners." As the Bush and Clinton administrations of the 1990s and the second Bush administration continued Reagan's policy trajectories, American anthropology turned inward, increasingly analyzing the tropes of agency with language of self-referential alienation and with a resounding call for inaction. As Laura Nader observes, some postmodern anthropologists captured "a reason to reinvent armchair anthropology, and, intentionally or not, legitimated a retreat from responsibility" (Nader 1997a:134; see also Nader 1989). It is not that activism is the opposite of analysis, but rather that analysis without action, or even a focus on action, is as pointless as action without analysis.

McCarthyism's intersection with anthropology teaches us that historically there has been safety in the nonactivist stances promulgated by postmodern anthropologists. The safety of postmodernism's disarticulation of praxis through endless layers of reflections can be traced to the cardinal lesson of McCarthyism: that, in a world where activism brings trouble, the inaction of unending deconstructions is a safe haven even if decisive inaction is a betrayal of anthropology's promise. Hoover's FBI knew that activism mattered and that action and advocacy threatened institutionalized inequality. Contemporary anthropologists need to relearn this lesson and anthropology must ethically recommit itself to serve those it studies.

The Heart that Fed

Cold War anthropologists followed funding opportunities at least as often as they followed questions and concerns of their own design (although the best scholars found ways of subverting the former to the whims of the latter). There were few funding incentives for pursuing radical research venues, while near-Pavlovian rewards awaited those who could comfortably work and think in ways amenable to the interests of the national security state (Nader 1997a, 1997b; Price 1998a, 2003d). As noted by Jerome Rauch in his first and only anthropological article, most of this had to do with following the funding made available by the Cold War's flourishing area study centers, with little or no control over the slants or spins of research (Rauch 1955). In some instances this meant that the Office of Naval Intelligence funded Ruth Benedict's culture and personality studies focusing on the Soviet Union and its satellite nations instead of funding Gene Weltfish's work on patterns of global inequality (a prospect that would have conflicted with Kennan's "Policy Planning Study 23"). There also was a wealth of funds for anthropologists willing to work on classified research projects, and this is the subject of ongoing research indicating a troubling coalescence of the interests of the state and the academy (Nader 1997; Price 2000a, 2002d; Roseberry 1996).

That the FBI and other intelligence agencies used anthropological data for their own means should cause anthropologists to reevaluate many of their standard fieldwork practices (Price 2002a). As the files of Stefansson, Newman, Lewis, and others indicate, the FBI gathered information on the subjects of their anthropological inquiries. That anthropologists would be even unwitting participants in such activities raises serious ethical questions (Bigwood 2001; Price 2002d).

The actions and inactions of various professional and civil rights associations during McCarthyism's attacks on academic freedom raise important questions regarding the functions and duties of professional organizations during times of crises. The AAA, the AAUP, and the ACLU did little to battle threats to free inquiry (see Salisbury 1984; Schrecker 1998). It is unfortunate that professional and legal associations did so little to assist scholars under attack, but it is important to note that in instances where scholars were attacked and colleagues or organizations came to their defense, such actions at times did have if not positive then less disastrous outcomes. Ralph Beals's AAA presidency brought aggressive protections to scholars under attack, and his proactive stance helped solve Leonard Broom's problems with the Department of State. Further, the AAA's investigation of the firing of Kathleen Gough sent a clear message that such purges would no longer be met with silence. When Bernhard Stern and Gene Weltfish were attacked at Columbia, Stern's colleagues in sociology organized and protested his firing, while Weltfish's colleagues in anthropology quietly expressed regrets that they did not organize any opposition to her termination. Stern retained his position and Weltfish was fired.

It is important to stress that organized defenses during attacks on intellectual freedom mattered, and this has important implications for scholars living in times of present or future witch-hunts and purges—whatever the issues. Academic associations exist to promote the interests of a given field of study, and protecting freedom of inquiry is an important and proper undertaking for such associations. It is not only appropriate for professional associations, civil rights organizations, and groups of academic colleagues to help defend the academic rights of colleagues, but they must recognize that the use of such group advocacy is the best way to protect those under attack and to prevent future attacks, no matter how distasteful the views expressed by those at the heart of a controversy.

It is likely that the AAA would have been attacked had it aggressively come to the aid of Melville Jacobs, Richard Morgan, Bernhard Stern, Gene Weltfish, and other members, but such defensive actions could have changed the outcome of these cases or prevented the abuses that followed. The silence of the association empowered those attacking its members. The AAA framed its refusal to assist members attacked under McCarthyism by proclaiming that such actions would be political actions and hence inappropriate for a professional organization. This argument ignores the extent that the AAA was involved in politics. Far from being apolitical, the association was selectively political. During the 1940s and 1950s the AAA was increasingly involved in forging its ties to political bodies such as the War Department, Department of State, the Central Intelligence Agency, and various military-linked social science research agencies (Price 2003a). When members of the AAA claimed it was an apolitical organization, in reality, as David Aberle wrote during the Vietnam era, it was "those who . . . urge an apolitical course of action . . . [who] mean that we should be 'apolitical' *for* the U.S. Government, not *against* it" (1967:7). Professional associations exist for political reasons, and "the only question [is] what kind of political positions [it] should adopt" (7). Serving the political interests of state is every bit as political as opposing them, although opposing such interests brings punishments rather than the rewards brought by support.

McCarthyism's Past, Present, and Future

This book was written prior to the terrorist attacks of 2001, and as I edited the final manuscript I found myself in a world growing increasingly accepting of repressive and invasive actions by agencies such as the CIA, FBI, and NSA. Many Americans now appear to welcome a return to the oppressive FBI tactics of the past. Today, much as in the past, free thought, civil liberties, and academic freedom are curtailed under conditions of fear as America appears to be preparing for another lengthy, ill-defined war.

Anthropologists understand that beneath the nationalistic claims to the contrary, nation-states share common modes of social management. As cultural forms, the differences between the FBI, CIA, Homeland Security, Stasi, KGB, MI5, and Mossad are differences of degree, not of kind. Whatever past legislative controls limited American domestic surveillance and persecutions have suddenly been removed with little public debate. With the adoption of the Patriot Act, the FBI, CIA, and NSA were taken off their leashes. The restoration of old surveillance powers and the granting of new ones stands to bring new levels of oppression to those challenging American domestic or foreign policies. Much as the Smith Act and Hatch Act undermined the civil rights of individuals and groups vaguely defined as "subversive" or "communistic," today the Patriot Act undermines the rights of similarly ill-defined "suspect terrorists." It took the judiciary decades to dismantle the unconstitutional features of the Smith and Hatch Acts and it remains to be seen how the courts will rule on the similar features of the Patriot Act.[8] New fears of terror encourage Americans to forget a past they barely knew; and vague assurances that the rights of the "innocent" will be protected ignores well-documented past violations of privacy and civil liberties. Perhaps future historians will view the few years following the mid-1970s Church Committee hearings as a brief interglacial period in which America's federal domestic surveillance and harassment campaigns were momentarily curtailed.

Today, American academic freedom and the freedom of political dissent are threatened with an intensity not seen since the McCarthy period. The names of scholars expressing unpopular views are being collected by governmental and private agencies with the view that unchecked ideas are a dangerous thing. And once again anthropologists find themselves front and center of such warped and dangerous accounting systems (Price 2001a). But if the past can shed any useful light on our current predicament, we know that anthropologist activists are sorely needed. Anthropologists must join the voices speaking out against the war on terrorism's threats to the world's indigenous peoples, the threats to academic freedom, and threats posed by intelligence agencies to our life, liberty, and inalienable rights. The lessons of McCarthyism teach us that professional organizations such as the AAA must be pressured to assist individuals attacked by McCarthyistic opponents of academic freedom (Price 2001a; Bonifield 2002).

During the postwar period, Hoover's FBI and congressional committees subverted democracy by precluding the free discussion of ideas and demonizing those who challenged the dominant economic and social order of the day. Democracy depends on the public's access to information and on an atmosphere allowing the free discussion of issues. McCarthyism precluded the possibility of such inquiry, and in McCarthyism's attacks on anthropologists promoting equality these limitations on inquiry restricted the possibility of informed democratic reforms.

Just as McCarthyism subverted democratic processes, the purges of progressive intellectuals from governmental policy positions limited America's national braintrust. The informed and questioning views of scholars like Jack Harris, John Embree, or Cora Du Bois are now rarely heard in the back rooms of the U.S. State Department or the United Nations. Instead, a prevailing atmosphere of self-reinforcing bureaucratic groupthink pervades these important agencies—an atmosphere that still precludes hatching policy decisions without the now-tired militaristic assumptions and blinders of the Cold War. This constrained arena of free thought is part of the enduring legacy of McCarthyism. Today we find the State Department purged of analysts advocating the legitimacy of the Palestinian cause, and given President Bush's threat that those who are not with him are "with the terrorists," we should not be surprised to find an absence of State Department analysts examining the relationships between U.S. neocolonial policies and the rise of anti-American sentiments and terrorism. These contemporary constraints remain as publicly unexamined as the enduring legacies of McCarthyism.

Perhaps some future generation living in a foreign, as yet articulated, political economy will come to view the hearings of the 1940s and 1950s as having been just what they were advertised to be at the time: loyalty hearings. Although a different age may be afforded a view allowing those yet to be born to clearly see that these individuals were simply being asked (in unimaginably obscure ways) if they were *loyal* supporters of an economic system based on racial, gender, and ethnic inequality that redistributed in a biased and stratified fashion economic resources, justice, education, health, and longevity. That anthropologists could be counted among those protesting the innumerable injustices and indignities of our socioeconomic system is a credit to the potential of anthropology.

On Using the Freedom of Information Act

> One might nearly be tempted to define a revolution by the
> willingness of the regime to open the archives of its
> predecessor's political police. Measured by this yard-stick,
> few revolutions have taken place in modern history.
>
> —Otto Kirchheimer

Because this book relies heavily on documents
released under the Freedom of Information Act
(FOIA) it is important to provide an overview of
FOIA, to describe how I have used it, and to discuss the pitfalls of an uncritical reliance on FOIA
documents.

In 1966 FOIA was enacted to allow access to
records held by federal governmental agencies. In
the mid-1970s the FOIA was briefly strengthened
as part of wider post-Watergate governmental reforms during a time when Americans were inun-
dated with revelations of covert programs ranging
from domestic surveillance under the FBI's COIN-
TELPRO to the CIA's attempts to assassinate various foreign leaders. However, the post-Watergate
1970s provided only a brief window of opportunity for FOIA researchers to access documents before the Reagan administration ushered in a return
to greater opposition, on the part of governmen-

tal and agency heads, to the free dissemination of information. The Reagan presidency further weakened FOIA through a number of executive orders and congressional acts allowing the CIA's now routine practice of denying most FOIA requests on national security grounds, blessing their predilections to "err on the side of silence" (Corn 1994:370). Because the U.S. Congress and Senate do not exert much meaningful oversight of the CIA's abuse of FOIA exemptions, the CIA refuses to comply with most requests for documents under FOIA.

All federal agencies are bound by law to respond (in some way) to FOIA requests, but different agencies respond with varying degrees of promptness and each agency follows its own internal guidelines. Some agencies almost never release *anything*; for example, agencies such as the National Security Agency (NSA) often respond to even the simplest request with a flat-out denial. During the dozen years I spent researching this book I found a wide variation in agency responses to FOIA requests. Some agencies sent requested FOIA documents within weeks of my initial requests (e.g., USDOE), while others (e.g., FBI) took six or more years to send records or denials of records. In some cases, when I appealed such FBI denials, hundreds of pages of files directly relevant to my request were released. It is impossible to know if the FBI's frequent initial denials are simply part of the FBI's sloppy standard of professionalism, or if they are part of an intentional plan. The FBI's slipshod approach to fulfilling FOIA requests is a serious matter and merits the examination of a congressional oversight committee, but Congress shows decreasing interest in monitoring America's intelligence agencies. As the late FOIA scholar Sigmund Diamond once advised, "the intelligence agencies (especially the FBI and CIA) are not there to help you. They are there to make matters as difficult as possible for you. They do not want the Freedom of Information Act to be of assistance to you; they want to emasculate it, to negate it without having to repeal it or even to amend it seriously. They administer it to death." (Diamond to Price 5/18/94)

FOIA Request and Exemptions

Numerous factors led me to file specific FOIA requests. In some instances I requested an individual anthropologist's FBI file as a result of stories I heard while interviewing older anthropologists. In other instances I came across information while reading the letters and correspondence of anthropologists at various archives. The obituaries of anthropologists often contained valuable information on those affected by McCarthyism (see for example Gould 1971; Thompson 1978). In some instances I filed FOIA requests to learn more about an individual's wartime work and then unexpectedly found evidence of FBI investigations. I established a detailed logging system recording when and why I made specific requests, and I made my requests as wide as possible by asking for any and all information held by agencies.

Typically, all that is needed to file an FOIA request is a letter addressed to the FOIA officer at the government agency of interest, specifying exactly what records are sought (see Adler 1987, 1991; Price 1997b). If the request is for records pertaining to an individual, the requestor is required to provide proof of death of the individual in question. This step is required because the Privacy Act protects living individuals from the inquiries of others. The dead, however, do not have these same privacy rights. As Sigmund Diamond successfully argued in a federal suit against the FBI, "if this were not the case, the writing of history would cease" (Diamond to Price 11/95).

The Freedom of Information Act requires all federal agencies to release documents, but it also provides a multitude of disclosure exemptions. Military and intelligence agencies often claim exemptions for documents under the "methods of intelligence gathering" clauses, which exempt the disclosure of information that might reveal methods of intelligence collection.

In April 1995 President Clinton signed Executive Order 12958 instructing all federal agencies to release records created more than twenty-five years before the request. Prior to the 2001 terrorist attacks, many FOIA scholars believed order 12958 could have been a watershed for FOIA researchers relying on lengthy appeal processes to access unaltered records. But, in practice, many governmental agencies have been slow to implement the order. In response to order 12958 the CIA created a new division known as the CIA Declassification Factory. This division, according to Richard Warshaw, is directed to oversee "over 60 million pages of classified records subject to automatic declassification [under 12958] . . . [which is] a stack [of paper] as high as 50 Washington Monuments" (1996:3). However, this task is being undertaken without any useful index retrieval system and documents are being released without context or indexing, thus making the identification and retrieval of information a highly problematic undertaking.

Despite order 12958's clear dictate to release documents older than twenty-five years in age, the FBI continues to resist complying with even basic requests. For example, I have accessed hundreds of FBI files indicating that at one point the FBI created an index of names mentioned in the Communist Party's *Daily Worker* newspaper, but my 1998 request for documents relating to such an index resulted in the FBI's denial that such an index exists (similar requests for FBI files on the Alternative Press Index resulted in FBI claims that they had no such holdings [Kelso to Price 8/2/99]). It is unfortunate that the FBI resists efforts to publicly release their comprehensive indexes of the *Daily Worker* as well as other unindexed publications because they could be an invaluable resource for scholars studying the radical left.

FOIA Appeals

I filed over 500 FOIA requests and over 250 appeals in the course of researching this book. I aggressively filed numerous administrative appeals to obtain the release of records that were initially withheld. I made it a practice to appeal many of the FBI's routine denials that they held any records on a particular anthropologist or organization—and in many instances these appeals led to the release of FBI records. Needless to say, not knowing what is being withheld creates difficulties in creating appellate arguments, and at times some appeals are shots in the dark. Accordingly, my appeal strategies varied. In appealing the FBI's finding (after more than five years of waiting for them to complete my FOIA request) that they held no records on anthropologist Gene Weltfish, I successfully got members of an FOIA processing team to look once again for Weltfish's records, when I wrote:

> The basis of my appeal is that the FBI obviously made one of two mistakes: either they really missed the boat fifty years ago and didn't even consider putting a prominent American with suspected ties to the Communist Party who reportedly supported North Korea during the Korean Conflict on the Security Index, or they've made a mistake these last five years that this request has been pending and did not adequately search for records pertaining to Dr. Gene Weltfish.
>
> I do not believe that the FBI FOIA processors adequately searched the FBI's indexes for materials pertaining to Dr. Weltfish. Call it a crazy hunch, but I find it unbelievable that the FBI would not have maintained an investigatory file on a woman who was fired from Columbia University after she was reported in the New York Times and other newspapers of record to have stated that the Americans were using biological warfare agents during the Korean Conflict.
>
> Dr. Weltfish appeared before House Committee of Un-American Activities and Senate Subcommittee to Investigate the Administration of the Internal Security Act and Other Internal Security Laws, and was accused of being a communist by Senator Joe McCarthy and others. (Price to FBI 7/26/00)

With the assistance of Senator Patty Murray and Congressman Brian Baird I convinced the FBI to reexamine their files, after which 412 pages of FBI files on Professor Weltfish were released to me. In other instances, the FBI's denial of holding records was actually a denial that the individual had ever been the subject of an FBI inquiry, and thus my appeals revealed that some of these individuals were known to the FBI, although FBI investigations had never been launched.

When I thought it was important to discover the identity of an anthropologist whose name was redacted under Privacy Act exemptions, I successfully used a broad-sweeping appeal strategy in which I sent an index of all obituaries ever published in the *American Anthropologist* and the *Anthropology Newsletter* as part of my appeal, arguing that this index constituted proof that these individuals were dead and thus their records could be released to me. This tactic worked with some success, although as with most appeals the process took years of waiting before records were released. This was how I secured the release of George P. Murdock's identity as the author of the January 1949 informant letter to FBI Director Hoover, and it was how the FBI came to release the names of most of the dozen anthropologists named by Hoover as Communists. This approach was also used in the appeal for numerous redactions in materials released from Leslie White's FBI files, and led to the identification of John Cornell as the job applicant that first brought Leslie White to the FBI's attention. Unfortunately, the workings of FOIA processing are such that another pair of researchers requested information on White while Bill Peace and I were undertaking further appeals, and these researchers were sent the information that Peace and I had worked over seven years to have released. These scholars then back-mined our FOIA request and then rushed into print with the fruits of our requests and appeals while we were still carefully working through the appeals process (Peace and Price 2001). This sort of FOIA request back-mining of information is a hazard for researchers patiently working their way through the appeal process if other scholars do not follow the basic dictates of embargoed news stories followed by journalists.

Evaluating FOIA Results: A "D+" for Effort

FOIA requests do not automatically lead to the release of all requested documents. The FBI and CIA often release files with significant portions redacted by the felt pens of government censors. On an initial request it is not uncommon to be sent only a few hundred pages of a thousand-page file. It is also common to receive pages with large redacted portions. Agencies are required to inform requesters under what category (e.g., privacy, national security, etc.) each exemption falls, but this does little to inform the requester about what has been rendered illegible. Theoharis (1994) and Buitrago (1981) offer guides to the "margin codes" written in the margins of FBI documents.

The FBI's efforts to avoid full compliance with FOIA suggests that the organization resents requirements that it comply with FOIA, and FOIA censors frequently fail with impunity to comply with basic FOIA standards. The FBI has a standard practice of withholding requested records unless the FOIA requestor specifically asks for identifiable documents. Retired FBI agent M. Wesley Swearingen indicates it is a standard bureau practice to obstruct the release of information through this technique. He writes: "[If] a person does not name a document, the FBI will deny that it exists. Of course, anyone not having been in the FBI will not know the name of a particular document, and so the FBI will deny they have it" (1995:158). Two other techniques used by the FBI to obstruct FOIA requests are the practice of not searching the FBI's precomputerized card files for subjects, and not sending records held on individuals who were not the primary subjects of FBI investigations. These practices are clear violations of both the spirit and letter of the Freedom of Information Act, but the lack of congressional oversight allows these practices to continue.

It Ain't Necessarily So: Rightly Divining the Word of Truth

FBI files are frequently full of mistakes and misinformation, and it is generally impossible to evaluate the validity and reliability of the information. This is an important issue, and the "facts" in each FBI report cited and quoted in this book should be viewed with skepticism. These FBI documents are a record of the FBI and its violations of privacy and academic freedom. As such they help us study the FBI but they are not records to be trusted unto themselves (Nader 1972).

The FBI's practice of not releasing informants' names greatly hinders the ability to evaluate information in files. If informants' names were known it might be possible to attribute ulterior motivations for the statements and information given to FBI agents, but in most cases the identity of FBI sources is unknown. The FBI seldom critically evaluates the information they collected. More often than not, they simply gathered as much gossip as they could about an individual of interest and then typed up reports uncritically, repeating the tales as they were told.

Agents from the FBI are also known to invent fictional informants to suit their purposes, so the nonidentification of "confidential informants" presents a very real problem for scholars (see Swearingen 1995). As Sigmund Diamond observed, "the FBI very often referred to 'confidential informants T1 or T7, when there was no such person. This was done to make it seem as if there was lots of 'evidence' about the person" (Diamond to Price 2/28/99).

I have adopted a skeptical view of the FBI materials reported in this book.

When derogatory information from FBI reports was examined, the intent was to examine the FBI's relentless collection of rumors and innuendo for its own political ends, not to pass on derogatory information on individuals. The FBI is notorious for its use of unscrupulous and unreliable informants, especially its paid informants, so it is important that this information not be considered reliable without further, independent information. The information in FBI files is useful as a fossilized remnant of the FBI's mindset, not necessarily as proof of an event or accusation.

I have avoided passing on a variety of salacious reports given in the FBI files I examined because I see no value in reproducing such speculations and rumors unless there is reason to believe the FBI or others took actions on the basis of these reports. Many FBI agents seem to have delighted in collecting scandalous details on the subjects of their inquiry, including reports ranging from sexual indiscretions to offensive body odor, or in one case, several pages of reports detailing one anthropologist's excessive masturbatory habits while serving in World War II. I have avoided reporting such overly intrusive, unverified details unless they have a direct bearing on the nature or direction of the FBI's investigations. The FBI had no right to collect this private information, and we have no need to examine it unless it adds to our understanding of the FBI's manipulation of free discourse in American society.

The FBI conducted hundreds of reference and background interviews on anthropologists. The questions changed from time to time, but the thrust remained the same: has this individual indicated by public or private action, or by opinion or professional research, any resistance to the socioeconomic status quo (or, put another way, the status quo of racial and economic inequality that the FBI protects). In the private papers of anthropologists housed in various archives, there are scarce records of visits from FBI agents. In some instances I tracked down the correspondence or diaries of individual anthropologists contacted by the FBI as part of background checks to see if they left records of these contacts, but they rarely did.

NOTES

Preface

1 It must be noted that a number of Marxist, Communist, and Socialist anthropologists are not discussed in this text. Irving Goldman's FBI file was released too late to be included in this book. In some cases the FBI has not complied with Freedom of Information Act's (FOIA) requirement that requests be processed in a timely manner, and I am still waiting for the completion of several FOIA requests. For example, I initially requested files on Marxist anthropologist Alexander Lesser more than a decade ago in 1993, but I have yet to receive all files pertinent to this request (see Mintz 1985; Vincent 1988). I have written nine letters (this gets tedious when conducting over five hundred FOIA requests) inquiring into the status of this request. Likewise, the FBI has not released files on Eleanor Leacock, a committed activist who published a popular introduction to a reissued version of Engels's *The Origin of the Family, Private Property and the State* (1972) at the Communist Party's International Publishers. Leacock was reportedly denied wartime security clearance by the Office of War Information over concerns she was a Communist (Gailey 1989:216). While many anthropologists maintain Leacock was a Communist Party member, one former party member insisted that she never belonged to the party—a point that is supported by her divergence from party doctrine in her writings on Engles. In other cases the FBI claims to have no records regarding individuals of interest; for example, the FBI claims to hold no records on anthropologist Willard Z. Park despite the Senate Judiciary Committee assertion that Parks was a key Communist Party functionary (U.S. Senate 1953a:656).

A number of Marxist anthropologists died before the postwar period discussed in this book; no doubt anthropologists such as Alexander Goldenweiser or Roy Barton (Price 2001b) would have been hauled in before the tribunals of the later 1940s and 1950s had they been alive (see Ebihara 1985 for more on American anthropology in the 1930s).

Marxist anthropologists Gitel Poznansky (Steed), Edward Haskell, Richard Slobodin (Slobodin to Price 8/10/00) and Paul Robeson's wife, anthropologist Eslanda Robeson are likewise passed over in this text but should provide good research subjects for future scholars. Marxist anthropologist Robert Armstrong is also not discussed in this text, but future work by George Stocking should shed valuable light on this scholar who left the academy for the field after the FBI's harassment and investigation (Stocking 2000:231–32, 2002). Future work should be undertaken to document the impact on anthropologists Angel Palerm, Clifton Amsbury, John Murra, and Elman Service of their experiences in the Spanish Civil War.

2 The actions of radical anthropologists during the 1960s through 1980s is a ripe topic for research, and one that is still waiting to be explored by those anthropologists who lived through this time. I had to end my narrative somewhere, however, and I had already written too much: over 350 pages of manuscript had to be removed before publication.

3 See the case of Judi Bari v. FBI, "Environmentalists Win Bombing Lawsuit," *New York Times*, June 12, 2002, 18(A).

4 This is still a controversial research topic, and one that has difficulty finding venues for publication. It is possible that the subject matter itself led to the rejection of proposals for research grants by the APS, NSF, Wenner-Gren, SSRC, and the Truman Library.

CHAPTER 1 *A Running Start at the Cold War*

1 As discussed in Price 2003a, the files presently released by the FBI under FOIA indicate the FBI monitored what they (correctly) suspected were CIA efforts to collect data on AAA members. For information on the FBI's more broad-ranging monitoring of the American Psychological Association, see Harris 1980.

2 See the appendix for a discussion of the Freedom of Information Act (FOIA), and the release of documents used in this book. For citation format information, see "A Note on Reference Abbreviations."

3 In the 1931 Scottsboro case, nine young black men were sentenced to death after being found guilty of rape at a sham trial. The Communist Party was an instrumental factor in bringing national publicity to the case and in saving the lives of the accused.

4 The 1939 Index Program extended the FBI's powers to monitor and prepare for the detention of individuals or organizations suspected of engaging in espionage or illegal activities related to the European or Pacific war (see Theoharis 1999:20).

5 Between 1936 and 1952 the FBI's budget increased by over 1,800 percent (Theoharis 2002:11).

6 Just a month into his presidency, Harry Truman worried about Hoover's power, writing, "we want no Gestapo or Secret Police. [The] FBI is tending in that direction. They are dabbling in sex life scandals and plain blackmail when they should be catching criminals" (Ferrell 1980:22). As Hoover's former assistant director of Domestic Intelligence, William C. Sullivan recalled that Hoover used his files not merely to blackmail politicians but to destroy them. According to Sullivan, Hoover "was saving everything he had on [President] Kennedy, and on Martin Luther King, Jr. too, until he could unload it all and destroy them both. He kept

this kind of explosive material in his personal files, which filled four rooms on the fifth floor of headquarters" (1979:50).

7 It is revealing of the AAUP's lack of commitment to academic freedom that it did not censor the University of California Board of Regents until 1956, when legal decisions clarified the impropriety of their loyalty oath (see Schrecker 1986:123). The AAUP similarly stalled for six years before issuing its report on the University of Washington's tenure committee's investigations of Communist professors (Schrecker 1986:322).

8 In 1911 Bingham made world news when he led a group of explorers to rediscover Machu Picchu, the lost city of the Peruvian Inca Empire. See WF062-93755 for Bingham's FBI file and limited correspondence with Hoover.

9 Although arguably it was social psychologists Kenneth B. Clark and Mamie Phipps (Clark's wife) who made perhaps the most significant contribution to mid-century racial public policy when their research on the harmful effects of racism on the self-image of schoolchildren became the basis of the linchpin footnote 11 of Chief Justice Earl Warren's unanimous decision in *Brown v. Board of Education* (J. Patterson 2001).

10 The FBI records released on Steward are incomplete but do not appear to provide any evidence of an FBI investigation of him. The released portions of Steward's FBI file pertain to background investigations of other individuals, but one document inexplicably refers to an unreleased FBI report "dated 9-14-42 at Washington, D.C. captioned, 'Julian H. Steward, Espionage'" (WF040-21495-111).

CHAPTER 2 *A Message Sent*

1 As discussed in chapter 13, these efforts were rewarded by FBI surveillance and job loss during the McCarthy period.

2 Arguably, these special elite sections of the party went against the basic tenets of the Communist Party by segregating the intelligentsia from the proletariat rank and file.

3 The FBI's files on Lauer do not indicate any secret contact between him and the FBI regarding these hearings (WF09-6343).

4 The six faculty appearing before the tenure committee were Joseph Butterworth, Harold Eby, Garland Ethel, Ralph Gundlach, Melville Jacobs, and Herbert Phillips.

5 Jacob's FBI file contains a highly redacted wiretap report summary from the week of his appearance before the tenure committee meeting. This document states: "▬▬▬▬ & JACOBS are bowing and scraping and boot-licking-vowing to devote their lifes [*sic*] exclusively to research" (WF0100-4082-85).

CHAPTER 3 *Syncopated Incompetence*

1 Interestingly enough, the FBI investigated A. I. Hallowell as a suspected Communist after his name appeared in 1938 on the letterhead of the Citizens Anti-Nazi

Committee of the American League for Peace and Democracy. A June 21, 1950, FBI memo reported that "it was reliably reported in 1945 that Professor A. Irving Hallowell, 401 South 21st Street, was a present or past member of the Communist Party (FBI 100-3-7-865 cited in WF062-60527-16878).

2 The Ohio State Archaeological and Historical Society received letters from over sixty anthropologists protesting Morgan's dismissal—though most of these were generated due to the efforts of Morgan not the AAA (WJP: RM/JG 4/20/48).

3 Shapiro explained, "Stout took it upon himself to prepare this resolution to wire Morgan without consulting me at all. He has been guilty of a number of such performances and this was the last straw, so I wrote him a rather angry letter protesting such irregularities" (RAAA: Box 3, HS/AH 5/12/48; cf. AAANB 2[3]:37).

4 Morgan later recounted the events of the Board's July 23 meeting in a letter to James Griffin: "It was agreed between Bennett and myself on July 22 that if I were called to the 'hearing' on the following day that I should not stay in the meeting if Bennett were not allowed to be present as the official observer of the American Anthropological Association. I followed this agreement faithfully, for we had agreed that if I were to stay without the observer it would mean that the AAA would lose its means of entry into the case and that its position would be greatly weakened. Hence, I told the Board members that I would be glad to discuss the case if the AAA representative were called in. You should also remember that Dr. Shapiro had officially requested of Mr. Arthur C. Johnson that an observer be allowed to attend the meeting. Since no observer was present and since I was not allowed to speak, the AAA does not know what went on in the meeting and does not have the evidence it was seeking in the case. Under such circumstances you must understand why I took the action I did. I could do nothing else. Believe me, the pressure placed on me to stay was very great" (Morgan to Griffin 9/7/48).

5 This correspondence by James Griffin was provided by William J. Peace, who was granted access to Leslie A. White and James Griffin's voluminous correspondence, housed at the University of Michigan, as part of his research on White.

6 Of course, during World War II the association did find the authority to organize itself to support the country's war effort, and it likewise had no qualms about committing itself to secret agreements with the CIA during the historical period of McCarthyism's attacks on Morgan and others in the association (Price 2000a, 2003a).

CHAPTER 4 *Hoover's Informer*

1 This January 1, 1949, letter from Murdock to Hoover was first described in a paper at the annual meeting of the AAA in Chicago in November 1999 (Price 1999).

2 The likelihood of my inference here is supported by Irving Goldman himself, whom I interviewed by phone on 10/21/99. Goldman's FBI files were released after the completion of this book, but they document his firing by the State Department in July 1947 (along with anthropologist Alexander Lesser) under the McCarran Rider for past membership in the Communist Party. Goldman later avoided

possible contempt charges for refusing to name other past party members when appearing before the Senate Judiciary Committee. After newspaper accounts of his refusal to cooperate reached the Sarah Lawrence College campus (where he taught), campus administrators supported Goldman's decision as being an individual moral choice. Goldman was allowed to maintain his job and his honor (WF0077-23351; NY100-91710). Goldman remained at Sarah Lawrence for the rest of his career.

3 Alexander Lesser was fired by the State Department on June 23, 1947, under provisions of the McCarran Rider designed to remove radicals from public service. Lesser was one of seven State Department employees first fired then allowed to "resign" under suspicions of disloyalty, but the reliance on secretive hearings and evidence prevent us from knowing the exact nature of these charges (see *Washington Post* 11/18/47). Released FBI records on Lesser indicate that known Communist informers identified him as a member of the Communist Party (WFO100-345118-5).

4 This paragraph was redacted in the released version from Jacobs's FBI file and is added here from Morgan's FBI file.

5 The FBI has yet to comply with my FOIA request in 1994 for records on Morris Siegel (Price to O'Brien 1/20/94).

6 This is likely to be Morris Swadesh because his FBI file (NY100-80694 5/10/49) indicates that Murdock identified him as a Communist in this letter, and his name would fit here in the alphabetical organization of the letter.

7 This is likely to be Gene Weltfish. The following paragraph was not released in the in-house FOIA appeal leading to the release of other withheld names, but rather was released in Gene Weltfish's FBI file and clearly comes from this Murdock letter of January 1, 1949: "On January 1, 1949 Confidential Informant [George Murdock] of unknown reliability, advised that Dr. Gene Weltfish was one of the Communist members of the American Anthropological Association. According to the informant, Gene Weltfish was brought into the Communist Party rather unwillingly at first by her former husband, Alexander Lesser, but since has become an active worker. According to the informant Dr. Weltfish had been active at the Annual Convention of the American Anthropological Association in Toronto in December, 1948, at which convention, according to the informant, the Communist members of the association attempted to propagandize. The informant further advised that Dr. Gene Weltfish had been previously responsible for temporarily involving the association in ties with 'front organizations.' The informant added that he mentioned the name of the subject with full assurance that he was correct about his statement, and that he had positive evidence of the above fact" (WFO100-287225-23).

8 In the aftermath of the 1971 AAA business meeting, Ester Goldfrank wrote a letter to Margaret Mead detailing how John Moore and others in the "radical caucus" (ARPA) had used similar tactics against Mead and her conservative position. Goldfrank wrote that "the Radical Caucus in the evening, you will remember, had an attendance of about 700 and the applause for the speakers was certainly not exu-

berant. I had enough by 8:30 and left. I wasn't surprised to learn that the meeting ended at 1:20 A.M. The vote was 248 to 14 against your report [investigating the Thailand Affair (see Wakin 1992)]. So almost 500 persons who had been at the earlier meeting that evening had melted away. There is a good old Communist tactic—you wear down your opponent with endless and not too relevant discussion and amendment, and when you are sure you can win, you call for a vote. In the afternoon Pete Murdock said if he were ten years younger he would start a new *scientific* association" (E. G.: EG/MM 1/3/72). In her reply, Mead thanked Goldfrank for this information and noted that "after all, there has been boring from within before, as you and I well know," which perhaps is a reference to the events at the 1948 AAA meeting in Toronto (E.G.: MM/EG 1/25/72).

9 In 1935 Communist Party functionary Joseph Peters described the structure and function of fractions in the following passage of his classic party text, *The Communist Party: A Manual on Organization*: "The fraction is an instrument in the hands of the Party through which the Policy of the Party is brought to the organized masses, and through which the Party gives leadership to members of the mass organization . . . in all conventions and conferences of such organizations where there are at least three Communists, a Communist Fraction must be organized . . . In all questions in which there is a decision of the corresponding Party organization, the Fractions must carry out these decisions. The policy for a mass organization is made in the Party Committee, but before the decisions are made on any basic question concerning the mass organization, the Party Committee invites the representatives of the given Fraction to participate in the discussion. The Fraction at this meeting has a consultative role. After the discussion, the decision is made by the Party committee. The Party Committee can decide that the Fraction members express their *opinion* on the problem through consultative voting. The *decision*, however, is made by the majority vote of the members of the *Party Committee*" (Peters 1935:99–100; emphasis in original). It is possible that some anthropologists at this meeting orchestrated these events using some of the tactics described by Murdock, although the extent to which this may have occurred is unknown.

10 This reference is apparently to Roman Jakobson, who held strongly anti-Soviet views. Jakobson's FBI file indicates he was cooperating with FBI's investigations, which produced a file on him of over 550 pages (WF0100-345400).

11 A security report dated 2/28/49 in Oscar Lewis's FBI file notes that Murdock was "being carried as an [FBI] informant at this time in view of the fact that he has apparently been quite active in the American Anthropological Association, [and has] furnished information regarding a number of individuals" (WF0101-6392-22:14 2/28/49). This suggests the possibility that Murdock maintained continued contact with the FBI during this period, although this is not known. Released portions of Murdock's FBI file indicate that the FBI did interview him the following July "in connection with an official investigation" of a suspected Communist. Murdock "stated that one of the reasons he believed this individual to be a Communist was because he was closely associated with an individual who Murdock was reliably

informed, was a member of the Communist Party. Professor Murdock, however, declined to reveal the name of this alleged Communist associate as he said it would be a breach of ethics to do so" (WFO100-190297-81).

CHAPTER 5 *Lessons Learned*

1 Leslie White's FBI records state that the FBI investigated the contributors to this volume of materialist essays because they represented a "grave problem for the Bureau" in their effect on "our operations and our efforts to safeguard the security of this Nation." The FBI noted that all the contributors' views were "widening and deepening the world trend toward materialism, socialism and communism." The FBI further observed that the authors "are day in and day out influencing the minds of countless youths. Their influence goes beyond the classroom. They are also writers issuing books and articles designed to influence educated and articulate adults in positions of importance. There can be little doubt that these materialists are subtly preparing the minds of at least a percentage of those reached by them for the acceptance of communism. Further, they probably are preparing a greater percentage of educated minds to be sympathetic or soft on communism . . . It is not unlikely that the majority of the educated enemies of the Bureau who are regularly attacking us or opposing in one form or another are philosophic materialists. And, they are not decreasing in numbers. *Philosophy for the Future* is our problem of the future" (WFO100-426562-1:2 7/8/57).

2 However, he was removed from the FBI's Security Index file on the recommendation of J. Edgar Hoover on March 15, 1949 (WFO100-4082-87).

3 "Lanted" refers to the process of coating a substance with lant (stale urine) in order to keep animals at a distance. As described by Sidney Addy, "[Lant] was preserved in a tank, and having been mixed with lime, used for dressing wheat before it was sown to prevent birds from picking up the seeds" (1888:27).

4 The AAA *News Bulletin* was sent a copy of this letter, which they did not reprint, though a brief mention of his travails was made in vol. 3, no. 4, of the bulletin.

5 There is no record of Aginsky having any contact with the FBI regarding Swadesh. However, in 1950 the FBI investigated Aginsky and a group of CCNY students who raised suspicions when they conducted survey research in Block Island, Rhode Island. The FBI's investigation determined that regardless of their "suspicious" activities they were only investigating the causes of past agricultural declines (WFO 62-92613-8).

6 In January 1950, G. S. Reed, director general of the Australian Security Intelligence Organization, mailed Hoover a copy of one of Swadesh's November 10, 1949, mass mailings to anthropologists wherein he outlines his travails (WFO100-344641-10). Reed apparently intercepted this document through an Australian mail surveillance operation.

7 Other *Daily Worker* articles discussing Swadesh's firing include: 5/19/50, p. 5; 6/4/50, p. 2 (*Sunday Worker*); 6/14/50, p. 4; 6/16/50, p. 4.

8 For example, in 1957 the FBI conducted an interview with a faculty member at

Mexico City College who had previously reported an interest in hiring Swadesh (e.g., WF0100-344641-53 12/30/57).

9 Two years earlier anthropologist Felix Keesing had found himself in a somewhat similar position regarding syndicated muckraking columnist Drew Pearson. Pearson's article suggested that Keesing's receipt of a federal administrative appointment in the South Pacific was because he was a friend of controversial attorney Milton Shalleck. After receiving strong criticism from AAA President Shapiro, Pearson apologized to Shapiro and corrected his comments in his column (RAAA: Series 2, Box 1 5/1948).

10 While no records establish direct contact between the FBI and administrators at CCNY, the timing of his sudden notification of nonrenewal of contract within days of his name being added to the FBI's Security Index suggests the likely possibility that someone from the FBI was secretly in contact with someone in CCNY's administration.

CHAPTER 6 *Public Show Trials*

1 According to the FBI's Manual of Rules and Regulations (part 2, section 5, p. 7), a blind memorandum is a memo shielding the FBI's identity. Here it is the illegal source of information given to the McCarran committee (WF0100-287225-42).

2 Weltfish's problems at Columbia may have been somewhat compounded by the absence of department chair Duncan Strong during the 1952–1953 winter semester. Charles Wagley served as the interim chair during his absence and would not have had the same level of administrative contacts as did Strong (AAANB 1952 6[3]:12). The FBI files for Strong (WF065-59840-14; WF0105-109031-3; WF0100-154696-16) and Wagley (WF0105-HQ-109031; WF0138-HQ-3015) show no evidence of any contact with the FBI regarding Weltfish.

3 The American Legion maintained long-standing relationships with Hoover's FBI, under which the legion's rank-and-file scoured the editorial pages of newspapers across the country to locate letters to the editor that they believed identified subversives and crypto-Communists. The letters were clipped by legion members then mailed to the FBI along with reports of their suspicions (see Theoharis 1984).

4 Ruth Benedict's FBI file (WF077-28923) lists her as affiliated with so many civil rights organizations appearing on the Attorney General's list of subversives that her appearance before such committees would have been guaranteed had she lived into the mid-1950s.

5 The arts were not a neutral ground, however, as demonstrated by the CIA's attempts during the Cold War to manipulate the public's appreciation of abstract impressionism as an anti-Soviet tactic (Saunders 1999:252–78).

6 Although she clearly stated her alignment with Stanley Diamond and Marvin Harris regarding an absolutist position in these matters.

CHAPTER 7 *Atrophy Among Those Who Fear*

1 The FBI monitored the journal *Science and Society* for years, compiling over 378 (released) pages of files on the journal (BA100-20644; WF0100-44562).

2 The FBI's Publication Services Division that produced these book reports was established in 1920 so that the FBI could "monitor the written word and discover writers who should be deemed suspicious" (Robins 1992:50).

3 A copy of this pamphlet was located for me at the Niebyl-Proctor Library, thanks to the diligent efforts of Bob Patenaude.

4 It is remarkable how similar Stern's tone and analysis are to the writings and lectures of Leslie White, although a long history of antagonism persisted between these two Marxist scholars (see Peace 1998).

5 As Schrecker notes, some elements within the Catholic worker movement did in fact work with labor groups as a means of subverting the Communist Party's influence on unions and other organizations concerned with social justice (1998:73–75).

CHAPTER 8 *Persecuting Equality*

1 Senator McCarran distrusted the United Nations, believing that "the worst decision he ever made was to have voted in the Senate for the UN Charter" (Melvern 1995:50). McCarran waged a reckless campaign pursuing supposed Communist Americans working at the UN, a campaign with numerous casualties. Chief among the casualties was UN general council member Abe Feller, who committed suicide by jumping out the window of his twelfth-floor Manhattan apartment (Melvern 1995:63, 67).

2 Moses Finkelstein, who later anglicized his name to M. I. Finley, once worked as a research assistant for Boas at Columbia. After being identified as a Communist by Karl Wittfogel, Finley was called to appear before McCarren's subcommittee in 1952. His use of the Fifth Amendment created serious problems at Rutgers, where he was a celebrated history professor. Due to problems associated with McCarthyism, Finley left the United States for Great Britain in 1954, where he taught first at Oxford and then at Cambridge. Finley settled at Cambridge and became a British citizen; later he was knighted by Queen Elizabeth for his groundbreaking historical work at Cambridge—work that shows a breadth of analysis and approach betraying an anthropological influence (see Goldfrank 1977:116; Schrecker 1986:171–79, 292–93; Reinhold 1994. Finely's FBI file is WF0100-116407).

3 The FBI claims to hold no records on Park.

4 In an apparent reference to Harris, Mort Fried wrote in *The Study of Anthropology* that "one brilliant student of the American Indian became a victim of McCarthyism and started a taxicab company in a Middle American country. It is said that he became a millionaire, but his success seems to have had nothing to do with his anthropology" (1972:210). Harris discounted the specific veracity of this report, telling Marc Edelman that he'd written a reply to Fried that stated "it's true

that I'm a millionaire, but I'm a *colon* millionaire and not a dollar millionaire, and there's quite a difference" (1997:13).

CHAPTER 9 *The FBI's Means and Methods*

1 This was likely Raymond Kennedy. Kennedy was murdered under false accusations that he was a CIA operative in Indonesia (Winks 1987:50–51; see also Kennedy's State Department file, FOIA no. 199802178; CIA files 23951-962, 236064-965, 242744-754, 242761-767).

2 The identities of the individuals discussed in this report are not known, but only four people received their doctorates in anthropology from Yale in 1937. They were Edwin Grant Burrows, William N. Fenton, Alfred E. Hudson, and Weston LaBarre. Hudson's left-leaning tendencies were well known, and he conducted fieldwork among the Kazak in the 1930s.

3 The FBI inadvertently released documents identifying anthropologist John Murra owing to FOIA processing errors. This type of accidental release of FOIA information referencing living individuals is a somewhat regular occurrence in FOIA research (see Diamond 1992:141–42; Robins 1992).

4 As a Romanian youth, Murra's radical politics led to a number of jail terms. He once "spent a month in a provincial jail, the only 'red' among twenty-five or so Iron Guardists who had just assassinated the prime minister," but reportedly his skills as a soccer player allowed him to avoid some of the beatings by his cellmates (Rowe 1984:636). In 1934, his uncle made arrangements for him to attend the University of Chicago, where he "drifted to the social sciences" (Murra quoted in Rowe 1984:636) and studied anthropology under Fay-Cooper Cole, Edward Sapir, A. R. Radcliffe-Brown, and Charles Fairbanks. At the age of nineteen, Murra graduated with a B.A. in anthropology and left for Spain in early 1937, joining the Lincoln Brigade fighting Franco's fascist army. Murra experienced fighting, and later was interned in a French concentration camp outside Perpignan in Spain (Murra to Price 5/15/98; Rowe 1984:637). It was during his membership in the Lincoln Brigade that Murra learned Spanish, which opened the door for a career of work studying Andean prehistory and culture. Back in Chicago, Murra fused anthropology with activism and he "was active in anti-Hitler parades and sit-downs throughout 1935–1936. I came with those ideas from Rumania. Upon returning to the U of C my ideas were pretty much as they are today. It takes two years of living in a Stalinist army to discover there was more to all that than I thought" (Murra to Price 5/15/98). At the war's end Murra was funded by the Social Science Research Council to conduct Andean ethnographic research, but, as he describes, "[as I was getting] ready to leave, I discovered that the United States government would not let me travel, nor would the Justice Department tolerate my naturalization. The Spanish war and earlier associations flagged my file. My petition was repeatedly rejected; even when the federal Circuit Court ordered my naturalization in 1950, the State Department withheld my passport until 1956. So my return to the Andes was delayed and some good fieldwork years were lost"

(quoted in Rowe 1984:639). During this period Murra went to Puerto Rico, but he returned to the Andes once his passport was restored, and he became one of the most important American Andeanists of the second half of the twentieth century.

Murra's Cold War experiences affected his research orientation. In writing about his reevaluation in the early-1950s of his position a decade earlier that the Inca system had been feudal, he wrote that this change in perspective resulted first from the fact that his "participation in the Spanish war had distanced [him] from Stalinist orthodoxy; [and second, and] more important, [he had] discovered the great monographs of British social anthropologists" (Rowe 1984:641; Mintz 1993).

5 The FBI uses the phrase "technical surveillance" to characterize a wide variety of espionage activities—including the use of wiretaps, bugs, and other surreptitious recording devices.

6 Although the name of Newman's supervisor is not released by the FBI, T. Dale Stewart was Newman's supervisor during this period, and on page four of the released document the word "St wart" appears in washed-out ink (WFO121-34169-6:4).

7 In 1968 the Alice Ferguson Foundation donated large riverfront land holdings to the National Park Service, and Accokeek became an environmental educational center with federal and state funding (see www.fergusonfoundation.org).

8 Newspaper summaries collected by the ONI indicate that the Loup City Riot began after "a group of Loup City (Nebraska) residents told a group of alleged 'outside agitators' to leave town" (WFO121-34169-38). Among this group of agitators was the renowned seventy-two-year-old radical Socialist labor organizer Ella Bloor Ombolt, aka Mother Bloor (see Raymond 1952).

9 This project employed Harold Hickerson, who was already being monitored by the FBI (see BAAA 1956 4[4]:16). Hickerson's work on this project may have brought the FBI's attention to Voegelin.

10 In an interesting parallel, the FBI's description of Hockett is reminiscent of Neal Stephenson's fictional brilliant but socially inept cryptographer, Lawrence Waterhouse, in his book *Cryptonomicon*.

11 According to retired U.S. Air Force intelligence officer Raymond S. Sleeper the Russian Research Center was funded with seed money from the CIA (O'Connell 1990:186).

12 Although I made FOIA requests and appeals for FBI records pertaining to Robert Lowie at both Washington and San Francisco FBI offices, the FBI maintains they have no records on Robert Lowie, including any records reflecting Lowie's association with the California Labor School.

13 That Shimkin informed on Lewis to this Pentagon official and to the FBI is seen in a redacted portion of this report that refers to FBI files WFO100-7573 and WFO101-6392—file numbers both referring to anthropologist Oscar Lewis.

14 Within Wagley's foreign counter-intelligence file there is a highly censored "secret" document examining Wagley's association with radical and subversive individuals, which also makes mention of anthropologist Richard Slobodin (WFO105-109031-

2). This file indicates that the FBI investigated Slobodin after he published a letter in the *Daily People's World* (5/5/48) castigating the paper for obfuscating useful information through its heavy reliance on hyperbolistic jargon. The FBI read and cataloged the frequent mentions of anthropologist activists in the American Communist, Socialist, and progressive press.

15 One of Field's neighbors reported her suspicions of him to the FBI after observing at numerous social events hosted by the Fields that, "seventy-five percent or more people [were] of Russian descent . . . [and that Henry Field] carried on a conversation with his guests in a foreign language she presumed to be Russian" (WFO65-47510-6).

CHAPTER 10 *Known Shades of Red*

1 Ruth Benedict's FBI file (WFO77-28923) reflects FBI concerns that her activism for gender, poverty, and racial issues indicated Communist or Socialist leanings (Krook 1993). The FBI conducted background investigations of Benedict as part of her wartime security clearance, and they documented her involvement in a number of progressive causes. They also collected information pertaining to her involvement in department politics at Columbia (see Krook 1993:105–6), and they interviewed numerous friends and riffled through her garbage. Further, according to Susan Krook (1993:108), the FBI tapped her phone, although I found no record of this in the FBI records released to me. In the end, the FBI found no concrete information connecting Benedict to any Communist or Socialist group or party.

2 Archie Phinney was a Nez Percé Indian who studied anthropology with Boas at Columbia in the 1920s and 30s. He lived in the Soviet Union from 1933 to 1938, then worked for the Bureau of Indian Affairs until his death in 1949. His interest in Communism, his years spent in the Soviet Union, his attempts to bring more communal structures to U.S. Indian reservations would have provided Senator McCarthy with plenty of material for a show trial (see Price 2003b; Willard 2000; WFO100-350068).

3 As described elsewhere (Price and Peace 2003d), Morris Opler accused Leslie White (through his student Betty Meggers) of engaging in Stalinistic anthropological analysis (see Meggers 1960, 1961; Opler 1961, 1962). Although Morris Opler's McCarthyistic attack occurred after Senator McCarthy's fall from power, this episode of red-baiting was a dangerous attack on Meggers and others who embraced materialist research strategies. As Marvin Harris observed in *The Rise of Anthropological Theory*, "Opler's incredulity is misplaced; what is hard to believe is that Opler does not know from firsthand experience the real reason for the avoidance of Marxist references by anthropologists who have discovered, or rediscovered, Marx's contribution to the strategy of cultural materialism. It is incredible, since Opler himself, with his political innuendo, reveals himself fully prepared to expose and jeopardize his colleague before the political passions of the times" (1968a:639).

4 This explanation is counter to Du Bois's comment in Radin's festschrift that "Radin is essentially an urban man and could never resign himself long to a limited and bucolic environment" (1960:xv).

5 In 1947 Abraham Brothman was questioned before a federal grand jury about his associations with Harry Gold and Jacob Golos, as well as other members of the Soviet espionage underground operating in America with links to Klaus Fuchs (see Weinstein and Vassiliev 1999:318–19). In 1950 Brothman was found guilty of espionage charges and sentenced to two years in prison (see West 1990:57).

6 The reasons for the FBI's lack of investigation of White are unknown. Sigmund Diamond speculates that the most likely explanation for the lack of investigation was that White had worked as an FBI informer, but Bill Peace and I have found no evidence of this (Diamond to Price 2/28/99).

7 When Service and his wife conducted fieldwork in Paraguay in 1949 and 1950 the FBI increased its interest in Service's associations with radical individuals and organizations because Service had notified the embassy in Asuncion that he had fought in the Spanish Civil War against the fascists (WFO100-212233-16).

CHAPTER 11 *Red Diaper Babies*

1 Anthropologists identified as radicals at times also endangered the career advancements of parents, siblings, children, and spouses working for the federal government.

2 The *National Legislative Letter* was published twice a month by Bernard Conal, 305 Broadway, New York, New York. The edition referred to here is vol. 1, no. 7.

3 Johnson was the only anthropologist then at the University of North Carolina who had worked on this Carnegie-funded project (see CIRA 1950).

4 George Harold Hickerson was known as "Harold," like his son. In order to reduce confusion, however, in this text I refer to him as "George."

5 This gentle consideration during an FBI investigation stands out in marked contrast to the usual intrusive, suspicion-generating investigations carried out by field agents. One is left to wonder what became of the career of this agent and his or her rare sensibilities.

6 The meaning of the final entries in Harold Hickerson's FBI file are unclear. The entries date from 1981 when some unidentified governmental agency undertook inquiries regarding Hickerson, a second individual in San Francisco and the Legal Attache in Ottawa, Canada. These documents are heavily censored, but they appear possibly to relate to the CIA (or some other bureau concerned with national security issues) that for reasons unknown suddenly became interested in Hickerson.

CHAPTER 12 *The FBI, Oscar Lewis, and Margaret Mead*

1 This *New York Times* advertisement was a message from CPUSA's general secretary, Earl Browder, asserting that Congressman Martin Dies's effort to persecute

American Communists was playing into Hitler's hand and weakening America's war effort. Browder argued that "American democracy needs more confidence in itself in order to win the war. It needs to snap out of the hypnosis induced by Hitler and Martin Dies, in which the cry of 'Communists' raises hysterical fear and sets the democrats to examining one another for hidden 'Reds' and protesting each his own innocence of the 'terrible' charge of which few know the meaning. American democracy must grow up, and stop believing in ghosts and witches" (2/24/43, p. C15).

2 The letter's author is possibly referring to the controversies surrounding Soviet biologist Trofim Lysenko.

3 A total of eleven addresses of specific interest to the FBI were recorded. Of these only four have been released under FOIA: the Progressive Party (Champaign, Illinois), the National Office of Youth Argosy (Northfield, Massachusetts), the N.H.J.C. (full name not known) (Denver, Colorado) and the Delmar Bank (University City, Missouri) (S1100-7573-3 5/4/50).

4 In the last three decades dozens of scholars have mounted significant critiques of Lewis's culture of poverty concept. These scholars generally agree that Lewis inconsistently used the term—at times describing the overall effect of individuals living in poverty while at other times referring to contributing causes of poverty. Even the sympathies of Susan Rigdon led to the observation that Lewis's use of the culture of poverty concept was contradictory and confusing, and that he sometimes contradicted his own usage of the phrase "not infrequently within a single article or letter" (1988:xi). A broad criticism of Lewis's conceptualization of the culture of poverty emerged in the 1960s and 1970s (see Butterworth 1972:752; Harvey and Reed 1996; Leacock 1971; Parker and Kleiner 1970).

5 The FBI investigated the *Children of Sanchez* after J. Edgar Hoover received a letter on March 6, 1965, from an unknown individual reporting on the controversy. Hoover's reply to this unnamed individual stated, "you may be assured that Oscar Lewis is not a Special Agent of the FBI" (WFO101-6392-60 3/17/65).

6 Other anthropologists were vocal in their criticism of U.S.-Cuban policy. John Whiting's FBI file was opened after he signed an open letter protesting U.S. policy in Cuba (NYT 5/10/61:48c; BS105-6796), and Kathleen Gough's protests on Cuba caught the FBI's attentions (see chapter 15).

7 It appears that his claims that an article for *Harper's* would be forthcoming was part of Lewis's efforts to get a difficult-to-obtain Cuban visa. Lewis tried to use a reporter's visa to gain access to Cuba several times, although he did not publish articles in *Harper's* concerning his 1946 or 1969–1970 Cuban travels.

8 For example, see Mead's "Suggested Materials for Training of Regional Specialists Army Program" (MM M25).

9 In 1969 Mead suggested to Henry Kissinger that one means of making better use of the (claimed) reduced troop numbers in Vietnam would be to replace military personnel working for civilian construction companies in Vietnam with local laborers. She wrote that it was her understanding that "if we were to return many more activities, such as construction and certain kinds of services, to contractors,

this would reduce the visibility of America, improve morale among Asians and release a very large number of troops who could then be brought home" (see MM: MM/HK 5/23/69). Kissinger replied that he found Mead's suggestion to be interesting and that he had passed it on for consideration by officials at the Department of Defense (MM: HK to MM 7/12/69). Although these actions have been excluded from the public views of Mead as a nurturer, her conservative military stance in 1971 led her to suppress the release of a report criticizing American anthropologists accused of working for U.S. intelligence agencies in Southeast Asia (Wakin 1992).

10 Joan Gordan's (1976) comprehensive bibliography of Mead's work also indicates no writings by Mead on this topic.

11 The CIA has resisted my efforts under FOIA to access Margaret Mead's complete CIA files. The only files the agency has released consist of clippings from newspapers.

12 That Montague was able to establish these funding interventions may be due to two factors. First, his FOIA requests were made prior to the Reagan, Bush, Clinton, and Bush Jr. administrations' drastic limitations on FOIA, and thus fewer exemptions were likely to have been used by these agencies. Second, Montague personally knew the details of this specific incident, and thus he knew exactly what information to seek, rather than having to make broad FOIA requests.

CHAPTER 13 *Crusading Liberals*

1 Charley Cherokee's true identity is now known to be Alfred E. Smith, an administrative assistant and staff advisor to the WPA and a member of President Roosevelt's "Black Cabinet." Smith's position in the administration gave him access to key information relating to racial issues, and these facts and rumors regularly made their way into his column (see Alfred E. Smith papers, University of Arkansas Special Collections, Series 2, Boxes 5–8).

2 Alfred Smith founded the Capital Press Club, Washington, D.C.'s only organization for black journalists.

3 This is the same private Quaker school that Chelsea Clinton attended and that Al Gore III attended after reportedly being expelled from St. Alban's for smoking marijuana (Cockburn and St. Clair 2000:4).

4 Background information on the informant states that he is "now sponsored by the University of Washington, Seattle, Washington, in cooperation with Columbia University, New York City. He is an economic historian by training, who has for twenty-five years been a student of Chinese Institutional History" (WFO121-12262-40), and describes him as the Director of "the Chinese History Project."

5 For more on Goldfrank's anti-Communist views, see EG:1, EG/Murdock 9/14/49, in which she bemoans the Communist inclinations of Edward Haskell, Conrad Arensberg, Ruth Benedict, and others, writing: "Collier, Thompson, even Cora Du Bois and Gillen, and there are many others [who] felt that there is something sacred about integration. The question is integration for what? But what could

be more comforting to a Stalinist than to cite well-known authorities whose political affiliations are clearly non-Stalinist to bolster a theory that attaches positive
[value] to integration, and thus by implication raises Stalinist Russia to the peak of
societal ordering. Some of us may feel with Orwell that at many levels integration
has devastating drawbacks." Goldfrank's correspondence shows her to be consistent and forthright in her anti-Communist views; indeed; in her correspondence
is a fan letter she wrote to Whittaker Chambers (EG:2, EG/Chambers 6/4/50).

6 The FBI identified Edith Nash as a "founding mother" of Georgetown Day
School, and Nash's two daughters were among the school's first seven enrollees.
Edith Nash later became the Georgetown Day School's "head of school" when
original founder Agnes Inglis O'Neil retired in 1961.

7 As a defensive measure against the red-baiting attacks by the National Action
Movement group, Nash's campaign made public a letter from the White House
Loyalty Board dated May 27, 1952, giving him full clearance as a government em-
ployee (*Milwaukee Journal* 9/18/60:20).

8 Montagu was born Israel Ehrenberg in London, England, in 1905. Thirty-five
years later in Philadelphia he legally changed his name.

CHAPTER 14 *The Suspicions of Internationalists*

1 After the crew of the *Karluk* summered on the island in 1914 it was believed that it
could support a large (imported) caribou population as well as serve as a strategic
airbase in the development of polar flight routes (Stefansson 1925, 1964:256).

2 Sometime earlier there had been some discussion about the Stefanssons' property
holdings at a dinner party. Their friend Judge Learned Hand assured them that "if
the matter ever came before him, if [they] had selected the right lawyer to plead
[their] case, and if both Evelyn and Vilhjalmur agreed that [they] wished to vote
in different states, he would decide in [their] favor. He suggested, however, that
[they] would do well to act and talk as if [they] were living on [their] Vermont
Farm and just visiting New Hampshire" (Stefansson 1964:372).

3 Irving Goldman's personal knowledge of Sarah Lawrence's history provided no
insight into the identity of this individual (Goldman interview with Price 10/21/
99).

4 A 1954 confidential FBI memo establishes there was no comprehensive investigation of Robert Lowie; the memo only lists various suspect organizations to which
he belonged (WF062-60527-39827 9/27/54).

5 For example Du Bois was "the first woman to eat in the main dining room of the
Harvard Faculty Club, an event that was found worthy of mention in her obituary years later." Laura Nader pressed further frontiers when she climbed in the
window of the Berkeley Men's Faculty Club when denied entrance to attend an
important faculty meeting (Rossiter 1995:142).

CHAPTER 15 *A Glimpse of Post-McCarthyism*

1 In the years after her marriage, Kathleen Gough published articles under the names Kathleen Gough and Kathleen Gough Aberle, but here I use Gough for simplicity and to avoid narrative confusion with her husband, David Aberle.

2 C. L. R. James scholar Scott McLemee generously provided me with copies of a number of Gough's Johnson Forest Tendency publications, as well as patiently answered my questions about the organization (McLemee to Price 4/5/2000; 4/9/2000)

3 The first such anomaly is a memo dated March 27, 1963, from the London legal attaché to Hoover with the subject heading "Kathleen Aberle, aka. SM—JFG." This brief memo has one uncensored line indicating that the Boston FBI office requested that FBI personnel in London check for information on Gough (WFO100-433636-4 2/8/63). This is an odd entry because Gough's FBI file contains only minimal information on the FBI's investigation into her activities after her speech to the student group yet this memo would suggest she was the subject of a more thorough investigation. Released portions of President Sachar's FBI file contain no indication that the FBI was in contact with Sachar concerning Gough during this period (Sachar's FBI file is WFO161-5109).

4 Sachar concluded he should have better protected himself by bureaucratically shifting the action taken against Gough to another body of the school. He wrote: "The issues of academic freedom are so sensitive that, though the times were tense and emotions ran high, I should have protected myself and the University by having the dean of faculty or a faculty committee undertake the responsibility" (1976:201).

5 The eight striking faculty included Kathleen Gough, John C. Leggett, Mordecai Briemberg, Louis Feldhammer, Saghir Ahmed, Nathan Popkin, Prudence Wheeldon, and David C. Potter.

6 Reynolds was not in fact a "former member of the Atomic Energy Commission."

7 The selection of this as a stopping point for the book is somewhat arbitrary, but I chose it in part to establish that while the 1960s did not see a reduction in the FBI's monitoring of radical activist anthropologists, a growing number of activist anthropologists engaged in radical critiques of the American military and fought for civil rights without the penalties suffered by their colleagues just a few years earlier.

8 Wolf's FBI file had been redacted and released prior to my FOIA request; FOIA stamps by the FBI indicate that the file was first processed for release in 1981, while other stamps indicate a release date of 1985. These files were likely released to Eric Wolf at this time.

9 The FBI conducted an extensive investigation of Angel Palerm (aka Angel Palerm Vich), amassing over 556 pages of (released) FBI files from the 1950s to the 1970s. His movements were tracked both inside and outside the United States, and extensive notes were made of his involvement in numerous Marxist and progressive organizations (WFO105-19110; WFO105-5516). This report contains some informa-

tion on (apparently) Palerm's past affiliation with the Communist Party. An informant, "made available information indicating that Palerm ▬▬▬▬▬ admitted to having formerly been a member of the Communist Party from before the time of the Spanish Civil War until 1956. Palerm indicated ▬▬▬▬▬ that he was no longer a communist but a socialist" (WFO100-444509-2).

10 The absurdity of maintaining FBI files on scholars who published in journals affiliated with the IPR is illustrated when as part of a background check the FBI notified Lawrence Walsh, then deputy attorney general, that E. Adamson Hoebel had published a one-half page article in *Far Eastern Survey* (WFO77-02348). Even politically conservative scholars like Lauriston Sharp raised the FBI's suspicions when it became known they had past connections to the IPR, *Pacific Affairs*, or the *Far Eastern Survey* (see WFO123-7625-1; NY123-5045).

11 This is a rich history in which Jack Stauder lost his position at Harvard after protesting ROTC as well as Harvard's campus expansions that displaced working-class families. Later, however, Stauder adopted more conservative views and even appeared as a supportive guest on Rush Limbaugh's radio program (see Stauder 1995; Nader 1997a:115). Many anthropologists, including Jim Farris, Nina Glick Schiller, Elliot Fratkin, Peter Newcomer, David Hakken, Al Zagarell, and many others, experienced career setbacks for their activism. John Moore's SDS and antiwar activism at Washington University brought Military Intelligence special agents to campus in an attempt in 1966 to intimidate Moore and his sociology professor, Irving Louis Horowitz (see Hochschild 1967; Moore 1971).

CHAPTER 16 *The Cold War's Impact on Free Inquiry*

1 For example, the discipline's leading historian and "erstwhile Marxist," George Stocking (Stocking 1992:178) provides an analysis of the impact of philanthropic funding opportunities that not only fails to mention the absence of funding for Marxist critiques but fails to find discernable trends in the selected instances of Rockefeller Foundation funding (Stocking 1985). The interests of these particular robber barons are not found to have promulgated their particular "ulterior corporate or class interest" in selecting particular anthropological research projects to fund (Stocking 1985:135; cf. Colby and Dennett 1995; Fisher 1983).

2 Stocking argues that presentism limits our understanding "because it wrenches the individual historical phenomenon from the complex network of its contemporary context in order to see it in abstracted relationship to analogues in the present, it is prone to anachronistic misinterpretation" (1982:4). Stocking instead advocates that historians practice a "historicism" approach marked by its "commitment to the understanding of the past for its own sake" (4).

3 Over a dozen years after dismissing Marvin Harris's *Rise of Anthropological Theory* in a review published in *Science* (1968), Stocking revised his initial view on the futility of Harris's presentist interpretations of anthropology: "I am . . . much more inclined today than when I first read Marvin Harris' *Rise of Anthropological Theory* to grant the historical utility of a strongly held present theoretical perspective.

However one may feel about the reading of particular figures which seem to be required to align ancestors in the two moieties of 'techno-environmental determinism' and 'idealism,' it seems to me that Harris not only provided a productive synthetic interpretation but in fact directed attention to problems which are historically significant, but which were not likely to be raised so long as one tried to work from within the perspective of the historical actors" (Stocking 1982:xvii).

4 Over the years Rauch was surprised to see his work completely ignored, and he observed that "I had no great expectation that this analysis would be received as front page news, but I was taken aback by the way it was totally rejected and assigned to oblivion" (Rauch to Price 2/22/01).

5 This distinction highlights the difference between the credos of "speak truth to power" and "will discover desired findings for hire."

6 L. B. Nichols of the FBI to Clyde Tolson. Nichols mocked Hooton's proposal, writing: "You will recall Dr. Hooton has always been a first-rate fool. His latest on scientific child breeding as set forth in the attached clipping is one for the books. It is too bad that some epidemic cannot strike a lot of our college professors" (WFO62-73410).

7 There are important exceptions to this trend as anthropologists strive to edge the discipline back to its socially engaged, activist roots: see, for example, Nancy Scheper-Hughes (1992), Paul Farmer (1994), Janice Harper (2002), Karen Sacks (1988), Laura Nader (1989), Carolyn Fluehr-Lobban (2003), Catherine Lutz (2002), Ida Susser (1998), and Philippe Bourgois (1996).

8 A few months following the rapid production and adoption of the 342-page Patriot Act, I heard Robert Meeropol (the youngest son of Ethel and Julius Rosenberg) speculate that Congress produced the Patriot Act so quickly by recycling provisions of the Smith and Hatch Acts and substituting the words "terrorist" for "subversive" and "communist."

BIBLIOGRAPHY

Archival and manuscript sources

AES   Records of the American Ethnological Society, National Anthropological Archives, Smithsonian Institution

BSC   Bernhard Stern Collection, Special Collections, Knight Library, University of Oregon

EG   Esther Goldfrank Papers, National Anthropological Archives, Smithsonian Institution

JBP   John Bennett Papers, private collection held by John Bennett

MM   Margaret Mead Papers, Manuscript Division, Library of Congress

MJ   Melville Jacobs Papers, Special Collections, University of Washington

NARA   United States National Archives and Records Administration

NAA   National Anthropological Archives, Smithsonian Institution

NAPNR   National Archives, Pacific Northwest Region, Sand Point, Seattle, Washington

NPML   Niebyl-Proctor Marxist Library for Social Research

PN   Philleo Nash Papers, National Archives and Records Administration, Truman Library

RAAA   Records of the American Anthropological Association, National Anthropological Archives, Smithsonian Institution

RR   Robert Redfield Papers, University of Chicago Library, Special Collections Research Center

ST   Sol Tax Papers, University of Chicago Library, Special Collections Research Center

USDOE   United States Department of Energy

WJP   William J. Peace Papers, private collection held by William J. Peace

Publication abbreviations

AA   *American Anthropologist*

AAANB   *American Anthropological Association News Bulletin*

AN   *Anthropology Newsletter*
BAAA   *Bulletin of the American Anthropological Association*
DW   *Daily Worker*
FN   *Fellows' Newsletter*, American Anthropological Association

FBI Field Office Abbreviations

AL   Albany, New York
BA   Baltimore, Maryland
BU   Buffalo, New York
BS   Boston, Massachusetts
CG   Chicago, Illinois
CI   Cincinnati, Ohio
DE   Detroit, Michigan
HON   Honolulu, Hawaii
IP   Indianapolis, Indiana
LA   Los Angeles, California
MC   Mexico City, Mexico
MI   Milwaukee, Wisconsin
NY   New York, New York
PD   Portland, Oregon
PH   Philadelphia, Pennsylvania
SA   San Antonio, Texas
SE   Seattle, Washington
SF   San Francisco, California
SI   Springfield, Illinois
SJ   San Juan, Puerto Rico
WFO   Washington Field Office, Washington, D.C.

Books and Journals

AAUP [American Association of University Professors] 2001. *Policy Documents and Reports*, 9th ed. Washington, D.C.: AAUP.

Aberle, David F. 1967. "Correspondence." *Fellows' Newsletter* (AAA) 8 (5):7.

Aberle, Kathleen. See Kathleen Gough.

Acenca, Albert A. 1975. "The Washington Commonwealth Federation: Reform Politics and the Popular Front." Ph.D. diss., University of Washington.

Addy, Sidney. 1888 [1965]. *A Glossary of Words Used in the Neighbourhood of Sheffield.* London: Vaduz, Kraus.

Adler, A. R. 1987. *Using the Freedom of Information Act: A Step by Step Guide*. New York: ACLU Foundation.

———. 1991. *Litigation under the Federal Open Government Laws*. Washington, D.C.: ACLU Foundation.

Asad, Talal, ed. 1973. *Anthropology and the Colonial Encounter*. London: Ithaca Press.

Babcock, Barbara, and Nancy Parezo. 1986. *Daughters of the Desert: Women Anthropologists in the Southwest (1880–1980)*. Tucson: Arizona State Museum.

Barsky, Robert F. 1997. *Noam Chomsky: A Life of Dissent*. Toronto: ECW Press.

Bateman, Chris. 1990a. "End of Commies' Trail: Twain Harte." *Union Democrat* (November 29): 1.

————. 1990b. "From Khruschev to Rosenbergs to the Arch." *Union Democrat* (November 29): 1.

Baumann, Gerd. 1998. "How Ideological Involvement Actually Operates: An Interview with Eric Wolf." *European Association of Social Anthropology Newsletter* 25:8–12.

Beals, Ralph L. 1950a. "Settlement Regarding the Dismissal of Richard G. Morgan as Curator of the Ohio State Museum." *American Anthropologist* 52 (3):443–44.

————. 1950b. "Academic Freedom and the University of California." AAA *News Bulletin* (November): 7–8.

————. 1951. "Proceedings of the American Anthropological Association for the Year Ending December 1950." *American Anthropologist* 53:431–39.

————. 1969. *Politics of Social Research*. Chicago: Aldine.

————. 1982. "Fifty Years in Anthropology." *Annual Reviews in Anthropology* 11:1–23.

Beck, Hubert. 1947. *Men Who Control Our Universities*, New York: King's Crown Press.

Benedict, Ruth, and Gene Weltfish. 1943. *The Races of Mankind*. New York: Public Affairs Committee.

————. 1947. *In Henry's Backyard*. New York: H. Schuman.

Bennett, Michael J. 1996. *When Dreams Came True*. Washington, D.C.: Brassey.

Bennett, Windell Clark. 1947. *The Ethnogeographic Board*. Washington, D.C.: Smithsonian.

Bernard, H. Russell, and Alan Burns. 1988. "Video Dialogues in Anthropology: Zunia Henry and Murray Wax." Human Studies Film Archives, Smithsonian, SC-89.10.15.

Bernstein, Carl. 1989. *Loyalties: A Son's Memoir*. New York: Simon and Schuster.

Bernstein, Michael A. 1995. "American Economics and the National Security States, 1941–1953." *Radical History Review* 63:8–26.

Berreman, Gerald D. 1981. *The Politics of Truth: Essays in Critical Anthropology*. New Delhi: South Asian Publishers.

Bigwood, Jeremy. 2001. "The Accidental Spy." *American Journalism Review* 23 (6):64–69.

Bloch, Maurice. 1985. *Marxism and Anthropology*. Oxford: Oxford University Press.

Bloom, Samuel W. 1990. "The Intellectual in a Time of Crisis: The Case of Bernhard J. Stern, 1894–1956." *Journal of the History of the Behavioral Sciences* 26:17–37.

Boas, Franz. 1941. "The Myth of the Race." *New Masses* (June 29): 6.

Boggs, Grace Lee. 1998. *Living for Change*. Minneapolis: University of Minnesota Press.

Boggs, James, Grace Boggs, Freddy Paine, and Lyman Paine. 1978. *Conversations in Maine*. Boston: South End Press.

Bonifield, Aaron. 2002. "The Rise of Fascism and the Decline of Humanity in the Homeland of Democracy." Unpublished manuscript.

Bourgois, Philippe. 1996. *In Search of Respect: Selling Crack in El Barrio*. Cambridge: Cambridge University Press.

Buhle, Mari Jo. 1994. "Ruth Fulton Benedict." In *The American Radical*, ed. Mari Jo Buhle, Paul Buhle, and Harvey J. Kaye, 251–263. New York: Routledge.

Buitrago, Ann Mari, and Leon Andrew Immerman. 1981. *Are You Now or Have You Ever Been in the FBI Files? How to Secure and Interpret Your FBI Files*. New York: Grove Press.

Butterworth, Douglas. 1972. "Oscar Lewis." *American Anthropologist* 74:747–56.

Caffrey, Margaret M. 1989. *Ruth Benedict: Stranger in This Land*. Austin: University of Texas Press.

Capra, Doug. 1996. Foreword to *Wilderness: A Journal of Quiet Adventure in Alaska*, by Kent Rockwell, xx. Hanover, N.H.: Wesleyan University Press.

Carneiro, Robert L. 1981. "Leslie A. White." In *Totems and Teachers: Perspectives on the History of Anthropology*, ed. Sydel Silverman, 207–52. New York: Columbia University Press.

Carstens, Peter, and Laura Nader. 1971. "Final Report Regarding the Position of Kathleen Gough Aberle at Simon Fraser University, Submitted to the Executive Board of the American Anthropological Association." Copy in Sol Tax Papers, Box 16, Folder 4, stamp dated February 1971.

Chalou, George C., ed. 1992. *The Secrets War: The Office of Strategic Studies in World War II*. Washington, D.C.: National Archives and Records Administration.

Charns, A., and Green, P. M. 1998. "Playing the Information Game: How It Took Thirteen Years and Two Lawsuits to Get J. Edgar Hoover's Secret Supreme Court Sex Files." In *A Culture of Secrecy: The Government versus the People's Right to Know*, ed. A. G. Theoharis, 97–114. Lawrence: University Press of Kansas.

Chase, Alan. 1943. *Falange*. New York: Putnam.

Cherokee, Charley. 1944. "National Grapevine: The Hell of It." *Chicago Defender* (October 7): 13.

Chomsky, Noam. 1997. "The Cold War and the University." In *The Cold War and the University*, 171–94. New York: New Press.

Christopher, George W., Theodore J. Cieslak, Julie A. Pavlin, and Edward M. Eitzen. 1997. "Biological Warfare: A Historical Perspective." *JAMA* 278 (5):412–17.

Churchill, Ward, and Jim Vander Wall. 1990. *The COINTELPRO Papers*. Boston: South End Press.

CIRA (Committee on International Relations in Anthropology). 1950. *International Directory of Anthropologists*. Washington, D.C.: CIRA.

Cockburn, Alexander, and Jeffrey St. Clair. 2000. *Al Gore: A User's Manual*. New York: Verso.

Colby, Gerard, and Charlotte Dennett. 1995. *Thy Will Be Done—The Conquest of the Amazon*. New York: Harper Collins.

Cole, Sally. 2002. "'Mrs. Landes Meet Mrs. Benedict': Culture Pattern and Individual Agency in the 1930s." *American Anthropologist* 104 (2):533–43.

Coon, Carelton. 1980. *A North Africa Story: The Anthropologist as OSS Agent, 1941–1943.* Ipswich, Mass.: Gambit.

Cooper, J. M. 1947. "Anthropology in the United States during 1939–1945." *Société des Americanistes des Paris Journal* 36:1–14.

Corn, David. 1994. "CIA vs. FOIA." *Nation* (November 10): 369–70.

Countryman, Vern. 1951. *Un-American Activities in the State of Washington.* Ithaca: Cornell University Press.

Criley, Richard. 1990. *The FBI v. the First Amendment.* Los Angeles: First Amendment Foundation.

Dailes, Ida (translator). *Fairy Tales for Workers' Children.* Chicago: Daily Worker.

Dallin, David J. 1956a. "Mark Zborowski: Soviet Agent, Part One." *New Leader* (March 19): 8–10.

———. 1956b. "Mark Zborowski: Soviet Agent, Part Two." *New Leader* (March 26): 15–16.

Deutscher, Isaac. 1963. *The Prophet Outcast: Trotsky, 1929–1940.* New York: Vintage.

Diamond, Sigmund. 1982. "The Arrangement: The FBI and Harvard University in the McCarthy Period." In *Beyond the Hiss Case: The FBI, Congress, and the Cold War,* ed. A. Theoharis, 341–71. Philadelphia: Temple University Press.

———. 1992. *Compromised Campus: The Collaboration of Universities with the Intelligence Community, 1945–1955.* New York: Oxford University Press.

Diamond, Stanley, ed. 1960. *Culture in History: Essays in Honor of Paul Radin.* New York: Columbia University Press, for Brandeis University.

———. 1980a. *History and Practice: Essays Presented to Gene Weltfish.* The Hague: Mouton.

———. 1980b. *Anthropology: Ancestors and Heirs.* The Hague: Mouton.

Dillings, Elizabeth. 1935. *Red Network: A Who's Who and Handbook of Radicalism for Patriots.* Chicago: self-published.

———. 1936. *Roosevelt's Red Record.* Chicago: self-published.

Doob, Leonard W. 1947. "The Utilization of Social Scientists in the Overseas Branch of the Office of War Information." *American Political Science Review* 61 (4):649–67.

Draper, Theodore. 1957. *The Roots of American Communism.* New York: Viking.

Drinnon, Richard. 1987. *Keeper of Concentration Camps: Dillon S. Meyer and American Racism.* Berkeley: University of California Press.

Du Bois, Cora. 1944. *People of the Alor.* Minneapolis: University of Minnesota Press.

———. 1960. "Paul Radin: An Appreciation." In *Culture in History,* ed. Stanley Diamond. ix–xvi. New York: Columbia University Press.

———. 1980. "Some Anthropological Hindsights." *Annual Review of Anthropology* 9:1–13.

Eberhart, Richard. 1984. *The Long Reach.* New York: New Directions.

Ebihara, May. 1985. "American Ethnology in the 1930s: Contexts and Currents." In *Social Context of American Ethnology, 1840–1984,* ed. June Helm, 101–21. Washington, D.C.: American Ethnological Society.

Edelman, Marc. 1997. "Anthropologist, Secret Agent, Witch-Hunt Victim, Entrepreneur: An Interview with Jack Harris ('40)." *AnthroWatch* 5:8–14.

Edwardson, Mickie. 1999. "James Lawrence Fly, the FBI, and Wiretapping." *Historian* 61 (2):361–81.

Eggan, Fred. 1986. "Abraham M. Halpern." *Anthropology Newsletter* 27 (1):3.

Embree, John. 1943. "Dealing with Japanese Americans." *Applied Anthropology* (January–March): 37–41.

———. 1945. "Applied Anthropology and Its Relationship to Anthropology." *American Anthropologist* 47:635–37.

Endicott, Stephen, and Edward Hagerman. 1999. *The United States and Biological Warfare: Secrets from the Early Cold War*. Bloomington: University of Indiana Press.

Evans-Pritchard, E. E. 1937. *Witchcraft, Oracles, and Magic among the Azande*. Oxford: Clarendon Press.

Farmer, Paul. 1994. *The Uses of Haiti*. Monroe, Mass.: Common Courage Press.

Ferrell, Robert. 1980. *Off the Record: The Private Papers of Harry S. Truman*. New York: Harper and Row.

Fisher, Donald. 1983. "The Role of Philanthropic Foundations in the Reproduction and Production of Hegemony: Rockefeller Foundations and the Social Sciences." *Sociology* 17 (2):206–33.

———. 1986. "J. Edgar Hoover's Concept of Academic Freedom and Its Impact on Scientists during the McCarthy Era, 1950–1954." Ph.D. diss., University of Mississippi.

Fluehr-Lobban, Carolyn, ed. 2003. *Ethics and the Profession of Anthropology*. Walnut Creek, Calif.: AltaMira.

Foerstel, Lenora, and Angela Gilliam, eds. 1992. *Confronting the Margaret Mead Legacy*. Philadelphia: Temple University Press.

Foner, Philip S. 1947. *History of the Labor Movement in the United States*. New York: International Publishers.

Ford, Clellan S. 1970. "Human Relations Area Files: 1945–1969." *Behavioral Science Notes* 5:1–27.

Foucault, Michel. 1977. "Intellectuals and Power: A Conversation between Michel Foucault and Giles Deleuze." In *Language, Counter-Memory, Practice*. Ithaca: Cornell University Press.

———. 2000. *Power*, ed. James D. Faubion. New York: New Press.

Frantz, Charles. 1974. "Structuring and Restructuring of the American Anthropological Association." Paper presented at the annual meeting of the American Anthropological Association, Mexico City, Mexico, November 22.

Frederick, Timothy (interviewer). 1997. *Albert F. Canwell: An Oral History*. Olympia, Wash.: Office of the Secretary of State.

Fried, Morton. 1972. *The Study of Anthropology*. New York: Crowell.

Fried, Morton, Marvin Harris, and Robert Murphy, eds. 1968. *War: The Anthropology of Armed Conflict and Aggression*. New York: Natural History Press.

Gaddis, John Lewis. 1992. *The United States and the End of the Cold War*. New York: Oxford University Press.

———. 1993. "The Tragedy of Cold War History." *Diplomatic History* 17 (1):1–16.

Gailey, Christine Ward. 1989. "Eleanor Burke Leacock." In *Women Anthropologists*, ed. Ute Gacs et al. 215–21. Urbana: University of Illinois Press.

Garfinkel, Harold. 1956. "Conditions of Successful Degradation Ceremonies." *American Journal of Sociology* 61 (1):420–24.

Gettleman, Marvin. 2001. "Lost World of U.S. Labor Education: Curricula at East and West Coast Community Schools, 1944–1957." Paper presented at Gotham History Festival, New York City, November 7.

Gillmor, Daniel S., ed. 1949. *Speaking of Peace*. New York: National Council of the Arts, Sciences, and Professions.

Goldfrank, Esther. 1977. *Notes on an Undirected Life*. Queen's College Publications in Anthropology, no. 3. New York: Queen's College.

Gordan, Joan, ed. 1976. *Margaret Mead: The Complete Bibliography, 1925–1975*. The Hague: Mouton.

Gornick, Vivian. 1977. *The Romance of American Communism*. New York: Basic Books.

Gough, Kathleen. 1961. *When the Saints Go Marching In: An Account of the Ban-the-Bomb Movement in Britain*. Correspondence Pamphlet, Detroit: Correspondence Publishing Co.

———. 1962. *The Decline of the State and the Coming of World Society: An Optimist's View of the Future*. Correspondence Pamphlet no. 4. Detroit: Correspondence Publishing Co.

———. 1963. "Student Movement in the South." *Correspondence* (June): 1.

———. 1964a. "The Peace Movement, Part One." *Correspondence* (March): 6–7.

———. 1964b. "The Peace Movement, Part Two." *Correspondence* (April): 6.

———. 1968. "Anthropology and Imperialism." *Monthly Review* (April): 12–27.

———. 1978. *Ten Times More Beautiful: The Rebuilding of Vietnam*. New York: Monthly Review Press.

———. 1990. *Political Economy in Vietnam*. Berkeley: Folklore Institute.

———. 1993. "'Anthropology and Imperialism' Revisited." *Anthropologica* 35 (2): 279–89.

Gould, Harold A. 1971. "Jules Henry." *American Anthropologist* (73):788–92.

Hallowell, A. Irving. 1950. "Report of the Executive Board, December 1948–November 1949." *American Anthropologist* 52 (1):134–38.

Hamilton, Neil. 1995. *Zealotry and Academic Freedom*. New Brunswick: Transaction.

Harner, Michael. 1973. *Hallucinogens and Shamanism*. New York: Oxford University Press.

Harper, Janice. 2002. *Endangered Species: Health, Illness, and Death among Madagascar's People of the Forest*. Durham: Carolina Academic Press.

Harris, Benjamin. 1980. "The FBI's Files on APA and SPSSI: Description and Implications." *American Psychologist* 35:1141–44.

Harris, Jack. 1941. "The Position of Women in a Nigerian Society." *Transactions of the New York Academy of Sciences* 2 (5):1–8.

———. 1942. "Human Relationship to the Land in Southern Nigeria." *Rural Sociology* 7 (1):89–92.

Harris, Marvin. 1968a. *The Rise of Anthropological Theory*. New York: Thomas C. Crowell.

———. 1968b. "Big Bust on Morningside Heights." *Nation* (June 10): 757–63.

———. 1974. *Cows, Pigs, Wars, and Witches*. New York: Random House.

———. 1979. *Cultural Materialism*. New York: Random House.

———. 1995. *Cultural Anthropology*. 4th ed. New York: Harper Collins.

Harris, Mary Emma. 1987. *The Arts and Black Mountain College*. Cambridge: MIT Press.

Harvey, David, and Michael H. Reed. 1996. "The Culture of Poverty: An Ideological Analysis." *Sociological Perspectives* 39 (4):465–96.

Heale, M. L. 1990. *American Anticommunism: Combating the Enemy Within, 1830–1970*. Baltimore: Johns Hopkins University Press.

Hellman, Lillian. 1976. *Scoundrel Time*. Boston: Little, Brown.

Henry, Charles. 1999. *Ralph Bunche: Model Negro or American Other?* New York: New York University Press.

Hess, Jerry N. 1973. "Oral History Interview with Philleo Nash." Philleo Nash Papers, Harry S. Truman Library, Independence, Missouri.

Hickerson, Harold. 1962. *The Southwestern Chippewa: An Ethnohistorical Study*. American Anthropological Association, memoir no. 92. Washington, D.C.: AAA.

———. 1967. *Land Tenure of the Rainy Lake Chippewa at the Beginning of the Nineteenth Century*. Washington, D.C.: Smithsonian Institution Press.

———. 1988. *The Chippewa and Their Neighbors: A Study in Ethnohistory*. Prospect Heights, IL: Waveland Press.

Higman, Howard. 1998. *Higman: A Collection*. Lafayette, Calif.: Thomas Berryhill Press.

Hill, Frances. 1995. *A Delusion of Satan: The Full Story of the Salem Witch Trials*. New York: Doubleday.

Hochschild, Adam. 1967. "The Army Escalates Its Spying on Students; Bizarre New Incident." *The Sunday Ramparts* 2/12–26/67, p. 1.

Holmes, David R. 1989. *Stalking the Academic Communist: Intellectual Freedom and the Firing of Alex Novikoff*. Hanover, N.H.: University Press of New England.

Holmes, T. Michael. 1994. *The Specter of Communism in Hawaii*. Honolulu: University of Hawaii Press.

Hook, Sidney. 1949. "What Shall Be Done about Communist Teachers?" *Saturday Evening Post* (September): 18–22.

———. 1987. *Out of Step: An Unquiet Life in the Twentieth Century*. New York: Carroll and Graf.

Horne, Gerald. 1986. *Black and Red: W. E. B. Du Bois and the Afro-American Response to the Cold War, 1944–1963*. Albany: State University of New York Press.

Huizer, G. 1979. "Appendix: Foundations on the Move." In *The Politics of Anthropology*, ed. G. Huizer and B. Mannheimeds. The Hague: Mouton.

Humphrey, Norman. 1943. *Race Riot*. New York: Dryden Press.

Hunt, William R. 1986. *Stef: A Biography of Vilhjalmur Stefansson*. Vancouver: University of British Columbia Press.

Hyatt, Marshall. 1990. *Franz Boas: Social Activist*. New York: Greenwood Press.

Hymes, Dell. 1999. "Introduction." In *Reinventing Anthropology*, ed. Dell Hymes, v–xlix. Ann Arbor: University of Michigan Press.

Isserman, Maurice. 1982. *Which Side Were You On? The American Communist Party during the Second World War*. Middletown, Conn.: Wesleyan University Press.

Jacobs, Melville, and Bernhard J. Stern. 1947. *General Anthropology*. New York: Barnes and Noble.

James, C. L. R. 1938. *The Black Jacobins*. New York: Vintage Books.

Jeffreys-Jones, Rhodi. 1989. *The CIA and American Democracy*. New Haven: Yale University Press.

Jenkins, Mark F. 2000. *All Powers Necessary and Convenient*. Seattle: University of Washington Press.

Kaplan, Craig, and Ellen Schrecker, eds. 1983. *Regulating the Intellectuals: Perspectives on Academic Freedom in the 1980s*. New York: Praeger.

Kaplan, Judy, and Lynn Shapiro. 1998. *Red Diapers: Growing Up in the Communist Left*. Urbana: University of Illinois Press.

Kahn, E. J. 1975. *The China Hands: America's Foreign Service Officers and What Befell Them*. New York: Viking.

Katz, Naomi, and David Kemnitzer. 1989. "Mary Thygeson Shepardson." In *Women Anthropologists*, ed. Ute Gates et al., 322–26. Urbana: University of Illinois Press.

Keen, Mike. 1999. *Stalking the Sociological Imagination: J. Edgar Hoover's FBI Surveillance of American Sociology*. Westport, Conn.: Greenwood Press.

Kennan, George F. 1948. "Review of Current Trends [in] U.S. Foreign Policy," Policy Planning Study 23. In *The State Department Policy Planning Staff Papers, 1947–1949*. Vol. 2. 1948, 103–34. New York: Garland.

Kirchheimer, Otto. 1961. *Political Justice*. Princeton: Princeton University Press.

Klehr, Harvey, John Earl Haynes, and Fridrikh Igorevich Firsov. 1995. *The Secret World of American Communism*. New Haven: Yale University Press.

Klehr, Harvey, and Ronald Radosh. 1996. *The Amerasia Spy Case: Prelude to McCarthyism*. Chapel Hill: University of North Carolina Press.

Kleinman, David Lee, and Mark Solovey. 1995. "Hot Science / Cold War: The National Science Foundation after World War II." *Radical History Review* 63:110–39.

Krook, Susan. 1989. "Franz Boas (a.k.a. Boaz) and the FBI." *History of Anthropology Newsletter* 16 (2):4–11.

———. 1993. "An Analysis of Franz Boas' Achievements and Work Emphasis during the Last Five Years of His Life, Based on Documentation and Interpretation of the Federal Bureau of Investigation File Maintained on Him from 1936 to 1950." Ph.D. diss., University of Colorado.

Landes, Ruth S. 1940. "A Cult Matriarchate and Male Homosexuality." *Journal of Abnormal and Social Psychology* 33:14–33.

———. 1945. "What about This Bureaucracy?" *Nation* 161:365–66.

Lazarsfeld, Paul, and Wagner Thielens Jr., 1958. *The Academic Mind: Social Scientists in a Time of Crisis*. New York: Free Press.

Leacock, Eleanor Burke. 1971. *The Culture of Poverty: A Critique*. New York: Simon and Schuster.

———. 1972. Introduction to *The Origin of the Family, Private Property, and the State, in Light of the Researches of Lewis H. Morgan*, by Frederick Engels, 7–67. New York: International Publishers.

———. 1985. "Marxism and Anthropology." In *The Left Academy*, ed. Bernard Ollman and E. Vernoff, 242–76. New York: McGraw-Hill.

Lee, Richard, and Karen B. Sacks. 1993. "Anthropology, Imperialism, and Resistance: The Work of Kathleen Gough." *Anthropologica* 35 (2):179–93.

Lehman, F. K. 1992. "Demitri Boris Shimkin." *Anthropology Newsletter* (3):41–42.

Leighton, Alexander H. 1949. *Human Relations in a Changing World: Observations on the Use of the Social Sciences*. New York: E. P. Dutton.

di Leonardo, Micaela. 1996. "Patterns of Culture Wars: The Right's Attack on 'Cultural Relativism' as Synecdoche for All that Ails Us." *Nation* (April 8): 25–29.

———. 1998. *Exotics at Home: Anthropologies, Others, American Modernity*. Chicago: University of Chicago Press.

Leopold, Tom, Harry Shearer, and Peter Matz. 1994. *J. Edgar!* Los Angeles: L.A. Theatre Works Production.

Lewis, Herbert. 2001. "The Passion of Franz Boas." *American Anthropologist* 103 (2): 447–67.

Lewis, Lionel S. 1993. *The Cold War and Academic Governance: The Lattimore Case at Johns Hopkins*. Albany: State University of New York Press.

Lewis, Oscar. 1959. *Five Families: Mexican Case Studies in the Culture of Poverty*. New York: Basic Books.

———. 1960. *Tepoztlán: Village in Mexico*. New York: Holt.

———. 1961. *The Children of Sánchez: Autobiography of a Mexican Family*. New York: Random House.

———. 1966. *La Vida: A Puerto Rican Family in the Culture of Poverty—San Juan and New York*. New York: Random House.

Lewis, Oscar, Ruth M. Lewis, and Susan M. Rigdon. 1977. *Four Men: Living the Revolution, an Oral History of Contemporary Cuba*. Urbana: University of Illinois Press.

Linton, Adelin, and Charles Wagley. 1971. *Ralph Linton*. New York: Columbia University Press.

Lippman, Walter. 1947. *The Cold War: A Study in U.S. Foreign Policy*. New York: Harper.

Lissner, Will. 1953. "Columbia Is Dropping Dr. Weltfish, Leftist." *New York Times* (April 1): 1, 19.

Lonergan, David. 1991. "Morris Swadesh." In *International Dictionary of Anthropologists*, ed. Christopher Winters, 678–80. New York: Garland.

Lowen, Rebecca S. 1997. *Creating the Cold War University: The Transformation of Stanford*. Berkeley: University of California Press.

Lutz, Catherine. 2002. *Homefront: A Military City and the American Twentieth Century*. Boston: Beacon.

McBride, Carol Ann. 1980. "A Sense of Proportion: Balancing Subjectivity and Objectivity in Anthropology." M.A. thesis, Columbia University.

McCormick, Charles H. 1989. *The Nest of Vipers: McCarthyism and Higher Education in the Mundel Affair, 1951–1952*. Urbana: University of Illinois Press.

McLemee, Scott, ed. 1996. *C. L. R. James on the "Negro Question."* Jackson: University Press of Mississippi.

McLemee, Scott, and Paul Le Blanc. 1994. *C. L. R. James and Revolutionary Marxism: Selected Writings of C. L. R. James, 1939–1949*. Atlantic Highlands, N.J.: Humanities Press.

McMillan, Robert. 1986. "The Study of Anthropology, 1931 to 1937, at Columbia University and the University of Chicago." Ph.D. York University.

McQuown, Norman. 1968. "Morris Swadesh." *American Anthropologist* 70:755–56.

Mabee, Carleton. 1987. "Margaret Mead and Behavioral Scientists in World War II: Problems of Responsibility, Truth, and Effectiveness." *Journal of History of the Behavioral Sciences* 23:3–13.

Madden, David K. 1999. "A Radical Ethnographer at Work in the Columbia Anthropology Department, 1936–1937." *History of Anthropology Newsletter* 26 (2):3–10.

Marro, Anthony. 1982. "FBI Break-In Policy." In *Beyond the Hiss Case: The FBI, Congress, and the Cold War*, ed. A. Theoharis, 78–128. Philadelphia: Temple University Press.

Marx, Karl. 1859. *Contribution to the Critique of Political Economy*. New York: International Publishers.

Massar, Ivan, and William Hedgepeth. 1967. "A Troubling Voyage to North Vietnam." *Look* 31 (13):17–21.

Matthews, J. B. 1953. "Communism and the Colleges." *American Mercury* (May): 111–44.

May, Ernest R., ed. 1993. *American Cold War Strategy: Interpreting NSC 68*. Boston: Bedford Books.

Mead, Margaret. 1928. *Coming of Age in Samoa*. New York: Morrow.

———. 1941. "On Methods of Implementing a National Morale Program." *Applied Anthropology* 1:20–24.

———. 1951. *Soviet Attitudes Towards Authority: An Interdisciplinary Approach to Problems of Soviet Character*. Rand Corporation Series. New York: McGraw-Hill.

Meggers, Betty. 1960. "The Law of Cultural Evolution as a Practical Research Tool." In *Essays in the Science of Culture*, ed. Gertrude Dole and Robert Carneiro, 302–16. New York: Crowell.

———. 1961. "Field Testing of Cultural Law, a Reply to Morris Opler." *Southwestern Journal of Anthropology* 17:352–54.

Melby, E. O., and M. B. Smith. 1953. "Academic Freedom in a Climate of Insecurity." *Journal of Social Issues* 9 (3):2–55.

Melman, Seymour. 1974. *The Permanent War Economy*. New York: Simon and Schuster.

Melvern, Linda. 1995. *The Ultimate Crime: Who Betrayed the UN and Why*. London: Allyn and Busby.

Meranto, Philip, Oneida Meranto, and Matthew Lippman. 1985. *Guarding the Ivory Tower: Repression and Rebellion in Higher Education*. Denver: Lucha.

Merton, Robert K. 1957. "In Memory of Bernard J. Stern." *Science and Society* 21 (1): 7–9.

Miller, Arthur. 1987. *Timebends: A Life*. New York: Grove.

Mintz, Sidney W., ed. 1985. *History, Evolution, and the Concept of Culture*. Cambridge: Cambridge University Press.

———. 1993. "Clio Rediviva." In *Configurations of Power: Holistic Anthropology in Theory and Practice*, ed. John Hudson and Patricia J. Netherly. Ithaca: Cornell University Press.

Mishkin, Bernard. 1949. "Democracy in Latin America, 'Good Neighbors'—Fact and Fancy." *Nation* (November 26), 510–51.

Mitgang, Herbert. 1988. *Dangerous Dossiers*. New York: Balantine.

Montagu, Ashley. 1942. *Man's Most Dangerous Myth: The Fallacy of Race*. New York: Columbia University Press.

———. 1972. *Statement on Race*. 3rd ed. New York: Oxford University Press.

Montague, Joel B. Jr. 1991. *Cohort of One*. Seattle: Frontier Press.

Moore, John. 1971. "Perspective for a Partisan Anthropology." *Liberation* (November): 34–43.

Morgan, Richard Guy. 1946. *Fort Ancient*. Columbus: Ohio State Archaeological and Historical Society.

Morgan, Richard Guy, and Edward S. Thomas. 1948. *Fort Hill*. Columbus: Ohio State Archaeological and Historical Society.

Moynihan, Daniel P. 1968. *On Understanding Poverty*. New York: Basic Books.

Murphy, Robert F. 1976. "Introduction: A Quarter Century of American Anthropology." In *Selected Papers from the "American Anthropologist," 1946–1970*, ed. Robert Murphy, 1–22. Washington, D.C.: AAA.

———. 1991. "Anthropology at Columbia: A Reminiscence." *Dialectical Anthropology* 16:65–81.

Myrdal, Gunnar. 1944. *An American Dilemma: The Negro Problem and Modern Democracy*. New York: Harper and Row.

Nader, Laura. 1972. "Up the Anthropologist—Perspectives Gained from Studying Up." In *Reinventing Anthropology*, ed. Dell Hymes, 284–311. New York: Pantheon.

———. 1989. "Post-Interpretive Anthropology." *Anthropological Quarterly* 61 (4): 149–59.

———. 1997a. "The Phantom Factor: Impact of the Cold War on Anthropology." In *The Cold War and the University*, 107–46. New York: New Press.

———. 1997b. "Postscript on the Phantom Factor: More Ethnography of Anthropology." *General Anthropology* 4 (1):1–8.

Nash, Edith. 1989. "Philleo Nash and Georgetown Day School." In *Applied Anthropologist and Public Servant: The Life and Work of Philleo Nash*. NAPA Bulletin 7, 32–41. Washington, D.C.: AAA.

Nash, Philleo. 1980. "Philleo Nash." In *The Truman Whitehouse*, ed. Francis Heller, 52–56. Lawrence: Regents Press of Kansas.

———. 1986. "Science, Politics, and Human Values: A Memoir." *Human Organization* 45 (3):189–201.

———. 1989. "Anthropologist in the White House." In *Applied Anthropologist and Public Servant: The Life and Work of Philleo Nash.* NAPA Bulletin 7, 3–6, Washington, D.C.: AAA.

Navasky, Victor. 1980. *Naming Names.* New York: Viking.

———. 2001. "Cold War Ghosts: The Case of the Missing Red Menace." *Nation* (July 16): 36–43.

Newman, Matthew. 1995. "UM Faculty's Historic Teach-In of 30 Years Ago: A Vital Service to Their Country." *Michigan Today* (October): 10–12.

Newman, Stanley. 1967. "Morris Swadesh." *Language* 43:948–57.

O'Connell, Charles Thomas. 1990. "Social Structure and Science: Soviet Studies at Harvard." Ph.D. diss., University of California at Los Angeles.

Olsen, Jack. 2000. *Last Man Standing: The Tragedy and Triumph of Geronimo Pratt.* New York: Doubleday.

Opler, Morris. 1961. "Cultural Evolution, Southern Athapaskans, and Chronology in Theory." *Southwestern Journal of Anthropology* 17:1–20.

———. 1962. "Two Converging Lines of Influence in Cultural Evolutionary Theory." *American Anthropologist* 64:524–47.

Orwell, George. 1949. *Nineteen Eighty-Four.* London: Secker & Warburg.

Oshinsky, David. 1983. *A Conspiracy So Immense: The World of Joe McCarthy.* New York: Free Press.

Ottanelli, Fraser M. 1991. *The Communist Party of the United States: From the Depression to World War II.* New Brunswick: Rutgers University Press.

Parezo, Nancy J., ed. 1993. *Hidden Scholars: Women Anthropologists and the Native American Southwest.* Albuquerque: University of New Mexico Press.

Park, George, and Alice Park. 1989. "Ruth Schlossberg Landes." In *Women Anthropologists*, ed. Ute Gacs et al. 209–14, Urbana: University of Illinois Press.

Parker, Seymour, and Robert J. Kleiner. 1970. "The Culture of Poverty: An Adjustive Dimension." *American Anthropologist* 72:516–27.

Parks, Douglas R., and Ruth E. Pathé. 1985. "Gene Weltfish, 1902–1980." *Plains Anthropologist* 30:59–64.

Pathé, Ruth. 1989. "Gene Weltfish." In *Women Anthropologists*, ed. Ute Gacs et al. Urbana: University of Illinois Press.

Patterson, James T. 2001. *Brown v. Board of Education: A Civil Rights Milestone and Its Troubled Legacy.* Oxford: Oxford University Press.

Patterson, Thomas. 1999. "The Political Economy of Archaeology in the United States." *Annual Review of Anthropology* 28:155–74.

———. 2001. *A Social History of Anthropology in the United States.* Oxford: Berg.

Peace, William J. 1993. "Leslie White and Evolutionary Theory." *Dialectical Anthropology* 18:123–51.

———. 1995. "Vere Gordon Childe and the Cold War." In *Childe and Australia: Archaeology, Politics, and Ideas*, ed. P. Gathercole, I. Terry, and M. Gregory, 135–51. Brisbane: University of Queensland Press.

———. 1998. "Bernhard Stern, Leslie White, an Anthropological Appraisal of the Russian Revolution." *American Anthropologist* 100:84–93.

———. 2004. *Leslie A. White: Evolution and Revolution in Anthropology*. Lincoln: University of Nebraska Press.

Peace, William J., and David H. Price. 2001. "The Cold War Context of the FBI's Investigation of Leslie A. White." *American Anthropologist* 103 (1):164–67.

Peters, J. 1977 [1935]. *The Communist Party: A Manual on Organization*. San Francisco: Proletarian Press.

Pintzuk, Edward C. 1997. *Reds, Radical Justice, and Civil Liberties: Michigan Communists during the Cold War*. Minneapolis: MEP Publications.

Powell, J. V. 1995. "To See Ourselves as Others See Us." *American Anthropologist* 97 (4):661–63.

Powers, Richard. 1987. *Secrecy and Power: The Life of J. Edgar Hoover*. New York: Free Press.

Price, David H. 1995. "Cold War Anthropology." Paper presented at the annual meeting of the American Anthropological Association, Washington, D.C., November.

———. 1997a. "Anthropologists on Trial: The Lessons of McCarthyism." Paper presented at the annual meeting of the American Anthropological Association, Washington, D.C., November.

———. 1997b. "Anthropological Research and the Freedom of Information Act." *CAM: Cultural Anthropology Methods* 9 (1):12–15.

———. 1998a. "Cold War Anthropology: Collaborators and Victims of the National Security State." *Identities* 4 (3–4): 389–430.

———. 1998b. "Mark Zborowski." *Anthropology Newsletter* 39 (6):31.

———. 1998c. "Earle L. Reynolds." *Anthropology Newsletter* 39 (6):29.

———. 1998d. "Gregory Bateson and the OSS." *Human Organization* 57 (4):379–84.

———. 1999. "The FBI and Oscar Lewis: Political Surveillance and the Culture of Poverty." Paper presented at the annual meeting of the American Anthropological Association, Chicago, Illinois, November 18.

———. 2000a. "The AAA and the CIA." *Anthropology News* 41 (8): 13–14.

———. 2000b. "Anthropologists as Spies." *Nation* 271 (16):24–27.

———. 2001a. "Academia under Attack: Sketches for a New Blacklist." *CounterPunch* (November, 21): 1–3.

———. 2001b. "Fear and Loathing in the Soviet Union: Roy Barton and the NKVD." *HAN* 28 (2):3–8.

———. 2001c. "'The Shameful Business': Leslie Spier on the Censure of Franz Boas." *HAN* 28 (2):9–12.

———. 2002a. "Present Dangers, Past Wars, and Past Anthropologies." *Anthropology Today* 18 (1):3–5.

———. 2002b. "Lessons from Second World War Anthropology: Peripheral, Persuasive, and Ignored Contributions." *Anthropology Today* 18 (3):14–20.

———. 2002c "Reply to van Bremen, Kopytoff, and Hardiman." *Anthropology Today* 18 (4):22.

———. 2002d. "Interlopers and Invited Guests: On Anthropology's Witting and Unwitting Links to Intelligence Agencies." *Anthropology Today* 18 (6):16–21.

———. 2003a. "Anthropology *Sub Rosa*: The AAA, the CIA, and the Ethical Problems Inherent in Secret Research." In *Ethics and the Profession of Anthropology: The Dialogue Continues.* 2nd ed., ed. Carolyn Fluehr-Lobban, 29–49. Walnut Creek, Calif.: AltaMira Press.

———. 2003b. "Tribal Communism under Fire: Archie Phinney and the FBI." *Journal of Northwest Anthropology* (fall).

———. 2003c. "Applied Anthropologist as Cold War Dissident: Earle Reynolds, an Informed Protester of Conscience." Paper presented at the annual meeting of the Society for Applied Anthropology, Portland, Oregon, March 23.

———. 2003d. "Subtle Means and Enticing Carrots: The Impact of Funding on American Cold War Anthropology." *Critique of Anthropology* 23 (4):1373–401.

Price, David H., and William J. Peace. 2003. "Un-American Anthropological Thought: The Opler / Meggers Exchange." *Journal of Anthropological Research* 59 (2):183–203.

Pynchon, Thomas. 1973. *Gravity's Rainbow.* New York: Viking Press.

Quigley, Carroll. 1966. *Tragedy and Hope.* New York: Macmillan.

Radin, Paul. 1932. *Social Anthropology.* New York: McGraw Hill.

———. 1933. *The Method and Theory of Ethnology.* New York: Basic Books.

———. 1934. *Racial Myth.* New York: Whittlesey House.

———. 1949. *The Culture of the Winnebago.* Baltimore: Waverly Press.

Rauch, Jerome. 1955. "Area Institute Programs and African Studies." *The Journal of Negro Education* (fall): 409–25.

Raymond, Anan. 1952. "Mother Bloor and the Communist Revolution in America." *American Bar Association Journal* 38 (11):911–14.

Redfield, Robert. 1951. "The Dangerous Duty of the University." *School and Society* 74:161–65.

———. n.d. (ca. 1951) "Communists Should Teach in American Universities." Robert Redfield Papers, University of Chicago, Box 61, Folder 7.

Reeves, Thomas C. 1982. *The Life and Times of Joe McCarthy.* New York: Stein and Day.

Reinhold, Meyer. 1994. "Moses Isaac Finley." In *Biographical Dictionary of North American Classicists*, ed. Ward Briggs, 179–80. Westport, Conn.: Greenwood.

Rendon, Juan José. 1967. "Mauricio Swadesh, 1909–1967." *América Indígena* 27:735–46.

Reynolds, Earle. 1960. "Irradiation and Human Evolution." In *The Process of Human Evolution*, ed. Gabriel Lasker, 89–108. Detroit: Wayne State University Press.

———. 1961. *The Forbidden Voyage.* New York: D. McKay.

Reynolds, Earle, and Barbara Reynolds. 1962. *All in the Same Boat.* New York: D. McKay.

Rice, Elmer. 1944. "The U.S.O. and 'The Races of Mankind.'" *Saturday Review of Literature* (July 15): 13.

Rigdon, Susan M. 1988. *The Culture Facade: Art, Science, and Politics in the Work of Oscar Lewis*. Urbana: University of Illinois Press.

Roberts, John A. 1968. "Columbia Crisis: Marvin Harris." Interview 5/13/1968. Oral History Research Office, Columbia University.

Robins, Natalie. 1992. *Alien Ink: The FBI's War on Freedom of Expression*. New York: William Morrow.

Rodney, Lester. 2001. "They Were Principled Idealists." *Nation* (January 22): 2, 24.

Rogin, Michael Paul. 1967. *The Intellectuals and McCarthy: The Radical Specter*. Cambridge: MIT Press.

Roseberry, William. 1996. "The Unbearable Lightness of Anthropology." *Radical History Review* 65:5–25.

Rosenfeld, Susan. 1999. "Doing Injustice to the FBI: The Negative Myths Perpetuated by Historians." *Chronicle of Higher Education* (October 8): B6–8.

Ross, Eric B. 1998. *The Malthus Factor: Poverty, Politics, and Population in Capitalist Development*. New York: Zed Books.

———. 1999. "Axel Wenner-Gren: The Nazi Connection and the Origins of the Viking Fund." Paper presented at the annual meeting of the American Anthropological Association, Chicago, Illinois, November 19.

———. 2002. "To Interpret the World or to Change It? On the Contradictory Relationship of Cultural Materialism to Marxism." Paper presented at the annual meeting of the American Anthropological Association, New Orleans, Louisiana, November 21.

Rossiter, Margaret W. 1995. *Women Scientists in America: Before Affirmative Action, 1940–1972*. Baltimore: Johns Hopkins University Press.

Rowe, John Howland. 1984. "An Interview with John V. Murra." *Hispanic American Historical Review* 64 (4):633–53.

Sachar, Abraham L. 1976. *A Host at Last*. Boston: Little, Brown.

Sacks, Karen Brodkin. 1988. *Caring by the Hour: Women, Work, and Organizing at Duke Medical Center*. Urbana: University of Illinois Press.

Sahlins, Marshall. 2000. *Culture in Practice*. New York: Zone Books.

Salisbury, Harrison E. 1984. "The Strange Correspondence of Morris Ernst and John Edgar Hoover, 1939–1964." *Nation* (December 1): 575–89.

Sanders, Jane. 1979. *Cold War on Campus: Academic Freedom at the University of Washington 1946–1964*. Seattle: University of Washington Press.

Sanjek, Roger. 1995. "Politics, Theory, and the Nature of Cultural Things." In *Science, Materialism, and the Study of Culture*, ed. M. Murphy and Maxine Margolis, 39–61. Gainesville: University Press of Florida.

Saunders, Frances Stoner. 1999. *The Cultural Cold War: The CIA and the World of Arts and Letters*. New York: New Press.

Saunders, Lucie Wood. 1989. "Vera Dourmashkin Rubin." In *Women Anthropologists*, ed. Ute Gacs et al., 316–21. Urbana: University of Illinois Press.

Sayre, Nora. 1995. *Previous Convictions: A Journey through the 1950s*. New Brunswick: Rutgers University Press.

Scates, Shelby. 2000. "Cold Warrior: Albert Canwell Is Still Alive, Still Living in Spokane, and Still Hates Commies." *Law and Politics* (February–March): 12–15.

Scheper-Hughes, Nancy. 1992. *Death without Weeping: The Violence of Everyday Life in Brazil*. Berkeley: University of California Press.

Schrecker, Ellen. 1986. *No Ivory Tower: McCarthyism and the Universities*. New York: Oxford University Press.

———. 1994. *The Age of McCarthyism: A Brief History with Documents*. Boston: Bedford Books.

———. 1998. *Many Are the Crimes: McCarthyism in America*. New York: Little, Brown.

Schultz, Buel, and Ruth Schultz. 1989. *It Did Happen Here*. Berkeley: University of California Press.

Scott, Peter Dale. 1975. "Exporting Military-Economic Development: America and the Overthrow of Sukarno, 1965–1967." In *Ten Years' Military Terror in Indonesia*, ed. Malcolm Caldwell, 209–61. Nottingham, Eng.: Spokesman Books.

Selcraig, James T. 1982. *The Red Scare in the Midwest, 1945–1955: A State and Local Study*. Ann Arbor: UMI Research Press.

Seymour, Susan. 1989. "Cora Du Bois." In *Women Anthropologists*, ed. Ute Gacs et al., 72–79. Urbana: University of Illinois Press.

Shepardson, Mary. 1963. *Navajo Ways in Government*. American Anthropological Association Memoir no. 96. Washington, D.C.: AAA.

———. 1965. "Problems of the Navajo Tribal Courts in Transition." *Human Organization* 24 (3):250–53.

———. 1983. "Development of Navajo Tribal Government." In *Handbook of North American Indians. Vol. 10: Southwest*, 624–35. Washington, D.C.: Smithsonian.

Shepardson, Mary, and Blodwen Hammond. 1970. *The Navajo Mountain Community: Social Organization and Kinship Terminology*. Berkeley: University of California Press.

Sillen, Samuel. 1949. "Behind the Ivy Curtain." *Masses and Mainstream* 2 (3):7–17.

Singh, Hira. 1993. "Colonialism, Rural Social Structure, and Resistance: The Relevance of Kathleen Gough's Work." *Anthropologica* 35 (2):202–12.

Smith, Julie. 1999. "Modernism and Cultural Criticism in Anthropology at the New School for Social Research: 1919–1940." M.A. thesis, New School for Social Research.

Sperling, Susan. 2000. "Ashley Montagu, 1905–1999." *American Anthropologist* 102 (3):583–88.

Spitzer, Steven. 1980. "Toward a Marxian Theory of Deviance." In *Criminal Behavior: Readings in Criminology*, ed. Dellos Kelly, 175–191. New York: St. Martin's Press.

Starobin, Joseph R. 1972. *American Communism in Crisis, 1943–1957*. Cambridge: Harvard University Press.

State of Washington. 1948. *Report of the Joint Legislative Fact-Finding Committee on Un-American Activities*. Olympia, Wash.: Washington State Government.

Stauder, Jack. 1972. "The 'Relevance' of Anthropology Under Imperialism." *Critical Anthropology* 2:65–87.

———. 1995. "Changing Course: Teaching Both Sides of Environmental Issues." *Liberal Education* 81 (3):36–41.

Stefansson, Vilhjalmur. 1913. *My Life with the Eskimos*. New York: Macmillan.

———. 1921. *The Friendly Arctic*. New York: Macmillan.

———. 1925. *The Adventure of Wrangel Island*. New York: Macmillan.

———. 1964. *Discovery: The Autobiography of Vilhjalmur Stefansson*. New York: McGraw Hill.

Stern, Bernhard J. 1928. *Lewis Henry Morgan: American Ethnologist*. Baltimore: Social Forces.

———. 1934. *The Lummi Indians of Northwest Washington*. New York: Columbia University Press.

———. 1943. "Franz Boas as Scientist and Citizen." *Science and Society* 7 (4):289–320.

Stevens, Bennett [Bernhard Stern]. 1932. *The Church and the Workers*. New York: International Pamphlets.

Stocking, George W. 1968. "A Historical Brief for Cultural Materialism." *Science* 162:108–10.

———. 1976. "Ideas and Institutions in American Anthropology." In *Selected Papers from the American Anthropologist, 1921–1945*, ed. George W. Stocking, 1–54. Washington, D.C.: AAA.

———. 1982 [1968]. *Race, Culture, and Evolution*. Chicago: University of Chicago Press.

———. 1985. "Philanthropoids and Vanishing Cultures: Rockefeller Funding and the End of the Museum Era in Anglo-American Anthropology." In *Objects and Others. Vol. 3: History of Anthropology Series*, ed. G. W. Stocking, 112–45. Madison: University of Wisconsin Press.

———. 1992. *The Ethnographer's Magic*. Madison: University of Wisconsin Press.

———. 2000. "Do Good, Young Man." In *Excluded Ancestors, Inevitable Traditions. Vol. 9: History of Anthropology Series*, ed. R. Handler, 171–264. Madison: University of Wisconsin Press.

———. 2002. "Society, Matter, and Human Nature: Robert Gelston Armstrong and Marxist Anthropology at the University of Chicago." *HAN* 29 (1):3–10.

Stockwell, John. 1991. *The Praetorian Guard: The U.S. Role in the New World Order*. Boston: South End Press.

Sullivan, William C. 1979. *The Bureau: My Thirty Years in Hoover's FBI*. New York: Norton.

Summers, Anthony. 1993. *Official and Confidential: The Secret Life of J. Edgar Hoover*. New York: Putnam.

Susser, Ida. 1998. "Inequality, Violence, and Gender Relations in a Global City: New York." *Identities* 5 (2):219–47.

Suzuki, Peter T. 1981. "Anthropologists in the Wartime Camps for Japanese Americans." *Dialectical Anthropology* 6 (1):23–60.

Swadesh, Morris. 1971. *The Origin and Diversification of Language*. Chicago: Aldine.

Swearingen, M. Wesley. 1995. *FBI Secrets: An Agent's Exposé*. Boston: South End Press.

Taylor, George E. 1985. "Karl A. Wittfogel." In *International Encyclopedia of the Social Sciences* Vol. 19, 812–14. New York: Free Press.

Theoharis, Athan G. 1984. *FBI American Legion Contact Program*. Wilmington, Del.: Scholarly Resources.

———. 1991. *From the Secret Files of J. Edgar Hoover*. Chicago: I. R. Dee.

———. 1994. *The FBI: An Annotated Bibliography and Research Guide. Vol. 9: Organizations and Interest Groups*. New York: Garland.

———. 1995. *J. Edgar Hoover, Sex and Crime*. Chicago: I. R. Dee.

———. 1999. "A Brief History of the FBI's Role and Powers." In *The FBI: A Comprehensive Reference Guide*, ed. A. Theoharis, 1–43. Phoenix: Oryx Press.

———. 2002. *Chasing Spies: How the FBI Failed in Counterintelligence but Promoted the Politics of McCarthyism in the Cold War Years*. Chicago: I. R. Dee.

Thomas, Robert. 1999. "Eric W. Wolf, 76, An Iconoclastic Anthropologist." *Society for Applied Anthropology Newsletter* 10 (2):14–15.

Thompson, Laurence C. 1978. "Obituary of Melville Jacobs." *American Anthropologist* 80:640–49.

Trencher, Susan R. 2002. "The American Anthropological Association and the Values of Science, 1935–70." *American Anthropologist* 104 (2):450–62.

Ulmen, G. L. 1978. *The Science of Society: Toward an Understanding of the Life and Work of Karl August Wittfogel*. The Hague: Mouton.

U.S. Congress. 1939–1940. House. "Special Committee on Un-American Activities in the United States of the House of Representatives," 76th Congress, Vol. 7. Washington, D.C.: Government Printing Office.

———. 1944. House. "House Report 1311 on CIO Political Action Committee, March 29, 1944." Washington, D.C.: Government Printing Office.

———. 1951. Senate. "Institute of Pacific Relations Hearings." Subcommittee to Investigate the Administration of the Internal Security Act, Committee of the Judiciary, part 1, July 25–August 5, 1951. Washington, D.C.: Government Printing Office.

———. 1952a. Senate. "Activities of United States Citizens Employed by the United Nations." Committee of the Judiciary, Hearings, October 18–December 17, 1952. Washington, D.C.: Government Printing Office.

———. 1952b. Senate. "Subversive Influence in the Educational Process Hearings." Subcommittee to Investigate the Administration of the Internal Security Act, Committee of the Judiciary. September 8–October 13, 1952. Washington, D.C.: Government Printing Office.

———. 1953a. Senate. "Activities of United States Citizens Employed by the United Nations." Committee of the Judiciary, Hearings, October 2, 29, and December 22, 1953. Washington, D.C.: Government Printing Office.

———. 1953b. Senate. "Hearings before the Permanent Subcommittee on Investigations of the Committee on Government Operations." March 27, April 1 and 2, 1953. Washington, D.C.: Government Printing Office.

———. 1953c. House. "Investigation of Communist Activities in the Los Angeles

Area, part 5." United States House of Representatives Committee on Un-American Activities, Hearings, "Testimony of Paul Benedict Radin." March 12, 1953. Washington, D.C.: Government Printing Office.

———. 1957. House. "Hearings Held in San Francisco, California, June 18–21, 1957." Part 2: Congressional Session 85-1, House Committee on Un-American Activities, Francis E. Walter, chairman. "Testimony of Mary Thygeson (Scott) Shepardson, Accompanied by Council, Francis J. McTernana, Jr." June 20, 1957. Washington, D.C.: Government Printing Office.

Velasco, Manuel Larenas. 1965. "Estricamente Confidential." *Foro Politico* 146:1–15.

Vidal, Gore. 1988. "The National Security State." *Nation* (June 4): 782–86.

Vincent, Joan. 1988. "Ahead of His Time: Production and Reproduction in the Work of Alexander Lesser." *American Ethnologist* 15:743–51.

———. 1990. *Anthropology and Politics: Visions, Traditions, and Trends*. Tucson: University of Arizona Press.

Vonnegut, Kurt. 1997. *Timequake*. New York: Putnam.

Wagley, Charles. 1955. "Bernard Mishkin, 1913–1954." *American Anthropologist* 57: 1033–35.

Waite, Elmont. 1957a. "Balky Bookseller Snarls Red Probe." *San Francisco Chronicle* (June 21): 1, 4.

———. 1957b. "S.F. Red Inquiry Ends in New Row." *San Francisco Chronicle* (June 22): 1, 4.

Wakin, Eric. 1992. *Anthropology Goes to War: Professional Ethics and Counterinsurgency in Thailand*. Madison: University of Wisconsin Center for Asian Studies.

Warshaw, Richard. 1996. "CIA Plans for Automatic Declassification." Paper presented at the George Washington University Symposium on Executive Order 12958, Washington, D.C.

Wax, Murray. 1997. "On Negating Positivism: An Anthropological Dialectic." *American Anthropologist* 99 (1):17–23.

———. n.d. [ca. 1997]. "My Life as a Commie-Trotskyite Menace, Blacklisted: A Personal Account." Unpublished manuscript.

Weinstein, Allen, and Alexander Vassiliev. 1999. *The Haunted Wood: Soviet Espionage in America—The Stalin Era*. New York: Random House.

Weisberg, Jacob. 1999. "Cold War without End." *New York Times* (November 28): 16.

Weltfish, Gene. 1949. "Racialism, Colonialism and World Peace." In *Speaking of Peace*, ed. Daniel S. Gillmore. New York: The National Council of the Arts, Sciences, and Professions.

———. 1953. *The Origins of Art*. Indianapolis: Bobbs-Merrill.

———. 1965. *The Lost Universe*. New York: Basic Books.

West, Nigel. 1990. *Games of Intelligence: The Classified Conflict of International Espionage*. London: Weidenfeld and Nicolson.

White, Leslie A. 1949. *The Science of Culture*. New York: Farrar, Straus.

Willard, William. 2000. "American Anthropologists on the Neva: 1930–1940." *History of Anthropology Newsletter* 27 (1):3–9.

Winkler, Allan M. 1978. *The Politics of Propaganda: The Office of War Information, 1942–1945*. New Haven: Yale University Press.

Winks, Robin W. 1987. *Cloak and Gown: Scholars in the Secret War, 1939–1961*. New York: Morrow.

Wittfogel, Karl. 1955. "Developmental Aspects of Hydraulic Societies." In *Irrigation Civilizations: A Comparative Study*, ed. J. Steward, 43–56. Washington, D.C.: Pan American Union.

———. 1957. *Oriental Despotism*. New Haven: Yale University Press.

Wittman, S. A. 1987. "Voyage of a Peace Activist." *Progressive* (February): 16.

Wolf, Eric. 1969. *Peasant Wars of the Twentieth Century*. New York: Harper and Row.

Wormser, Rene A. 1993. *Foundations: Their Power and Influence*. Sevierville, Tenn.: Covenant House Books.

Yans-McLaughlin, Virginia. 1986a. "Science, Democracy, and Ethics: Mobilizing Culture and Personality for World War II." In *Malinowski, Rivers, Benedict, and Others. Vol. 4: History of Anthropology Series*, ed. G. W. Stocking, 184–217. Madison: University of Wisconsin Press.

———. 1986b. "Mead, Bateson, and 'Hitler's Peculiar Makeup': Applying Anthropology in the Era of Appeasement." *History of Anthropology Newsletter* 13 (1):3–8.

David H. Price is an associate professor of Anthropology
at St. Martin's College.

Library of Congress Cataloging-in-Publication Data

Price, David H.

Threatening anthropology : Mccarthyism and the FBI's

surveillance of activist anthropologists / David H. Price.

p. cm.

Includes bibliographical references and index.

ISBN 0-8223-3326-0 (cloth : alk. paper) —

ISBN 0-8223-3338-4 (pbk. : alk. paper)

1. Anthropology—United States—History—20th century—

Sources.   2. Anthropologists—United States—Political

activity.   3. Marxist anthropology—United States—History—

20th century.   4. Blacklisting of anthropologists—United

States—History—20th century.   5. United States. Federal

Bureau of Investigation—History—Sources.   6. McCarthy,

Joseph, 1885–1943—Relations with anthropologists.   I. Title.

GN17.3.U5P75   2004

301'.0973'09045—dc22   2003019214